MODERN JAPANESE

Third Edition

Mieko Shimizu Han, Ph.D.
University of Southern California

 Institute for Intercultural Studies Press

Printed in the United States of America

ISBN: 1-878463-09-8

Institute for Intercultural Studies Press
Los Angeles

For book orders, address to: Sannean Press
11727 Gateway Blvd., Los Angeles, CA 90064
Phone: (310) 478-3800, FAX (310) 478-8001

Preface

This book, *Modern Japanese: Third Edition*, is intended for beginning students of Japanese who wish to learn how to speak, read and write the language as it is spoken and written by educated native speakers. It is intended for young adult learners who speak English as their primary language.

The type of language presented in this book is the polite conversational style, or the *desu-masu* style, which is appropriate for foreigners to use in most social situations. Although Japanese men and women may speak differently in informal situations -- when they are at home, or when they are with intimate friends -- the *desu-masu* style is the standard conversational mode in modern Japanese society. In short, the dialogues in this book should sound natural and tasteful to educated speakers of Japanese, and will be practical and useful to the students.

To achieve the goal of making the book interesting and relevant to the intended learners, the lessons are built around the imaginary character, or the role model, Mr. Brown, a young American who is studying Japanese in Tokyo. His association with Japanese friends makes it possible to introduce a variety of practical and authentic language situations. The use of this fictitious character has proven, since the first publication of *Modern Japanese* in 1963, to be a useful device for classroom drills and activities.

The *Third Edition* represents an improved version of *Modern Japanese: Second Edition*. The author has incorporated new ideas, materials, and teaching techniques in this edition while retaining the useful basic elements of the previous editions. At the requests of teachers who developed workbooks, drills and testing materials based on the book, the revision in the *Third Edition* is rather restricted.

The order of grammatical and vocabulary introductions has been kept unchanged: the order of kana and kanji remains the same. The readers will notice, however, that the hiragana syllabary is introduced in Lesson 4 instead of Lesson 5 as was in the *Second Edition*. Introduction of katakana, therefore, begins one lesson earlier allowing extra time for the students to master hiragana and katakana before launching the study of kanji. Changes made in the *Third Edition* are found in the following: updating facts, improving authenticity and naturalness of expressions which resulted in some change in the dialogues of Lesson 3, 7, 12, 13, and 16.

To enhance communicative skills of the learners, activities are added in the exercises for the instructors to choose from.

The book is composed of twenty-eight lessons and is roughly divided into two major parts: Lesson 1 through Lesson 16 present recommended study materials for the first semester. Here, emphasis is placed on the spoken language and basics of reading and writing. Lesson 17 through Lesson 28 are intended for the classes in the second half of the first year in college or the second year in high school. The materials are presented in hiragana, katakana, and kanji. For the convenience of conversation classes the romanized texts of the central dialogues are continued through Lesson 22. After Lesson 23, emphasis is directed toward introduction of Japanese culture in authentic writing.

Each lesson is structured around a main dialogue or a text and appears with a complete English equivalent; the main dialogue or text is followed by grammatical and cultural notes on the specific linguistic and cultural elements introduced in the lesson. Exercises are built on the new vocabulary and grammar for additional practice; for the purpose of review, elements from preceding lessons are incorporated as re-entry. Activities are added to give the students meaningful output of the lesson. Most new vocabulary items are introduced in the main dialogue, but additional vocabulary may appear in the exercises. New VERBS are listed first, followed by ADJECTIVES and NOUNS; OTHERS include particles, adverbs, conjunctions and other grammatical elements and idiomatic expressions. The vocabulary introduced in the exercises are listed as ADDITIONAL VOCABULARY at the end.

The writing of this book has taken a long time. During this time the author has received encouragements, advice and technical assistance from a number of colleagues, students and friends, without whose cooperation this book could not have been completed. Words cannot adequately express the gratitude felt by the author to all persons who have helped make this book a reality.

Mieko Shimizu Han, Ph.D.
Professor of East Asian Languages and Cultures
University of Southern California
November, 1997

Contents

1

Tanaka:	hajimemashite.
Brown:	hajimemashite.
Tanaka:	watakushi wa Tanaka desu.
Brown:	watakushi wa Buraun desu.
Tanaka:	doozo yoroshiku.
Brown:	doozo yoroshiku.
Tanaka:	Buraun-san wa nihongo ga wakarimasu ka?
Brown:	hai, sukoshi wakarimasu.
	Tanaka-san wa eigo ga wakarimasu ka?
Tanaka:	iie, wakarimasen.
Brown:	dewa, nihongo de hanashimashoo.
Tanaka:	hai, soo shimashoo.

ENGLISH EQUIVALENT

Tanaka: How do you do?
Brown: How do you do?
Tanaka: My [last] name is Tanaka. (I am Tanaka.)
Brown: My [last] name is Brown. (I am Brown.)
Tanaka: Pleased to meet you.
Brown: Pleased to meet you.
Tanaka: Do you [Mr. Brown] understand Japanese?
Brown: Yes, I understand a little.
         Do you [Miss Tanaka] understand English?
Tanaka: No, I don't.
Brown: Then, let's speak in Japanese.
Tanaka: Yes, let's do that.

GRAMMATICAL AND CULTURAL NOTES

1.1   hajimemashite

When a Japanese speaker meets someone for the first time, or when he or she is introduced to a person, the speaker says **hajimemashite**. This expression means something like ' beginning' or 'this is the first time [I have the pleasure of meeting you], ' and is equivalent to the English 'How do you do?'

1.2   watakushi

In English the word 'I' can be used by anybody in any circumstance referring to himself or herself. In Japanese there are several words that mean 'I.' They have slightly different stylistic connotations: some of them are more formal and polite, while others are informal and casual; some words are preferred by men while some are used by women. You should choose the one which suits yourself best according to your age, sex, and profession. It is always recommendable for a foreigner to be a little bit formal and polite in the beginning rather than risk being too informal. It is for this reason that the most formal word for ' I ' **watakushi** is introduced in this lesson. Some people prefer **watashi**. In a less formal style, men can use **boku** and women can use [**w**]**atashi**.

1.3   Particles

There is a class of words called 'particles' in Japanese. Particles occur at the end of a word, phrase or sentence to give grammatical meaning such as 'subject,' 'object' or 'question' to what precedes them. A particle is usually very short, generally one syllable, and is pronounced without a pause between it and the preceding word. Particles are the most important element in Japanese grammar. The particles **wa**, **ka**, **ga** and **de** are introduced in this lesson.

1.4   wa

The particle **wa** as in **watakushi wa** and **Buraun-san wa** indicates that the preceding word is the topic of the sentence. It means something like 'as for' or 'in reference to.' This idea is very similar to the subject of a sentence in English, but there is a small difference between the idea of 'subject' in English and that of 'topic' in Japanese. In English, all sentences other than imperatives must have a subject, but in Japanese the topic can be left out if the meaning is clear from the context.

> **watakushi wa** Tanaka desu.   (**I** am Tanaka.)
> **Buraun-san wa** nihongo ga   wakarimasu ka?
> > (Do **you** [**Mr. Brown**] understand Japanese?)
> hai, [**watakushi wa**] nihongo ga   wakarimasu.
> > (Yes, **I** understand Japanese.)

In the above sentence [**watakushi wa**] can be left out, but in the corresponding English sentence the subject '**I**' cannot be omitted.

1.5   Japanese Names

Japanese people usually identfy themselves by their family names.

> watakushi wa **Tanaka** desu.   (My [last] name is **Tanaka**.)

When they say their full names they say their family names (last names) first and their given names (first names) last. Usually Japanese people have no middle names.

> watakushi wa **Tanaka Masako** desu. (I am **Masako Tanaka**.)

In case of the name of a foreigner, the order usually is unchanged from the foreigner's native language.

> watakushi wa **Jooji Buraun** desu.   (I am **George Brown**.)

If a person has a Japanese family name and an English given name, as with many Japanese-Americans, the practice varies.

> One may say: watakushi wa **Merii Tanaka** desu.   (I am **Mary Tanaka**.)
> Or one may say: watakushi wa **Tanaka Merii** desu.   (I am **Mary Tanaka**.)

1.6   desu

The word **desu** is a member of a unique set of inflected forms called the **copula**. Although there is no exact equivalent to **desu** in English, the closest English meaning is 'to be' or 'to equal' as opposed to 'to exist.' The word **desu** may be added to a noun to make it the predicate of a sentence.

> watakushi wa **Buraun desu**.   (**I am Brown**.)
> watakushi wa **Tanaka desu**.   (**I am Tanaka**.)

3

1.7   doozo yoroshiku

In English, when you meet someone for the first time you exchange such greeting as 'How do you do?' or 'Pleased to meet you.' A similar greeting in Japanese is **doozo yoroshiku**. The word **doozo** means 'please' and **yoroshiku** means 'be favorable [to me].' The Japanese people bow politely and exchange this greeting when they are introduced to someone or meet someone for the first time. When someone greets you with **doozo yoroshiku** you may repeat the same expression, or you may say **'kochira koso doozo yoroshiku.'** **kochira** means 'my way' or 'this side' and along with the emphatic marker **koso** it expresses that it's the speaker who wanted to say that expression.

> **doozo yoroshiku.**   **(Pleased to meet you.**)
> **kochira koso** doozo yoroshiku.   (It's **my pleasure** to meet you.)

1.8   Word for 'you' in Japanese

The simplest word for 'you' in Japanese is **anata**. You hear **anata** quite often on TV commercials, but not so in natural conversations among native speakers. Instead of using the word **anata** Japanese people usually use the name of the person he or she is speaking to **+san**. There are several words meaning 'you' in Japanese and it requires social and cultural rules to select the correct word to mean 'you.' It would be a good idea to address your teacher as **sensei** (Teacher) and call your friends by their names **+ san**. The suffix **-san** means Mr., Mrs., or Miss. This is an honorific suffix and it should **not** be added to **one's own name**.

> **anata** wa   eigo ga   wakarimasu ka? (Do **you** understand English?)
>> This sentence sounds straight forward and a bit like a foreigner
>> speaking, or a TV commercial speaking to the viewers.
> **Tanaka-san** wa   eigo ga wakarimasu ka? (Do **you** [**Miss Tanaka**] understand
>> English?
>> This sentence is more natural and sounds like a native Japanese speaker
>> asking Miss Tanaka a question.
> **Buraun-san** wa   eigo ga   wakarimasu ka? (Do **you** [**Mr. Brown**] understand
>> English?)

1.9   wakarimasu

The word **wakarimasu** comes from the verb **wakaru** (to understand) ending in its polite conversational form **-masu**. In Japanese dictionaries verbs are listed in dictionary forms ending in **-ru** or **-u**, as **wakaru** (to understand), **hanasu** (to speak), or **suru** (to do). However, in most social conversations people speak in **the polite conversational style** which is characterized by the predicate verbs ending in **-masu** or its variants. Most native speakers recommend this style for the students of Japanese to use over more informal or familiar style. This style which is often called **'the desu-masu style'** is introduced and maintained throughout this book.

1.10   Predicate Verbs

In a Japanese sentence the predicate verb usually comes at the end. The subject is followed by the object and then the verb. That is why Japanese is often called a **SOV** language by linguists. English is called a **SVO** language because the verb comes before the object.

Japanese verbs are inflected in a number of categories that are quite different from those of Indo-European languages such as English, French, or German. They will be explained as each ending is introduced in the subsequent lessons.

Japanese verbs have no ending changes for the first, second, and third persons, (I, you, he or she). No singular or plural distinction is required: the same word, e.g. **wakarimasu** (understand) can be used to mean 'I understand,' 'you understand,' 'he or she understands,' 'we understand,' and 'they understand.' In the vocabulary sections of this book verb meanings are listed with the pronoun 'I' as (I understand) for simplicity's sake, but the same verb can be used for other persons.

The verb **wakarimasu** is in its **polite non-past form**. This form corresponds roughly to the present indicative in English. The ideas expressed by the present tense of English verbs such as 'I sometimes (usually, every day) do such and such,' are usually expressed by the polite, non-past verb forms in Japanese.

1.11   ga

In the English sentence 'I understand Japanese' the word 'Japanese' is the object of the verb, as the verb 'to understand' takes a direct object. In the corresponding Japanese sentence, **nihongo ga wakarimasu**, the verb is an intransitive verb which does not take a direct object. The verb **wakarimasu** means 'something is clear or comprehensible.' The word **nihongo** is marked by **ga** and is the subject of the verb **wakarimasu**. The Japanese sentence literally means 'English is comprehensible [to me].'

nihongo **ga** **wakarimasu**. (Japanese **is comprehensible** [to me]. or
                          I **understand** Japanese.)
eigo **ga** **wakarimasu** ka? (Is English **comprehensible** [to you]? or
                          Do you **understand** English?)

1.12   ka

The particle **ka** makes a sentence interrogative. A statement can be made into a question by adding the particle **ka** at the end.

Statement: nihongo ga   wakarimasu.   ([I] understand Japanese.)
Question: nihongo ga   wakarimasu **ka**?   (**Do you** understand Japanese?)

1.13   -masen

The **-masu** form of a verb can be made into the negative form by changing **-masu** to **-masen**.

Affirmative: eigo ga   **wakarimasu**.   (I **understand** English.)
Negative: eigo ga   **wakarimasen**.   (I **don't understand** English.)

1.14   de

The particle **de** marks the preceding word as the agent by which the activity expressed by the verb is accomplished. It means something like 'by means of' or 'using ...' In English the same concept is expressed by various prepositions such as 'with,' 'in,' or 'by.' If the preceding word is the name of a language such as **eigo** or **nihongo**, then the resulting expression **eigo de** or **nihongo de** means 'using English,' 'in English,' or 'using Japanese,' ' in Japanese.'

> **nihongo de** hanashimashoo.   (Let's speak **in Japanese**.)
> **eigo de** hanashimashoo.   (Let's speak **in English**.)

1.15 -mashoo

The **-mashoo** form is a variant of **-masu**, and it means 'let's ... ' as in "Let's speak' or 'Let's go.'

> nihongo de **hanashimashoo**.   (**Let's speak** in Japanese.)
> soo **shimashoo**.   (**Let's do** that.)

PRONUNCIATION NOTES

1P.1 Japanese Vowels

To speak Japanese well, it is important to know the sounds of Japanese and how they are combined to form words and sentences. Japanese has five vowel phonemes: /i/, /e/, /a/, /o/ and /u/. These five vowels are phonetically described by linguists as in the following diagram. The phoneme /u/ is pronounced as [ɯ], rounded or unrounded, and more fronted than [u] in other languages.

	Front	Central	Back
High	i		ɯ
Mid	e		o
Low		a	

The Japanese usually pronounce these vowels in the order of /a/, /i/, /u/, /e/, /o/. In the romanized writing system, **Romaji**, the five vowels are represented by the letters 'a,' 'i,' 'u,' 'e,' 'o,' respectively.

[a]	is like the 'a' in 'father.'
[i]	is like the 'ea' in 'eat.'
[ɯ]	is like the 'oo' in 'book.'
[e]	is like the 'e' in 'bet.'
[o]	is like the 'oa' in 'toast.'

Pronounce each vowel distinctly. Avoid the vague English vowel schwa [ə] as in 'but' or 'us.' Also, the English [I] as in 'pit' or 'sit' may sound vague and confusing to the Japanese ear.

Exercise: The following forty-six syllables represent the basic sound patterns in modern Japanese, and also form the basis of the Japanese syllabic writing system. Each of the syllables is represented by a **kana** symbol.

The students practice pronouncing the following syllables, repeating them after the instructor.

a	i	u	e	o
ka	ki	ku	ke	ko
sa	shi	su	se	so
ta	chi	tsu	te	to
na	ni	nu	ne	no
ha	hi	fu	he	ho
ma	mi	mu	me	mo
ya	_	yu	_	yo
ra	ri	ru	re	ro
wa	_	_	_	(w)o
N				

1P.2   Vowel Quality and Rhythm

Each syllable in Japanese must be evenly stressed; for example, the four vowels in the word **Tanaka-san** must all have the same clear / a / sound.

Exercise: The students pronounce each vowel distinctly in the following Japanese names, avoiding the English vague schwa sound [ə]. The instructor checks the students' pronunciation.

Tanaka-san   Yamada-san   Sakata-san

1P.3   Short Vowels and Long Vowels

In Japanese, all five vowels may be either short or long. It is important that students of Japanese learn to distinguish, in hearing and speaking, a short vowel from a long one at the beginning stage of their study. A difference in vowel length brings a difference in meaning. Many students are unaware of this distinction since vowel duration is not distinctive feature in English. To make the distinction clear, a short vowel is represented in this book with a single letter and a long vowel with two letters. The long vowel 'i i' must be pronounced at least twice as long as its short counterpart 'i.' The results of the author's acoustic phonetics research indicate that a long vowel is approximately 2.8 times as long as a short one. A helpful hint for good Japanese pronunciation is to pronounce a long vowel longer and a short vowel shorter than you normally would in speaking English.

Exercise: The students pronounce the following words correctly, repeating after the model provided by the instructor or the tape paying special attention to the underlined vowel length.

obasan (aunt)   obaasan (grandmother)
ojisan (uncle)   ojiisan (grandfather)
ie (house)   iie (no)
biru (building)   biiru (beer)
imasu (to exist)   iimasu (to say)
to (door)   too (ten [objects])

The instructor checks the students' pronunciation, first with the above paired words, and then with each of the words individually. Use English words as cues.

1P.4   Japanese Consonants

There are twenty different consonants and two semi-vowels in Japanese. The following chart describes these sounds.

Manners of Articulation		Bilabial	Dental-Alveolar	Palatal	Pre-velar	Velar	Glottal
Stops	Voiceless	p	t			k	
	Voiced	b	d			g	
Fricatives	Voiceless	ɸ	s	ʃ	ç		h
	Voiced		z				
Affricates	Voiceless		ts	tʃ			
	Voiced		dz	dʒ			
Flap	Voiced		ɾ				
Nasals	Voiced	m	n			ŋ	
Semivowels	Voiced	w		y			

Most of these consonants are familiar to the English speakers, but the following symbols may require some explanations.

> [ɸ] is represented by the letter 'f'
> [ʃ] is represented by the letter 'sh'
> [tʃ] is represented by the letter 'ch'
> [dz] is represented by the letter 'z'
> [dʒ] is represented by the letter 'j'
> [ɾ] is represented by the letter 'r'
> [ç] is represented by the letter 'h'

The sounds represented by other symbols are generally similar to the corresponding English sounds. As new sounds and difficult distinctions are introduced, special notes on pronunciation and exercises will be provided. In Lesson 1 the following two points are called to attention.

1P.5   Flapped 'r'

The [r] sound in Japanese is called a 'flap' sound by phoneticians. The sound is produced by a very quick tap of the tip of the tongue against the alveolar ridge (the alveolar ridge is the bumpy mass of gum tissue just behind the upper teeth). The English [r] is produced without the tap--in other words, without any contact between the tongue and the alveolar ridge. English speakers often pronounce their [t] or [d] sounds as flapped consonants when these sounds occur between two vowels (e.g., water, letter, ladder). That is why the Japanese [r] may sound something like [t] or [d] to English speakers at first. The difference between the Japanese [r] and the English flapped sounds is that the Japanese [r] is much shorter and quicker. The regular ' r ' symbol will be used for [r] in this book.

Exercise: The students try to imitate the pronunciation of the instructor and pronounce [r] correctly in the following words, avoiding the English [r].

1. yoroshiku
2. wakarimasen
3. ra, ri, ru, re, ro
4. roku (six); doku (poison)
5. sore (that); sode (sleeve)

1P.6   Alternation of [g] and [ŋ]

The letter 'g' at the beginning of a Japanese word is pronounced like the [g] in English 'go' or 'get.' The same 'g' in the middle of a Japanese word or utterance may become nasalized, that is, pronounced like the [n] or 'ng' in the English words 'sing' or 'song.' The particle **ga** is normally pronounced [ŋa]. The nasalized sound [ŋ] is more common with Tokyo speakers than with the speakers of other dialects. The difference in pronunciation makes no significant difference in meaning; thus the student can use either [g] or [ŋ] when imitating the instructor's model or recorded models.

Exercise: The students pronounce the following words correctly.

1. eigo
2. nihongo
3. eigo ga wakarimasu.

EXERCISES

1E.1   Say the following expressions in Japanese. When another expression is
suggested in parentheses, take the suggestion as a reminder of the form used in the
main dialogue. The words in [   ] are not expressed in Japanese.

1. How do you do? (This is the first time I have the pleasure of meeting you.)
2. My name is [Mr.] Brown. (I'm Brown.)
3. I'm [Miss] Tanaka. (I'm Tanaka.)
4. Pleased to meet you. (Please be favorable to me.)
5. Do you understand Japanese?
6. Do you understand English?
7. Yes, I understand English.
8. No, I don't understand English.
9. I understand a little English.
10. Mr. Brown understands Japanese.
11. Docs Mr. Brown understand Japanese?
12. Yes, he understands a little Japanese.
    (Yes, Mr. Brown understands a little Japanese.)
13. No, he (Mr. Brown) doesn't understand Japanese.
14. Let's speak in English.
15. Let's speak in Japanese.
16. Yes, let's do that.

1E.2   Activity: Meeting a classmate. The instructor divides the students into
pairs. Each pair practices the dialogue at the beginning of Lesson 1 using their own
names. The instructor may go around and meet individual students.

1E.3   Additional dialogues for practice: The instructor orally presents the
following dialogues with brief explanations. The students repeat after the instructor
twice, and then, practice the dialogues in pairs.

(1) A: Yamada-san desu ka?
     B: hai, soo desu. Yamada desu.
     A: watakushi wa Buraun desu.
     B: hajimemashite.
     A: hajimemashite.
     B: doozo yoroshiku.
     A: kochira koso, doozo yoroshiku.

(2) A: Yamamoto-san desu ka?
     B: iie, chigaimasu.
     A: doomo shitsurei shimashita.
     B: iie.

(3) A: onamae wa?
     B: Santosu desu.
     A: watakushi wa Kimura desu.
     B: hajimemashite.
     A: hajimemashite.
     B: doozo yoroshiku.
     A: kochira koso, doozo yoroshiku.

(4) A: Sumisu-san desu ka?
     B: hai, soo desu.
     A: Sumisu-san wa amerika kara desu ka?
     B: hai, amerika kara desu.
     A: nihongo ga wakarimasu ka?
     B: hai, sukoshi wakarimasu.

(5) A: chuugokugo ga wakarimasu ka?
     B: iie, wakarimasen.
     A: eigo ga wakarimasu ka?
     B: hai, sukoshi wakarimasu.
     A: dewa, eigo de hanashimashoo.
     B: hai, eigo de hanashimashoo.

(6) A: Toomasu-san desu ka?
     B: iie, chigaimasu. Buraun desu.
     A: shitsurei shimashita. watakushi wa Aoki desu.
     B: hajimemashite.
     A: hajimemashite.
     B   Aoki-san wa dochira kara desu ka?
     A: watakushi wa Hawai kara desu.
     B: watakushi wa Kariforunia kara desu.
         doozo yoroshiku.
     A: kochira koso, doozo yoroshiku.

1E.4   The instructor reads the following expressions and the students give appropriate responses including correct bodily gestures such as bowing, if necessary. The second time, Student A reads the sentences and Student B gives responses.

1. Tanaka-san desu ka?
2. onamae wa?
3. hajimemashite.
4. doozo yoroshiku.
5. kankoku kara desu ka?
6. kankokugo ga wakarimasuka?
7. chuugokugo ga wakarimasu ka?
9. nihongo ga wakarimasu ka?
10. eigo ga wakarimasu ka?
11. watakushi wa _____ desu.
12. watakushi wa nihongo ga wakarimasen.

1E.5   Activity: Getting to know more classmates. The instructor asks the students to get a sheet of paper and a pencil. Then the instructor asks the students to stand up and move around in the classroom to meet **five new classmates** and greet them in Japanese. After introduction, each student writes (1) **the names** of the five classmates he or she met, (2) **which language** each person understands, and (3) **where the person is from**. Then the student reports the findings to the instructor in Japanese.

1E.6   Activity: Introducing oneself. The instructor asks each student to introduce himself or herself to the class. Each student must tell his or her language background and where he or she is from.

1E.7   Activity: Finding a person. If time allows, the following activity may be added. The instructor writes the names of the students on small pieces of paper, and pass them out in class. Each student must find the person by asking other students **"onamae wa?"** or **"...-san desu ka?"** until he or she meets the person on the slip. Only Japanese is spoken in class.

VOCABULARY

VERBS

wakarimasu	(I or someone understand[s]: -masu form of wakaru, 1.9)
wakaru	(to understand)
wakarimasen	(I [or someone] don't [doesn't] understand: negative of wakarimasu, 1.13)
hanashimashoo	(let's speak: -mashoo form of hanasu, 1.15)
hanasu	(to speak)
shimashoo	(let's do ...: -mashoo form of suru, 1.15)
suru	(to do)

ADJECTIVES   (---)

NOUNS

watakushi	(a formal and polite form for 'I', 1.2)
Tanaka	(a Japanese surname)
Buraun	(the English surname 'Brown' as pronounced in Japanese)
anata	(you, 1.8)
nihongo	(the Japanese language)
eigo	(the English language)

OTHERS

hajimemashite	(How do you do? 1.1)
wa	(a particle marking the topic, 1.4)
desu	(is; equivalent to: a copula, 1.6)
doozo	(please, 1.7)
yoroshiku	(be favorable [to me], 1.7)
-san	(Mr., Mrs., Miss, 1.8)
ga	(a particle marking the subject, 1.11)
ka	(a particle marking the question, 1.12)
hai	(yes)
iie	(no)
sukoshi	(a little)
dewa	(well; then; hmmm)
de	(by means of; in (the ... language): a particle marking the agent, 1.14)

ADDITIONAL VOCABULARY

Masako	(a Japanese name for girls, 1.5)
Jooji	(the English name 'George' as pronounced in Japanese, 1.5)
Merii	(the English name 'Mary' as pronounced in Japanese, 1.5)
Yamada	(a Japanese surname)
soo	(in that way; so)
soo desu	(that's right; you are correct)
kochira	(this way; my way; for me to say)
koso	(indeed, 1.7)

13

kochira koso	(it's for me to say that; it's my pleasure to say that, 1.7)
onamae	(your name: the exalted form of namae meaning 'name')
Yamamoto	(a Japanese surname)
Santosu	(the Spanish name 'Santos' as pronounced in Japanese)
Kimura	(a Japanese surname)
Sumisu	(the English name 'Smith' as pronounced in Japanese)
amerika	(America; USA)
chigaimasu	(that is incorrect; that's wrong; you are mistaken)
doomo	(very much)
shitsurei shimashita	(I'm sorry; pardon me; I was rude)
chuugoku	(China)
chuugokugo	(the Chinese language)
Toomasu	(the English name 'Thomas' as pronounced in Japanese)
Aoki	(a Japanese surname)
dochira	(which way; where [politely spoken])
dochira kara desu ka?	(Where are you from?)
Hawai	(Hawaii)
Kariforunia	(California)
Taiwan	(Taiwan)
supeingo	(the Spanish language)
kankoku	(South Korea)
kankokugo	(the Korean language)

2

Brown:	Tanaka-san, ohayoo gozaimasu.
Tanaka:	Buraun-san, ohayoo gozaimasu.
Brown:	kyoo wa ii (o)tenki desu ne!
Tanaka:	honto ni ii (o)tenki desu ne!
Brown:	ogenki desu ka?
Tanaka:	hai, okagesamade genki desu.
	Buraun-san mo ogenki desu ka?
Brown:	hai, okagesamade.
Tanaka:	gakkoo wa doo desu ka?
Brown:	totemo tanoshii desu.
Tanaka:	kurasu wa omoshiroi desu ka?
Brown:	hai, totemo omoshiroi desu.
Tanaka:	sore wa yokatta desu ne!
	ja, mata.
Brown:	ja, mata.
Tanaka:	sayoonara.
Brown:	sayoonara.

ENGLISH EQUIVALENT

Brown: Good morning, Miss Tanaka.
Tanaka: Good morning, Mr. Brown.
Brown: It's beautiful today, isn't it! (Today, the weather is good, isn't it!)
Tanaka: It certainly is beautiful [isn't it] !
Brown: How are you? (Are you well?)
Tanaka: Yes, I'm fine, thank you. (Thank you for asking. I'm in good health.)
         Are you also in good health?
Brown: Yes, thank you.
Tanaka: How is school?
Brown: It's very enjoyable.
Tanak: Are [your] classes interesting?
Brown: Yes, they are very interesting.
Tanaka: That's good. (That was good to hear!)
         Well, [I'll see you] again.
Brown: Okay, see you again.
Tanaka: Good-bye.
Brown: Good-bye.

GRAMMATICAL AND CULTURAL NOTES

2.1   Greetings

The following are the common greetings in Japanese.

ohayoo gozaimasu.	(Good morning.)
konnichiwa.	(Hello! or Good afternoon.)
kombanwa.	(Good evening.)
ja mata, or dewa mata.	(Well, then, I'll see you.)
sayoonara, or sayonara.	(Good-bye, or bye!)
oyasuminasai.	(Good night.)
gokigenyoo	(Farewell; Good-bye)

The following are other useful daily exchanges.

ogenki desu ka?	(Are you in good health? or How are you?)
ikaga desu ka?	(How are you doing?)
okagesamade.	(Thank you for asking [implying a good answer].)
genki desu.	(I'm fine. or I'm in good health.)
maa maa desu.	(I'm so so. or Not bad, thank you.)

2.2   -san

When Japanese people address someone they usually add the suffix **-san** to a family name (as in **Tanaka-san**), a given name (as in **Masako-san**), or the full name (as in **Tanaka Masako-san**).   Japanese people will call Mr. Brown '**Buraun-san**.' As mentioned in **1.8**, the suffix **-san** is basically an honorific form, so it should **not** be added to **your own name**. **-san** has no component of gender, as in the English Mr., Mrs., and Miss.   You can address anybody with their name + **-san**.

Tanaka-**san**,	ohayoo gozaimasu.	(Good morning, **Miss** Tanaka.)
Buraun-**san**,	ohayoo gozaimasu.	(Good morning, **Mr.** Brown.)

Japanese people usually call their friends by their **surnames + -san** .

2.3   Commenting on the Weather

Japanese people comment on the weather as part of their daily greetings. This custom may stem from the fact that Japan is an island country with changeable weather. So, Japanese people would naturally be concerned about the weather. The polite prefix **o-** is optional.

kyoo wa ii (o)tenki desu ne!	(It's beautiful today, isn't it!)
honto ni ii (o)tenki desu ne!	(It certainly is beautiful!)

2.4   ne meaning 'isn't it'

The particle **ne** means 'isn't it?' and it may be added to many sentences.   Different intonations may change its meaning slightly; a sharp rising intonation signals a question, whereas a rising-falling intonation with an extra vowel length as /**nee**/ makes the sentence exclamatory. Both intonations are heard in commenting on the weather; but in a response, if the exclamatory intonation is intended, the exclamation mark ' **!** ' is added. If it is a question, a question mark ' **?** ' is added.

kyoo wa ii (o)tenki desu **ne?**	(It's beautiful today, **isn't it?** **[Please tell me if I am correct.]**)
kyoo wa ii (o)tenki desu **ne!**	(It's beautiful today, **isn't it!** **[How nice it is!]**)

2.5   (o)genki: Exalted Forms

The question '**ogenki desu ka?**' means 'Are you in good health?' The polite prefix **o-** makes the word **genki** (good health) polite or **exalted**.   The exalted word refers to the person addressed to, i.e. '**your** good health.' For your own health you should use **genki** without the polite prefix. This prefix is an optional feature, and, as such, is placed in parentheses (   ) in this book.

ogenki desu ka?	(Are **you in good health**?)
hai, **genki** desu.	(Yes, **I**'m **fine**.)

'**ikaga desu ka?**' is the equivalent of the English 'How are you?' The word **ikaga** means 'how. In English, we say 'How are you?' to everybody, and we almost automatically answer, 'Fine, thank you.' In Japanese, it is common to comment on the weather instead of asking about each other's health. Some Japanese people say that '**ikaga desu ka?**' sounds more like an English translation of 'How are you?' and not natural in Japanese. Others have no objection to this expression.

> **ikaga** desu ka?   (**How** are you?)

2.6   okagesamade

The literal meaning of **okagesamade** is something like 'Thanks to the favors of others' or 'fortunately,' and it implies that the speaker is fine. '**okagesamade, genki desu**' is one of the commonest ways to respond when someone asks you '**ogenki desu ka?**' or '**ikaga desu ka?**'

> **okagesamade,** genki desu.   (**Thank you for asking,** I'm fine.)

2.7   mo

The particle **mo** has the meaning of 'also' or 'too,' and it may replace the particle **wa** and other particles. As a particle, **mo** is added to a word, and not used independently to mean 'also.'

> **watakushi mo**   genki desu.   (**I'm** fine, **too.**)
> **watakushi mo**   nihongo ga wakarimasu.   (**I, too,** understand Japanese.)
> watakushi wa   **eigo mo** wakarimasu.   (I understand **English as well.**)

2.8   doo

The word **doo** is an interrogative word meaning 'how?' or 'in what way?' Both **ikaga** and **doo** mean 'how?' but **ikaga** is more polite. When referring to a person's health, one is apt to use the more polite word **ikaga**. In other cases, such as the one here, **doo** is used to mean 'how.' There are other pairs of words which mean the same but differ in their degrees of politeness. Politeness level is one of the important dimensions of the Japanese language.

> gakkoo wa   **doo desu ka?**   (**How is** school?)
> nihongo wa   **doo desu ka?**   (**How is** Japanese?)

2.9   Adjectives

The word **omoshiroi** (interesting, fun) is an adjective. In their dictionary forms the Japanese adjectives end with an **-i** as in **omoshiroi** (interesting), **tanoshii** (enjoyable), or **ii** (good). The adjectives are inflected in several ways and the ending **-i** may be replaced by other endings in different expressions. The dictionary form may precede a noun as a modifier, or it may be followed by **desu** to make the predicate of a sentence.

> **ii** (o)**tenki** desu.   (It's **good weather**.)
> kurasu wa   **omoshiroi desu.**   (The class **is interesting**.)
> Gakkoo wa   **tanoshii desu.**   (The school **is enjoyable**.)

2.10   Adverbs

Words like **totemo** (very much) and **honto ni** (truely, really) are adverbs. Adverbs may modify adjectives or verbs just like in English.

honto ni ii otenki desu.	(It **really** is good weather.)
totemo omoshiroi desu.	(It's **very** intresting.)
sukoshi wakarimasu.	(I understand **a little**.)

2.11   ja mata

The word **ja** is the contracted form of **dewa** which means 'well, then,' and is commonly heard in causal conversations. In a more formal style of speech **dewa** is proper. The choice of style depends upon a number of factors: circumstances where the conversation takes place and the speaker's age, sex, and social status. In classroom situations and most social occasions both **ja** and **dewa** are spoken. **mata** means 'again.' **ja mata** is the Japanese equivalent of the English 'I'll see you.'

ja, mata.   sayoonara.   (**I'll see you**. Good-bye.)

PRONUNCIATION NOTES

2P.1   [y]

The [y] sound in Japanese may occur in the initial position of the syllables ya, yu, yo, or may occur between one of the following consonants, k, g, n, h, b, m, r, and one of the vowels a, u, o. It is pronounced together with the vowel following it to form a single syllable. In English, the [y] sound is more like a syllable-end sound, thus, the native speakers of English erroneously tend to pronounce the Japanese [y] as they are accustomed to doing in English. The word **ohayoo** should be pronounced in four moraic units as in **o-ha-yo-o**, not as in **o-hay-o**, which may sound like the English word 'Ohio.'

Exercise: Practice pronouncing the following syllables and words correctly.

ya	yu	yo
kya	kyu	kyo
gya	gyu	gyo
nya	nyu	nyo
hya	hyu	hyo
bya	byu	byo
mya	myu	myo
rya	ryu	ryo

1. o-ha-yo-o   ohayoo   ohayoo gozaimasu
2. kyo-o   kyoo   kyoo wa ii (o) tenki desu
3. kyoo   (today)
    kiyo   (personal name)
    ki-o   (tree as direct object)

19

2P.2   Review: Long Vowels

Problem sounds must be repeated as many times as required in order to develop good pronunciation. The importance of making the long vowels longer should be reviewed. (See 1P.3)

Exercise: Make the long vowels long enough as you pronounce the following words.

1. ohay<u>oo</u> gozaimasu.
2. ky<u>oo</u> wa ii (o) tenki desu.
3. gakk<u>oo</u> wa d<u>oo</u> desu ka?
4. s<u>oo</u> desu ka?
5. say<u>oo</u>nara
6. d<u>oo</u>zo yoroshiku
7. s<u>oo</u> shimash<u>oo</u>.

EXERCISES

2E.1   Say the following expressions in Japanese.

1. Good morning!
2. Good morning, Mr. Yamada.
3. Good morning, Miss Tanaka.
4. How are you?
5. Fine, thank you.
6. How are you, Mr. Brown?
7. Fine, thank you. And you [Miss Tanaka]?
8. I'm fine, too.
9. It's beautiful today, isn't it! (Today, the weather is good, isn't it!)
10. It really is beautiful, isn't it! (Really, the weather is good, isn't it!)
11. It's hot today, isn't it!
12. Yes, it really is hot!
13. Is it hot today?
14. Yes, it is hot today.
15. Is it cold today?
16. Yes, it is cold today.
17. How is school?
18. How is Japanese?
19. It's very interesting.
20. Japanese is very interesting.
21. Well, I'll see you.
22. Good-bye.

2E.2 Additional dialogues: The instructor introduces the dialogues with brief explanations. Then the students practice in pairs.

(1) Kim: Buraun-san, ohayoo gozaimasu.
     Brown: aa, Kimu-san, ohayoo gozaimasu.
     Kim: ogenki desu ka?
     Brown: maa maa desu. Kimu-san wa?
     Kim: watakushi mo maa maa desu.
     Brown: isogashii desu ka?
     Kim: hai, totemo isogashii desu.
     Brown: ja, mata.
     Kim: ja, mata. sayoonara.

(2) Yamada: Buraun-san, konnichiwa.
     Brown: aa, konnichiwa.
     Yamada: kyoo wa atsui desu ne!
     Brown: honto ni atsui desu ne!
     Yamada: ogenki desu ka?
     Brown: okagesamade genki desu.
              Yamada-san mo ogenki desu ka?
     Yamada: hai, okagesamade.
     Brown: kurasu wa doo desu ka?
     Yamada: totemo omoshiroi desu.
     Brown: sore wa yokatta desu ne!
     Yamada: ja, mata.
     Brown: ja, mata. sayoonara
     Yamada: sayoonara.

(3) Brown: kombanwa.
     Kimura: kombanwa.
     Brown: samui desu ne!
     Kimura: honto ni samui desu ne!
     Brown: ogenki desu ka?
     Kimura: ee, demo chotto kaze o hikimashita.
     Brown: ikemasen ne... odaiji ni.
     Kimura: arigatoo gozaimasu.
     Brown: ja, mata ashita.
     Kimura: oyasuminasai!

2E.3   The instructor reads the following expressions and the students give an appropriate response to each, including correct gestures, if necessary. The second time, Student A reads the sentences and Student B gives the responses.

1. ohayoo gozaimasu.
2. ikaga desu ka?
3. kyoo wa   ii   (o)tenki desu ne!
4. ja, mata.
5. sayoonara.
6. konnichiwa.
7. gakkoo wa   doo desu ka?
8. nihongo wa   omoshiroi desu ka?
9. kombanwa.
10. kyoo wa   samui desu ne!
11. nihongo wa   omoshiroi desu ne!
12. ja, oyasuminasai.
13. hajimemashite.
14. anata wa   nihongo ga   wakarimasu ka?
15. dewa,   nihongo de   hanashimashoo.

2E.4   Answer the following questions. The first time, the instructor asks the questions and the students answer. The second time, Student A asks Student B.

1. Tanaka-san wa   genki desu ka?
2. Buraun-san wa   genki desu ka?
3. anata mo ogenki desu ka?
4. gakkoo wa   omoshiroi desu ka?
5. kyoo wa   atsui desu ka?
6. anata wa   eigo ga   wakarimasu ka?
7. anata wa   nihongo ga   wakarimasu ka?
8. anata wa   furansugo ga wakarimasu ka?
9. ja, anata wa   supeingo mo   wakarimasu ka?
10. Buraun-san wa   eigo ga   wakarimasu ne?
11. furansugo mo   wakarimasu ka?
12. Tanaka-san wa   nihongo ga   wakarimasu ne?
13. Tanaka-san wa   eigo ga   wakarimasu ka?
14. nihongo wa   doo desu ka?

2E.5   Role Play: Greeting in the morning. Work in pairs. Memorize the dialogue at the beginning of Lesson 2, and act out the scene.

2E.6   Role Play: Greeting in the afternoon. It's a warm afternoon. You meet your friend on your way to school. Greet him or her and ask a few questions. Your friend is enjoying school, and you are glad to hear about it. As you are in a hurry, you will have to say good-bye.

2E.7   Role Play: Greeting in the evening. It's after the evening class. It's cold, and you have a slight cold. You meet your Japanese friend who is taking French. You are taking Japanese. Greet your friend and exchange questions and answers on the following:

1. weather
2. how he or she feels this evening
3. how school is
4. if your friend finds the class interesting
5. say 'good-night' in Japanese

2E.8   In Japanese, tell your classmates the following things:

1. that it is very warm today
2. that you understand Spanish a little
3. that school is enjoyable
4. that Mr. Yamada does not understand Spanish
5. that you are pleased to meet your classmate (ask your classmate to be favorable to you)
6. that class is enjoyable
7. that Japanese is interesting
8. that you'll have to leave

VOCABULARY

VERBS   (---)

ADJECTIVES

ii	(good: colloquial form of yoi, 2.9)
tanoshii	(enjoyable, 2.9)
omoshiroi	(interesting; fun, 2.9)
yokatta	([sometnig] was good): the past form of ii)

NOUNS

kyoo	(today)
(o)tenki	(weather, 2.3)
(o)genki	(in good health; fine, 2.5)
gakkoo	(school)
kurasu	(class)

OTHERS

ohayoo gozaimasu	(good morning, 2.1)
honto ni	(really; truly, 2.10)
okagesamade	(fortunately; thank you for asking, 2.6)
mo	(also; too, 2.7)
doo	(how, 2.8)
totemo	(very much, 2.10)
sore	(that)
sore wa yokatta desu ne!	(I'm glad to hear that; that was good!)
ja, mata	(I'll see you, 2.11)
sayoonara	(good-bye, 2.1)

ADDITIONAL VOCABULARY

gokigenyoo	(Farewell; good-bye, 2.1)
ikaga desu ka?	(How are you? 2.5)
aa	(oh; ah; well)
Kimu	(the Korean name 'Kim' as pronounced in Japanese)
maa maa desu	(I'm so so; not too bad)
isogashii	(busy)
ashita	(tomorrow)
mata ashita	(I'll see you [again] tomorrow)
konnichiwa	(good afternoon; good day; hello, 2.1)
atsui	(hot)
kombanwa	(good evening, 2.1)
samui	(cold weather; [to feel] cold)
ee	(yeah; informal way to say 'yes')
demo	(but)
chotto	(a littel bit)
kaze o hikimashita	(I've caught a cold; I have a cold)
ikemasen ne!	(that's too bad!)
odaiji ni	(please take care of yourself)
arigatoo gozaimasu	(thank you very much)
oyasuminasai	(good night, 2.1)
furansugo	(the French language)
supeingo	(the Spanish language)

3

Instructor:	minasan, kochira o mite kudasai. ii desu ka?
Students:	hai.
Instructor:	kiite kudasai. 'kore wa hon desu.'
	ja, itte kudasai. 'kore wa hon desu.'
Students:	kore wa hon desu.
Instructor:	ja, kotaete kudasai. kore wa hon desu ka?
Students:	hai, sore wa hon desu.
Instructor:	kore wa hon desu ka, empitsu desu ka?
Students:	sore wa empitsu desu.
Instructor:	*(Pointing to an object near Student A,)*
	sore wa nan desu ka?
Student A:	kore wa shimbun desu.
Instructor:	*(Pointing to a desk in distance,)*
	ja, minasan, are o mite kudasai.
Students:	dore desu ka?
Instructor:	are desu. are wa isu desu ka, tsukue desu ka?
Students:	are wa tsukue desu.
Instructor:	ja, are mo tsukue desu ka?
Students:	iie, chigaimasu. are wa tsukue de wa arimasen.
	are wa mado desu.
Instructor:	hai, soo desu.

ENGLISH EQUIVALENT

Instructor: Everybody. May I have your attention please. (Please look this way.)
Are you ready? (Is it OK [to begin]?)
Students: Yes.
Instructor: Please listen [to me]. 'This is a book.'
Now, please say [it]. 'This is a book.'
Students: This is a book.
Instructor: Now, please answer. Is this a book?
Students: Yes, that is a book.
Instructor: Is this a book or [is it] a pencil?
Students: That is a pencil.
Instructor: *(Pointing to an object near Student A,)*
What is that [thing near you]?
Student A: This is a newspaper.
Instructor: *(Pointing to a desk in distance,)*
Well, everyone, please look at that [thing over there].
Students: Which one?
Instructor: That [one] over there. Is that a chair or [is it] a desk?
Students: That [one over there] is a desk.
Instructor: Then, is that [thing over there] also a desk?
Students: No, it isn't. That [thing over there] is not a desk.
That is a window.
Instructor: Yes, that is right.

GRAMMATICAL AND CULTURAL NOTES

3.1   minasan

When you address a group of people such as a class, you use the word **minasan**. This means everybody. The teacher usually begins speaking to the class by saying **minasan** to catch attention of everyone.

minasan,	kochira o mite kudasai.	(**Everybody,** please look this way.)
minasan,	ohayoo gozaimasu!	(Good morning, **everyone!**)
minasan,	ogenki desu ka?	(How's **everyone?**)
minasan,	sayoonara!	(Good-bye, **everyone!**)

3.2   kochira o mite kudasai

kochira means 'this direction' and **...o mite kudasai** means 'please look at ...' This sentence means 'Please look this [speaker's] direction' or 'Please look at me.' The teacher usually says this expression to catch attention of the students to begin his or her class. The students are expected to stop talking and be ready to begin the lesson. In English the teacher may say, 'May I have your attention, please.' for the same purpose.

minasan, kochira o mite kudasai. (Everyone, please look this way.)

3.3 ii desu ka?

ii desu ka? literally means 'Is it good?' or 'Is it OK?' When the teacher asks this question at the beginning of the class it means 'Is it OK to begin the class?' or 'Are you ready to begin?' If you are ready, you say '**hai**' or nod.

ii desu ka?	**(Are you ready?)**
hai.	**(Yes.)**

3.4 kiite kudasai

kiite is the **-te form** of the verb **kiku** (to hear or to listen). **mite** is the **-te form** of the verb **miru** (to see or to look). The **-te** is one of the verb endings. **kudasai**, when spoken independently, means 'please give me [something].' When **kudasai** is added to the **-te form** of a verb, it means 'please give me the favor of your doing such and such,' or 'please do such and such.' In Japanese dictionaries, verbs are listed in their dictionary forms. When you learn a new verb it is a good idea to learn both the **dictionary form** and the **-te form** along with the **-masu form**.

Dictionary form		-masu form	-te form	-te form + kudasai
kiku	(to hear)	kikimasu	kiite	kiite kudasai
miru	(to see)	mimasu	mite	mite kudasai
i[w]u	(to say)	iimasu	itte	itte kudasai
kotaeru	(to answer)	kotaemasu	kotaete	kotaete kudasai
hanasu	(to speak)	hanashimasu	hanashite	hanashite kudasai

3.5 kore, sore, are, and dore

The word **kore** means 'this' or 'this one' and it usually refers to a thing or things near the speaker, or to what he or she is holding. The word **sore** means 'that' or 'that one' and it usually refers to a thing or things which are located near the person addressed. The word **are** refers to a thing or things 'over there' or 'over yonder,' removed from both the speaker and the hearer, either within sight or out of sight. The word **kore** is maintained when both the speaker and hearer are near the object discussed. The word **dore** is an interrogative word meaning 'which' or 'which one.'

kore wa hon desu.	**(This** is a book.)
sore wa hon desu.	**(That** is a book.)
are wa hon desu.	**(That over there** is a book.)
kore wa hon desu ka?	(Is **this** a book?)
hai, **sore** wa hon desu.	(Yes, **that** is a book.)
dore desu ka?	**(Which one** is it?)

In English the distinction is made only between **this** and **that**, whereas in Japanese the distinction is three-way: **kore** (this), **sore** (that), and **are** (that over there). This distinction, however, is basically relative; the same object may be called **kore**, **sore**, or **are**, depending upon how the speaker perceives it in relation to other people or objects.

3.6   kochira, sochira, achira, and dochira

The word **kochira** means 'this way,' or 'my way,' and **sochira** 'that way' or 'your way,' and **achira**, 'that way ' or 'away from both you and me.' The word **dochira** is an interrogative word meaning 'which way.' The segments **ko-, so-, a-,** and **do-** in this set of words as well as in the set in **3.5** are related. There are more of these words which will be introduced later.

> **kochira** o   mite kudasai.   (Please look **this way**. Please look **at me**.)
> **sochira** o   mite kudasai.   (Please look **that way**. Please look **your way**.)
> **achira** o   mite kudasai.   (Please look **that way over there**.)
>
> **dochira** desu ka?   (**Which way** is it?)

3.7   Nouns

Japanese nouns are not inflected. In many languages such as English, German, or French, a word like 'pencil' has specific endings to make such grammatical distinctions as singularity-plurality. A Japanese nouns such as **empitsu** can mean 'a pencil' or 'pencils.' There is no article in Japanese, so the word **empitsu** can also mean 'a pencil,' 'pencils,' 'the pencil,' or 'the pencils.' The Japanese use other devices to express these subtle meanings, if required.

3.8   ... ka, ... ka?

When two or more short sentences, each ending with the question marker **ka**, are combined into one longer interrogative sentence as in **kore wa hon desu ka, empitsu desu ka?** the result is a question which asks that a choice be made between the alternatives. In English the word 'or' represents the same idea.

> kore wa   hon desu **ka**, empitsu desu **ka**?   (Is this a book **or** is this a pencil?)
> are wa   isu desu **ka**, tsukue desu **ka**?   (Is that over there a chair **or** is it a desk?)

3.9   o marking the Direct Object

The particle **o** is a direct object marker. When **o** is added to a word, it makes that word as the direct object of the verb in the sentence.

> **are** o   mite kudasai.   (Please look at **that thing over there**.)
> **mado** o   mite kudasai.   (Please look at **the window**.)
> **kokuban** o   mite kudasai.   (Please look at **the chalkboard**.)
> **kochira** o   mite kudasai.   (Please look at **me [this way or this direction]**.)

3.10   de wa arimasen

To make the negative form of **Noun + desu**, change **desu** to **de wa arimsen**.

iie, are wa **tsukue de wa   arimasen**.   (No, that **i s not a desk**.)
iie, kore wa **hon de wa   arimasen**.   (No, this **i s not a book**.)

When **desu** follows an adjective the negation is made in a different way which will be introduced later.

3.11   Contractions

There are contractions in Japanese just as there are in English. Contracted forms are spoken frequently among native speakers in casual conversations at a normal tempo. In written Japanese, contracted forms are less commonly used. The classroom use of contractions may vary according to the size of the class and the type of students. The instructor may apply his or her judgment and advise the students on how to use the contracted forms. **ja** is the contracted form of **dewa**. Thus **de wa arimasen** may be spoken as **jà arimasen** in a conversational style. Similarly, **dewa** for 'well, then' can be spoken as **ja**. In writing, **de wa** should be retained.

iie,   are wa   tsukue **ja arimasen**.   (No, that **isn't** a desk.)
ja,   are wa   nan desu ka?   (**Then**, what is that?)

3.12   'hai, soo desu' and 'iie, chigaimasu'

hai, soo desu means 'Yes, that's right.' When a Japanese speaker agrees with what he or she hears, this expression is a suitable response. The word **s o o** means 'in that way' or 'that is correct.' This is one of the most frequently spoken words in Japanese conversations.

iie, chigaimasu is the opposite of **hai, soo desu**. The word **iie** means 'no' and **chigaimasu** means 'you are mistaken' or 'that is not correct.'

PRONUNCIATION NOTES

3P.1   [ts] and [s]

The consonants [ts] and [s] are two different sounds, and they occur before the vowel [u]. The difference between [tsu] and [su] distinguishes a number of words in Japanese. For example, **tsuki** means 'the moon' and **suki** means 'I like'; **tsumi** is 'a crime' and **sumi** is 'a corner.' The students are often unaware of this distinction since the [ts] sound does not occur at the beginning of a word in English. They tend to leave the initial [t] off from the [tsu] syllable, thus neglecting the distinction between [tsu] and [su].

Exercise: The students practice pronouncing the following words correctly. The instructor checks their pronunciation.

tsuki	(the moon)	suki	(I like)
tsumi	(a crime)	sumi	(a corner)
tsuri	(fishing)	suri	(pickpocket)
tsukue	(desk)		

Some students may confuse **'tsu'** and **'chu.'**   The instructor should check the students' pronunciation of these sounds to make sure they can make the correct **'tsu'** sound.

3P.2 Syllabic or Moraic Nasals

There is a unique class of sounds in Japanese called syllabic nasals or moraic nasals. These sounds are unique in the sense that each of the nasal consonants [m, n, ŋ] that are usually non-syllabic in other languages may be lengthened to form syllables or moras by themselves. A 'mora,' is a unit of duration; and moras are basic units of Japanese utterances. A mora can be a vowel as in [a], a consonant + a vowel as in [ka], a consonant + the semi-vowel [y] + a vowel as in [kya], or a consonant as the [t] in [itte], or it can be a syllabic nasal by itself as the [n] in [hon]. Immediately before a vowel within a syllable [m], [n], and [ŋ] are regular consonants, but when they come at the end of a word or immediately before another consonant they are syllabic or moraic. Occasionally, there are cases in which a 'n' before a vowel or [y] may be syllabic or non-syllabic. Consult with your instructor or a native speaker for the syllable division. When you encounter a syllabic nasal it is important to give extra length to that sound.

Exercise: The students identify syllabic or moraic nasals in the following words by adding dot under them. The instructor checks the students' pronunciation to make sure that their syllabic or moraic nasals are long enough.

1. empitsu	5. hon	9. Tanaka-san
2. nihongo	6. otenki	10. nan desu ka
3. shimbun	7. genki	11. hon'ya (book store)
4. pen	8. honto ni	12. kon'ya (this evening)

The students distinguish the following words:

kon'yaku	(marriage engagement)	[ko-n-ya-ku]
konnyaku	(Japanese yam cake or noodles used in sukiyaki)	[ko-n-nya-ku]
konyakku	(cognac)	[ko-nya-k-ku]

3P.3 Single Consonants and Double Consonants

Good pronunciation in speaking Japanese can be achieved only with accurate control over the lengths of sounds. The vowel-duration contrast was stressed in Lesson 1. In a similar manner, the single consonants and double consonants must be kept clearly contrasted. The Japanese native speakers normally make the double consonants -pp-, -tt-, or -kk- 2.5 to 3.0 times as long as their single counterparts. In the minds of native speakers, the first -k- of the double -kk- stands for one mora. This means that the word **gakkoo** is composed of four moras, **ga-k-ko-o**, and each of the four moras takes approximately the same length of time. If the student tries to pronounce -kk- three times as long as a -k-, the resulting sounds come out just about right in length. It is important that the beginning students of Japanese establish a good habit of pronouncing double consonants long enough.

Exercise: The students pronounce the words below, imitaing the instructor's model. Then the instructor checks the accuracy of each student's pronunciation individually.

machi	(town)	matchi	(match)
ichi	(one)	itchi	(agreement)
isho	(will)	issho	(together)
supai	(spy)	suppai	(sour)

saki	(ahead)	sakki	(a little while ago)
kite kudasai	(please come)	kitte kudasai	(please cut)

Exercise: Divide each of the following words into moras. Pronounce them correctly, giving one beat to each of the mora in the words.

1. gakkoo
2. empitsu
3. ohayoo gazaimasu
4. nihongo
5. shimbun

6. zasshi
7. kyoo wa ii tenki desu.
8. gakkoo wa omoshiroi desu.
9. tsukue desu ka, tokei desu ka?
10. zasshi desu ka, shimbun desu ka?

3P.4 [ɸ]

It was mentioned earlier that the consonant [ɸ] is represented by the letter ' f ' in this book. The consonant [ɸ] occurs only before the vowel [u]. Among the English consonants the [f] sound is the most similar sound to the Japanese [ɸ]. However, there is one slight difference between the Japanese [ɸ] and the English [f]: the former is a voiceless bilabial fricative whereas the latter is a voiceless labiodental fricative. The difference is in the point of articulation: the Japanese [ɸ] is pronounced with both lips brought together, while the English [f] is pronounced with the upper teeth touching the lower lip. To pronounce the Japanese [ɸ] correctly, first pucker your lips and blow air as though you were blowing out a candle, then reduce the air flow to a gentle puff.

Exercise: Pronounce the following words carefully with correct [ɸ] sounds wherever the letter ' f ' appears.

1. furansugo   (the French language)
2. saifu   (wallet)
3. naifu   (knife)
4. Fuji   (Mt. Fuji)

EXERCISES

3E.1   Physical Response: The instructor says the following expressions and the students respond in action.

1. mado o mite kudasai.
2. tokei o mite kudasai.
3. hon o mite kudasai.
4. ue o mite kudasai.
5. shita o mite kudasai.
6. migi o mite kudasai.
7. hidari o mite kudasai.
8. hon o akete kudasai.
9. hon o tojite kudasai.

10. empitsu o totte kudasai.
11. tatte kudasai.
12. suwatte kudasai.

3E.2 Repetition Drill: The instructor says the following expressions holding the appropriate objects, and the students repeat after the instructor correctly without looking at the book. The instructor checks the students' pronunciation.

1. (holding a pencil)   empitsu desu.
2. (holding a magazine)   zasshi desu.
3. (holding a book)   hon desu.
4. (holding a newspaper)   shimbun desu.
5. (holding a pen)   pen desu.
6. (touching a desk)   tsukue desu.
7. (touching a chair)   isu desu.
8. (touching a wristwatch)   tokei desu.
9. (holding a sheet of paper)   kami desu.
10. (holding a key)   kagi desu.

3E.3 Response Drill: The instructor asks the questions holding or touching the objects, and the students answer affirmatively, replacing the word **kore** with **sore**.

1. (holding a book)   kore wa hon desu ka?
2. (holding a pen)   kore wa pen desu ka?
3. (holding a sheet of paper)   kore wa kami desu ka?
4. (holding a key)   kore wa kagi desu ka?
5. (holding a newspaper)   kore wa shimbun desu ka?
6. (holding a magazine)   kore wa zasshi desu ka?
7. (touching a wristwatch)   kore wa tokei desu ka?
8. (touching a desk)   kore wa tsukue desu ka?
9. (holding the pencil)   kore wa empitsu desu ka?
10. (touching the chair)   kore wa isu desu ka?

3E.4 Response Drill: The instructor points to various objects near the students and asks the following questions. The students answer affirmatively beginning with **hai** and using the word **kore**.

1. sore wa empitsu desu ka?
2. sore wa shimbun desu ka?

3. sore wa   kagi desu ka?
4. sore wa   kami desu ka?
5. sore wa   zasshi desu ka?
6. sore wa   seetaa desu ka?
7. sore wa   saifu desu ka?

3E.5   Response Drill: The instructor points to the various objects away from both himself or herself and the students, and asks the following questions. The students give correct responses.

1. are wa   isu desu ka,   tsukue desu ka?
2. are wa   tsukue desu ka,   mado desu ka?
3. are wa   hon desu ka,   zasshi desu ka?
4. are wa   tokei desu ka,   mado desu ka?
5. are wa   mado desu ka,   kokuban desu ka?
6. are wa   shimbun desu ka,   kami desu ka?
7. are wa   seetaa desu ka,   saifu desu ka?
8. are wa   empitsu desu ka,   pen desu ka?
9. are wa   kagi desu ka,   tokei desu ka?
10. are wa   kami desu ka,   kagi desu ka?

3E.6   Response Drill: The students give negative answers to the following questions first. Then the instructor asks the students to identify the names of the objects. The students give correct answers as demonstrated by the example.

Example:
Instructor: (holding a pen)	kore wa hon desu ka?
Student:	iie, sore wa hon de wa arimasen.
Instructor:	dewa kore wa nan desu ka?
Student:	sore wa pen desu.

1. kore wa   kami desu ka?
2. kore wa   saifu desu ka?
3. kore wa   empitsu desu ka?
4. sore wa   kagi desu ka?
5. sore wa   zasshi desu ka?
6. are wa   kokuban desu ka?
7. are wa   tsukue desu ka?
8. are wa   isu desu ka?

3E.7   Say the following expressions in Japanese.

1. Please look at this.
2. What is this?
3. That is a pencil.
4. Please look at the window.
5. Please stand up.
6. Please open the window.
7. Please sit down.
8. Please speak in Japanese.
9. Please speak in English.
10. It's warm today, isn't it!
11. Yes, it really is warm today.
12. How is Japanese?
13. It's very interesting.
14. Is that over there a newspaper?
15. No, that's not a newspaper.

3E.8   Activity: Naming objects. Work in pairs. Student A and Student B show each other's belongings, and ask each other to name the objects in Japanese. If the answer is correct, say **'hai, soo desu.'** If the answer is wrong, say **'iie, chigaimasu.'** Include the objects listed below.

Example.   A: kore o mite kudasai. ii desu ka?
           B: hai.
           A: kore wa nan desu ka?
           B: sore wa hon desu.
           A: hai, soo desu.

1. a book
2. a notebook
3. a pencil
4. a newspapaer
5. a pen
6. a sheet of paper
7. a wallet
8. a magazine
9. a key
10. a sweater

3E.9   Activity: Acting out. Work in pairs, A and B. First, A says the following expressions in Japanese. B acts out the commamd. If correctly done, say **'hai, soo desu.'** If the action is wrong, **'iie, chigaimasu.'** Next, reverse the roles.

1. Please look at the window.
2. Please look at the instructor.
3. Please look at [your] right.
4. Please look at [your] left.
5. Please stand up.
6. Please sit down.
7. Please open [your] book.
8. Please close [your] book.

VOCABULARY

VERBS

mite kudasai	(please look, 3.2, 3.4)
miru	(to look; to see, 3.4)
kiite kudasai	(please listen, 3.4)
kiku	(to listen; to hear, 3.4)
itte kudasai	(please say, 3.4)
i[w]u	(to say, 3.4)
kotaete kudasai	(please answer, 3.4)
kotaeru	(to answer; to respond, 3.4)
hanashite kudasai	(please speak, 3.4)

ADJECTIVES

ii desu ka?	(Are you ready? Is it okay to begin?)

NOUNS

minasan	(everyone, 3.1)
hon	(book)
empitsu	(pencil, 3.7)
pen	(pen)
zasshi	(magazine)
shimbun	(newspaper)
isu	(chair)
tsukue	(desk)
mado	(window)

OTHERS

kochira	(this way, 3.2, 3,6)
ii desu ka?	(Is it OK?; Are you ready?; Is it good? 3.3)
kore	(this, 3.5)
sore	(that, 3.5)
are	(that over there, 3.5)
dore	(which one, 3.5)
... ka, ... ka?	(a question giving a choice among alternatives, 3.8)
de wa arimasen	(is not: negation of NOUN + desu, 3.10)
hai, soo desu	(Yes, that's right, 3.12)
ja	(contracted form of de wa, 3.11)
nan	(what)
nan desu ka?	(What is it?)
sochira	(that way; that one; your way, 3.6)
achira	(that way over there, 3.6)
dochira	(which way; which one of the two, 3.6)
sore wa nan desu ka?	(What is that [thing near you]?)
kore desu ka?	(Do you mean this one?)
hai, sore desu.	(Yes, that is the one.)
are o mite kudasai.	(Please look at that thing over there.)
o	(direct object marker, 3.9)
dore desu ka?	(Which one?)

ADDITIONAL VOCABULARY

nooto	(notebook)
tokei	(clock)
kami	(paper)
kagi	(key)
seetaa	(sweater)
saifu	(wallet)
kokuban	(blackboard)
akete kudasai	(Please open)
tojite kudasai	(Please close [the book])
ue	(up; above; on top of)
shita	(down; below; under)
migi	(right hand side; right)
hidari	(left hand side; left)
tatte kudasai	(please stand up)
suwatte kudasai	(please sit down)

4

Tanaka:	ano kata wa donata desu ka?
Brown:	dono kata desu ka?
Tanaka:	ano onna no kata desu.
Brown:	aa, ano kata wa Sasaki-sensei desu.
Tanaka:	nihongo no sensei desu ka?
Brown:	hai, watakushitachi no nihongo no sensei desu.
Tanaka:	ja, ano hito wa dare desu ka?
Brown:	ano otoko no hito desu ka?
Tanaka:	hai, ano otoko no hito desu.
Brown:	ano hito wa Chen-san desu.
	watakushi no kurasu-meeto desu.
Tanaka:	*(Looking at the book Mr. Brown is holding,)*
	sore wa nihongo no kyookasho desu ka?
Brown:	hai, soo desu.
Tanaka:	chotto misete kudasai.
Brown:	hai, doozo.
Tanaka:	ii hon desu ne!
Brown:	ee, kanari ii hon desu.
Tanaka:	*(Looking at a briefcase on the floor,)*
	sono kaban wa dare no kaban desu ka?
Brown:	saa, wakarimasen. watakushi no ja arimasen.

ENGLISH EQUIVALENT

Tanaka: Who is that person over there?

Brown: Which person [are you talking about]?

Tanaka: That lady over there.

Brown: Oh, she [that person over there] is Professor Sasaki.

Tanaka: Is she [your] Japanese teacher?

Brown: Yes, she is our Japanese teacher.

Tanaka: Then, who is that person over there?

Brown: [Do you mean] that [young] man over there?

Tanaka: Yes, I mean that [young] man over there.

Brown: He [that person over there] is Mr. Chen.
         [He] is my classmate.

Tanaka: *(Looking at the book Mr. Brown is holding,)*
         Is that the Japanese textbook?

Brwon: Yes, it is. [Yes, that is correct.]

Tanaka: Please let me see it a minute.

Brown: Yes, please.

Tanaka: It's a good book, isn't it!

Brown: Yes, it's a pretty good book.

Tanaka: *(Looking at a briefcase on the floor,)*
         Whose briefcase is that?

Brown: Well, I'm not sure. It's not mine.

GRAMMATICAL AND CULTURAL NOTES

4.1   kono, sono, ano, and dono

The words **kore** (this), **sore** (that), and **are** (that over there) have their corresponding forms **kono** (this [things]), **sono** (that [thing]) and **ano** (that [thing] over there) which are used before nouns. In English, the same word 'this' or 'that' can be used in both positions as in 'This is a book' or 'This book is mine.' In Japanese the above two grammatical slots require two different words: **kore** stands alone; while **kono** is used if the following word is a noun, animate or inanimate.

> **kore** (this) **sore** (that) **are** (that over there)
> **kono** hon (**this** book) **sono** hon (**that** book) **ano** hon (**that** book **over there**)
>
> **dore** (**which** one)
> **dono** hon (**which** book)
>
> **ano** kata wa donata desu ka? (Who is **that** person **over there**?)
> **dono** kata desu ka? (**Which** person are you talking about?)

4.2   donata, dare

Distinguishing between different levels of politeness is important in speaking a good Japanese. **donata** and **dare** both mean 'who' but they are different in the degree of politeness. When you ask 'who' referring to a person older in age and higher in social standing than yourself, you normally use the **exalted** word **donata**. You can use the less polite **dare** when you refer to someone who is not older or higher in social status. Similarly, the word **kata** (person) is an exalted word while the word **hito** (person) is neutral.

<table>
<tr><td>ano kata wa donata desu ka?</td><td>(Who is that person over there?)</td><td>Exalted</td></tr>
<tr><td>ano hito wa dare desu ka?</td><td>(Who is that person over there?)</td><td>Neutral</td></tr>
</table>

4.3   otoko, onna

otoko means 'male' and **onna** means 'female.' These words are used with **kata** (honorable person), **hito** (person), or **ko** (part of **kodomo** meaning 'child').

<table>
<tr><td>otoko no kata</td><td>(man or men)</td><td>Exalted expression</td></tr>
<tr><td>otoko no hito</td><td>(man or men)</td><td>Neutral expression</td></tr>
<tr><td>otoko no ko</td><td>(boy or boys)</td><td>Neutral expression</td></tr>
<tr><td>onna no kata</td><td>(lady or ladies)</td><td>Exalted expression</td></tr>
<tr><td>onna no hito</td><td>(woman or women)</td><td>Neutral expression</td></tr>
<tr><td>onna no ko</td><td>(girl or girls)</td><td>Neutral expression</td></tr>
</table>

The words **otoko** and **onna** should **not** be used **alone** to mean man or woman. They may sound offensive to Japanese because TV newscasters often use these words referring to crime suspects.

4.4   no meaning 'of'

The particle **no** linking two nouns marks that the first noun is the modifier of the second noun. The second noun is the head of the construction.

<table>
<tr><td>nihongo no hon</td><td>(Japanese book; book of the Japanese language)</td></tr>
<tr><td>eigo no hon</td><td>(English book; book of the English language)</td></tr>
<tr><td>nihongo no kyookasho</td><td>(Japanese textbook; textbook of the Japanese language)</td></tr>
<tr><td>nihongo no sensei</td><td>(Japanese teacher; a teacher of Japanese)</td></tr>
<tr><td>nan no hon</td><td>(what book; a book of what content)</td></tr>
</table>

In English a modifier and the head noun can be juxtaposed as in 'English book' or 'Japanese class' but in Japanese the particle **no** is required between the two nouns.

4.5   no meaning possesive 's'

There is no category of pronouns in Japanese. The similar idea is expressed by a set of nouns and particles. The particle **no** is added to the nouns **watakushi**, **anata**, **ano hito**, and so forth to express the idea of possesive pronouns. As English speakers are accustomed to using the personal pronouns in possesive forms, the following Japanese equivalents are given for convenience.

watakushi no hon	(**my** book)
anata no hon	(**your** book)
ano hito no hon	(**his/her** book; **that person's** book)
ano kata no hon	(**his/her** book; **that honorable person's** book)
watakushitachi no hon	(**our** book)
dare no hon	(**whose** book)
donata no hon	(**whose** [**which exalted person's**] book)
Tanaka-san no hon	(**Miss Tanaka's** book)
Buraun-san no hon	(**Mr. Brown's** book)

In the above phrases the head noun may be omitted when the context makes the meaning clear. The resulting expressions correspond to English 'mine,' 'yours,' 'his/hers,' and so forth.

kore wa **anata no** desu ka?	(Is this **yours** ?)
iie, kore wa **watakushi no** ja arimasen.	(No, this is not **mine**)
are wa **Sasaki-sensei no** desu.	(That is **Professor Sasaki's** .)

4.6 misete kudasai

misete is the **te-form** of the verb **miseru** (to show). As explained previously, the **te-form** of a verb followed by **kudasai** indicates 'request' or 'please do such and such.'

chotto **misete kudasai** .	(**Please show** [**it to me**] for a little while; **Please let me see it** a minute.)
sore o **misete kudasai** .	(**Pease let me see** that.)

4.7 hai, doozo

doozo means 'please.' This expression is used to accompany the gesture of offering something.

hai, doozo	(**Yes, please.**) or (**Here you are.**)

4.8 Adjectives as Noun Modifiers

An adjective can modify a noun. When an adjective is used as a modifier of a noun it takes the ending **-i** (the dictionary form). The word order in the 'modifier + head noun' is the same in English and in Japanese.

ii hon	(a **good** book)
ii tenki	(**good** weather)
chiisai hon	(a **small** book)
ookii hon	(a **large** book)

4.9 nanigo

The interrogative word **nani** (what) can be combined with certain other words to make a compound word. The word **-go** (language) in **nanigo** (what language) -- which also appears in **nihongo** or **eigo** -- is a **bound word** and cannot be used as a free, independent word. A compound word, **nanigo** , grammatically acts as a single word. There are many bound words in Japanese.

> **nanigo** no kyookasho desu ka? (**What language** textbook is it?)
> **nanigo** ga wakarimasu ka? (**What language(s)** do you understand?)

4.10 sensei

sensei means 'teacher,' 'master (as in 'a master of martial arts' or 'a master of traditional dance'), or 'doctor' (in the sense of 'college professor' as well as 'physician, 'dentist,' and so on). **sensei** is also used as a title of respect in addressing an older person who has a professional or scholarly air. **sensei** is attached to the surname as a suffix and replaces **-san.**

> **sensei, ohayoo gozaimasu** (Good morning, **Professor!**)
> **Sasaki-sensei** (**Professor** Sasaki)

PRONUNCIATION NOTES

4P.1 Accent

In English the noun 'import' is distinguished from the verb 'import' by its stress: the noun receives a strong stress on the first syllable, while the verb receives a strong stress on the second syllable. A similar phenomenon exists in Japanese. The word **kami** meaning 'god' receives accent on the first syllable, while the word **kami** meaning 'paper' receives accent on the second syllable. English stress and Japanese accent function similarly to distinguish words, but they are significantly different in their manifestations. A stressed syllable in English is spoken much louder, higher in pitch, and longer in duration. An accented syllable in Japanese is also higher in pitch, but not necessarily louder or longer. In Japanese, both accented and unaccented syllables must retain the basic durational unit, thus maintaining the equal length. The range of rise and fall in pitch is small, so the students may experience difficulty hearing the accents of Japanese words. The most important feature of Japanese accent is the **fall in pitch** ; the syllable preceding the fall is the accented syllable, or accent core, of the word.

Exercise: Listen carefully for the difference between the following pairs of words. The model should be a native speaker of standard Japanese or the tape. Practice pronouncing them correctly.

1.	**ka**mi	(God)	kami	(paper)
2.	**ka**ki	(oyster)	kaki	(persimmon)
3.	**ha**shi	(chopstick)	ha**shi**	(bridge)
4.	**a**me	(rain)	a**me**	(candy)

The complexity of Japanese pitch accent has been the object of studies by many linguists. Japanese words change their accents when they are compounded or in phrases. Also, different dialects in Japanese have different accent patterns. Although the native speakers of Japanese can tell by each others' accents where they are from, accent does not usually confuse them in speech, except for an occasional problem with words such as those listed above. Theoretically speaking, the student of Japanese should learn the accent of each word as he or she first encounters it. Some Japanese language textbooks mark accents with lines drawn above words or sentences. But the complex nature of accent phenomena and the wide variations between dialects and individuals make the use of these lines confusing and cumbersome. After some consideration the author of this book has decided not to mark accent in this textbook so that the students can imitate the speech of the instrucotr or the tape.

4P.2   Devoiced Vowels

You may already have noticed that some [i] and [u] sounds are not pronounced clearly in the speech of your models, even though they are spelled out in the text; these sounds are devoiced vowels. When the vowels [i] and [u] occur between two voiceless consonants such as [k], [s], [ts], [t] and so forth, or when they are after a voiceless consonant and at the end of an utterance, they may be devoiced, that is, whispered or not clearly enunciated. When a syllable is unaccented, it is more apt to be devoiced. Although native speakers devoice [i] and [u] automatically in these environments and may be unaware that they are doing so because devoicing does not change meanings. When the student of Japanese acquires the habit of devoicing, his or her pronunciation improves, sounding more like that of a native speaker.

Exercise: Listen carefully to the speech model provided by the instructor or by the tape. Learn how to pronounce the devoiced vowels in the following words. Devoiced vowels are marked by underlines.

1. watak<u>u</u>shi	6. watak<u>u</u>sh<u>i</u>tachi
2. yorosh<u>i</u>ku	7. rek<u>is</u>hi
3. s<u>u</u>koshi	8. Sasak<u>i</u>-sensei
4. emp<u>it</u>su	9. s<u>u</u>peingo
5. ts<u>u</u>kue	10. nandes<u>u</u> ka?

EXERCISES

4E.1   Drill on **kono, sono, ano, & dono**. The instructor shows several pictures of different people or draws stick figures on the chalkboard. First, the instructor identifies them as in the following examples.

Examples:
1. kono kata wa Sasaki-sensei desu.
2. kono kata wa Tomita-sensei desu.
3. kono hito wa Buraun-san desu.
4. kono hito wa Tanaka-san desu.
5. kono hito wa Chen-san desu.

Next, the instructor(A) asks questions, and the students(B) respond using the word **sono** as in the following examples.

Examples:

    1. A: kono kata wa donata desu ka?

          B: sono kata wa Sasaki-sensei desu.

    2. A: kono hito wa dare desu ka?

          B: sono hito wa Tanaka-san desu.

    3. A: kono hito wa Chen-san desu ka?

          B: hai, soo desu. sono hito wa Chen-san desu.

Then, the instructor moves away from the pictures, point to the figures from distance and asks questions. The students first clarify which figure the instructor is pointing to. Then they answer the questions by correctly choosing **sono** and **ano**.

Examples:

    1. A: ano kata wa donata desu ka?

          B: dono kata desu ka?

          A: ano onna no kata desu.

          B: ano onna no kata wa Sasaki-sensei desu.

    2. A: ano hito wa dare desu ka?

          B: dono hito desu ka?

          A: ano otoko no hito desu.

          B: ano otoko no hito wa Chen-san desu.

4E.2   Activity: Identifying names of people. Work in pairs, A and B. Using the pictures and/or the stick figures on the chalkboard, A and B ask questions to each other and identify the names of the people and if they are teachers or students. Make sure that your partner uses **kono**, **sono**, **ano**, and **dono** correctly.

Examples:

    1. A: ano kata wa donata desu ka?

          B: dono kata desu ka?

          A: ano onna no kata desu.

          B: ano kata wa Sasaki-sensei desu.

          A: Sasaki-sensei wa nan no sensei desu ka?

          B: ano sensei wa nihongo no sensei desu.

    3. A: ano hito wa dare desu ka?

          B: dono hito desu ka?

          A: ano otoko no hito desu.

    B: ano hito wa Kimu-san desu.

    A: Kimu-san wa sensei desu ka, gakusei desu ka?

    B: Kimu-san wa gakusei desu.

4E.3   Activity: Identify names of your classmates. Work in small groups. Point to the person sitting next to you and call him or her as **kono kata** (or **kono hito**), and the person near your partner as **sono kata** (or **sono hito**), and the person away from both you and your partner as **ano kata** (or **ano hito**). Ask each other the names of the classmates. If you don't know the person's name, ask **'onamae wa nan desu ka?'** Find the names of at least five people.

4E.4   Response Drill: The instructor shows various books and identifies them. The students listen and repeat.

    1. kore wa nihongo no kyookasho desu.

    2. kore wa supeingo no kyookasho desu.

    3. kore wa furansugo no kyookasho desu.

    4 kore wa nihongo no shimbun desu.

    5. kore wa nihongo no jisho desu.

    6. kore wa nihongo no zasshi desu.

Using the same objects and some other objects near the students or that are visible in class, the instructor asks questions and the students respond using **kor**e, **sore** , **are** and **kono...** , **sono...** , **ano...** correctly. Ask **'dore desu ka?'** or **'dono...desu ka?'** if the object in question is not clear.

    1. kore wa nihongo no kyookasho desu ka?

    2. sore mo nihongo no kyookasho desu ka?

    3. sono hon wa nanigo no hon desu ka?

    4. sono shimbun wa nanigo no shimbun desu ka?

    5. sono zasshi wa nanigo no zasshi desu ka?

4E.5   Dialogue Practice: First as a repetition drill, and next as a pair practice.

    1. A: sore wa nihongo no zasshi desu ka?

        B: hai, soo desu.

        A: chotto misete kudasai.

        B: hai, doozo.

        A: zuibun omoshiroi zasshi desu ne!

        B: ee, totemo omoshiroi zasshi desu.

2. A: sore wa nihon no empitsu desu ka?
   B: hai, soo desu.
   A: chotto misete kudasai.
   B: hai, doozo.
   A: ii empitsu desu ne!
   B: ee, totemo ii empitsu desu.

3. A: sore wa nan no hon desu ka?
   B: kore wa rekishi no kyookasho desu.
   A: chotto misete kudasai.
   B: hai, doozo.
   A: zuibun ookii hon desu ne!
   B: ee, totemo ookii hon desu.

4E.6   Response Drill: The instructor points to the objects near the students and asks the questions. The students answer **affirmatively** as shown in the example.

Example: Instructor: sono hon wa anata no hon desu ka?
         Student: hai, kono hon wa watakushi no hon desu.

1. sono empitsu wa anata no empitsu desu ka?
2. sono jisho wa anata no jisho desu ka?
3. sono saifu wa anata no saifu desu ka?
4. sono kagi wa anata no kagi desu ka?
5. sono seetaa wa anata no seetaa desu ka?
6. sono kaban wa anata no kaban desu ka?

4E.7   Response Drill: The instructor holds or points to objects and asks the questions. The students answer **negatively**. Then the instructor asks whose objects they are. The students give correct responses.

Example: Instructor: kono hon wa anata no desu ka?
         Student: iie, sono hon wa watakushi no ja arimasen.
         Instructor: ja, kore wa donata no desu ka?
         Student: sore wa Tanaka-san no desu.

1. kono kaban wa anata no desu ka?
2. kono seetaa wa anata no desu ka?
3. sono jisho wa anata no desu ka?
4. ano kyookasho wa anata no desu ka?

5. ano eigo no jisho wa anata no desu ka?
6. ano nihongo no shimbun wa anata no desu ka?

4E.8   Activity: Identifying owners.   The instructor goes around with a bag collecting from students small items such as pencils, pocket dictionaries, erasers, notebooks, and so forth.   Then the instructor picks out the objects from the bag, one by one, asks '**kore wa dare no ... desu ka?**' The students try to guess who each object belongs to, and respond by using the form '**... -san no ... desu.** Continue the activity until the owners of all the objects are identified.

VOCABULARY

VERBS

misete	(-te form of miseru, 4.6)
miseru	(to show; to let someone see)
misete kudasai	(please show [it] to me; please let me see [it], 4.6)
wakarimasen	(I'm not sure; I don't know: -masen form of wakarimasu)

ADJECTIVES   (---)

NOUNS

kata	(person [exalted]; honorable person, 4.2, 4.3)
onna	(female, 4.3)
onna no kata	(lady, 4.3)
onna no ko	(girl, 4.3)
sensei	(teacher; instructor, 4.10)
watakushitachi	(we)
watakushitachi no	(our, 4.5)
nihongo no sensei	(teacher of Japanese; Japanese language instructor, 4.4)
otoko	(male, 4.3)
hito	(person [neutral], 4.2, 4.3)
otoko no hito	(man; gentleman, 4.3)
otoko no ko	(boy, 4.3)
Chen-san	(Mr. [Mrs. or Miss] Chen)
kurasu-meeto	(classmate)
kyookasho	(textbook)
kaban	(briefcase; bag)

OTHERS

kono	(this ..., 4.1)
sono	(that ..., 4.1)
ano	(that ... over there, 4.1)
dono	(of which, 4.1)

donata	(who [exalted], 4.2)
dare	(who [neutral], 4.2)
ano hito	(that person over there; that person mentioned; he; she, 4.2)
chotto	(a little bit)
hai, doozo	(yes please; here you are, 4.7)
ii hon desu ne!	(It's a nice book!)
kanari	(quite; considerablly; pretty much)
dare no	(whose, 4.5)
saa	(well; let me think)
watakushi no	(my...; mine, 4.5)

ADDITIONAL VOCABULARY

gakusei	(student)
(o)tomodachi	(friend)
rekishi	(history)
jisho	(dictionary)
zuibun	(quite; extremely)
nihon no	(of Japan; Japanese ...)
nihongo no	(of the Japanese language; Japanese...)
ruumu-meeto	(roommate)

READING AND WRITING

Most Japanese books, magazines, and newspapers are written in vertical columns. The columns are written and read by moving downward from the top of the page, from right to left. The first column appears on the right side of the page so that the columns themselves progress from right to left. Such books and magazines open from what Westerners consider the back, or end. Mathematics and science books, however, contain equations and formulas, so they necessarily use horizontal writing. Also, in recent years young people are using horizontal writing more and more in their personal correspondence. College students usually take class notes in horizontally-lined notebooks. This book obviously follows the Western method of pagination and moves from left to right. The author has adopted the horizontal system of writing in this book for the sake of convenience. The instructor can add supplementary readings written in the vertical manner to acquaint the students with the original Japanese style of writing. The companion workbook titled *Introduction to Writing Japanese* was prepared for this purpose.

Three categories of symbols are used to write Japanese: the **hiragana** syllabary, the **katakana** syllabary, and **kanji** (Chinese characters). The **hiragana** syllabary with its **forty-six symbols** is the basis of modern Japanese writing. Each **kana** (**hiragana** and **katakana**) symbol represents one **syllable**, not one sound as in English. Any Japanese sentences can be written in **hiragana** alone, but the Japanese normally use **katakana** and **kanji** in addition to **hiragana**. The **katakana** syllabary is used to write Western loan words. Each **kanji** character represents one unit of meaning. There are approximately 1900 **kanji** in common use. Japanese children learn **hiragana** first and **katakana** next. They acquire **kanji** characters gradually as they progress in grades. A high-school graduate usually reads and writes most of 1900 **kanji**.

47

The following chart shows the first forty-six **hiragana** and the corresponding **katakana** symbols.

		Hiragana						**Katakana**		
a	i	u	e	o		a	i	u	e	o
あ	い	う	え	お		ア	イ	ウ	エ	オ
ka	ki	ku	ke	ko		ka	ki	ku	ke	ko
か	き	く	け	こ		カ	キ	ク	ケ	コ
sa	shi	su	se	so		sa	shi	su	se	so
さ	し	す	せ	そ		サ	シ	ス	セ	ソ
ta	chi	tsu	te	to		ta	chi	tsu	te	to
た	ち	つ	て	と		タ	チ	ツ	テ	ト
na	ni	nu	ne	no		na	ni	nu	ne	no
な	に	ぬ	ね	の		ナ	ニ	ヌ	ネ	ノ
ha	hi	fu	he	ho		ha	hi	fu	he	ho
は	ひ	ふ	へ	ほ		ハ	ヒ	フ	ヘ	ホ
ma	mi	mu	me	mo		ma	mi	mu	me	mo
ま	み	む	め	も		マ	ミ	ム	メ	モ
ya		yu		yo		ya		yu		yo
や		ゆ		よ		ヤ		ユ		ヨ
ra	ri	ru	re	ro		ra	ri	ru	re	ro
ら	り	る	れ	ろ		ラ	リ	ル	レ	ロ
wa				(w)o		wa				(w)o
わ				を		ワ				ヲ
N						N				
ん						ン				

In learning how to write any Japanese symbols, it is important to observe two things.
(1) You must know the **stroke order**.
(2) You must know **how each stroke ends**; that is, you must know whether it ends with a definite stop or it trails off.

The **stop ending**: When the stroke ends in a **stop**, press your pen firmly to mark a clear stop, then lift your pen quickly. A small circle at the end of each stroke indicates a stop ending.

Examples:　　こ。　　て。　　は。　　よ。

The **trailing ending**: To make the end trail off, move the pen slowly and lift it gradually so that the ending of the stroke thins until it disappears. Three dots at the end of a stroke iindicates trailing ending.

Examples:　　の　　し　　け　　つ

The Japanese used to write with brushes; the difference between a stop ending and a trailingending is more apparent when the writing instrument is a brush. Modern Japanese use pens and pencils to write, but they still observe the distinction in stroke endings when they write.

Beginning with this lesson, a reading and writing section is added atthe end of each lesson. The exercises in this section are based upon the materials presented prior to that page.

Exercise: Learn how to write each **hiragana** with the correct stroke order and stroke endings.

a　　あ　　て　あ
i　　い　　い　い
u　　う　　う
e　　え　　え
o　　お　　おお

ka	か	カ	か
ki	き		き
ku	く		く
ke	け		け
ko	こ		こ

sa	さ		さ
shi	し		し
su	す		す
se	せ		せ
so	そ		そ

ta	た	ナ	た
chi	ち		ち
tsu	つ		つ
te	て		て
to	と		と

na　な　ナ　ナ　な

ni　に　し゚　じ　に

nu　ぬ　し゚　ぬ　ぬ

ne　ね　し゚　ね　ね

no　の　の　の

ha　は　じ　は

hi　ひ　ひ

fu　ふ　ふ　ふ　ふ

he　へ　へ

ho　ほ　じ　じ　ほ

ma　ま　ニ　ま

mi　み　み　み

mu　む　む　む

me　め　め　め

mo　も　も　も

ya	や	つや や
yu	ゆ	ロ ゆ
yo	よ	よ

ra	ら	ら
ri	り	り
ru	る	る
re	れ	れ
ro	ろ	ろ

wa	わ	わ
wo	を	を
N	ん	ん

5

Tanaka: nihongo wa yasashii desu ka?

Brown: iie, yasashiku arimasen.

Tanaka: muzukashii desu ka?

Brown: hai, kanari muzukashii desu.

Tanaka: nihongo no kurasu wa ookii desu ka?

Brown: iie, sonna ni ookiku arimasen. choodo ii desu.

Tanaka: ii kurasu desu ka?

Brown: hai, totemo ii kurasu desu.

Tanaka: gakusei wa minna yoku benkyoo shimasu ka?

Brown: hai, minna totemo yoku benkyoo shimasu.

Tanaka: kyooshitsu wa doko desu ka?

Brown: ano tatemono no nikai desu.

Tanaka: ano ookii tatemono desu ka?

Brown: iie, are wa toshokan desu. ano chiisai tatemono desu.

Tanaka: aa, asoko desu ka.

               nihongo no kurasu de wa nihongo dake hanashimasu ka?

Brown: hai, taitei nihongo dake hanashimasu ga, sensei wa

             tokidoki eigo de setsumei shimasu.

Tanaka: Buraun-san wa uchi de mo nihongo o hanashimasu ka?

Brown: iie, hanashimasen. uchi de wa eigo o hanashimasu.

ENGLISH EQUIVALENT

Tanaka: Is Japanese easy [to learn] ?
Brown: No, it isn't easy.
Tanaka: Is it hard?
Brown: Oh, yes. It's quite difficult.
Tanaka: Is [your] Japanese class big?
Brown: No, it's not that big. It's just about right.
Tanaka: Is it a good class?
Brown: Yes, it's a very good class.
Tanaka: Do the students all study hard (well)?
Brown: Yes, they all study very hard (well).
Tanaka: Where is the classroom?
Brown: It's on the second floor of that building.
Tanaka: Do you mean [it's in] that large building?
Brown: No, that is the library. It's that small building.
Tanaka: Oh, [I see]. It's over there.
　　　　Do you speak only Japanese in class?
Brown: Yes, we usually speak only Japanese, but sometimes the professor
　　　　explains in English.
Tanaka: Do you [Mr. Brown] speak Japanese at home, too?
Brown: No, I don't. At home, I speak English.

GRAMMATICAL AND CULTURAL NOTES

5.1　　Adjectives

A Japanese adjective is a descriptive word, e.g. **ookii**, **chiisai**, **ii**, **warui**, that ends with **-i** in its dictionary form. Words that describe size, length, quality, form, and basic colors are usually adjectives.

There are, however, other types of descriptive words that do not have the characteristic adjective endings. These other words are called by other names in this book and will be introduced later.

An adjective in its dictionary form can occur before a noun as a modifier of a head noun.

kore wa　**ookii kurasu** desu.	(This is a **large class**.)
kore wa　**ii hon** desu.	(This is a **good book**.)
kore wa　**muzukashii hon** desu.	(This is a **difficult book**.)

An adjective may be followed by **desu** to form the predicate of a sentence.

nihongo wa　**yasashii desu**.　　　　(Japanese **is easy**.)

54

nihongo wa **muzukashii desu.**   (Japanese **is difficult.**)
kurasu wa **tanoshii desu.**   (The class **is enjoyable.**)

The adjective is inflected in several categories that are quite different from the English adjective. These inflectional endings will be introduced gradually as they appear in the text. In this lesson the ending **-ku** is introduced in negative adjectives as explained in the next section.

Basic color words, namely 'white,' 'black,' 'blue', 'red,' and 'yellow' are adjectives but more subtle colors such as green, pink, purple, and others are nouns.

kono hon wa **akai desu.**   (This book **is red.**)
kore wa **akai hon** desu.   (This is a **red book.**)
kono hon wa **midoriiro desu.**   (This book **is green.**)
kore wa **midoriiro no hon** desu.   (This is a **green book.**)

5.2   -ku arimasen

The predicate construction, **Adjective + desu** can be made **negative** by replacing the **-i** ending with the **-ku** ending and **desu** with **arimasen**, as in **ookii desu ---> ookiku arimasen.** In a formal style of speech, **wa** may be added between **-ku** and **arimasen.** The particle **wa** in this position is optional, and the students are more likely to hear the sentences without it.

nihongo wa **yasashiku (wa) arimasen.**   (Japanese is **not easy.**)
kurasu wa **ookiku (wa) arimasen.**   (The class is **not big.**)
kyoo wa **samuku (wa) arimasen.**   (It's **not cold** today.)

The only irregular adjective in Japanese is **ii** (good). The stem **i-** of **ii** changes to **yo-** when the ending **-i** is changed to **-ku**, resulting in the form **yoku.**

ii desu.   ([It] is **good.**)
yoku arimasen.   ([It] is not **good.**)

5.3   Negations

So far, the following three types of predicate constructions have been introduced: **Noun + desu**; **Adjective + desu**; and **Verb** ending in **-masu**. These three types take different ways to make the corresponding negative forms.

Noun + desu   kore wa **hon desu.**   ---> kore wa **hon de wa arimasen.**
Adjective + desu   kyoo wa **atsui desu.** ---> kyoo wa **atsuku arimasen.**
Verb in -masu   eigo ga **wakarimasu.** ---> eigo ga **wakarimasen.**

5.4   sonna ni

sonna ni is an adverb meaning 'in that manner,' or 'in that way.' The word is often used along with a negative form to express a moderate degree of negation. The English expressions for this idea are '**not so** [good]' or '**not that** [big].'

kurasu wa **sonna ni** ookiku arimasen.   (The class is **not so** large.)

nihongo wa **sonna ni** muzukashi**ku arimasen**.   (Japanese is **not that** hard.)

5.5   yoku

yoku is the adverbial form of **i i** and means 'well.' **yoku** modifies verbs just as other adverbs do.

gakusei wa **yoku** benkyoo shimasu.	(The students study **well**.)
nihongo ga **yoku** wakarimasu.	([I] understand Japanese **well**.)
yoku kiite kudasai.	(Please listen [to me] **well**.)
yoku mite kudasai.	(Please look [at this] **carefully**.)

5.6   benkyoo shimasu

benkyoo is a noun meaning 'studying' or 'study.' **shimasu** is the **-masu** form of the verb **'suru'** (to do). **benkyoo suru** is grammatically a compound verb, literally meaning 'to do studying.' This compound verb is used to mean 'to study.' Similarly, **setsumei shimasu** is a compound verb made up of **setsumei** (explanation) and **suru** (to do). There are many other such compound verbs but they are used just like other non-compound verbs. The part **suru** may be changed but the noun part stays unchanged.

gakusei wa yoku **benkyoo shimasu**.   (The students **study** well.)
saa, **benkyoo shimashoo**!   (OK, **let's study!**)
sensei wa tokodoki eigo de **setsumei shimasu**.
                (The teacher sometimes **explains** in English.)

5.7   doko

doko is an interrogative word meaning 'where.' This word **doko** belongs to a group of related words forming a paradigm.

koko	soko	asoko	doko
(here)	(there)	(over there)	(where)

The sentence pattern '**... wa   doko desu ka?**' is mainly used to ask identification of whereabout of certain places such as offices, classrooms, or buildings.

kyooshitsu wa **doko** desu ka?   (**Where** is the classroom?)
gakkoo wa **doko** desu ka?   (**Where** is the school?)
koko wa **doko** desu ka?   (**Where** is **this place**? [**Where am I?**])
taitei **doko de** benkyoo shimasu ka?   (**Where** do you usually study?)

5.8   de

The particle **de** as in **uchi de** (at home) marks the preceding word as the place of activity of the predicate verb. It means that such and such an action takes place at such and such place. If the predicate verb indicates existence rather than an action, a different particle is used; this usage will be introduced later. Students should be careful not to confuse Japanese with English, where the prepositions 'at,' 'in or 'on' may indicate both the place of activity and the place of existence.

uchi de nihongo o **hanashimasu**. ([I] **speak** Japanese **at home**.)
anata wa **uchi de** nihongo o **hanashimasu** ka?
                     (Do you **speak** Japanese **at home**?)
sensei wa **kurasu de** nihongo o **hanashimasu** ka?
                     (Does the teacher **speak** Japanese **in class**?)
doko de benkyoo shimasu ka? (**Where** do you **study**?)

5.9   o

As noted in 3.9, the particle **o** indicates that the preceding word is the **direct object** of the predicate verb of a sentence. The transitive verbs such as 'speak,' 'eat,' and 'read' require a direct object. In English, word order marks the verb-object relationship. For example, 'eat fish' and 'fish eat' convey two different meanings because of the order of the words. In Japanese the particle **o** is more essential than the word order in determining the verb-object relationship.

anata wa	uchi de	**nihongo o**	hanashimasu	ka?
topic	place	direct object	verb	question marker
'you'	'at home'	'Japanese'	'speak'	' ? '

(Do you speak **Japanese** at home?)

uchi de wa **eigo o** hanashimasu. ([I] speak **English** at home.)

5.10   dake

The word **dake** means 'limiting to,' or 'only.' It may replace the direct object marker **o** when the meaning is clear without it, or may be used in the sequence, **dake o** or sometimes **o dake**. The latter is more formal and specific while the former is more common and conversational.

    sensei wa   kurasu de   nihongo **dake**   hanashimasu ka?
                    (Does the teacher speak **only** Japanese in class?)
    nihongo no   kurasu de wa   nihongo **dake** o   hanashimashoo.
                    (Let's speak **only** Japanese in the Japanese class.)

5.11   Particle Sequence

The particle **wa**, the topic marker, can be added to a phrase such as **uchi de** (at home) to mark that phrase as the topic. In such a case, a sequence of two or more particles may result. The topic marker **wa** directs the attention of that phrase as the focal point of the sentence, or placing 'emphasis' on that section of the conversation.

    uchi de wa   eigo o   hanashimasu.   ([I] speak English **at home**.)
       [The implication is that I may speak other languages somewhere else.]
    kurasu de wa   nihongo o   hanashimasu.   ([I] speak Japanese **in class**.)
       [The implication is that I may speak some other languages when I am not in class.]

5.12   ga meaning 'but'

The particle **ga** at the end of a clause means 'but,' and acts as a conjunction. This particle **ga** combines two clauses into one sentence. This conjunctive particle meaning 'but' is different from the nominative particle **ga** as in **eigo ga wakarimasu**. While they happen to have the same form, their functions are very different. It is easier to learn them simply as different particles.

sensei wa   taitei   nihongo dake   hanashimasu **ga**,   tokidoki   eigo mo   hanashimasu.
(The teacher usually speaks only Japanese in class, **but** he/she sometimes speaks English, too.)
kono kurasu wa   ookii desu **ga,**   totemo ii kurasu desu.
(This class is very big, **but** it's a very good class.)

EXERCISES

5E.1   Grammar Drill: Make the following sentences negative.

1. nihongo wa yasashii desu.
2. eigo wa   muzukashii desu.
3. kyoo wa   atsui desu.
4. kyoo wa   samui desu.
5. rekishi no   kurasu wa   tanoshii desu.
6. kono empitsu wa   mijikai desu.
7. sono empitsu wa   nagai desu.
8. kono jisho wa   ii desu.
9. kono nooto wa   ii desu.
10. tenki wa   warui desu.

5E.2   Response Drill: Answer the following questions negatively, beginnng each answer with '**iie.**' Choose correct ways to form negative sentences.

1. kono kurasu wa   chiisai desu ka?
2. Tanaka-san wa   eigo ga   wakarimasu ka?
3. Sasaki-sensei wa   otoko no sensei desu ka?
4. nihongo wa   yasashii desu ka?
5. kono kurasu wa   rekishi no   kurasu desu ka?
6. anata wa   uchi de   doitsugo o   hanashimasu ka?
7. kono empitsu wa   nagai desu ka?
8. Buraun-san wa   uchi de   nihongo o   hanashimasu ka?
9. anata wa   kyoo   isogashii desu ka?
10. kyoo wa   samui desu ka?

5E.3 Activity: Stating opinions about their Japanese class. Work in pairs. Students A and B ask each other's opinion about their Japanese class. Discuss the following.

    1. If the class is interesting or not
    2. If the class is large or small
    3. If the class is easy or hard
    4. If he or she studies hard or not
    5. If the students in class study hard or not
    6 If the textbook is easy or hard

5E.5 Activity: Talking about books. Work in small groups. The instructor and students collect several books, newspapers, magazines, and dictionaries found in the class. The student who contributes a book marks his or her name on the cover. Ask questions to each other and find out the following:

    (1) The content of the book.
    (2) The language used in the book.
    (3) The owner of the book.
    (4) The level of difficulty.
    (5) The appearance of the book.

Examples:

    1. kore wa nan no hon desu ka?
    2. kore wa jisho desu ka, kyookasho desu ka?
    3. kono kyookasho wa nan no kyookasho desu ka?
    4. kono jisho wa dare no jisho desu ka?
    5. kono shimbun wa donata no desu ka?
    6. kono hon wa muzukashii desu ka, yasashii desu ka?
    7. kono hon wa ookii desu ka, chiisai desu ka?

5E.6 Repetition Drill: The instructor says the following sentences and the students repeat after him or her with their books closed. Orally check the meanings.

    1. Sasaki-sensei wa kurasu de nihongo dake hanashimasu.
    2. Sasaki-sensei wa tokidoki eigo mo hanashimasu.
    3. Sasaki-sensei wa taitei kurasu de nihongo dake hanashimasu ga, tokidoki eigo de setsumei shimasu.

4. Buraun-san wa uchi de eigo dake hanashimasu.
5. Buraun-san wa uchi de eigo dake hanashimasu ga, gakkoo de wa nihongo mo hanashimasu.
6. Tanaka-san wa uchi de nihongo dake hanashimasu.
7. Tanaka-san wa gakkoo de mo nihongo dake hanashimasu.

5E.7 Response Drill: The instructor asks the following questions and the students give appropriate answers. Next, Student A asks and Student B answers.

1. Buraun-san wa uchi de nanigo o hanashimasu ka?
2. Tanaka-san wa uchi de nanigo o hanashimasu ka?
3. anata wa uchi de nanigo o hanashimasu ka?
4. Sasaki-sensei wa kurasu de nanigo o hanashimasu ka?
5. kono kurasu no gakusei wa kurasu de nanigo o hanashimasu ka?
6. Chen-san wa uchi de nanigo o hanashimasu ka?
7. Santosu-san wa uchi de nanigo o hanashimasu ka?
8. Kimu-san wa uchi de nanigo o hanashimasu ka?
9. kono kurasu no gakusei wa yoku benkyoo shimasu ka?
10. Buraun-san wa yoku nihongo o benkyoo shimasu ka?
11. watakushitachi mo nihongo o benkyoo shimasu ka?
12. watakushitachi wa yoku benkyoo shimasu ka?

5E.8 Fill in the blanks with correct particles.

1. kore _____ anata _____ zasshi desu _____?

   hai, soo desu. sore _____ watakushi _____ zasshi desu.

   sono jisho _____ anata _____ desu _____?

   iie, kono jisho _____ watakushi _____ de wa arimasen.

2. are _____ zasshi desu _____, shimbun desu _____?

   are _____ zasshi desu. shimbun _____ _____ arimasen.

3. kyoo _____ ii tenki desu _____!

   honto ni ii tenki desu _____!

4. nihongo _____ wakarimasu _____?

   hai, sukoshi wakarimasu.

   ja, nihongo _____ hanashimashoo!

5E.9   Say the following sentences in Japanese.

1. Where is your Japanese class [class room]?
2. Where is Professor Sasaki's office (research room)?
3. Where is the library?
4. Where is the restroom?
5. Where do you study?
6. Let's study in the library.
7. Please speak only Japanese in class.
8. Please explain in English.

VOCABULARY

VERBS

hanashimasu	(I speak/ someone speaks; the -masu form of hanasu)
hanashimasen	(I don't speak/ someone doesn't speak: negative form of hanashimasu)
benkyoo shimasu	(I study/ someone studies; the -masu form of benkyoo suru 'to study')
setsumei shimasu	(I explain; someone explains; the -masu form of setsumei suru)

ADJECTIVES

yasashii	(easy, 5.1)
yasashiku arimasen	(not easy, 5.2)
muzukashii	(difficult; hard, 5.1)
ookii	(large; big, 5.1)
ookiku arimasen	(not large, 5.2)

NOUNS

gakusei	(students)
kyooshitsu	(classroom)
nikai	(second floor)
tatemono	(building)
toshokan	(library)
uchi	(home; house)

OTHERS

minna	(all)
yoku	(well)
sonna ni	(in that manner; that way; not so ..., 5.4)
choodo	(just, exactly)
koko	(here, 5.7)
soko	(there, 5.7)
asoko	(over there, 5.7)

doko	(where, 5.7)
taitei	(usually)
tokidoki	(sometimes)
de	(at; in; on: a particle marking the place of activity, 5.8)
o	(a particle marking the direct object of the verb, 5.9)
dake	(only, 5.10)
ga	(but: a conjunctive particle, 5.12)
-ku arimasen	(negation of ADJECTIVE + desu, 5.2)

ADDITIONAL VOCABULARY

kuroi	(black)
akai	(red)
shiroi	(white)
aoi	(blue)
midori iro	(green)
warui	(bad)
nagai	(long)
mijikai	(short)
nani	(what)
watakushitachi	(we)
tsumaranai	(uninteresting; dull; boring)
kenkyuushitsu	(professor's office; research room)
otearai	(restroom; place to wash hands; toilet)

READING AND WRITING

Exercise 1: Read the following symbols aloud. The second time through, note the differences carefully, and write each symbol correctly as your instructor reads it.

1.	あ：お		11.	さ：き
2.	い：こ		12.	れ：わ
3.	さ：ち		13.	な：た
4.	ね：ぬ		14.	り：い
5.	う：ら		15.	の：め
6.	え：そ		16.	に：た
7.	ろ：る		17.	こ：に
8.	す：む		18.	ぬ：め
9.	ま：ほ		19.	わ：ね
10.	く：し		20.	け：は

Exercise 2: Indicate the stroke order of the following **hiragana** symbols as shown in the example. Also mark a stop ending by a small circle and a trailing ending by three small dots.

Example: み   み。   み

1. も		6. ふ
2. き		7. せ
3. か		8. を
4. え		9. よ
5. お		10. ほ

Exercise 3: Write the following syllables in **hiragana**.

1. nu _____
2. re _____
3. hi _____
4. sa _____
5. ma _____

6. ho _____
7. so _____
8. fu _____
9. yu _____
10. mu _____

Exercise 4: Write a complete **hiragana** chart in the conventional vertical style in the following boxes. Write them in the correct order beginning the first line at the right hand side with a, i, u, e, o, the second line ka, ki, ku, ke, ko, and so on, eventually ending with N at left.

N	w	r	y	m	h	n	t	s	k	vowels

Exercise 3: Read the following **hiragana** words.

1. ほん
2. いす
3. つくえ
4. かみ
5. さいふ
6. いい
7. わるい
8. あつい
9. さむい
10. おおきい

11. ちいさい
12. やさしい
13. たのしい
14. おもしろい
15. おとこのひと
16. おんなのひと
17. おとこのせんせい
18. おんなのせんせい
19. おもしろいほん
20. やさしいほん

6

Brown: sumimasen, chotto shitsumon ga arimasu.

Tanaka: hai, nan desu ka?

Brown: kore wa nihongo de nan to iimasu ka?

Tanaka: sore wa nihongo de 'keshigomu' to iimasu.

Brown: sumimasen, moo ichido itte kudasai.

Tanaka: hai. sore wa nihongo de 'keshigomu' to iimasu.

Brown: motto yukkuri itte kudasai.

Tanaka: hai. sore wa 'ke-shi-go-mu' to iimasu.

Brown: hai, wakarimashita. ja, 'keshigomu' wa hiragana de kakimasu ka, katakana de kakimasu ka?

Tanaka: 'keshigomu' wa hiragana de kakimasu.

Brown: sumimasen ga, kokuban ni kaite kudasai.

Tanaka: hai. 'keshigomu' wa koo kakimasu.

Brown: muzukashii desu ne!

              sumimasen, sono ji o yonde kudasai.

Tanaka: ja, issho ni yomimashoo.

Brown & Tanaka: 'ke-shi-go-mu.'

Brown: doomo arigatoo gozaimashita.

Tanaka: iie, doo itashimashite.

ENGLISH EQUIVALENT

Brown: Excuse me, I just have a question.

Tanaka: Yes. What is it?

Brwon: What do you call this in Japanese?

               (Excuse me, what do you say for this thing in Japanese?)

Tanaka: That's called 'keshigomu' in Japanese.

Brown: Excuse me, please say it once more.

Tanaka: All right. That's called 'keshigomu' in Japanese.

Brown: Please say it more slowly.

Tanaka: All right. That's called 'ke-shi-go-mu.'

Brown: Fine; I've understood [it]. Hmm-- Do you write 'keshigomu' in hiragana or katakana?

Tanaka: We [usually] write 'keshigomu' in hiragana.

Brown: I'm sorry, but please write it on the blackboard.

Tanaka: All right. 'keshigomu' is written this way.

Brown: How difficult! Excuse me, please read those characters.

Tanaka: Well, okay, let's read them together.

Brown & Tanaka: 'ke-shi-go-mu.'

Brown: Thank you very much.

Tanaka: Not at all. You're welcome.

GRAMMATICAL AND CULTURAL NOTES

6.1   sumimasen

sumimasen literally means 'I'm sorry [to disturb you].' or 'Excuse me.' In English when you want to interrupt someone to ask a question or favor, it is customary to say 'Excuse me, but ...' In a similar way, the Japanese say **sumimasen** or **sumimasen ga ...** with a sustaining intonation to convey that the speaker has a question to ask. In a more casual speech of daily conversation, the sounds [**m**] is left out and **suimasen** is generally heard. The word **ga** here is a conjunctive particle meaning 'but.' This **ga** is optional, and it may be left out.

> **sumimasen**, chotto shitsumon ga arimasu.
> > (**Excuse me**, I just have a question.)
>
> **suimasen**, kore wa nan desu ka?
> > (**Excuse me**, what is this?)
>
> **sumimasen**, chotto misete kudasai.
> > (**Excuse me**, may I see [it] a minute?)
>
> **sumimasen ga**, onamae wa nan desu ka?
> > (**Excuse me, but** what is your name?.)

6.2   shitsumon ga arimasu

The word **shitsumon** means 'question.' The word **arimasu** is the -**masu** form of the verb 'aru' meaning 'to exist' or 'there is.' The subject of the verb is marked by the particle **ga**. The expression **shitsumon ga arimasu** means 'there is a question [in my mind and I'd like to ask].' In English you would say 'I **have** a question.' The idea of 'have' is often expressed by the verb **arimasu** referring to an inanimate object.

chotto **shitsumon ga arimasu.**	(Excuse me, I just **have a question.**)
shitsumon ga **arimasu ka?**	(**Do you have** a question?)
empitsu **ga arimasu ka?**	(**Do you have** a pencil?)
kami **ga arimasu ka?**	(**Do you have** paper?)

6.3   nan to iimasu ka?

When a Japanese speaker wants to know the name of an object or when the speaker wants to find out how to say certain things, he or she asks '**nan to iimasu ka?**' **nan** is the short form of **nani** (what). **to** is a particle indicates something like a quotation mark in English. **iimasu** is the -**masu** form of the verb **i[w]u** meaning 'to say.' The [w] is a part of the stem pronounced only when the following sound is [a]. Otherwise it is hidden. The expression '**nan to iimasu ka?**' literally means 'what do you say [for it]? or 'how do you say it?' This expression is introduced in this lesson for the purpose of utility. In and out of the classroom, the student may use this expression as a means for vocabulary enrichment.

kore wa nihongo de **nan to iimasu ka?**	
	(**What do you say** for this thing in Japanese?) or
	(**What do you call** this in Japanese?)
sore wa nihongo de **'keshigomu' to iimasu.**	
	(**We say 'keshigomu'** for that in Japanese.) or
	(**It's called 'keshigomu'** in Japanese.)

6.4   moo ichido

moo means 'additional,' **ichi** means 'one,' and **do** means 'time,' and when spoken in one phrase it is an equivalent of 'one more time,' 'once more,' or 'again.' This expression is spoken very often with the verb 'to say.'

moo ichido itte kudasai.	(Please say that **again.**)
moo ichido iimashoo.	(Let's say that **once more.**)
moo ichido kaite kudasai.	(Please write it **once more.**)

6.5   itte kudasai and the -te forms

itte is the -**te** form of the verb **i[w]u** (to say) which is pronounced as [yuu]. Every Japanese verb has its -**te** form. All verbs in their -**te** form end with either -**te** or -**de**. The -**te** form is an inflectional ending. It may combine with various words, with different resulting meanings. As previously explained, in **itte kudasai**, the word **kudasai** itself means 'please give me.' When it follows the -**te** form of a verb it expresses the polite request, 'Please give (do) me the favor of your doing such and such' or 'please do such and such.' **itte kudasai**, then, means 'Please say.'

67

Here are the **-te forms** of the verbs introduced in this lesson or in the previous lessons.

Dictionary Form	(Meaning)	-masu Form	-te Form + kudasai	
i[w]u	(to say)	iimasu	**itte** kudasai	(Please say.)
hanasu	(to speak)	hanashimasu	**hanashite** kudasai	(Please speak.)
kaku	(to write)	kakimasu	**kaite** kudasai	(Please write.)
yomu	(to read)	yomimasu	**yonde** kudasai.	(Please read.)
suru	(to do)	shimasu	**shite** kudasai.	(Please do.)
wakaru	(to understand)	wakarimasu	**wakatte** kudasai	(Please understand.)

Japanese verbs are classified into several types, and each type has a grammatical rule to make the **-te form**. The grammatical rules to form the **-te forms** of other verbs will be introduced later, when the students have learned more verbs. In this lesson, the students are advised to learn the separate **-te forms** as separate vocabulary words. Each of these verbs will serve later as a model to formulate the **-te forms** of new vocabulary entries.

6.6   motto yukkuri

motto is an adverb meaning 'more,' or 'furthermore,' and it may modify another adverb of manner as **yukkuri** (slowly), **yoku** (well), **kuwashiku** (in detail), and other adverbs of manners.

motto yukkuri hanashite kudasai.	(Please speak **slower**.)
motto yoku benkyoo shimashoo.	(Let's study **harder**.)
motto kuwashiku hanashite kudasai.	(Please tell me **in more detail**.)
motto hakkiri itte kudasai.	(Please say it **more distinctly**.)

6.7   motto, moo

motto and **moo** both mean 'more,' but they are different in usage. **moo** is used with adverbs of quantity or numbers such as **ichido** (one time), **sukoshi** (a little bit) and so forth, while **motto** is used with manner words as explained above.

moo ichido itte kudasai.	(Please say it **once more**.)
moo sukoshi kudasai.	(Please give me **a little bit more**.)
moo sukoshi yukkuri hanashite kudasai.	(Please speak **a little bit slower**.)
moo chotto hayaku hanashite kudasai.	(Please speak **a littel bit faster**.)

6.8   -mashita

The form **-mashita** is the past form of **-masu**. A verb in the **-mashita** form indicates that the action has been completed. Strictly speaking, **-mashita** is not the past tense as in English; it expresses 'completion' rather than the time of action. In a practical sense, **-mashita** expresses both the English past and present perfect tenses. Thus **wakarimashita** -- depending on context -- could mean either '[I] understood' (past tense) or '[I] have understood' (present perfect tense).

wakarimashita ka?	(**Did** [you] **understand**? **Have** [you] **understood**?)
hai, **wakarimashita**.	(Yes, [I] **understood**. Yes, [I] **have understood**.)

iimashita.   ([I] said.; [I] have said.)
hanashimashita.   ([I] spoke.; [I] have spoken.)

6.9   doomo arigatoo gozaimashita

The word **arigatoo** means 'thank you.' If a speaker wants to say it politely, **gozaimasu** may be added. **arigatoo** is usually preceded by **doomo** (very much). The form **-mashita** indicates that a person is thanking for the favor completed.

arigatoo   (Thanks.) or (Thank you.)
doomo arigatoo   (Thank you **very much**.)
doomo arigatoo **gozaimasu**.   (Thank you very much for **what you are doing for me**.)
doomo arigatoo gozaimashita.   (Thank you very much for **what you have done for me**.)

The reply to the expression of 'thank you' is '**iie, doo itashimashite**' (No, don't mention it; You're welcome.)

6.10   ni (kaku)

In English we write **on** paper or write **on** the chalkboard, and we normally use the preposition 'on' to express the place for writing. In Japanese, the particle **ni** is used to express the same idea. The particle **ni** has the basic meaning of 'onto,' 'attaching to,' or 'directed toward' and the concept is more like 'we write **onto** the paper' or 'I write **onto** the blackboard.'

kokuban **ni**   kaite kudasai.   (Please write it **on** the board.)
kami **ni**   kaite kudasai.   (Please write it **on** a sheet of paper.)
nooto **ni**   kaite kudasai.   (Please write it **in** [your] notebook.)

6.11   koo

koo means 'in this way.' This word belongs to a group of words forming a paradigm.

kore	**sore**	**are**	**dore**
(this one)	(that one)	(that one over there)	(which one?)
kono	**sono**	**ano**	**dono**
(this ...)	(that ...)	(that ... over there)	(which ...?)
koo	**soo**	**aa**	**doo**
(in this way)	(in that way)	(in that other way)	(in what way; how)

keshigomu wa   **koo** kakimasu.   (We write 'keshigomu' **this way**.)
soo shimashoo.   (Let's do it **that way**, just as you have said.)
aa shimashoo.   (Let's do it **the other way**.)
doo kakimasu ka?   (**How** [in what way] do you write it?)
gakkoo wa   **doo** desu ka?   (**How** is school?)

EXERCISES

6E.1   Response Drill: The instructor holds or points to the objects and asks the following questions, and the students answer. Next, Student A asks and Student B answers.

```
 1. (pencil)      kore wa  nihongo de  nan to  iimasu ka?
 2.               kore wa  eigo de  nan to  iimasu ka?
 3. (eraser)      kore wa  nihongo de  nan to  iimasu ka?
 4.               kore wa  eigo de  nan to  iimasu ka?
 5. (notebook)    kore wa  nihongo de  nan to  iimasu ka?
 6.               kore wa  eigo de  nan to  iimasu ka?
 7. (key)         kore wa  nihongo de  nan to  iimasu ka?
 8.               kore wa  eigo de  nan to  iimasu ka?
 9. (wallet)      kore wa  nihongo de  nan to  iimasu ka?
10.               kore wa  eigo de  nan to  iimasu ka?
11. (blackboard) are wa  nihongo de  nan to  iimasu ka?
12.               are wa  eigo de  nan to  iimasu ka?
13. (window)      are wa  nihongo de  nan to  iimasu ka?
                  are wa  eigo de  nan to  iimasu ka?
```

6E.2   Response Drill: The instructor asks the questions and the student who knows the correct answer raises his or her hand and answers.

```
 1. 'Thank you' wa  nihongo de  nan to  iimasu ka?
 2. 'Good morning' wa  nihongo de  nan to  iimasu ka?
 3. 'Good-bye' wa  nihongo de  nan to  iimasu ka?
 4. 'Good-bye' wa  supeingo de  nan to  iimasu ka?
 5. 'Thank you' wa  furansugo de  nan to  iimasu ka?
 6. 'Thank you' wa  doitsugo de  nan to  iimasu ka?
 7. 'Thank you' wa  chuugokugo de  nan to  iimasu ka?
 8. 'Good-bye' wa  chuugokugo de  nan to  iimasu ka?
 9. 'Good-bye' wa  kankokugo de  nan to  iimasu ka?
10. 'Pencil' wa  kankokugo de  nan to  iimasu ka?
```

6E.3   Say the following expressions in Japanese.

1. Excuse me, please say it again.
2. Please say it slowly.

3. Please say it more slowly.
4. Please say it a little bit slower.
5. Please say it in English.
6. Please say it in Japanese.
7. Please say it again in Japanese.
8. Let's say it in Japanese.
9. Let's say it again together.
10. Please say your name once more.
11. Please speak slowly in Japanese.
12. Please explain that word in English.

6E.4 Response Drill: The instructor asks the following questions and the students answer. The second time, Student A asks and Student B answers.

1. 'keshigomu' wa hiragana de kakimasu ka, katakana de kakimasu ka?
2. 'kokuban' wa hiragana de kakimasu ka, katakana de kakimasu ka?
3. 'mado' wa hiragana de kakimasu ka, katakana de kakimasu ka?
4. 'seetaa' wa hiragana de kakimasu ka, katakana de kakimasu ka?
5. 'pen' wa hiragana de kakimasu ka, katakana de kakimasu ka?
6. Buraun-san no namae wa katakana de kakimasu ne?
7. Tanaka-san no namae wa kanji de kakimasu ne?
8. anata no namae wa katakana de kakimasu ka, kanji de kakimasu ka?

6E.5 Directed Conversation: The instructor writes on flash cards or on the blackboard **hiragana** letters such as 'a,' 'i,' 'u,' 'e,' 'o,' or simple words, and carries on the following conversation with the students. Next, Student A and Student B repeat the dialogue using different letters or words.

A: (The instructor writes 'a' in hiragana.)
1. kono ji wa nan to yomimasu ka?
2. kono ji o yonde kudasai.
3. kono ji wa hiragana desu ka, katakana desu ka?
4. kono ji o moo ichido yonde kudasai.
5. ja, issho ni moo ichido yomimashoo.

71

6. nooto ni kono ji o kaite kudasai.
7. nooto ni kono ji o kakimashita ka?

B: (The instructor writes 'hon' in hiragana.)
1. kono kotoba wa nan to yomimasu ka?
2. kono kotoba o yonde kudasai.
3. kono kotoba wa eigo de nan to iimasu ka?
4. kono kotoba o nooto ni kaite kudasai.
5. kakimashita ka?
6. muzukashii desu ka, yasashii desu ka?
7. ja, motto muzukashii kotoba o kakimashoo.

C: (The instructor writes 'kami' in hiragana.)
1. kono kotoba wa nan to yomimasu ka?
2. kono kotoba o yonde kudasai.
3. kono kotoba wa eigo de nan to iimasu ka?
4. nooto ni kaite kudasai.
5. moo ichido yonde kudasai.
6. moo ichido yukkuri yonde kudasai.

6E.6   Activity: Home language survey. Work in pairs. Student A and Student B ask each other what language he or she speaks at home. Also, find out more about each other.

1. what language he or she speaks at home
2. if he or she understands Chinese
3. how he or she writes his or her name
4. if he or she sometimes speaks Japanese at home
5. if he or she thinks Japanese is easy [to learn]
6. if he or she studies hard

6E.7   Activity: Vocabulary expansion. Each student writes on a sheet of paper a few objects he or she wants to learn to say in Japanese. The students, in turn, ask the instructor '**... wa   nihongo de   nan to iimasu ka?**' The instructor gives the answers. The students may further ask the instructor '**sumimasen ga kokuban ni   kaite kudasai.**' or '**Roomaji de   kaite kudasai.**' Make comments or ask more questions to expand the vocabulary in Japanese.

VOCABULARY

VERBS

arimasu	(there is; there are; I have: -masu form of aru, 6.2)
aru	(to have; to exist)
iimasu	(-masu form of i[w]u 'to say'; I say /someone says, 6.3)
itte kudasai	(please say: -te form of i[w]u + kudasai, 6.5)
hanashite kudasai	(please speak: -te form of hanasu + kudasai, 6.5)
wakarimashita	(I have understood: -mashita form of wakaru 'to understand, 6.8)
kakimasu	(I write/ someone writes: -masu form of kaku 'to write')
kaku	(to write)
kaite kudasai	(please write: -te form of kaku + kudasai, 6.5)
yonde kudasai	(please read: -te form of yomu + kudasai, 6.5)
yomu	(to read)
yomimashoo	(let's read: -mashoo form of yomu, 1.13)

ADJECTIVES   (---)

NOUNS

shitsumon	(question, 6.2)
keshigomu	(eraser)
hiragana	(hiragana syllabary)
katakana	(katakana syllabary)
ji	(written symbol, character or letter)
namae	(name)
kotoba	(word)
kanji	(Chinese characters adopted in Japanese)

OTHERS

motto	(more, 6.6, 6.7)
yukkuri	(slowly; slow, 6.6)
issho ni	(together)
koo	(this way, 6.11)
nan to iimasu ka?	(How do you say it? 6.3)
ni	(onto; towards: a particle of direction, 6.10)
sumimasen	(excuse me)
moo ichido	(once again, 6.4)
doomo arigatoo gozaimashita	(thank you very much for what you have done, 6.9)
doo itashimashite	(you are welcome, 6.9)

ADDITIONAL VOCABULARY

kuwashiku	(in detail)
hakkiri	(clearly; distinctly)
hayaku	(fast; rapidly)

READING AND WRITING

In addition to the basic 46 **hiragana** symbols there are a few diacritical marks and combination rules used to represent other syllables that the basic symbols cannot represent by themselves. Two dots may be added to the upper righthand corner of some of the **hiragana** to represent voiced consonants. A small circle is added to the upper righthand corner of the symbols for syllables beginning with 'h' to represent syllables beginning with the [p] sound.

ka	ki	ku	ke	ko	ga	gi	gu	ge	go
か	き	く	け	こ	が	ぎ	ぐ	げ	ご
sa	shi	su	se	so	za	ji	zu	ze	zo
さ	し	す	せ	そ	ざ	じ	ず	ぜ	ぞ
ta	chi	tsu	te	to	da	ji	zu	de	do
た	ち	つ	て	と	だ	ぢ	づ	で	ど
ha	hi	fu	he	ho	ba	bi	bu	be	bo
は	ひ	ふ	へ	ほ	ば	び	ぶ	べ	ぼ
					pa	pi	pu	pe	po
					ぱ	ぴ	ぷ	ぺ	ぽ

There are two symbols, 'じ' and 'ぢ' representing the syllable **ji**. In most cases the syllable **ji** is written as 'じ' in modern Japanese. There are, however, a limited number of special words which use 'ぢ.'

Similarly, there are two symbols 'ず' and 'づ' representing the syllable **zu**. The symbol 'ず' is used in most cases. Exceptions to the rule will be explained as the specific situations arise.

Three 'small size' symbols, や, ゆ, よ, may be combined with certain syllables to represent the semivowel [y] sound, or palatalized sounds. The following list summarizes the pronunciation of such syllables.

kya	きゃ	kyu	きゅ	kyo	きょ
sha	しゃ	shu	しゅ	sho	しょ
cha	ちゃ	chu	ちゅ	cho	ちょ
nya	にゃ	nyu	にゅ	nyo	にょ
hya	ひゃ	hyu	ひゅ	hyo	ひょ
mya	みゃ	myu	みゅ	myo	みょ
rya	りゃ	ryu	りゅ	ryo	りょ
gya	ぎゃ	gyu	ぎゅ	gyo	ぎょ

ja	じゃ	ju	じゅ	jo	じょ
ja	ぢゃ	ju	ぢゅ	jo	ぢょ
bya	びゃ	byu	びゅ	byo	びょ
pya	ぴゃ	pyu	ぴゅ	pyo	ぴょ

The two sets of symbolization, じゃ, じゅ, じょ and ぢゃ, ぢゅ, ぢょ are available to represent the syllables **ja, ju, jo.** Of these two the first set is more commonly used, leaving the second set almost useless in modern Japanese.

In most cases, long vowels are represented simply by doubling the appropriate symbol.

aa	ああ
ii	いい
uu	うう
ee	ええ
oo	おお

Exceptions to this rule are noted as follows: When a syllable comprised of a consonant and an **'o'** vowel is lengthened as in **koo** or **too**, the second syllable **'o'** is written by the symbol for **'u.'** It is for this reason **ookii** is written おおきい, while **otoosan** is written おとうさん.

A small size symbol 'つ' is used to represent the first part of a long consonant, or a syllabic or moraic consonant, except in the case of nasals.

yukkuri is written	ゆっくり
zasshi is written	ざっし
gakkoo is written	がっこう
motto is written	もっと

A special symbol 'ん' represents syllabic nasal **'N'** (pronounced [m], [n], or [ŋ]). The syllabic nasals do not occur at the beginning of a word, but occur in the word-ending position or in the middle of many words.

hon is written	ほん
kanji is written	かんじ
honto ni is written	ほんとに
onna is written	おんな

Exercise 1: Read and write the following words, and give their meanings in English.

1. けしごむ
2. ともだち
3. ひらがな
4. がくせい
5. こくばん
6. しんぶん
7. えんぴつ
8. にほんご
9. ときどき
10. しつもん
11. がっこう
12. ざっし

Exercise 2: Read and write the following words and expressions written in hiragana. Give their meanings in English.

1. まど
2. りんご
3. げんき
4. だれ
5. どなた
6. えいご
7. みじかい
8. きょう
9. きょうしつ
10. べんきょう
11. としょかん
12. けんきゅうしつ
13. ゆっくり
14. はっきり

Exercise 3: Read and write the following expressions.

1. みてください
2. いってください
3. こたえてください
4. よんでください
5. かいてください
6. おはようございます
7. ありがとうございます
8. はじめまして
9. わかりません
10. はなしましょう

7

Brown:	ii shuuji no sensei o shitte imasu ka?
Tanaka:	(o)shuuji no sensei desu ka? soo desu ne...
	aa, shitte imasu yo. sono kata wa Okada-sensei to
	iimasu ga, totemo ii sensei desu yo.
	watakushi no shiriai desu.
Brown:	sono sensei wa otona ni shuuji o oshiemasu ka?
Tanaka:	mochiron! kodomo ni mo otona ni mo oshiemasu yo.
Brown:	Okada- sensei wa eigo ga dekimasu ka?
Tanaka:	hai, Okada-sensei wa eigo ga kanari joozu desu.
Brown:	donna kata desu ka?
Tanaka:	nempai no otoko no kata desu.
Brown:	ja, kondo shookai shite kudasai.
Tanaka:	hai, ii desu yo.
Brown:	Okada-sensei no denwa-bangoo o shitte imasu ka?
Tanaka:	hai, shitte imasu. chotto matte kudasai...
	Okada-sensei no denwa-bangoo wa ni-ichi-san ,
	yon-nana-hachi, roku-san-kyuu-go desu. (213-478-6395).
Brown:	juusho mo shitte imasu ka?
Tanaka:	iie, juusho wa shirimasen.

ENGLISH EQUIVALENT

Brown: Do you know a good calligraphy teacher?

Tanaka: A calligraphy teacher? Well, let me see... Oh, I know [a person].
He is called Okada-sensei, and is a very good teacher.
He is an acquaintance of mine.

Brown: Does he teach calligraphy to adults?

Tanaka: Of course! He teaches [it] to both children and adults

Brown: Can he speak English?

Tanaka: Yes. Mr. Okada speaks pretty good English. (Mr. Okada is quite
proficient in English.)

Brown: What sort of person is he?

Tanaka: He is an older gentleman.

Brown: Well, will you sometime introduce me [to him] ?

Tanaka: I'd be happy to. (Yes, that's fine.)

Brown: Do you know Mr. Okada's telephone number?

Tanaka: Yes, I do. Just a moment. Mr. Okada's telephone number is
213-478-6395.

Brown: Do you know [his] address, too?

Tanaka: I'm sorry, I don't know [his] address.

GRAMMATICAL AND CULTURAL NOTES

7.1   ...o shitte imasu ka?

The verb **shitte imasu** is composed of the **-te** form of the verb **shiru** (to know) followed by
imasu , the **-masu** form of **iru** (to be). The phrase **-te** + **imasu** is called the **descriptive
present** and it expresses the present 'state of being.' The verb **shiru** means 'to acquire knowledge
of' or 'to get to know [something].' This verb, in most cases, is used in the **descriptive present**
form to mean 'to have the knowledge of [something],' or simply 'I know [something].' The
particle **o** goes with this verb to mark the direct object of the verb **shiru** (to know).

        ii shuuji no sensei o **shitte imasu ka?**
                           (Do you know a [any] good calligraphy teacher?)
        Okada-sensei no denwa-bangoo o **shitte imasu ka?**
                           (Do you know Mr. Okada's telephone number?)
        Buraun-san o **shitte imasu ka?**
                           (Do you know Mr. Brown?)
        hai, **shitte imasu.**   (Yes, **I do.** [**I know.**])

To give a negative reply, **shirimasen** is commonly used to express 'I don't know.'

        iie, **shirimasen.**   (No, **I don't** [**know**].)

7.2   soo desu ne...

A Japanese speaker often responds to a question by saying 'soo desu nee...' with a sustaining intonation. This indicates that the speaker has understood the question but he or she is thinking for a moment how to answer. This is similar to the English expression, 'Well, let me see...'

> soo desu nee... aa, shitte imasu yo.
> > (Well, let me see... Oh, [I think] I know [a person].)

7.3   (o)shuuji

(o)shuuji is a traditional, Japanese brush-writing or calligraphy. Japanese people value artistic writing and thus encourage children to take up calligraphy lessons while they are young. It is included in the school curriculum, but they often take private lessons. Here Mr. Brown is trying to learn the calligraphy art and to find a good private teacher.

> ii shuuji no sensei o   shitte imasu ka?
> > (Do you know a good calligraphy teacher?)

7.4   shiriai

shiriai expresses the relationship of mutual acquaintance. In English you may say 'someone I know' or 'an acquaintance of mine.'

> watakushi no shiriai desu. (He is an acquaintance of mine.)

7.5   yo

The particle yo may be added at the end of a sentence to give it an assertive tone or emphasis. The speaker shows that he or she is speaking with confidence. In English there are many similar expressions, e.g. 'I tell you...' or 'You'd better listen.' The use of yo gives a touch of informal tone to the conversation, because yo is not used much in formal speeches.

> Okada-sensei wa totemo ii sensei desu yo.
> > (Mr. Okada is a very good teacher, I tell you.)
> nihongo wa totemo muzukashii desu yo.
> > (Japanese is very difficult, believe me.)

7.6   ni marking Indirect Object

The particle ni marks the indirect object of the predicate verb. In English this idea is usually expressed by the preposition 'to,' as in 'He teaches English to his students.' Or it may also be expressed through word order (S-V-IO-O) as in 'He teaches his students English.' For this reason, the particle ni may or may not be translated as 'to' in English.

> Sasaki-sensei wa gakusei ni nihongo o   oshiemasu.
> > (Professor Sasaki teaches Japanese to students.)
> Buraun-san wa Tanaka-san ni   nihongo de   hanashimasu.
> > (Mr. Brown speaks in Japanese to Miss Tanaka.)

Okada-sensei wa **otona ni** mo shuuji o oshiemasu ka?

> (Does Mr. Okada teach calligraphy **to adults**, too?)

dare ni shuuji o oshiemasu ka?

> (**To whom** does he/she teach calligraphy?)

7.7   (A) **mo** (B) **mo**

When the particle **mo** is used twice as in (A) **mo** (B) **mo** it means '**both** (A) **and** (B).'

eigo **mo** nihongo **mo** hanashimasu ka?

> (Do you speak **both** English **and** Japanese?)

otona ni **mo** kodomo ni **mo** shuuji o oshiemasu.

> (He/she teaches calligraphy to **both** adults **and** children.)

Tanaka-san **mo** Buraun-san **mo** yoku benkyoo shimasu.

> (**Both** Miss Tanaka **and** Mr. Brown study very hard.)

7.8   **donna**

The interrogative word **donna** is used primarily to elicit descriptions of a person, an object or an activity. The best literal translation of the word is 'what sort of.' It is usually used immediately before a noun. When a Japanese speaker asks a question using **donna**, he or she expects 'description' and not 'identification' in response.

donna kata desu ka?   (**What sort of** person is he?; **How** is he?)
donna hon desu ka?   (**What sort of** book is it?; **How** is the book?)

donna belongs to a set of related words.

konna	**sonna**	**anna**	**donna**
(this sort of)	(that sort of)	(that sort of)	(what sort of)

7.9   Numbers: 0 - 10

The following are the Japanese numbers 0 through 10.

0	rei or zero	6	roku
1	ichi	7	(s)hichi or nana
2	ni	8	hachi
3	san	9	ku or kyuu
4	shi or yon	10	juu
5	go		

These basic numbers are used in math, or when talking about numbers such as telephone numbers or zipcodes. The numbers 4, 7, and 9 vary according to different usages or in regional dialects.

7.10   Telephone Numbers

In the case of a telephone number, the numbers for **4, 7, 9** are spoken **yon**, **nana**, and **kyuu**, because telephone communication is less confusing if one avoids strong hissing sounds like 'sh,' and if the short numbers **ni** or **go** are lengthened to make them clearly audible. For **0** some people use the word **maru** (circle), while others use **zero** or **rei**. Japanese speakers may insert **no** to mark a short break in the sequence of numbers. The vowels in **ni** and **go** are often lenghtened to two moras.

$$213 - 478 - 6395 \quad \text{(ni ichi san [no]- yon nana hachi [no]- roku san kyuu goo)}$$
$$818 - 326 - 4275 \quad \text{(hachi ichi hachi [no]- san nii roku [no]- yon nii nana goo)}$$

The telephone services and the telephone numbering system in Japan are very similar to those in the United States. Public telephones are color coded and available almost everywhere in Japan.

7.11   wa in Negative Sentences

The particle **wa** in a negative sentence marks the focus of negation.

juusho o   shitte imasu. (I know [his] **address**.)
juusho wa   shirimasen. (I don't know [his] **address** [though I know his telephone number].)
uchi de wa   nihongo o   hanashimasen. (He does not speak Japanese **at home** [implying that he speaks it in other places].)

EXERCISES

7E.1   Say the following expressions in Japanese.

1. Do you know a good calligraphy teacher?
2. Do you know a good French language teacher?
3. Do you know a good Spanish language teacher?
4. Do you know a good Japanese dictionary?
5. Do you know Miss Tanaka's address?
6. Do you know Professor Sasaki's telephone number?
7. Do you know that older gentleman over there?
8. Do you know that young lady over there?

Next, Student A asks the above questions in Japanese, and Student B answers. If the answere is positive, use the expresssion **'hai, ... o   shitte imasu.'** If negative, use the sentence **'iie, ... wa   shirimasen.'**

7E.2   Directed Conversation: The instructor draws on the board or show on flashcards three stick figures to represent Mr. Brown, Miss Tanaka and Professor Sasaki. The instructor asks the following questions about the three persons. The students answer. The class may expand the conversation by adding more figures.

1. kono hito no namae o shitte imasu ka?
2. kono hito no namae wa nan to iimasu ka?
3. kono hito wa daigakusei desu ka, sensei desu ka?
4. kono kata wa donata desu ka?
5. kono kata wa nanigo o oshiemasu ka?
6. kono hito wa kookoosei desu ka?
7. kono hito wa nihonjin desu ka, amerikajin desu ka?
8. kono hito wa nanijin desu ka?
9. kono kata wa sensei desu ka, gakusei desu ka?
10. kono kata wa nihongo ga dekimasu ka?
11. kono kata wa eigo mo nihongo mo dekimasu ka?
12. kono kata wa daigaku de nani o oshiemasu ka?

7E.3　Response Drill: Answer the following questions with correct indirect object markers.

1. Okada-sensei wa kodomo ni shuuji o oshiemasu ka?
2. Sasaki-sensei wa gakusei ni nihongo o oshiemasu ka?
3. Buraun-san wa tokidoki nihonjin no tomodachi ni eigo o oshiemasu ka?
4. Tanaka-san wa Buraun-san ni nihongo o hanashimasu ka?
5. Chen-san wa chuugokujin no tomodachi ni nanigo o hanashimasu ka?
6. Buraun-san wa tomodachi ni nihongo de hanashimasu ka?
7. Santosu-san wa okaasan ni supeingo de hanashimasu ka?
8. Buraun-san wa otoosan ni eigo de tegami o kakimasu ka?
9. Kimu-san wa kankoku no tomodachi ni nanigo de tegami o kakimasu ka?
10. anata wa kurasu-meeto ni nanigo de hanashimasu ka?

7E.4　Response Drill: Give appropriate responses. Remember that '**donna**' is the word asking description.

1. Okada-sensei wa donna sensei desu ka?
2. Tanaka-san wa donna hito desu ka?
3. Sasaki-sensei wa donna sensei desu ka?
4. kono kurasu wa donna kurasu desu ka?
5. kono gakkoo wa donna gakkoo desu ka?

6. kyoo wa donna (o)tenki desu ka?
7. anata no uchi wa donna uchi desu ka?
8. anata no kaban wa donna kaban desu ka?
9. anata no tsukue wa donna tsukue desu ka?
10. Buraun-san no nihongo no kurasu wa donna kurasu desu ka?

7E.5 Dictation: In Japanese, the instructor tells the students the **telephone numbers** of the following persons. The students repeat the numbers after the instructor. The second time, the students take notes while the instructor reads the numbers. Repeat the exercise with different numbers.

1. Okada-sensei no denwa-bangoo wa 213-478-6395 desu.
2. Tanaka-san no denwa-bangoo wa 310-956-0308 desu.
3. Sasaki-sensei no denwa-bangoo wa 818-274-6901 desu.
4. Yamada-san no denwa-bangoo wa 714-584-1749 desu.
5. Kimura-san no denwa-bangoo wa 202-743-4416 desu.
6. Tsuda-sensei no denwa-bangoo wa 405-474-9102 desu.
7. Suda-sensei no denwa-bangoo wa 653-747-8500 desu.

7E.6 In Japanese, Student A asks Student B the questions marked (a). If the response is affirmative, continue to ask (b). Student A then thanks Student B, and Student B gives an appropriate response.

1. (a) Ask your friend if he or she knows Mr. Brown's telephone number.
   (b) Ask your friend to tell you the number.

2. (a) Ask if he or she understands Japanese.
   (b) Ask him or her to speak to you in Japanese

3. (a) Ask if he or she knows Spanish.
   (b) Ask how to say 'Thank you' in Spanish.

4. (a) Ask if he or she knows Chinese.
   (b) Ask how to say 'Good morning' in Chinese.

5. (a) Ask if he or she knows the name of the person over there.
   (b) Ask to tell you his or her name.

6. (a) Ask if he or she sometimes reads Japanese magazines.
   (b) Ask to read you a little.

7. (a) Ask if he or she knows hiragana.
   (b) Ask to write 'a' in hiragana on a piece of paper.

8. (a) Ask if he or she knows Miss Tanaka's address.
   (b) Ask to write her address in your notebook.

7E.7   Activity: Making a telephone directory. The instructor divides the class into several groups. The members of each group ask each other's telephone number and write it down on a sheet of paper. Next, each group reports the telephone numbers to the instructor correctly. The students take notes. When all the telephone numbers are reported, a class directory is made.

7E.8   Fill in the blanks with correct particles.

1. Okada-sensei _____ eigo_____ dekimasu _____?

2. Buraun-san _____ tokidoki eigo _____ oshiemasu _____?

3. 'Thank you' _____ nihongo _____ nan _____ iimasu _____?

4. 'hon' _____ hiragana _____ kakimasu _____, katakana_____ kakimasu _____?

5. sumimasen. sono ji _____ yonde kudasai.

6. Okada-sensei _____ otona _____ _____ kodomo _____ ____ shuuji _____ oshiemasu _____?

7. anata _____ doitsugo _____ dekimasu _____?

8. Tanaka-san _____ denwa-bangoo _____ shitte imasu _____?

9. anata _____ tokidoki tomodachi _____ tegami _____ kakimasu _____?

10. anata _____ eigo _____ joozu desu _____!

VOCABULARY

VERBS

shitte imasu	(I [or someone] know[s]: -te form of shiru + imasu, 7.1)
shiru	(to know)
shirimasen	(I don't know, 7.1)
oshiemasu	(I [or someone] teach[es]: -masu form of oshieru 'to teach')
oshieru	(to teach; to inform; to instruct)
oshiete kudasai	(please teach; please inform: -te form of oshieru + kudasai)
dekimasu	([someone] is able to do such and such: -masu form of dekiru)
dekiru	(to be able to do such and such; to be able to speak the language)
matte kudasai	(please wait: -te form of matsu + kudasai)
matsu	(to wait)
shookai shite kudasai	(please introduce: a compound verb made up of shookai (introduction) + suru (to do))

ADJECTIVES   (---)

NOUNS

(o)shuuji	(traditional Japanese brush writing; calligraphy, 7.3)
shiriai	(acquaintance, 7.4)
otona	(adult; grown-up people)
kodomo	(child/children)
joozu	(being skillful at; be proficient in)
nempai	(mature age; older)
denwa	(telephone)
bangoo	(number)
ichi	(one; 1, 7.9)
ni	(two; 2, 7.9)
san	(three; 3, 7.9)
shi, yon	(four; 4, 7.9)
go	(five; 5, 7.9)
roku	(six; 6, 7.9)
(s)hichi, nana	(seven; 7, 7.9)
hachi	(eight; 8, 7.9)
kyuu, ku	(nine; 9, 7.9)
juu	(ten; 10, 7.9)
rei, zero	(zero; 0, 7.9)
juusho	(address)

OTHERS

konna	(this sort of, 7.8)
sonna	(that sort of, 7.8)
anna	(that ... sort of, 7.8)
donna	(what sort of, 7.8)
mochiron	(of course)

yo	(particle of emphasis, 7.5)
ni	(the particle marking indirect object, 7.6)
kondo	(next time; the coming occasion)

ADDITIONAL VOCABULARY

daigakusei	(college student: daigaku + [gaku]sei)
kookoosei	(high school student: kootoo-gakkoo 'high school' + [gaku]sei)
wakai	(young)
tegami	(letter; correspondence)
ikebana	(the art of flower arrangement)
okaasan	(mother)
otoosan	(father)
nihonjin	(Japanese national)
amerikajin	(US citizen)
chuugokujin	(Chinese person)
kankokujin	(Korean person)
maru	(circle)

READING AND WRITING

There are certain conventions that one must observe in writing Japanese sentences.

(a) The following punctuation marks are used.

o   A small circle is equivalent to an English period. It is called '**maru**' (circle) in Japanese.

、   A long dot called '**ten**' is similar to a comma in English, although rules for using commas are not rigidly observed by Japanese writers.

「 」 Quotation marks.

?   Although question marks are not usually used in Japanese, they are available. Normally, questions have a question particle such as **ka** or **ne**, so a question mark is not necessary. The question marks are sometimes used to indicate a rising pitch in intonation.

In the traditional Japanese writing style, which is vertical, writers usually employ only the '**maru**.' In modern writing styles, all punctuation marks are used. Spacing may be used between words or phrases to assist with reading and comprehension -- particularly in books for beginning readers -- but this 'spacing' is not governed by specific rules and is not consistent from one writer or text to another. In most modern styles, however, a '、 + **space**' is used to indicate a major pause in a sentence or clause. Otherwise, individual words or characters are not separated from one another; particles are written with no space between them and the characters which precede them. In this book individual phrases (usually a word + a particle) will be followed by a space to assist in comprehension and reading fluency. Spacing will gradually be reduced later to make the printed pages look more like those of authentic Japanese books.

(b) The particle **wa** is represented by the symbol ' は ' (ha). The **wa** syllable in other instances is represented by the symbol ' わ.'

koré **wa**   **wa**takushi no hon desu.

これは、わたくしの　ほんです。

de **wa**   soré **wa**   nan desu ka?

では、それは、なんですか。

soré **wa**   hon de **wa**   arimasen. den **wa** desu.

それは、ほんでは　ありません。でんわです。

(c) The particle **o** is represented by the symbol ' を ' (wo). This symbol is used exclusively for the particle **o**, while the symbol ' お ' is used for most other cases of the 'o' syllable.

okada-sensei **o**   shitte imasu ka?

おかだせんせいを　しっていますか。

sensei wa **o**shuuji **o** **o**shiemasu.

せんせいは、おしゅうじを　おしえます。

(d) The particle **e** is represented by the symbol ' へ ' (he). (This particle **e** is limited in use and has not been drilled yet. It will be introduced later.) Other cases of the **e** syllable are represented by ' え ' (e).

With these specific exceptions, every other particle is represented by the symbol which corresponds to its pronunciation.

Exercise 1: Read the following sentences and give their meanings in English.

1. これは、えんぴつですか。
   はい、それは、えんぴつです。
2. あれは、だれの　ざっしですか。
   あれは、やまださんの　ざっしです。
3. それは、なにごの　じしょですか。
   これは、ちゅうごくごの　じしょです。
4. きょうは、いい　おてんきですね！
   ほんとに、いい　おてんきですね！
5. こんにちは。きょうは、あついですね！
   ほんとに、あついですね！

Exercise 2: Read the following dialogue in pairs.

A: いい　いけばなのせんせいを　しっていますか。

B: はい、しっていますよ。そのかたは、とよたせんせい
と、いいます。わたくしの　しりあいです。
とても　いいせんせいですよ。

A: どんなかたですか。

B: ねんぱいの　おんなのかたです。

A: じゃ、こんど、しょうかいしてください。

B: はい、いいですよ。こんど、しょうかいしましょう。

Exercise 3: Write the Japanese equivalents of the following words in **hiragana**.

1. newspaper
2. teacher
3. history
4. weather
5. good-bye
6. good morning
7. pencil
8. magazine
9. blackboard
10. math

Exercise 4: Read the following sentences and write answers as homework.

1. あなたは、かんこくごが　できますか。
2. いい　ちゅうごくごの　せんせいを　しっていますか。
3. きょうは、あついですか、さむいですか。
4. にほんごは、やさしいですか、むずかしいですか。
5. がっこうは、どうですか。
6. 「こくばん」は、えいごで、なんと、いいますか。

8

Tanaka:	nihon-shoku ga suki desu ka?
Brown:	hai, suki desu.
Tanaka:	donna mono ga suki desu ka?
Brown:	sukiyaki ya tempura ga suki desu.
Tanaka:	(o)sushi wa doo desu ka?
Brown:	mochiron, daisuki desu.
Tanaka:	tokidoki nihon-shoku o tabemasu ka?
Brown:	hai, taitei mainichi tabemasu.
Tanaka:	(o)hashi de tabemasu ka?
Brown:	hai, mochiron hashi de tabemasu.
Tanaka:	hambaagaa to sukiyaki to dochira no hoo ga suki desu ka?
Brown:	sukiyaki no hoo ga suki desu.
Tanaka:	ja, sukiyaki to (o)sushi to dochira no hoo ga suki desu ka?
Brown:	ryoohoo to mo daisuki desu.
Tanaka:	tokidoki nihon no ocha o nomimasu ka?
Brown:	hai, mainichi nomimasu.
Tanaka:	nandaka onaka ga sukimashita ne...
Brown:	soo desu ne... ja, hirugohan ni (o)sushi demo tabemashoo.

ENGLISH EQUIVALENT

Tanaka: Do you like Japanese food?
Brown: Yes, I do. (Yes, I like it.)
Tanaka: What sort of things do you like?
Brown: I like things like sukiyaki and tempura.
Tanaka: How about sushi?
Brown: Of course, I like it very much.
Tanaka: Do you sometimes eat Japanese food?
Brown: Yes. I generally eat it every day.
Tanaka: Do you eat [it] with chopsticks?
Brown: Yes, of course, I do.
          (Yes, of course, I eat [it] with chopsticks.)
Tanaka: Which do you like better, hamburgers or sukiyaki?
Brown: I like sukiyaki better.
Tanaka: Hmm. Which do you like more, sukiyaki or sushi?
Brown: I like both of them very much.
Tanaka: Do you sometimes drink Japanese green tea?
Brown: Yes, I drink [it] every day.
Tanaka: I'm kind of getting hungry. Aren't you?
          (My stomach seems to be getting empty. How about you?)
Brown: I guess so... Okay, let's eat sushi or something for lunch, then.

GRAMMATICAL AND CULTURAL NOTES

8.1   ...ga suki desu

In English, the idea that you like something or someone is expressed by the verb 'to like,' as in 'I like oranges' or 'I like my teacher.' In Japanese the word **suki** expresses the same idea, but grammatically the word **suki** is a type of noun, not a verb, so it is usually followed by **desu** to make the predicate of a sentence. **suki** means 'pleasing' or 'likeable.' The object you like or find pleasing is marked by **ga**, the particle of subject marker. When you like something or someone very much you say '**daisuki desu**.' The opposite of **suki** is **kirai** (displeasing) or ([I] don't like).

nihon-shoku **ga suki desu ka?**   (**Do you like** Japanese food?)
hai, **suki desu**.   (Yes, **I do**.) or (Yes, **I like** it.)
hai, **daisuki desu**.   (Yes, **I like** it **very much**.)
iie, **kirai** desu.   (No, **I don't like** it.)

8.2   Short Answers

In English, when someone asks you a question, you often give a short answer, 'Yes, I do.' or 'No, I don't.' There are no equivalent expressions in Japanese; but answering with only the predicate gives a similar feeling of brief and concise response.

nihon-shoku ga **suki desu ka?**	(**Do you like** Japanese food?)
hai, **suki desu.**	(Yes, **I do.**)
mainichi nihon-shoku o **tabemasu ka?**	
	(**Do you eat** Japanese food every day?)
hai, **tabemasu.**	(Yes, **I do.**)
iie, **tabemasen.**	(No, **I don't.**)

8.3 ya, to

The particle **ya** joining two or more nouns or noun phrases means 'and' in incomplete enumeration. That is, **ya** indicates that more is implied than is actually listed in the series (A and B [and C] and so forth). In the case of complete enumeration (i.e., A and B and no more), the particle **to** is used.

sukiyaki **ya** tempura ga suki desu.	(I like sukiyaki **and** tempura **and such food.**)
sukiyaki **to** tempura ga suki desu.	(I like sukiyaki **and** tempura.)
ringo **ya** mikan ga suki desu ka?	(Do you like apples **and** oranges **and such fruits?**)

8.4 prefix o-

The prefix **o-** may be attached in front of a noun to make it sound more gentle or polite. Women use **o-** more often than men, especially with food items and utensils. In some words, the prefix **o-** is always used by both men and women and has become a part of the words, while in some other words it is optional. When the optional **o-** appears in this book it is placed in parentheses. Consult your instructor for his or her recommendation whether or not you should use the prefix **o-**.

	MEN	WOMEN
(o)hashi	hashi	ohashi
(o)sushi	sushi	osushi
(o)cha	(o)cha	ocha
(o)tenki	tenki	otenki

8.5 de

The particle **de** as in **(o)hashi de tabemasu** expresses 'agency.' It can be translated into English as 'by means of,' 'using such and such,' 'with' or 'by' depending upon the thing employed. This is the same particle **de** introduced in Lesson 1 as in **nihongo de hanashimashoo**, in which case 'in' is the right English.

ohashi **de** tabemasu ka?	(Do you eat **with** chopsticks?)
nihongo **de** hanashimashoo.	(Let's speak **in** English.)
kono ji wa hiragana **de** kakimasu.	(We write this word **in** hiragana.)

8.6 (A) to (B) to dochira no hoo ga (suki desu ka?)

When Japanese speakers want to know which of two alternatives, A and B, you like better, they ask **A to B to dochira no hoo ga suki desu ka?** This idiomatic expression may be broken down into the following components.

> **... ga suki desu ka?**   **(Do you like ...?)**
> **dochira no hoo**   **(Which one of the two)**
> **... to ... to**   **(... and ... compared)**

> **hambaagaa to** sukiyaki **to dochira no hoo ga** suki desu ka?
>   **(Which** do you like **better,** hamburger **or** sukiyaki?)

Here are two common ways to respond to the question, **A to B to dochira no hoo ga suki desu ka?**

> **[A yori] B no hoo ga** suki desu. (I like **B** better **[than A].**)
> **[A mo B mo] ryoohoo to mo** suki desu.
>   (I like **both [A and B].**)

ryoohoo to mo means 'inclusive of' or 'both of them.'

The expression, **... to ... to dochira no hoo ga ...** may be altered into other expressions to compare two things in various different ways. For example:

> **nihongo to** supeingo **to dochira no hoo ga muzukashii** desu ka?
>   **(Which** is **harder,** Japanese **or** Spanish?)
> supeingo **yori** nihongo **no hoo ga muzukashii** desu.
>   (Japanese is **harder than** Spanish.)

8.7   onaka ga suku

The word **onaka** means 'stomach,' and **...ga suku** means 'to become less filled.' When a Japanese speaker feels hungry, he or she says **onaka ga sukimashita.** Normally the verb is in the **-mashita** form to indicate that he or she 'has become and is hungry.'

onaka ga sukimashita ne...	(I'm hungry. Aren't you?)
onaka ga suki**mashita ka?**	(Are you hungry? The implication is "**Have you become** hungry?")
onaka ga sui**te imasu** ka?	(Are you hungry? The implication is '**Are you in the state of** being hungry?')

8.8   Japanese Food

sukiyaki - very thin slices of beef cooked with various kinds of vegetables such as green onions, Chinese cabage, bean sprouts, bamboo shoots, mushrooms, konnyaku (yam cake or noodle), and tofu. The dish is flavored with soy sauce, sugar, and sake, and is eaten hot from the cooking pan on the table. Each bite may be dipped in a bowl of beaten raw egg before being eaten.

tempura - deep fried shrimp or vegetables. The crust is pale yellow, very light and crisp. Each bite may be dipped into a bowl of specially prepared soy-sauce-based sauce.

(o)sushi - cold rice, flavored with salt, sugar and vinegar, which is formed into bite-size balls topped with a slice of sea food, such as tuna, octopus, or shrimp. The rice can be wrapped in a thin sheet of pressed seaweed, with cooked vegetables, pickled ginger, or fish cake in the center.

(o)cha - Japanese green tea, usually served in a Japanese-style small teacup which has no handle. One picks up the cup with both hands, one holding the cup and the other supporting the bottom of the cup to drink. Black tea or Lipton tea is referred to as **koocha**, which means 'red tea' in Japanese. **koocha** is served in a Western-styled teacup.

8.9   ni denoting Purpose

The particle **ni** expresses 'purpose.' The purpose marker **ni** may be added to a noun such as 'lunch,' or 'dinner' to indicate a purpose of the activity in question. In English the preposition 'for' expresses a similar idea.

hirugohan ni sushi o tabemashoo.	(Let's eat sushi **for lunch**.)
yuugohan ni nani o tabemasu ka?	(What do you eat **for dinner**?)
dezaato ni nani o tabemasu ka?	(What do you eat **for dessert**?)

8.10   demo

demo following a word or phrase means '... or something,' and is often used in casual conversation when suggesting some choice of activities or objects.

ja, sushi **demo** tabemashoo.	(Well, let's eat sushi **or something**, then.)
ocha **demo** nomimashoo.	(Let's have some tea **or something**.)

8.11   Loan Words

The Japanese language has borrowed many words from other languages of the world: earlier words were borrowed from Chinese; more recently, from European languages. Especially since World War II, a large number of English words have been adapted to become part of the every day Japanese vocabulary. Words like **hambaagaa** (hamburger) and **koora** (cola) are some of these.

When words are borrowed into the Japanese language, their sounds will normally change to fit the Japanese sound system. Thus, English 'coffee' becomes Japanese 'koohii.' Also, Japanese vowels may be added to make the word conform to the syllable structure of Japanese. There are still other ways in which loan words may be modified.

Often, too, the meaning of a loan word may be adjusted as it passes into the Japanese language. The word **manshon** has come to refer to condominiums.

It is customary to use **katakana** to write Western loan words.

EXERCISES

8E.1   Response Drill: The instuctor asks the following questions, and the students respond. The second time, Student A asks Student B.

1. anata wa nihon-shoku ga suki desu ka, kirai desu ka?
2. (o)sushi ga suki desu ka, kirai desu ka?
3. tempura ga suki desu ka, kirai desu ka?
4. nihon no ocha ga suki desu ka, kirai desu ka?
5. kudamono ga suki desu ka?
6. ringo ya mikan ga suki desu ka?
7. banana ya painappuru ga suki desu ka?
8. aisukuriimu ya keeki ga suki desu ka?

8E.2   Response Drill: The instructor asks the questions and the students answer. The second time, Student A asks Student B.

1. hambaagaa to sukiyaki to dochira no hoo ga suki desu ka?
2. sukiyaki to tempura to dochira no hoo ga suki desu ka?
3. ringo to banana to dochira no hoo ga suki desu ka?
4. mikan to painappuru to dochira no hoo ga suki desu ka?
5. aisukuriimu to keeki to dochira no hoo ga suki desu ka?
6. ocha to koohii to dochira no hoo ga suki desu ka?
7. niku to sakana to dochira no hoo ga suki desu ka?
8. nihon-ryoori to chuuka-ryoori to dochira no hoo ga suki desu ka?

8E.3   Activity: Likes and dislikes. Work in pairs. Student A asks Student B if he or she sometimes eats the following foods, or drinks the following beverages. If Student B does, Student A asks if he or she likes the item[s] in question.

1. Japanese food
2. Japanese green tea
3. Japanese tangerines
4. Japanese vegetables
5. fish
6. fruit
7. ice cream and cake
8. coffee

Student B asks Student A which one of the two he or she likes better. Student A gives his or her preference or says he or she likes or dislikes both.

1. meat or fish
2. apples or oranges

3. sukiyaki or hamburger
4. coffee or tea
5. pineapples or tangerines
6. vegetables or fruit
7. milk or orange juice

8E.4 Dialogue Practice: First, the students repeat after the instructor for pronunciation and intonation. Next, students work in pairs to practice.

1. A: tokidoki (o)hirugohan ni nihon-shoku o tabemasu ka?
   B: hai, tabemasu.
   A: donna mono ga suki desu ka?
   B: (o)soba ga suki desu.
   A: soo desu ka. ja, kondo issho ni (o)soba o tabemashoo.
   B: ee, soo shimashoo. (o)soba wa totemo oishii desu.

2. A: onaka ga sukimashita ne...
   B: soo desu ne...
   A: hambaagaa ga suki desu ka?
   B hambaagaa wa ammari suki ja arimasen.
   A: ja, nihon-shoku wa doo desu ka?
   B: aa, ii desu ne... sushi ya udon ga daisuki desu.

3. A: kyoo wa atsui desu ne!
   B: honto ni atsui desu ne!
   A: nodo ga kawakimashita ne...
   B: soo desu ne...
   A: ja, tsumetai mono demo nomimashoo.
   B: ii desu ne...
   A: orenji-juusu to koora to dochira no hoo ga suki desu ka?
   B: watakushi wa orenji-juusu no hooga suki desu.
   A: watakushi mo koora yori juusu no hoo ga suki desu.

4. A: chotto samui desu ne! atsui ocha demo ikaga desu ka?
   B: arigatoo gozaimasu. atsui nihon no ocha ga daisuki desu.
   A: nihon no okashi mo ikaga desu ka?
   B: arigatoo. nihon no okashi mo daisuki desu.
   A: nihon no okashi wa ammari amaku arimasen yo.
   B: demo totemo oishii desu.

8E.5   Activity: Favorite cuisine. First, practice the words for different types of cuisine. Interview three classmates and find out what types of cuisine they like. Ask them to compare two cuisines each of them like, find out which they like better for dinner.   Report the findings to the instructor.

1. nihon-ryoori   (Japanese cuisine)
2. chuuka-ryoori   (Chinese cuisine)
3. furansu-ryoori   (French cuisine)
4. kankoku-ryoori   (Korean cuisine)
5. mekishiko-ryoori   (Mexican cuisine)
6. itaria-ryoori   (Italian cuisine)

8E.6   Say the following sentences in Japanese.

1. Are you hungry?
2. Yes, I'm hungry.
3. Do you sometimes eat Italian food?
4. Yes, I eat Italian food very often.
5. Do Japanese people sometimes eat hamburgers ?
6. Yes, they do. They like hamburgers very much.
7. Do you write 'hamburger' in hiragana or katakana?
8. Please write 'hamburger' in katakana on this paper.
9. Do you eat with chopsticks every day?
10. Yes, I usually eat Japanese food with chopsticks.

8E.7   Fill in the blanks with correct particles. Say the meanings of the sentences in English.

1. anata wa nihongo _____ benkyoo _____ suki desu _____?

2. nihongo _____ supeingo _____ dochira _____ hoo _____

    muzukashii desu _____?

3. Buraun-san _____ nihon-shoku _____ hashi _____ tabemasu.

4. nihonjin _____ yoku hambaagaa _____ tabemasu _____?

5. anata _____ tokidoki sakana _____ tabemasu _____ ?

6. niku _____ sakana _____ dochira _____ hoo _____ suki desu ka?

7. ryoohoo _____ _____ daisuki desu.

VOCABULARY

VERBS

tabemasu	(I eat/someone eats: -masu form of taberu)
taberu	(to eat)
nomimasu	(I drink/someone drinks: -masu form of nomu)
nomu	(to drink)
sukimashita	(... has become empty/is empty: -mashita form of suku, 8.7)
suku	(to become less filled; to be hungry)
tabemashoo	(let's eat: -mashoo form of taberu)

ADJECTIVES   (---)

NOUNS

nihon-shoku	(Japanese food, 8.8)
mono	(thing; item)
sukiyaki	(a Japanese dish, 8.8)
tempura	(a Japanese dish, 8.8)
(o)sushi	(a Japanese dish, 8.8)
(o)hashi	(chopsticks, 8.4)
hambaagaa	(hamburger, 8.11)
ocha	(Japanese green tea, 8.8, 8.4)
onaka	(stomach, 8.7)
(o)hirugohan	(lunch)

OTHERS

suki	(pleasing; likeable; I like, 8.1)
kirai	(displeasing; I don't like; I dislike, 8.1))
mainichi	(every day)
ya	(and: a particle meaning 'and' in incomplete enumeration, 8.3)
mochiron	(of course)
daisuki	(very pleasing; I like ... very much, 8.1)
...to ...to	(... and ... compared, 8.6)
dochira no hoo	(which one of the two, 8.6)
ryoohoo	(both [of them], 8.6)
to mo	(inclusive of ... ; both of them, 8.6)
nandaka	(somehow; rather)
ni	(a prticle denoting purpose; for, 8.9)
...demo	(... or something, 8.10)
o-	(a prefix making the following noun sound more gentle or polite, 8.4)

ADDITIONAL VOCABULARY

(o)soba	(buckwheat noodles; Japanese people's favorite lunch item)
udon	(regular white noodles; a favorite lunch item)
oishii	(good tasting; delicious; good)

mazui	(bad tasting)
amai	(sweet tasting)
atsui	(warm; hot to touch)
tsumetai	(cold to touch; cold referring to food or other things but not to weather)
(o)kashi	(cookies, crackers; snacks)
mikan	(tangerine)
banana	(banana, 8.11)
painappuru	(pineapple, 8.11)
kudamono	(fruit)
yasai	(vegetable)
aisukuriimu	(ice cream, 8.11)
keeki	(cake, 8.11)
niku	(meat)
koohii	(coffee, 8.11)
sakana	(fish)
miruku	(milk, 8.11)
orenji-juusu	(orange juice, 8.11)
koocha	(red tea; black tea, 8.8)
ryoori	(cuisine)
nihon-ryoori	(Japanese cuisine or cooking)
chuuka-ryoori	(Chinses cuisine or cooking)
furansu-ryoori	(French cuisine or cooking)
kankoku-ryoori	(Korean cuisine or cooking)
itaria-ryoori	(Italian cuisine or cooking)
mekishiko-ryoori	(Mexican cuisine or cooking)
resutoran	(restaurant)

READING AND WRITING

The **katakana** syllabary has the same number of symbols as the **hiragana** syllabary. **Katakana** symbols use straight lines and sharp corners while **hiragana** use more cursive lines and rounded corners. As with **hiragana**, it is important to differentiate a trailing ending from a stop ending.

Exercise 1: Learn how to write **katakana** symbols.

a　ア　マ ア

i　イ　ノ イ

u　ウ　｀ ｀ ウ

e　エ　｀ エ エ

o　オ　一 オ オ

ka	カ	プ カ	
ki	キ	二 キ	
ku	ク	ノ ク	
ke	ケ	ノ ヒ ケ	
ko	コ	フ コ	
sa	サ	一 サ サ	
shi	シ	゛ シ シ	
su	ス	フ ス	
se	セ	フ セ	
so	ソ	ゝ ソ	
ta	タ	ノ ク タ	
chi	チ	二 チ チ	
tsu	ツ	゛ ツ ツ	
te	テ	二 テ テ	
to	ト	｜ ト	

na	ナ	一 ナ
ni	ニ	一 ニ
nu	ヌ	フ ヌ
ne	ネ	` ラ ネ ネ
no	ノ	ノ
ha	ハ	ノ ハ
hi	ヒ	一 ヒ
fu	フ	フ
he	ヘ	ヘ
ho	ホ	一 ナ オ ホ
ma	マ	フ マ
mi	ミ	` ミ ミ
mu	ム	ム ム
me	メ	ノ メ
mo	モ	一 ニ モ

ya	ヤ	
yu	ユ	
yo	ヨ	

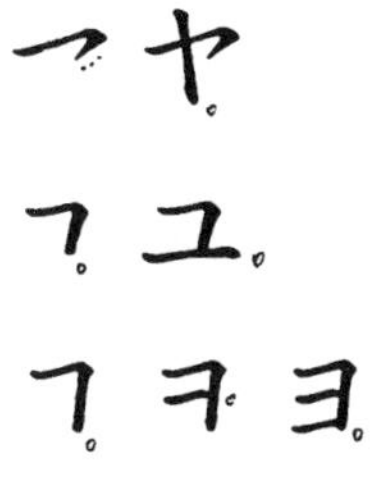

ra	ラ	
ri	リ	
ru	ル	
re	レ	
ro	ロ	

wa	ワ	
[w]o	ヲ	
N	ン	

Such procedures as using the two dotts for writing voiced consonants, the small circles for writing syllables with the [p] sound, and the small letters 'ヤ,' 'ユ,' 'ヨ' to write the syllables with internal [y] generally follow the corresponding rules used with **hiragana**.

ga ガ	gi ギ	gu グ	ge ゲ	go ゴ
za ザ	ji ジ	zu ズ	ze ゼ	zo ゾ
da ダ	ji ヂ	zu ヅ	de デ	do ド
ba バ	bi ビ	bu ブ	be ベ	bo ボ
pa パ	pi ピ	pu プ	pe ペ	po ポ

kya	キャ	kyu	キュ	kyo	キョ
sha	シャ	shu	シュ	sho	ショ
cha	チャ	chu	チュ	cho	チョ
nya	ニャ	nyu	ニュ	nyo	ニョ
hya	ヒャ	hyu	ヒュ	hyo	ヒョ
mya	ミャ	myu	ミュ	myo	ミョ
rya	リャ	ryu	リュ	ryo	リョ
gya	ギャ	gyu	ギュ	gyo	ギョ
ja	ジャ	ju	ジュ	jo	ジョ
bya	ビャ	byu	ビュ	byo	ビョ
pya	ピャ	pyu	ピュ	pyo	ピョ

The only major difference between the two systems is the way in which long vowels are written. In **katakana**, a short line ' ー ' which follows the direction of writing (a horizontal line in horizontal writing; vertical in vertical writing) represents a lengthening of the preceding syllable.

ノート	nooto	(notebook)
コーヒー	koohii	(coffee)
セーター	seetaa	(sweater)

The **katakana** syllabary is primarily used to write Western loan words, onomatopoetic words and exclamatory expressions.

Exercise 2: Write the follwoing pairs of syllables in **katakana** three times paying special attention to the differences between the two **katakana** symbols.

1. o na

2. so N

3. ra [w]o

4. ku wa

5. me   na

6. shi   tsu

7. ko   yu

8. u   fu

9. shi   N

10. o   ho

11. shi   so

12. chi   te

13. so   tsu

Exercise 3: The following words are loanwords from English. Read them and figure out the meanings. Write each word three times.

1. コーヒー   6. サラダ

2. バナナ   7. スープ

3. ケーキ   8. ピザ

4. コーラ   9. サンドイッチ

5. ミルク   10. レストラン

Exercise 4: Practice reading the following dialogues in pairs.

1. A: スープと　サラダと　どちらのほうが　いいですか。

   B: わたしは、サラダが　いいです。

   A: わたしは、スープに　します。

   B: ピザを　たべますか、サンドイッチを　たべますか。

   A: わたしは、サンドイッチを　たべます。

   B: わたしは、ピザを　たべます。

2. A: ミルクを　のみますか、コーヒーを　のみますか。

   B: わたしは、ミルクを　のみます。

   A: わたしは、コーヒーに　します。

   B: ケーキと　アイスクリームと　どちらのほうが
   すきですか。

   A: りょうほうとも　だいすきです。でも、きょうは、
   アイスクリームを　たべましょう。

   B: そう　しましょう。

3. A: にほんしょくが　すきですか。

   B: はい、もちろん、だいすきです。

   A: どんなものが　すきですか。

   B: すしや、おそばが　すきです。

   A: わたしは、すしより　てんぷらのほうが　すきです。

   B: じゃ、ひるごはんに　にほんしょくをたべましょう。

   A: ええ、そう　しましょう。

4. A: いい　にほんしょくのレストランを　しっていますか。

   B: しっていますよ。そのレストランは、「みやこ」と
   いいます。

   A: どんなレストランですか。

   B: ちいさい　レストランですが、とても　おいしいです。

   A: じゃ、そのレストランで、たべましょう。

   B: おなかが　すきましたね！

9

Brown:	maiasa nanji ni okimasu ka?
Tanaka:	taitei rokuji goro ni okimasu.
Brown:	zuibun hayaoki desu ne!
Tanaka:	soo omoimasu ka?
	ja, Buraun-san wa nanji goro ni okimasu ka?
Brown:	watakushi wa taitei hachiji goro ni okimasu.
Tanaka:	asagohan ni nani o tabemasu ka?
Brown:	taitei nihon-shoku o tabemasu.
Tanaka:	mainichi gakkoo ni ikimasu ka?
Brown:	hai, mainichi ikimasu.
Tanaka:	kurasu wa nanji ni hajimarimasu ka?
Brown:	gozen kuji ni hajimarimasu.
Tanaka:	nanji ni owarimasu ka?
Brown:	gogo sanji juugofun sugi ni owarimasu.
Tanaka:	nanji goro ni uchi ni kaerimasu ka?
Brown:	taitei yoji-han goro ni uchi ni kaerimasu.
Tanaka:	maiban benkyoo shimasu ka?
Brown:	hai, sukoshi benkyoo shimasu.
	sore kara terebi o mimasu.
Tanaka:	watakushi mo taitei soo desu.

ENGLISH EQUIVALENT

Brown: What time do you get up in the morning (every morning)?
Tanaka: I usually get up around six o'clock.
Brown: That's very early! (You're an early-riser aren't you?)
Tanaka: Do you think so?
         Well, about what time do you get up?
Brown: I usually get up around eight o'clock.
Tanaka: What do you eat for breakfast?
Brown: I usually eat Japanese food.
Tanaka: Do you go to school every day?
Brown: Yes, I go [to school] every day.
Tanaka: What time does your class begin?
Brown: It begins at 9:00 a.m.
Tanaka: What time does it end?
Brown: It ends at 3:15 p.m.
Tanaka: About what time do you get home?
Brown: I usually get home around 4:30.
Tanaka: Do you study every night?
Brown: Yes, I study a little. Afterwards, I watch T.V.
Tanaka: I usually do that, too.

GRAMMATICAL AND CULTURAL NOTES

9.1   How to Tell Time

The following list indicates how to tell time in Japanese. The bound word **-ji** means 'o'clock.'

ichiji	(one o'clock)	(s)hichiji	(seven o'clock)
niji	(two o'clock)	hachiji	(eight o'clock)
sanji	(three o'clock)	kuji	(nine o'clock)
yoji	(four o'clock)	juuji	(ten o'clock)
goji	(five o'clock)	juuichiji	(eleven o'clock)
rokuji	(six o'clock)	juuniji	(twelve o'clock)
		nanji	(what time)

9.2   gozen, gogo

The word for **a.m.** in Japanese is **gozen**, and that for **p.m.** is **gogo**. These words precede the time word.

   gozen kuji (9:00 **a.m.**)   **gogo** sanji (3:00 **p.m.**)

106

9.3　Numbers 1 - 100

The following list is the numbers 1 - 100.

1	ichi	51	gojuu-ichi
2	ni	52	gojuu-ni
3	san	53	gojuu-san
4	shi, yon	54	gojuu-shi, gojuu-yon
5	go	55	gojuu-go
6	roku	56	gojuu-roku
7	(s)hichi, nana	57	gojuu-(s)hichi, gojuu-nana
8	hachi	58	gojuu-hachi
9	ku, kyuu	59	gojuu-ku, gojuu-kyu
10	juu	60	rokujuu
11	juu-ichi	61	rokujuu-ichi
12	juu-ni	62	rokujuu-ni
13	juu-san	63	rokujuu-san
14	juu-shi, juu-yon	64	rokujuu-shi, rokujuu-yon
15	juu-go	65	rokujuu-go
16	juu-roku	66	rokujuu-roku
17	juu-(s)hichi, juu-nana	67	rokujuu-(s)hichi, rokujuu-nana
18	juu-hachi	68	rokujuu-hachi
19	juu-ku, juu-kyuu	69	rokujuu-ku, rokujuu-kyuu
20	nijuu	70	nanajuu, (s)hichijuu
21	nijuu-ichi	71	nanajuu-ichi
22	nijuu-ni	72	nanajuu-ni
23	nijuu-san	73	nanajuu-san
24	nijuu-shi, nijuu-yon	74	nanajuu-shi, nanajuu-yon
25	nijuu-go	75	nanajuu-go
26	nijuu-roku	76	nanajuu-roku
27	nijuu-(s)hichi, nijuu-nana	77	nanajuu-(s)hichi, nanajuu-nana
28	nijuu-hachi	78	nanajuu-hachi
29	nijuu-ku, nijuu-kyuu	79	nanajuu-ku, nanajuu-kyuu
30	sanjuu	80	hachijuu
31	sanjuu-ichi	81	hachijuu-ichi
32	sanjuu-ni	82	hachijuu-ni
33	sanjuu-san	83	hachijuu-san
34	sanjuu-shi, sanjuu-yon	84	hachijuu-shi, hachijuu-yon
35	sanjuu-go	85	hachijuu-go
36	sanjuu-roku	86	hachijuu-roku
37	sanjuu-(s)hichi, sanjuu-nana	87	hachijuu-(s)hichi, hachijuu-nana
38	sanjuu-hachi	88	hachijuu-hachi
39	sanjuu-ku, sanjuu-kyuu	89	hachijuu-ku, hachijuu-kyuu
40	yonjuu	90	kyuujuu
41	yonjuu-ichi	91	kyuujuu-ichi
42	yonjuu-ni	92	kyuujuu-ni
43	yonjuu-san	93	kyuujuu-san
44	yonjuu-shi, yonjuu-yon	94	kyuujuu-shi, kyuujuu-yon
45	yonjuu-go	95	kyuujuu-go
46	yonjuu-roku	96	kyuujuu-roku
47	yonjuu-(s)hichi, yonjuu-nana	97	kyuujuu-(s)hichi, kyuujuu-nana
48	yonjuu-hachi	98	kyuujuu-hachi
49	yonjuu-ku, yonjuu-kyuu	99	kyuujuu-ku, kyuujuu-kyuu
50	gojuu	100	hyaku

107

9.4 -fun, -pun for Minutes

The bound word **-fun** means 'minute(s),' and is attached to number stems in the following specific manner. The word **-fun** follows **ni, yon, nana,** and **kyuu**. When the word **-fun** is added to **ichi, san, roku, hachi** and **juu** it is changed to **-pun**. Either **-fun** or **-pun** may follow **yon**.

ippun	(1 minute)	juusampun	(13 minutes)
nifun	(2 minutes)	juuyonfun, juuyonpun	(14 minutes)
sampun	(3 minutes)	juugofun	(15 minutes)
yonfun, yompun	(4 minutes)	juuroppun	(16 minutes)
gofun	(5 minutes)	juunanafun	(17 minutes)
roppun	(6 minutes)	juuhappun	(18 minutes)
nanafun	(7 minutes)	juukyuufun	(19 minutes)
happun	(8 minutes)	nijuppun	(20 minutes)
kyuufun	(9 minutes)	sanjuppun	(30 minutes)
juppun	(10 minutes)	yonjuppun	(40 minutes)
juuippun	(11 minutes)	gojuppun	(50 minutes)
juunifun	(12 minutes)	rokujuppun	(60 minutes)

nampun (how many minutes)

9.5 mae, sugi

To indicate time before the hour, **mae** (before) is added, and to indicate time after the hour, **sugi** (past) is added. To indicate half past the hour, either **sanjuppun sugi** (30 minutes past) or **han** (half) is used.

gogo **sanji juugofun sugi** ni owarimasu.   (It ends at **3:15** p.m.)
gogo **goji sanjuppun sugi** desu.   (It's **5:30** p.m.)
rokuji **juppun mae** desu.   (It's **ten to** six.)

9.6 ni denoting Time of Activity

The particle **ni** is used with words that indicate specific times (such as 9:00 a.m. or 3:15 p.m.) for certain activities. In English the preposition 'at' is used to express the same idea.

nanji **ni** okimasu ka?   (**At** what time do you get up?)
taitei rokuji **ni** okimasu.   (I usually get up **at** 6:00.)
gakkoo wa gozen kuji **ni** hajimarimasu.   (School starts **at** 9:00 a.m.)

9.7 goro

goro means 'approximate time,' and is usually attached to a time word to mean 'about' or 'around that time.'

taitei rokuji **goro** ni okimasu.   (I usually get up **around** six o'clock.)
nanji **goro** ni uchi ni kaerimasu ka?   (**About** what time do you get home?)

9.8   ni denoting Direction/Destination

The particle **ni** used with verbs of movement such as 'to go,' 'to return,' or 'to come' indicates direction or destination. This idea is usually expressed by 'to' in English, as in 'I go to school' or 'We returned to our home.'

mainichi **gakkoo ni** ikimasu ka?	(Do you go **to school** every day?)
nanji goro ni **uchi ni** kaerimasu ka?	(About what time do you **get home**?) or (About what time do you return **to** your **home**?)

EXERCISES

9E.1   Repetition Drill: The instructor brings a paper clock on which he/she displays the times in the exercise below, reading the times aloud. The students repeat after the instructor.

1. ima   ichiji desu.
2. ima   niji desu.
3. ima   sanji desu.
4. ima   yoji desu.
5. ima   goji desu.
6. ima   rokuji desu.
7. ima   (s)hichiji desu.
8. ima   hachiji desu.
9. ima   kuji desu.
10. ima   juuji desu.
11. ima   juuichiji desu.
12. ima   juuniji desu.

The instructor sets the clock at half past the hour and reads the following times. The students repeat after the instructor.

1. ima   sanji-han desu. (3:30)
2. ima   yoji-han desu. (4:30)
3. ima   rokuji-han desu. (6:30)
4. ima   (s)hichiji-han desu. (7:30)
5. ima   hachiji-han desu. (8:30)
6. ima   kuji-han desu. (9:30)
7. ima   juuichiji-han desu. (11:30)

The instructor sets the clock at the following times and tells the time aloud. The students repeat each time after the instructor.

1. (3:01) ima sanji ippun sugi desu.
2. (3:02) ima sanji nifun sugi desu.
3. (3:03) ima sanji sampun sugi desu.
4. (3:04) ima sanji yonfun (~ yompun) sugi desu.
5. (3:05) ima sanji gofun sugi desu.
6. (3:06) ima sanji roppun sugi desu.
7. (3:07) ima sanji nanafun sugi desu.
8. (3:08) ima sanji happun sugi desu.
9. (3:09) ima sanji kyuufun sugi desu.
10. (3:10) ima sanji juppun sugi desu.
11. (3:11) ima sanji juuippun sugi desu.
12. (3:12) ima sanji juunifun sugi desu.
13. (3:15) ima sanji juugofun sugi desu.
14. (3:20) ima sanji nijuppun sugi desu.
15. (3:25) ima sanji nijuugofun sugi desu.
16. (3:30) ima sanji sanjuppun sugi desu.
17. (3:40) ima sanji yonjuppun sugi desu.
18. (3:45) ima yoji juugofun mae desu.
19. (3:50) ima yoji juppun mae desu.
20. (3:55) ima yoji gofun mae desu.

9E.2   The students tell the time in Japanese, indicating **a.m.** or **p.m.** as shown in the examples below:

Examples: 09:15 a.m. --> ima gozen kuji juugofun sugi desu.
                    10:30 p.m. --> ima gogo juuji sanjuppun sugi desu.
1. 06:00 a.m.
2. 06:15 a.m.
3. 07:30 a.m.
4. 07:55 a.m.
5. 09:05 a.m.
6. 11:57 a.m.
7. 12:45 p.m.
8. 02:13 p.m.
9. 04:25 p.m.
10. 09:20 p.m.

Next, the instructor and the students use the paper clock to set different times and ask each other such questions as **ima nanji desu ka?** (What time is it now?) or **ima nanji nampun desu ka?** (What time and how many minutes is it now?). Repeat the drill until everyone in class can tell time in Japanese with ease.

9E.3 Activity: Reading the digital clock. Work in pairs. Each student cuts a sheet of white paper into eight pieces, and write time (as shown in 9E.2 exercise) including a.m. or p.m. Student A asks Student B 'ima nanji nampun desu ka?' showing a piece of paper with time. If Student B answers correctly, then Student B asks A a question. The person who correctly answers all is the winner. Change the partner, and try more difficult ones to test each other, or hold a contest.

08:30 a.m.	03:15 p.m.
09:15 a.m.	05:20 p.m.
10:05 a.m.	07:36 p.m.
11:45 a.m.	12:55 p.m.

9E.4 Response Drill: The instructor asks the following questions and the students answer.

1. Tanaka-san wa maiasa nanji ni okimasu ka?
2. Buraun-san wa maiasa nanji ni okimasu ka?
3. anata wa maiasa nanji ni okimasu ka?
4. anata wa taitei nanji goro ni asagohan o tabemasu ka?
5. Buraun-san no kurasu wa maiasa gozen kuji ni hajimarimasu ne?
6. watakushitachi no kurasu wa mainichi nanji ni hajimarimasu ka?
7. Buraun-san no kurasu wa gogo sanji juugofun sugi ni owarimasu ne?
8. watakushitachi no kurasu wa nanji ni owarimasu ka?
9. Buraun-san wa taitei nanji goro ni uchi ni kaerimasu ka?
10. anata wa taitei nanji goro ni uchi ni kaerimasu ka?
11. anata wa taitei nanji goro ni yuugohan o tabemasu ka?
12. anata wa taitei nanji goro ni nemasu ka?

9E.5   Response Drill: The instructor asks the following questions and the students answer.

1. Tanaka-san wa maiasa rokuji ni nani o shimasu ka?
2. Tanaka-san wa maiasa (s)hichiji goro ni nani o shimasu ka?
3. anata wa maiasa hachiji goro ni nani o shimasu ka?
4. Buraun-san wa mainichi kuji goro ni nani o shimasu ka?
5. anata wa mainichi juuniji goro ni nani o shimasu ka?
6. Buraun-san wa mainichi gogo rokuji goro ni nani o shimasu ka?
7. anata wa mainichi gogo rokuji goro ni nani o shimasu ka?
8. anata wa maiban juuichiji goro ni nani o shimasu ka?

9E.6   Activity: Daily Schedules.   Interview five classmates and find out the following:

1. At what time he or she gets up every morning.
2. At what time he or she eats breakfast.
3. At what time he or she goes to school.
4. At what time his or her Japanese class begins.
5. At what time his or her Japanese class ends.
6. At what time he or she goes home.
7. At what time he or she goes to bed.

9E.7   Say the best Japanese equivalent of the following sentences.

1. Are you an early riser?
2. Do you study every night?
3. Do you watch TV every night?
4. At what time do you eat dinner?
5. What time do you go to bed every night?
6. What time is it now?
7. It's ten o'clock now. Let's have some coffee (drink coffee) or something.

VOCABULARY

VERBS

okimasu   (I get up: -masu form of okiru)
okiru   (to get up)

omoimasu	(I think: -masu form of omo[w]u)
omo[w]u	(to think)
ikimasu	(I go: -masu form of iku)
iku	(to go)
hajimarimasu	(it starts; it begins: -masu form of hajimaru)
hajimaru	(something begins)
owarimasu	(it ends: -masu form of owaru)
owaru	(something ends)
kaerimasu	(I go home: -masu form of kaeru)
kaeru	(to return; to go home)
benkyoo shimasu	(I study: -masu form of benkyoo suru, 9.9)
mimasu	(I see; I watch: -masu form of miru)
nemasu	(I go to bed: -masu form of neru)
neru	(to go to bed; to sleep)

ADJECTIVES   (---)

NOUNS

rokuji	(six o'clock, 9.1)
hayaoki	(earlybird; one who wakes up early)
hachiji	(eight o'clock, 9.1)
asagohan	(breakfast; morning meal)
gozen	(a.m., 9.2)
kuji	(nine o'clock, 9.1)
gogo	(p.m.; afternoon, 9.2)
sanji juugofun	(3:15, 9.1, 9.3, 9.4)
yoji-han	(4:30, 9.1, 9.4, 9.5)
terebi	(T.V.; a Japanese abbreviation for the English word 'television')

OTHERS

maiasa	(every morning)
maiban	(every night)
sore kara	(after that; afterwards; and then)
ima	(now)
nanji	(what time, 9.1)
ni	(at: a particle indicating the time for an activity, 9.6)
goro	(approximate time, 9.7)
ni	(for: a particle expressing purpose, 8.9)
-fun, -pun	(minute: bound words indicating minutes, 9.4)
sugi	(past the hour, 9.5)
ni	(to: a particle indicating direction when used with verbs of movement, 9.8)
mae	(before; till the hour, 9.5)
han	(half; half past the hour, 9.5)

ADDITIONAL VOCABULARY

ichiji	(one o'clock, 9.1)
niji	(two o'clock, 9.1)
goji	(five o'clock, 9.1)
shichiji	(seven o'clock, 9.1)
juuji	(ten o'clock, 9.1)
juuichiji	(eleven o'clock, 9.1)
juuniji	(twelve o'clock, 9.1)
yuugohan	(supper; dinner)
toosuto	(toast)
(o)hirugohan	(lunch)
dezaato	(dessert)
sandoitchi	(sandwich)
aisukuriimu	(icecream)
orenjijuusu	(orange juice)
miruku	(milk)
painappuru	(pineapple)
meron	(melon)
furuutsu	(fruit)
soshite	(and then)

READING AND WRITING

Exercise 1: Read and write the following **katakana** words, and give their meanings in English.

1. アメリカ
2. フランス
3. スペイン
4. イギリス
5. ドイツ
6. メキシコ
7. ハワイ
8. クラス
9. ブラウン
10. セーター

11. テレビ
12. ペン
13. ノート
14. デザート
15. フルーツ
16. メロン
17. アイスクリーム
18. パイナップル
19. オレンジジュース
20. ハンバーガー

Exercise 2: Fill in the blanks with correct particles.

1. あなた＿＿＿、フランスご＿＿＿、わかります＿＿＿。
2. これ＿＿＿、どなた＿＿＿セーターです＿＿＿。
3. イギリスじんは、えいご＿＿＿ はなします。
4. たなかさん＿＿＿、パイナップル＿＿＿、すきです。
5. アイスクリーム＿＿＿ たべましょう。
6. これは、とても、おいしいコーヒーです＿＿＿！
7. あなた＿＿＿、まいにち、テレビ＿＿＿ みます＿＿＿。
8. デザート＿＿＿、ケーキ＿＿＿ たべましょう。
9. アメリカじん＿＿＿、コーヒー＿＿＿、すきですね。
10. ときどき、オレンジジュース＿＿＿ のみます＿＿＿。

Exercise 3: Student A and Student B read the following dialogue aloud.

1. A: ブラウンさんは、イギリスじんですか。
   B: いいえ、ブラウンさんは、イギリスじんじゃ
      ありません。アメリカじんです。
   A: ブラウンさんは、スペインごが、じょうずですか。
   B: はい、あのかたは、スペインごも、フランスごも
      とても じょうずです。ドイツごも しっています。

2. A: アメリカじんは、デザートに、どんなものを、た
      べますか。
   B: たいてい、アイスクリームや、ケーキをたべます。
   A: にほんじんは、デザートに、フルーツをたべます。
   B: よく、メロンや、オレンジなどを、たべますね。

115

Exercise 4: Read the following passage aloud.

わたくしは、はやおきです。

まいあさ、6じに、おきます。

7じに、あさごはんを、たべます。

まいあさ、オレンジジュースを、のみます。

オレンジジュースは、とても、おいしいです。

それから、たいてい、トーストを、たべます。

ときどき、ミルクも、のみます。

コーヒーは、のみません。きらいです。

すこし、しんぶんを、よみます。

そして、8じに、がっこうに、いきます。

9じに、にほんごのクラスが、はじまります。

11じに、れきしのクラスに、いきます。

12じに、ひるごはんを、たべます。

ごごは、たいてい、としょかんで、べんきょうします。

そして、4じごろ、うちに、かえります。

よるは、たいてい、テレビをみます。

ときどき、ともだちと、でんわで、はなします。

まいばん、11じごろに、ねます。

10

Brown:	kyoo wa nangatsu nannichi desu ka?
Tanaka:	kyoo wa juunigatsu tsuitachi desu.
Brown:	ja, moosugu kurisumasu desu ne!
Tanaka:	honto ni soo desu ne!
Brown:	kyoo wa kin'yoobi desu ne?
Tanaka:	soo desu. ashita wa doyoobi desu.
Brown:	Tanaka-san wa ashita isogashii desu ka?
Tanaka:	iie, betsuni.
Brown:	ja, issho ni kaimono ni ikimasen ka?
Tanaka:	ii desu ne... ja, issho ni ikimashoo.
Brown:	doko ga ii deshoo ka?
Tanaka:	Ginza ga ii deshoo.
Brown:	ja, Ginza ni ikimashoo.
	nanji goro ni dekakemashoo ka?
Tanaka:	ohiru goro wa doo desu ka?
Brown:	ii desu ne. ja, doko de aimashoo ka?
Tanaka:	Tookyoo-eki wa doo desu ka?
Brown:	soo desu ne. ja, Tookyoo-eki no minami-guchi de
	juuniji ni aimashoo.
Tanaka:	ee, soo shimashoo.

ENGLISH EQUIVALENT

Brown: What is the date today? (Which month, which day is it today?)
Tanaka: Today is December 1st.
Brown: That means it will be Christmas pretty soon.
Tanaka: It certainly will.
Brown: It's Friday today, isn't it?
Tanaka: Right. Tomorrow will be Saturday.
Brown: Are you going to be busy tomorrow?
Tanaka: No, not in particular.
Brown: Then would you like to go shopping [together] with me?
Tanaka: That'll be fine. Let's go together.
Brown: Where would be a good place [to go shopping]?
Tanaka: The Ginza would probably be good.
Brown: Well, then let's go to the Ginza.
         Around what time shall we leave?
Tanaka: How about around noon?
Brown: That'll be fine. So where shall we meet?
Tanaka: How about Tokyo Station?
Brown: Hmmm. All right, let's meet at the south entrance of Tokyo Station at twelve.
Tanaka: Okay, let's do that.

GRAMMATICAL AND CULTURAL NOTES

10.1   Names of the Months

The following list indicates the names of the months of the year. The names of the months in Japanese are very simple: they are comprised of the words for one through twelve + **-gatsu**, the Japanese bound word for month. In other words, **ichigatsu** (January) means 'number one month'; **nigatsu** (February) means 'number two month'; and so on. **nangatsu** is comprised of **nani + -gatsu**, meaning 'what month.'

ichigatsu	(January)	(s)hichigatsu	(July)
nigatsu	(February)	hachigatsu	(August)
sangatsu	(March)	kugatsu	(September)
shigatsu	(April)	juugatsu	(October)
gogatsu	(May)	juuichigatsu	(November)
rokugatsu	(June)	juunigatsu	(December)
nangatsu	(what month)		

10.2   Names of the Days of the Month

The following list indicates the names of the days of the month.   As with the names of the months, the names for the days of the month are comprised of the numbers one through thirty-one + bound words **-ka** or **-nichi**, which both mean 'day.' The first day is an exception.

tsuitachi	(the first day of the month)
futsuka	(the second day of the month)
mikka	(the third day of the month)
yokka	(the fourth day of the month)
itsuka	(the fifth day of the month)
muika	(the sixth day of the month)
nanoka	(the seventh day of the month)
yooka	(the eighth day of the month)
kokonoka	(the ninth day of the month)
tooka	(the tenth day of the month)
juuichinichi	(the eleventh day of the month)
juuninichi	(the twelfth day of the month)
juusannichi	(the thirteenth day of the month)
juuyokka	(the fourteenth day of the month)
juugonichi	(the fifteenth day of the month)
juurokunichi	(the sixteenth day of the month)
juu(s)hichinichi	(the seventeenth day of the month)
juuhachinichi	(the eighteenth day of the month)
juukunichi	(the nineteenth day of the month)
hatsuka	(the twentieth day of the month)
nijuuichinichi	(the twenty-first day of the month)
nijuuninichi	(the twenty-second day of the month)
nijuusannichi	(the twenty-third day of the month)
nijuuyokka	(the twenty-fourth day of the month)
nijuugonichi	(the twenty-fifth day of the month)
nijuurokunichi	(the twenty-sixth day of the month)
nijuu(s)hichinichi	(the twenty-seventh day of the month)
nijuuhachinichi	(the twenty-eighth day of the month)
nijuukunichi	(the twenty-ninth day of the month)
sanjuunichi	(the thirtieth day of the month)
sanjuuichinichi	(the thirty-first day of the month)
nannichi	(what day of the month)

The seeming irregularities observed in naming the days stem from the fact that in an earlier stage of the Japanese language a mixing of two systems occurred: one, the days 1 through 10, 14, 20, and 24 resulted from the underlying old native Japanese way of counting; and two, the remaining days came from the Chinese numbers and the Chinese counting system which the Japanese language borrowed as loan words. The two systems merged to form the modern Japanese system.

10.3   Days of the Week

The following list indicates the names of the days of the week. The names of the days of the week are comprised of two bound words: a word for an important force or phenomena in nature + -**yoobi**, 'day of the week' or 'day.' The literal meanings of the days of the week in Japanese are included in the list below.

nichiyoobi	('sun day': Sunday)
getsuyoobi	('moon day': Monday)
kayoobi	('fire day': Tuesday)
suiyoobi	('water day': Wednesday)
mokuyoobi	('wood day': Thursday)
kin'yoobi	('gold day': Friday)
doyoobi	('earth day': Saturday)
nan(i)yoobi	(what day of the week)

10.4   Future

As mentioned earlier, the Japanese verbs have two dimensions in time: past and non-past. The non-past form covers the idea of future tense. In English, activities planned for 'tomorrow' are expressed in future tense; but in Japanese, activities for **ashita** (tomorrow) are normally expressed in the non-past forms.

ashita **isogashii desu ka?**	(Are you **going to be busy** tomorrow?) or
	(**Will you be busy** tomorrow?)
ashita .wa **doyoobi desu.**	(Tomorrow **will be Saturday**.)
ashita nani o **shimasu ka?**	(What **will** you **do** tomorrow?)
ashita kaimono ni **ikimasu.**	(I **will go** shopping tomorrow.)

10.5   -masen ka?

Questions such as **'ikimasen ka?'** or **'tabemasen ka?'** are used to ask someone's inclination or desire. In English, one asks 'won't you?' or 'wouldn't you like to ...?' in a similar situation. When a Japanese speaker asks a question using this sentence structure along with the word **issho ni** (together) he or she has the definite intention to participate in the activity and wishes to invite the other person to join him or her.

issho ni kaimono ni **ikimasen ka?**	(**Won't you go** shopping with me?) or
	(**Wouldn't you like to go** shopping with me?)
issho ni koohii o **nomimasen ka?**	
	(**Would you like to have** some coffee with me?)

10.6   deshoo

deshoo is a variant of **desu** in the tentative or indefinite form which the English words 'probably be' or 'may be' or 'would be' express. As with **desu**, **deshoo** can be added to a noun or an adjective to form the predicate of a sentence. A question '**... deshoo ka?** ' is more polite and indirect than '**... desu ka?**' English speakers express the idea in 'I wonder if ...' or 'would it be ..'

doko ga **ii deshoo ka?**	(Where **would be good?**) or
	(**I wonder** where **would be** a **good** place?)
Ginza ga **ii deshoo.**	(The Ginza **would be good.**) or
	(The Ginza **is probably fine.**)
ano hito wa **Tanaka-san deshoo.**	
	(That person over there **may be Miss Tanaka.**) or
	(That peson over there **is probably Miss Tanaka.**)

10.7   -mashoo ka?

-masu has a variant **-mashoo** form similar in construction to the **deshoo** variant of **desu**, though the meanings of **deshoo** and **-mashoo** are somewhat different. The meaning of **-mashoo** is similar to the English expression 'let's ...,' as introduced in Lesson 1. When a question is formed by **-mashoo + ka**, as in **aimashoo ka**, it takes on a meaning similar to an English question such as 'shall we ...?' or 'shall I ...?' in which the speaker asks the inclination of the other person with reference to a future activity.

nanji goro ni **dekakemashoo ka?**	(Around what time **shall we leave?**)
doko de **aimashoo ka?**	(Where **shall we meet?**)

10.8   ga with Interrogative Words

When a question begins with an interrogative word such as **doko** (where), **dare** (who) or **nani** (what), the particle **ga** is required to mark the subject. Such questions are answered by keeping the subject marker **ga** with the word replacing the interrogative word.

doko ga ii deshoo ka?	(**Where** would be a good place?)
Ginza ga ii deshoo.	(**The Ginza** would be fine.)
nani ga ii deshoo ka?	(**What** would be good?)
(o)sushi ga ii deshoo.	(**Sushi** would be good.)
dare ga eigo o hanashimasu ka?	(**Who** speaks English?)
Buraun-san ga eigo o hanashimasu.	(**Mr. Brown** speaks English.)

10.9   The Ginza

The **Ginza** is located in central Tokyo, and is the city's most famous shopping district. Because it is a beautiful and fascinating area, it attracts many visitors. It is, however, a rather expensive place to shop. Visitors engage in a lot of window-shopping. There are many fancy restaurants.

10.10   -guchi

-guchi is a bound word meaning 'entrance,' 'exit,' or 'mouth.' It may be combined with the direction words **minami** (south), **kita** (north), **higashi** (east), and **nishi** (west) to specify a specific entrance to or exit from a large train station. It may combine with the bound words **iri-** or **de-** to specify 'entrance' and 'exit,' respectively. Tokyo Station is an extremely large and very busy building cluster in downtown Tokyo. Its North, South, East, West, and Central Entrances are well-known and are frequently used as rendezvous points or as points of reference.

10.11   Arranging to Meet

In America, when one makes an appointment for dinner or shopping or business outside the home or the office, one usually offers to 'pick someone up.' In Japan, people arrange a rendezvous at a mutually-convenient and well-known place. Even dating couples will frequently arrange a rendezvous instead of planning that the man will stop by the woman's home or apartment to pick her up.

EXERCISES

10E.1   Repetition Drill: The instructor, with the aid of a calendar, says the names of the days of the months, and the students repeat the names after the instructor.

1.	ichigatsu	7.	(s)hichigatsu
2.	nigatsu	8.	hachigatsu
3.	sangatsu	9.	kugatsu
4.	shigatsu	10.	juugatsu
5.	gogatsu	11.	juuichigatsu
6.	rokugatsu	12.	juunigatsu

After the students have learned the names of the months, the instructor says the names of the days of the month. The instructor may continue the drill by pointing at the different days on the calendar and having the students name them in Japanese.

1.	tsuitachi	16.	juurokunichi
2.	futsuka	17.	juu(s)hichinichi
3.	mikka	18.	juuhachinichi
4.	yokka	19.	juukunichi
5.	itsuka	20.	hatsuka
6.	muika	21.	nijuuichinichi
7.	nanoka	22.	nijuuninichi
8.	yooka	23.	nijuusannichi
9.	kokonoka	24.	nijuuyokka
10.	tooka	25.	nijuugonichi
11.	juuichinichi	26.	nijuurokunichi
12.	juuninichi	27.	nijuu(s)hichinichi
13.	juusannichi	28.	nijuuhachinichi
14.	juuyokka	29.	nijuukunichi
15.	juugonichi	30.	sanjuunichi
		31.	sanjuuichinichi

10E.2   Repetition Drill: The instructor, with the aid of a calendar, says the names of the days of the week, and the students repeat the names after the instructor.

1. nichiyoobi   (Sunday)
2. getsuyoobi   (Monday)
3. kayoobi   (Tuesday)
4. suiyoobi   (Wednesday)
5. mokuyoobi   (Thursday)
6. kin'yoobi   (Friday)
7. doyoobi   (Saturday)

After the students have learned the names of the days of the week, the instructor asks the following questions, and the students respond. The second time, Student A asks Student B.

1. Kyoo wa   nan(i)yoobi desu ka?
2. kyoo wa   nangatsu nannichi desu ka?
3. ashita wa   nan(i)yoobi desu ka?
4. ashita wa   nangatsu nannichi desu ka?
5. *(pointing at one of the days on the calendar)*
    kono hi wa   nan(i)yoobi desu ka?
6. kono hi wa   nangatsu nannichi desu ka?
7. anata wa   getsuyoobi ni gakkoo ni ikimasu ka?
8. Buraun-san wa   getsuyoobi ni nihongo no kurasu ni ikimasu ka?
9. anata wa   kayoobi ni gakkoo ni ikimasu ka?
10. anata wa   nichiyoobi ni gakkoo ni ikimasu ka?
11. kurisumasu wa   nangatsu nannichi desu ka?
12. anata no (o)tanjoobi wa   nangatsu nannichi desu ka?

10E.3   Activity: Talking about dates. Work in pairs. Student A asks the following questions in Japanese. Student B responds. Next, reverse the role.

1. today's date
2. what day of the week today is
3. which day he or she likes better, Sunday or Friday
4. the date of his or her birthday
5. the date of Thanksgiving this year
6. the date of the final examination of this class

10E.4 Activity: Plan for tomorrow. In Japanese Student A asks Student B if he or she would like to do the following activities together with him or her tomorrow. Student B agrees and makes the appropriate response.

1. to go shopping
2. to watch T.V.
3. to go to the Ginza
4. to eat Japanese food
5. to study Japanese
6. to drink coffee
7. to go home
8. to go out
9. to write a letter to Mr. Brown
10. to read a Japanese newspaper

10E.5 Fill in the blanks with correct particles and say the meaning of the resulting sentences in English.

1. ashita doko _____ aimashoo ka?
    Tookyoo-eki _____ aimashoo.
2. ashita doko _____ ikimashoo ka?
    Ginza _____ ikimashoo.
3. ashita doko _____ benkyoo shimashoo ka?
    toshokan _____ benkyoo shimashoo.
4. ashita doko _____ kaimono o shimashoo ka?
    Shinjuku no depaato_____ kaimono o shimashoo.
5. ashita doko _____ ohirugohan o tabemashoo ka?
    gakkoo _____ tabemashoo.
6. nanji goro _____ dekakemashoo ka?
    ohiru goro _____ dekakemashoo.
7. nani _____ tabemashoo ka?
    (o)sushi _____ tabemashoo.
8. ashita dare _____ tegami _____ kakimashoo ka?
    Buraun-san _____ tegami _____ kakimashoo.
9. ashita issho ni kaimono _____ ikimashoo ka?
    ee, kaimono _____ ikimashoo.

10E.6 In Japanese, make an appointment to meet your friend at the places and times specified below. Your friend agrees and confirms the place and time.

1. at the south entrance of Tokyo Station at 12:00 noon.
2. at the north entrance of Tokyo Station at 11:30 a.m.
3. at the east entrance of Tokyo Station at 2:15 p.m.
4. at the west entrance of Shinjuku Station on Sunday at 3:00 p.m.
5. at the east entrance of Shinjuku Station tomorrow at 10:45 a.m.
6. at the south entrance of Shinjuku Station tomorrow at 6:30 p.m.
7. at the west entrance of Shibuya Station tonight at 7:15 p.m.

VOCABULARY

VERBS

ikimasen	(I don't go: negative form of ikimasu 'I go')
ikimasen ka	(wouldn't you like to go, 10.5)
ikimashoo	(let's go: -mashoo form of iku)
dekakemashoo	(let's go out; let's leave: -mashoo form of dekakeru)
dekakeru	(to leave home [to go somewhere]; to go out)
aimashoo ka	(shall we meet, 10.7)
aimashoo	(let's meet: -mashoo form of a[w]u)
a[w]u	(to meet [someone])

ADJECTIVES (---)

NOUNS

juunigatsu	(December, 10.1)
tsuitachi	(the first day of the month, 10.2)
kurisumasu	(Christmas)
kin'yoobi	(Friday, 10.3)
ashita	(tomorrow)
doyoobi	(Saturday, 10.3)
kaimono	(shopping)
Ginza	(Tokyo's most fashionable shopping district, 10.9)
(o)hiru	(noon)
Tookyoo-eki	(Tokyo Station)
minami-guchi	(south entrance, 10.10)

OTHERS

nangatsu	(what month, 10.1)
nannichi	(what day of the month, 10.2)
moosugu	(soon)

betsu ni ... [-masen] (not particularly; nothing in particular)
doko   (where)
deshoo   (probably is; maybe: tentative form of desu, 10.6)
nan(i)yoobi   (what day of the week, 10.3)

ADDITIONAL VOCABULARY

iriguchi	(entrance, 10.10)
deguchi	(exit, 10.10)
kita	(north, 10.10)
higashi	(east, 10.10)
nishi	(west, 10.10)
nichiyoobi	(Sunday, 10.3)
getsuyoobi	(Monday, 10.3)
kayoobi	(Tuesday, 10.3)
suiyoobi	(Wednesday, 10.3)
mokuyoobi	(Thursday, 10.3)
hi	(day)
(o)tanjoobi	(birthday)
kon'ya	(tonight)
itsu	(when: interrogative word)
zehi	(for sure; definitely: emphatic expression approving the proposed action)
purezento	(gift; present)
mada desu	(I [have] not yet [done that])

READING AND WRITING

Kanji, or Chinese characters, represent units of meaning while **hiragana** and **katakana** represent sounds. In modern Japanese writing, 'content words' such as nouns and the stems of verbs and adjectives are often written in **kanji**, while 'grammatical units' such as particles, conjunctions, and inflectional endings are written in **hiragana**.

The Chinese ideographic writing was originally invented in China many centuries ago, and the Japanese borrowed some of the characters during the sixth to tenth centuries A.D. During the long period of time since this initial borrowing, many changes have been made in the way both Chinese and Japanese characters are written. Some of the characters -- those for the moon '月' and the sun '日' for example -- look alike in modern Chinese and Japanese; there are other characters, however, that do not resemble each other any more. **Kanji**, the Chinese characters adopted in Japanese, have developed into something unique to the Japanese language.

To read and write Japanese like an educated native speaker requires the knowledge of approximately 2,000 **kanji** characters. During the first six grades of elementary education, native Japanese students learn approximately 900 characters. In their junior and senior high school they learn the remaining **Jooyoo kanji** (the approximately 1,900 characters in daily use).

Three things must be learned with each new **kanji**: (1) the core meaning it represents, (2) how to read it, and (3) how to write it. This book introduces the first 162 characters that are considered to be essential. Selections are based upon frequency of use, the order of introduction in Japanese grades, the usefulness of individual **kanji** characters, and the attempt to coordinate the learning of

126

specific **kanji** with the introduction of new vocabulary words.

One of the most difficult points of learning **kanji** is that each kanji character may have more than one pronunciation. The student of Japanese must know how to pronounce a **kanji** in a given context in order to read the word or phrase in which it occurs. Basically there are two types of 'readings' or pronunciations for any given **kanji**. The **On-yomi**, or the 'Chinese reading,' is basically the Japanese way of imitating the ancient Chinese pronunciation of the character. The **Kun-yomi**, or the 'Japanese reading,' represents the original Japanese word corresponding to the Chinese meaning of the **kanji** character and assigned to the character when it was borrowed anciently. Although there are many important exceptions it is frequently the case that a **kanji** occurring in a compound with other **kanji** characters will be read according to its **On-yomi**, while a character standing alone will be read according to its **Kun-yomi**. The challenges of learning **kanji** pronunciation are increased, however, by the fact that some characters have more than one **On-yomi** or **Kun-yomi**.

The following example may illustrate some of these points. The character '月' represents the moon and the idea of 'month.' By itself, it is read as '**tsuki**' (its **Kun-yomi**) to mean 'moon'; in the names of the months--such as '**ichigatsu**' (January) and '**nigatsu**' (February)--it is read as '**gatsu**' (its **On-yomi**) to mean 'month.' In other contexts, it has an additional **On-yomi**, '**getsu**,' also meaning 'month.'

The reading of **kanji** is difficult not only for the students of Japanese but also for the children who speak Japanese natively. To assist children in learning to read Japanese, the Japanese have adopted the convention of writing small **hiragana** at the side of **kanji** characters to indicate the pronunciation of **kanji** in particular contexts. These **hiragana** 'pronunciation guides' are called **yomigana** or **furigana** by the Japanese. They normally appear on the right-hand side of a character in conventional vertical writing, and above a character in horizontal writing.

There are basically three styles of kanji writing: the **kaisho** or the print style, the **gyoosho** or the cursive writing style, and the **soosho** or the 'grasshand' calligraphy style. For the most part, only the print style is used in books, magazines and newspapers, but educated native speakers often use the cursive style in personal correspondences. Artistic writings on screens and monuments and in paintings often use the grasshand style. In this book, the text materials are written in the print style font. When a new **kanji** is introduced it is written in the **kaisho calligrahpy** font to make the character look better. The same **kanji** in the three styles: (1) the normal print style, (2) the **kaisho calligraphy** style, (3) the **gyosho** cursive style may look like the following.

| (1) | (2) | (3) |

To learn the writing of **kanji** requires time and effort. It is important to know the stroke order and the way each stroke ends, either in trailing or in a stop. Each **kanji** is shaped to 'fit' in a square box. It is, therefore, advisable for the student of Japanese to practice writing **kanji** on paper lined to form square boxes.

Exercise 1: The instructor demonstrates on the board how to write the following **kanji** characters. The students practice writing them while the instructor checks the accuracy of the stroke order, the manners of stroke endings and the general artistic appearance of the characters written by the students.

1. 一 (one) いち 一 一

2. 二 (two) に 二 一 二

3. 三 (three) さん 三 一 二 三

4. 四 (four) し 四 丨 冂 冈 四 四

5. 五 (five) ご 五 一 丁 五 五

6. 六 (six) ろく 六 丶 二 六 六

7. 七 (seven) しち 七 一 七

8. 八 (eight) はち 八 丿 八

9. 九 (nine) きゅう 九 丿 九

10. 十 (ten) じゅう 十 一 十

11. 日 (sun; day) にちようび 日曜日 丨 冂 月 日

12. 月 (moon; month) げつようび 月曜日 丿 几 月 月

Exercise 2: Using **yomigana/furigana** as a guide, read the following words.

1. 一、 　 一月、 　 一日。

2. 二、 　 二月、 　 二日。

3. 三、 　 三月、 　 三日。

4. 四、 　 四月、 　 四日。

5. 五、 　 五月、 　 五日。

6. 六、 　 六月、 　 六日。

7. 七、 　 七月、 　 七日。

8. 八、 　 八月、 　 八日。

9. 九、 　 九月、 　 九日。

10. 十、 　 十月、 　 十日。

11. 十一月、 　 十二月。

12. 十三日、 　 十四日、 　 二十日。

In horizontal Japanese writing, numbers may be written using either Arabic numerals or **kanji** characters. The dates above (12) may also appear as 13日, 14日, and 20日, respectively. In the traditional vertical writing system, **kanji** characters are always used to write numbers.

Exercise 3: Say the following dates in Japanese and write them in **kanji**.

1. March 4th
2. April 10th
3. January 1st
4. October 2nd
5. May 3rd
6. February 24th
7. June 20th
8. July 14th
9. December 25th
10. November 7th
11. August 31st
12. September 5th

Exercise 4: Student A and Student B read the following dialogues.

1. A: きょうは、なん月なん日ですか。

   B: きょうは、十二月一日です。

   A: じゃ、もうすぐ、クリスマスですね。

   B: ほんとに、そうですね。

2. A: こんどいっしょに、コンサートに、いきませんか。

   B: いつですか。

   A: 十一月二十日の、ごご八じからです。

   B: 十一月二十日は、どようびですね。ちょっと、
      まってください。ああ、いいです。じゃ、ぜひ。

   A: じゃ、六じはんごろに、でかけましょう。

3. A: あしたは、ブラウンさんの、たんじょう日ですね。

   B: そうですね。もう、プレゼントをかいましたか。

   A: いいえ、まだです。

   B: じゃ、きょう、いっしょに、かいものにいきませんか。

   A: ええ、ぜひ、いっしょに、いきましょう。

   B: なんじごろに、でかけましょうか。

   A: 三じごろが、いいでしょう。

Exercise 4: Write the following words in **katakana**.

1. milk
2. coffee
3. cola
4. orange juice
5. icecream

6. cake
7. hamburger
8. sandwich
9. pizza
10. melon

11

Yamada: kinoo nanika shimashita ka?

Brown: ee. kinoo kaimono ni ikimashita.

Yamada: doko ni ikimashita ka?

Brown: tomodachi to issho ni Ginza e ikimashita.

Yamada: Ginza de nanika kaimashita ka?

Brown: iie, depaato de iroiro na mono o mimashita ga,

            nani mo kaimasen deshita.

Yamada: ja, dokoka de shokuji demo shimashita ka?

Brown: iie, shokuji wa shimasen deshita ga, kissaten de

            oishii koohii o nomimashita.

Yamada: aa, sore wa yokatta desu ne.

            norimono wa nan de ikimashita ka?

Brown: Tookyoo-eki kara Ginza made chikatetsu de ikimashita.

            kaeri wa takushii de kaerimashita.

Yamada: soo desu ka. watakushi wa kinoo densha de

            Shinjuku e ikimashita.

Brown: dareka to issho ni ikimashita ka?

Yamada: iie, hitori de ikimashita. Shinjuku de eiga o mimashita

            ga, ammari ii eiga ja arimasen deshita.

Brown: sore wa zannen deshita ne!

ENGLISH EQUIVALENT

Yamada: Did you do anything [special] yesterday?
Brown: Yes. I went shopping yesterday.
Yamada: Where did you go?
Brown: I went to the Ginza with a friend.
Yamada: Did you buy anything in the Ginza?
Brown: No, I saw various things at the department store, but I didn't buy anything.
Yamada: Then, did you have a meal or something somewhere?
Brown: No, we did not have a meal, but we had very good [delicious] coffee at a *kissaten* coffee-house.
Yamada: Oh, I'm glad you did.
What type of transportation did you go by? (How did you get there?)
Brown: From Tokyo station to the Ginza we went by the subway.
On our return [trip], we came home by taxi.
Yamada: Oh, I see. I went to Shinjuku by train yesterday.
Brown: Did you go with someone?
Yamada: No, I went alone. I saw a movie in Shinjuku, but it wasn't a very good movie.
Brown: Oh, that's too bad! (I'm sorry to hear that!)

GRAMMATICAL AND CULTURAL NOTES

11.1   -mashita

-mashita is the past form of **-masu**, and it indicates that the activity expressed by the verb has already happened. The most important concept expressed by the **-mashita** form is the completion of an activity. In many cases its meaning corresponds to the past tense in English, but it may also correspond to the present perfect tense.

kinoo kaimono ni **ikimashita**.	(I **went** shopping yesterday.)
kissaten de oishii koohii o **nomimashita**.	(We **drank** good coffee at a kissaten.)
Shinjuku de eiga o **mimashita**.	(I **saw** a movie in Shinjuku.)

11.2   -masen deshita

-masen conveys the idea of negation and **deshita** marks the predicate verb in the past. **-masen deshita** is the negative past form of the verb in the polite conversational **desu-masu** style.

nani mo **kaimasen deshita**.	(I **did not buy** anything.)
shokuji wa **shimasen deshita** ga ...	(We **did not have** a meal but...)

11.3   deshita

deshita is the past form of **desu**, and it may follow a noun to form the predicate of a sentence in the past. The same idea is expressed in English by such words as 'was' and 'were.'

sore wa zannen **deshita** ne!.	(That **was** too bad!)
kinoo wa nichiyoobi **deshita**.	(Yesterday **was** Sunday.)

11.4   de wa (ja) arimasen deshita

The negative form of the predicate, **NOUN + deshita**, is **NOUN + de wa (ja) arimasen deshita**. **de wa arimasen** indicates negation and **deshita** marks the construction as 'past' or 'completed.'

sore wa ii eiga **ja arimasen deshita**.	(It **was not** a very good movie.)
kinoo wa getsuyoobi **ja arimasen deshita**.	(Yesterday **was not** Monday.)

11.5   nanika, dokoka, dareka

Interrogative words such as **nani** (what), **doko** (where), and **dare** (who) may be followed by **ka** to form new compound words: **nanika** (something, anything), **dokoka** (somewhere, anywhere), **dareka** (somebody, anyone).

kinoo **nanika** shimashita ka?	(Did you do **anything** yesterday?)
Ginza de **nanika** kaimashita ka?	(Did you buy **anything** at the Ginza?)
dokoka de shokuji demo shimashita ka?	(Did you have dinner **somewhere**?)
dareka to issho ni ikimashita ka?	(Did you go with **someone**?)

11.6   e denoting Destination or Direction

The particle **e** is a free variant of **ni**, meaning direction or destination. Both particles are used with verbs of movement such as 'to come,' 'to go,' or 'to return,' and so forth. Some people prefer **e** while others prefer **ni**, and often both are used by one person. However, many people seem to avoid using **ni** where another **ni** has already occurred in the same sentence, and prefer to substitute **e** instead.

tomodachi to issho ni **Ginza e** ikimashita.	(I went **to the Ginza** with a friend.)
uchi e kaerimasu. = **uchi ni** kaerimasu.	(We'll **go home**.)
gakkoo e ikimasu. = **gakkoo ni** ikimasu.	(We'll **go to school**.)

11.7   (someone) to issho ni

The phrase **to issho ni** means 'together with' or 'accompanied by' and indicates that a person performs the activity with another person. In an informal, faster speech, **issho ni** may be left out and only **to** may be spoken for the same function. As presented in Lesson 6, **issho ni** means 'together.'

tomodachi **to   issho ni**   ginza e   ikimashita.

(I went to the Ginza **[together] with a friend**.)

Buraun-san to   Ginza e   ikimashita.   (I went to the Ginza **with Mr. Brown**.)

11.8   iroiro na: Copula Noun

iroiro na means 'various' and belongs to a small group of words called copula nouns. Copula nouns are descriptive words similar to adjectives modifying nouns. However, copula nouns are different from adjectives because the characteristic adjective endings such as **-i** and **-ku** do not combine with copula nouns. A copula noun takes **na** preceding a noun head. Copula nouns are known by various other names such as adjectival nouns, na-adjectives, or keiyoo-dooshi. In this book, however, the word **Copula Noun** is maintained to be consistent with the earlier editions of the same book. **kirei na** (pretty) and **shizuka na** (quiet) are some of the frequently used copula nouns. Also **suki na mono** (favorite things) and **kirai na mono** (things I dislike) are commonly used. **Copula nouns** are listed with **na** in the vocabulary section of this book.

> **iroiro na mono** o mimashita.   (We saw **various things**.)
> depaato de **iroiro na   mono** o kaimashita.
> > (We bought **various things** at the department store.)
>
> Tanaka-san wa **kirei na   kata** desu ne!
> > (Miss Tanaka is a **pretty person**, isn't she!)
>
> koko wa **shizuka na   tokoro** desu ne!
> > (This is a **quiet place**!)

11.9   nani mo kaimasen deshita

The interrogative word **nani + mo + negation** conveys the meaning of total, or complete, negation as expressed in English, 'not any.'

> **nani mo   kaimasen deshita**.   (**I did not buy anything**.)
> **nani mo   tabemasen**.   (**I don't eat anything**.)

Similarly, other interrogative words such as **dare** (who) and **doko** (where) may take the **'mo + negation'** ending to convey the similar meanings, 'not anybody' (or nobody) and 'not anywhere' (nowhere), respectively. In emphatic speech **nani mo** is often pronounced as **na-n-ni-mo** with an extra syllable.

> betsu ni **nani mo   shimasen**.   ([I'm] **not doing anything** in particular.)
> **doko ni mo   ikimasen**.   ([I'm] **not going anywhere**.)
> **dare mo   shirimasen**.   (**No one knows**.)

11.10   de denoting Means of Transportation

The particle **de** added to a word such as 'bus,' 'train,' or 'subway' indicates the means of transportation. This particle is considered to be the same 'agency' particle **de** previously presented in such sentences as **nihongo de hanashimashoo** (Let's speak in Japanese) or **hashi de tabemasu** (I eat with chopsticks.) In English, the preposition 'by' is used to express means of transportation as in 'I go by bus' or 'We went by train.' As several prepositions are used to convey the meaning of **de**, it might be easier to learn the particle **de** in terms of its core meaning, 'using such and such.'

> Tookyoo-eki kara Ginza made **chikatetsu de** ikimashita.
> > (We went from Tokyo Station to the Ginza **by subway**.)

densha de Shinjuku e ikimashita.   (I went to Shinjuku **by train**.)
kuruma de ikimashoo.   (Let's go **by car**.)

11.12 ... kara ... made

The particle **kara** denotes the point of departure or origination in space as well as in time. The same idea is usually expressed in English by the preposition 'from.' The particle **made** is often used with **kara**, denoting the point of destination or termination, also in space and time. This idea is often conveyed in English by such expressions as 'till,' 'up to,' and 'as far as ...' Both **kara** and **made** can be used together or independently.

> Tookyoo-eki **kara** Ginza **made** chikatetsu de ikimashita.
> > (We took the subway **from** Tokyo Station **to** the Ginza)

> (s)hichiji **kara** juuji **made** benkyoo shimashita.
> > (I studied **from** seven o'clock **till** ten o'clock.)

11.13 chikatetsu and Other Means of Transportation

The underground system, the **chikatetsu** (subway), is operative within most major cities. Cities are not usually linked by **chikatetsu** lines; rather, the **chikatetsu** lines and stations link together important neighborhoods and points of significance within cities. Each **chikatetsu** station is generally flanked by fairly large and elaborate underground shopping malls, interesting and appealing attractions in and of themselves. A network of **chikatetsu** provides especially fast, convenient transportation to the central area of Tokyo.

The main surface transportation system is the **JR Line**. The **Jeiaaru-sen** (JR Line), or the Japan Railway System is one of the finest mass transportation systems in the world, and is supported and operated now by private companies. Every city and town in the country has links to the system; major points within each city are also linked together by a well-organized and efficient railway network. Tokyo itself has a large number of train stations and thousands of kilometers of surface railway which link its various neighborhoods, districts, and sectors. One such line encircles each of the central metropolitan areas. Trains run approximately every five minutes and provide fast transportation services to many people. Added are many suburban trains running from major JR stations to different subrban residential areas. Buses and taxies run everywhere.

11.14 kissaten

Although **kissaten** is frequently translated in English as 'coffeeshop,' the translation is really not accurate. While the American 'coffeeshop' is inexpensive and very informal, the Japanese **kissaten** is elaborate, posh, and rather expensive. Its purpose is not to provide a place for an inexpensive cup of coffee and some quick chatter, but for relaxed and contemplative visiting with friends. People frequently stop with friends at the **kissaten** for a refreshing break from shopping or school. Or sometimes they arrange brief meetings with friends or acquaintances there.

11.15 Shinjuku

Shinjuku is one of the major stations in Tokyo where not only the JR, Japan Railway System, and the subway but also several other private suburban trains meet. Large shopping malls and underground shopping centers surround the station and attract huge crowds daily to this area. **Shinjuku** was rebuilt after having been completely burned down during World War II. In comparison with other areas such as the **Ginza**, the buildings in the Shinjuku district are newer and more modern.

Several major department stores, a variety of restaurants both domestic and foreign, and many movie theaters attract thousands of people to the area day and night. Prices are relatively reasonable in **Shinjuku** and maybe that is why young people frequently go to **Shinjuku** to shop and to enjoy themselves.

EXERCISES

11E.1   Answer the following questions.

1. kinoo Buraun-san wa kaimono ni ikimashita ka, eiga ni ikimashita ka?
2. Buraun-san wa Tanaka-san to issho ni ikimashita ka, Yamada-san to issho ni ikimashita ka?
3. kinoo Buraun-san wa kissaten de oishii koohii o nomimashita ka, nihon-shoku o tabemashita ka?
4. Buraun-san wa Tookyoo-eki kara Ginza made chikatetsu de ikimashita ka, basu de ikimashita ka?
5. kaeri wa arukimashita ka, takushii de kaerimashita ka?
6. kinoo Yamada-san wa kaimono ni ikimashita ka, eiga o mimashita ka?
7. Yamada-san wa Ginza ni ikimashita ka, Shinjuku ni ikimashita ka?
8. Yamada-san wa dareka to issho ni ikimashita ka, hitori de ikimashita ka?
9. anata wa kinoo dokoka ni ikimashita ka?
10. anata wa kinoo asagohan ni nanika tabemashita ka?
11. anata wa kinoo dareka to denwa de hanashimashita ka?
12. kinoo nani ka kaimashita ka?

11E.2   Give negative answers to the following questions.

1. kinoo Tanaka-san wa gakkoo ni ikimashita ka?
2. kinoo Buraun-san wa benkyoo shimashita ka?
3. kinoo Buraun-san wa shuuji no renshuu o shimashita ka?
4. kinoo Tanaka-san wa Buraun-san to issho ni eiga o mimashita ka?

5. Tanaka-san wa kinoo zasshi o yomimashita ka?
6. Buraun-san wa kinoo tegami o kakimashita ka?
7. Buraun-san wa Ginza de shokuji o shimashita ka?
8. Buraun-san wa Ginza de iroiro na mono o kaimashita ka?
9. Yamada-san wa kinoo kaimono ni ikimashita ka?
10. Yamada-san wa kinoo Buraun-san to issho ni koohii o nomimashita ka?
11. anata wa kinoo nihon no eiga o mimashita ka?
12. anata wa kinoo Ginza e ikimashita ka?

11E.3   Give appropriate answers to the following questions.

1. kinoo Buraun-san wa Tookyoo-eki kara Ginza made norimono wa nan de ikimashita ka?
2. Ginza kara uchi made takushii de kaerimashita ka, arukimashita ka?
3. Yamada-san wa uchi kara Shinjuku made norimono wa nan de ikimashita ka?
4. kaeri wa eigakan kara eki made arukimashita ka?
5. Shinjuku kara uchi made nan de kaerimashita ka?
6. anata wa mainichi uchi kara gakkoo made kuruma de ikimasu ka, arukimasu ka?
7. kaeri wa gakkoo kara uchi made nan de kaerimasu ka?
8. anata wa getsuyoobi kara kin'yoobi made gakkoo ni ikimasu ka?
9. taitei mainichi nanji kara nanji made benkyoo shimasu ka?
10. kinoo wa nanji goro kara nanji goro made benkyoo shimashita ka?

11E.4   Activity: Let's do something.   Student A asks Student B if he/she would like to join him/her in each of the following activities. Student B gives a positive answer to each, and makes a suggestion. Student A agrees; then Student B confirms the appointment.

Example: Let's go somewhere.

A: issho ni dokoka e ikimasen ka?
B: ee, ikimashoo. Ginza wa doo desu ka?
A: ee. Ginza ga ii deshoo.
B: ja, Ginza ni ikimashoo.

1. Let's drink something.
2. Let's eat something.
3. Let's do something tomorrow.
4. Let's read something in Japanese.
5. Let's go somewhere on Sunday.
6. Let's eat some Japanese food at the Ginza.
7. Let's meet [each other] at some place at noon.
8. Let's study together somewhere.
9. Let's see a movie somewhere.
10. Let's drink good coffee or something somewhere.
11. Let's eat good sushi or something somewhere.
12. Let's go shopping somewhere.

11E.5   Review Grammar: Negation forms. Make the following sentences negative. Give the meanings of the resulting sentences in English.

1. Buraun-san no denwa-bangoo wa 579-6238 desu.
2. Yamada-san wa Buraun-san no denwa-bangoo o shitte imasu.
3. Tanaka-san wa kinoo asagohan ni toosuto o tabemashita.
4. Buraun-san wa hayaoki desu.
5. ima juuji gofun mae desu.
6. kinoo wa ii otenki deshita.
7. kinoo wa Buraun-san no (o)tanjoobi deshita.
8. kinoo wa doyoobi deshita.
9. watakushi wa kinoo tomodachi ni tegami o kakimashita.
10. Buraun-san wa aisukuriimu ga daisuki desu.
11. Yamada-san wa sakana ga kirai desu.
12. Buraun-san wa Ginza kara Tookyoo-eki made arukimashita.

11E.6   Response Drill: Give complete negative responses to the following questions, as shown in the example. Give the meanings of the questions in English.

Example: kinoo nanika kaimashita ka?   (Did you buy anthing yesterday?)
          iie, nani mo kaimasen deshita. (No, I didn't buy anything.)

1. anata wa kinoo dokoka ni ikimashita ka?
2. kinoo dareka ni aimashita ka?
3. kesa nanika tabemashita ka?
4. kesa nanika omoshiroi nyuusu o kikimashita ka?

5. kesa nanika nomimashita ka?
6. anata wa ashita dokoka ni dekakemasu ka?
7. nichiyoobi ni nanika kaimasu ka?
8. ashita dareka to issho ni eiga o mimasu ka?
9. mainichi dokoka ni ikimasu ka?
10. mainichi nanika kakimasu ka?

VOCABULARY

VERBS

shimashita	(I have done; I did: -mashita form of suru, 11.1)
ikimashita	(I have gone; I went: -mashita form of iku, 11.1)
arukimashita	(I have walked; I walked: -mashita form of aruku, 11.1)
kaerimashita	(I have returned; I went home: -mashita form of kaeru, 11.1)
kaimashita	(I have bought; I bought: -mashita form of ka[w]u, 11.1)
mimashita	(I have seen; I saw: -mashita form of miru, 11.1)
kaimasen deshita	(I didn't buy: negative past form of ka[w]u, 11.2)
shimasen deshita	(I didn't do: negative past form of suru, 11.2)
nomimashita	(I have drunk; I drank: -mashita form of nomu, 11.1)

ADJECTIVES   (---)

NOUNS

kinoo	(yesterday)
Ginza	(The Ginza, the beautiful shopping center in Tokyo)
depaato	(department store)
mono	(thing)
shokuji	(meal)
kissaten	(the Japanese version of a coffeeshop, 11.14)
norimono	(means of transportation)
chikatetsu	(subway, 11.13)
kaeri	(returning home)
takushii	(taxi; cab)
densha	(train)
Shinjuku	(a major shopping center in Tokyo, 11.15)
eiga	(movie)

OTHERS

nanika	(something, 11.5)
...to issho ni	(together with..., 11.7)
de	(using such and such; by: a particle denoting the means of transportation, 11.10)

kara	(from: a particle denoting the point of departure, 11.12)
made	(till; to: a particle denoting the point of destination, 11.12)
iroiro (na)	(various: a copula noun, 11.8)
nani mo -masen	(not ... any, 11.9)
dokoka	(somewhere, 11.5)
deshita	(was: the past form of desu, 11.3)
ammari + -masen	(not very ...; not so ...)
e	(to: a particle denoting destination or direction, 11.6)
dareka	(someone, 11.5)
hitori de	(alone; by oneself)
zannen	(too bad; regrettable)
-mashita	(the past form of -masu, 11.1)
-masen deshita	(the negative past form of -masu, 11.2)
de wa arimasen deshita	(the negative past form of desu, 11.4)

ADDITIONAL VOCABULARY

basu	(bus)
kuruma	(car)

READING AND WRITING

A **kanji** character is often composed of two or more units which may recur in different characters.

言 of 語 and 話

These recurring units are referred to as 'graphemes.' The simple characters presented in the previous lesson are all 'one-grapheme' characters. When two or more graphemes make up a new **kanji**, each grapheme is somewhat modified in shape and reduced in size so that the resulting **kanji** will 'fit' in a box. A **kanji** is often composed of two graphemes which are placed side by side. For example, the character 明 , meaning 'bright' or 'light,' is composed of 日 and 月 in one character.

When such a character is described using Japanese terminology, the grapheme filling the left-hand side is called the **hen** and the one on the right-hand side is called the **tsukuri**. There are many characters composed of **hen** and **tsukuri**. Common graphemes appearing as **hen** have special names. For example the grapheme 日 (hi) in this space is called the **hi-hen**, and indicates that the character in which it appears has a meaning which relates to the concept of 'sun' or 'day.'

Some **kanji** characters are composed of more than two graphemes. One example of such a character is the kanji for 'language.' This character, 語 , is composed of three graphemes-- 言 (to say), 五 (five) and 口 (mouth) -- filling in the three slots indicated by the following diagram. Generally speaking, one of the graphemes of a compound character -- '五' in the case of '語' -- will indicate the pronunciation of the character.

語

140

Exercise 1: Practice writing the following kanji, using correct stroke order, until you can comfortably write each from memory.

13. 本 (book) 本(ほん) 一 十 才 木 本

14. 人 (person) 人(ひと)・人(じん) ノ 人

15. 語 (language) 日本語(にほんご) 、 二 三 三 言 言 言 言

訂 訝 語 語 語 語

16. 何 (what) 何(なに) ノ イ 亻 仃 仃 何 何

17. 英 (English) 英語(えいご) 一 十 艹 芢 芐 芇 英 英

18. 話 (to speak) 話(はな)します 、 二 三 三 言 言 言 言

訁 訐 訐 話 話

Exercise 2: Read the following words and expressions and give their meanings in English.

1. 日本(にほん)。日本人(にほんじん)。日本語(にほんご)。

2. この本(ほん)。その本。あの日本語の本。

3. 日本人は、日本語を話(はな)します。

4. アメリカ人は、英語(えい)を話します。

5. メキシコ人は、スペイン語を話します。

6. イタリア人は、何語を話しますか。

7. ブラウンさんは、うちでは、英語を話しますが、

　　がっこうでは、日本語を話します。

8. このかんじは、何とよみますか。

9. この本は、何語の本ですか。

10. あの人は、何人ですか。

11. きょうは、何月、何日ですか。

12. それは、四月八日のしんぶんです。

Exercise 2: As a homework assignment, write answers to the following questions using complete sentences and the **kanji** already introduced.

1. ブラウンさんは、アメリカ人ですか、イギリス人ですか。

2. たなかさんは、英語を話しますか。

3. ブラウンさんは、日本人に、英語をおしえますか。

4. あなたは、うちで、何語を話しますか。

5. "Good morning" は、日本語で、何といいますか。

6. 「おやすみなさい」は、英語で、何といいますか。

7. メキシコ人は、何語を話しますか。

8. フランス人は、何語を話しますか。

9. ブラウンさんは、アメリカ人のともだちに、何語で、

　　てがみをかきますか。

10. あなたは、ときどき、日本語のざっしをよみますか。

Exercise 3: Reading practice. Dialogue 11

やまだ　　きのう、何か、しましたか。

ブラウン　　ええ、きのう、かいものに、いきました。

やまだ　　どこに、いきましたか。

ブラウン　　ともだちといっしょに、ぎんざへいきました。

やまだ　　ぎんざで、何か、かいましたか。

ブラウン　　いいえ、デパートで、いろいろなものを、みま
　　　　　　したが、何も、かいませんでした。

やまだ　　じゃ、どこかで、しょくじでも、しましたか。

ブラウン　　いいえ、しょくじは、しませんでしたが、きっ
　　　　　　さてんで、おいしいコーヒーを、のみました。

やまだ　　それは、よかったですね。
　　　　　　のりものは、何で、いきましたか。

ブラウン　　とうきょうえきから、ぎんざまで、ちかてつで、
　　　　　　いきました。かえりは、タクシーで、かえりま
　　　　　　した。

やまだ　　そうですか。わたくしは、きのう、でんしゃで、
　　　　　　しんじゅくへ、いきました。

ブラウン　　だれかと、いっしょに、いきましたか。

やまだ　　いいえ、ひとりで、いきました。しんじゅくで、
　　　　　　えいがを、みましたが、あんまり、いいえいが
　　　　　　じゃ、ありませんでした。

ブラウン　　それは、ざんねんでしたね！

Exercise 4: Fill in the blanks with correct particles.

きのう、わたくし＿＿＿、ひとり＿＿＿ぎんざ＿＿＿いきました。
とうきょうえき＿＿＿ ＿＿＿ぎんざ＿＿＿ ＿＿＿、バス＿＿＿、いきま
した。ぎんざ＿＿＿ デパート＿＿＿、カメラ＿＿＿ コンピューター
＿＿＿とけい＿＿＿ みましたが、なに＿＿＿ かいませんでした。

それから、きっさてん＿＿＿、いきました。そこ＿＿＿、アイス
クリーム＿＿＿、たべました。おいしいコーヒー＿＿＿ のみまし
た。かえり＿＿＿、でんしゃ＿＿＿、かえりました。ごご、五じご
ろ、うち＿＿＿かえりました。

Exercise 4: Complete the following sentences using the correct predicate forms.

きのうは、土曜日＿＿＿＿＿＿＿＿＿。わたくしは、あさ、
九じごろ、＿＿＿＿＿＿＿＿＿。あさごはんに、トーストを
＿＿＿＿＿＿＿。ミルクと、オレンジジュースを＿＿＿＿＿
＿＿＿＿。それから、すこし、テレビを＿＿＿＿＿＿＿。

十一じごろ、かいものに＿＿＿＿＿＿＿＿。　スーパー
マーケットで、やさいや、くだものを＿＿＿＿＿＿＿＿＿。
にくや、さかなは、＿＿＿＿＿＿＿＿＿＿。

ごご、ともだちに、てがみを＿＿＿＿＿＿＿＿＿＿。
それから、テニスを、＿＿＿＿＿＿＿＿＿＿＿。

よる、すこしだけ、日本語のかんじを＿＿＿＿＿＿＿
＿＿＿＿＿＿＿＿。

12

Yamada:	teeburu no ue ni iroiro na mono ga arimasu ne!
	nanika tanoshii koto ga arimasu ka?
Brown:	hai, kyoo wa koko de paatii ga arimasu.
Yamada:	ii desu ne! (o)kyaku(sama) ga oozei kimasu ka?
Brown:	ee, kurasu-meeto ga oozei kimasu.
	Yamada-san mo issho ni ikaga desu ka?
Yamada:	arigatoo! sore wa ureshii desu.
Brown:	watakushi no kurasu-meeto o shookai shimashoo.
Yamada:	zehi shookai shite kudasai.
	ja, sukoshi tetsudaimashoo ka?
Brown:	ee, onegai shimasu. ja, sara o kazoete kudasai.
Yamada	hai, ii desu yo. eeto... , ichimai, nimai, sammai,
	yommai, gomai, rokumai, nanamai, hachimai,
	kyuumai, juumai. minna de juumai arimasu.
Brown:	ja, koora no bin wa nambon arimasu ka?
Yamada:	eeto..., ippon, nihon, sambon, yonhon, gohon, roppon,
	nanahon, happon, kyuuhon, juppon. juppon arimasu.
Brown:	sore de juubun deshoo. sorekara teeburu no shita ni
	hako ga arimasu ne? sono naka ni mikan ga arimasu.
	sore o too hodo dashite kudasai.
Yamada:	hai, wakarimashita. hitotsu, futatsu, mittsu, yottsu,
	itsutsu, muttsu, nanatsu, yattsu, kokonotsu, too.

ENGLISH EQUIVALENT

Yamada: [Oh, look,] there are a lot of things on the table, aren't there!
Is there going to be some fun activity?

Brown: Yes, there is going to be a party here.

Yamada: How nice! Are lots of people (guests) coming?

Brown: Yes. A lot of my classmates are coming.
How about joining us, Mr. Yamada?

Yamada: Oh, thanks! That's great. (That makes me happy!)

Brown: I'll introduce you to my classmates.

Yamada: Please be sure to introduce me [to them].
Well, shall I help [you] a little?

Brown: Oh, thanks, I'd appreciate it. Well, will you count the plates then?

Yamada: O.K. Let me see..., one, two, three, four, five, six, seven, eight,
nine, ten. There are ten [plates] in all.

Brown: Then, how many cola bottles are there?

Yamada: Let's see..., one, two, three, four, five, six, seven, eight, nine, ten.
There are ten.

Brown: That would be enough. And then, there is a box under the table, isn't
there? There are tangerines in it. Please take out about ten [of them].

Yamada: All right, I understand. One, two, three, four, five, six, seven, eight,
nine, ten.

GRAMMATICAL AND CULTURAL NOTES

12.1   ue, shita, naka and other Location Words

The word **ue** is a noun meaning 'on' or 'on top of,' and is used with **no** and a preceding noun as in
tsukue no ue (on top of the desk). **shita** (under or below) and **naka** (in or inside of) belong to
the same category of nouns of location. To express a similar idea of location in English, we use
prepositions followed by nouns, in which the word order is the opposite of the Japanese order.
Other frequently used words of location include **soba** (near), **mae** (in front of), and **ushiro**
(behind).

    teeburu no **ue**   (**on top** of the table)
    teeburu no **shita**   (**under** the table)
    hako no **naka**   (**in** the box)
    teeburu no   **ue ni** iroiro na mono ga arimasu ne!
            (There are a lot of things **on the table**, aren't there!)
    teeburu no   **shita ni** hako ga arimasu.
            (There is a box **under the table**.)
    tsukue no   **mae ni** isu ga arimasu. (There is a chair **in front of the desk**.)

12.2   mono ga arimasu, koto ga arimasu

arimasu is the **-masu** form of the verb **aru** which means 'to exist,' or 'to be located' with reference to **mono** (tangible things) as well as **koto** (abstract things such as events or activities). In English we normally express the same idea by saying 'we **have** such and such things,' or '**there is** (or there will be) such and such activity.' The subject of the verb **aru** is normally marked by the particle **ga**.

iroiro na mono **ga arimasu** ne!

> (**There are** a lot of (various) things, aren't there!) or
> (You **have** a lot of things, don't you!)

tsukue no ue ni hon **ga arimasu**.

> (**There is** a book on the desk.) or
> (**There are** books on the desk.)

teeburu no shita ni hako **ga arimasu**.

> (**There is** a box under the table.)

nanika tanoshii koto **ga arimasu** ka?

> (**Is there going to be** an enjoyable activity?)

kyoo wa koko de paatii **ga arimasu**.

> (**There is going to be** a party here today.) or
> (We'**ll have** a party here today.)

ashita nihongo no tesuto **ga   arimasu**.

> (We'll **have** a Japanese test tomorrow.)

mainichi kuji ni rekishi no kurasu **ga   arimasu**.

> (I **have** a history class every day at 9 o'clock.)

In negation, **wa** may be used to mark the subject as the focus of negation.

tsukue no ue ni **hon wa arimasen**.

> (**There is no book** on the desk [but there is something else].)

It is important for the students to distinguish the concepts of **aru** (to exist) from **desu** (to equal) as they are both expressed by the verb 'to be' in English.

kore wa hon **desu**.   (This **is** a book.) or (This object **equals** a book.)
koko ni hon **ga arimasu**.   (A book **is** here.) or (A book **exists** here.)

Animate objects, e.g. people, animals, birds or insects, take a different verb, **iru**, to express the idea of existance or location. The use of **iru** will be introduced in the next lesson.

12.3   ni marking Location of Existence

The particle **ni** means 'at [the place of]' and denotes that what precedes it is the place where a certain object or objects are located. The verb **aru** expresses existence of a certain thing. The two elements '[somewhere] **ni**' and '[something] **ga arimasu**' (something exists) occur together often.

teeburu no **ue ni** iroiro na mono **ga arimasu**.

> (**There are** various things **on top of** the table.)

       teeburu no **shita ni** hako **ga** **arimasu**.

                  (There is a box **under** the table.)

       hako no **naka ni** mikan **ga** **arimasu**.

                  (There are tangerines **in** the box.)

12.4　**de** marking Location of Activity

To mark the location of activities the particle **de** is used. In the sentence '**koko de　paatii ga arimasu.**' (There is going to be a party here.) the predicate verb **... arimasu** expresses activity, not the existence of an inanimate object. In such cases the location is marked by **de**, not by **ni**. The use of **de** and **ni** are known to be a difficult point for the students of Japanese to master.

koko de paatii ga arimasu.	(There is going to be a party **here**.)
koko de koohii o nomimashoo.	(Let's drink some coffee **here**.)
koko de mikan o tabemashoo.	(Let's eat some tangerines **here**.)
koko ni mikan ga arimasu.	(There are some tangerines **here**.)
toshokan de benkyoo shimashoo.	(Let's study **in the library**.)
toshokan ni ii hon ga arimasu.	(There are good books **in the library**.)

12.5　**y o** marking Emphatic Statements

The particle **yo** is added to a statement to make it emphatic. This particle is heard often in casual conversations in which speakers use more emphatic tone to statements. In English the same idea is conveyed by higher pitch in intonation.

hai, **ii desu yo!**	**(Yes, of course, it's all right!)**
atsui desu yo!	**(Be careful, it's hot!)**
soo desu yo!	**(That's right!)**

12.6　**-mai**: Counter for Thin and Flat Objects

In Japanese, different types and shapes of objects are counted in different ways. The counter **-mai** is used when counting thin and flat objects such as paper, plates, napkins, towels, sheets, and so forth. The counter **-mai** does not cause sound changes in the number words.

ichimai	(one sheet)	rokumai	(six sheets)
nimai	(two sheets)	nanamai	(seven sheets)
sammai	(three sheets)	hachimai	(eight sheets)
yommai	(four sheets)	kyuumai	(nine sheets)
gomai	(five sheets)	juumai	(ten sheets)
nammai	(how many sheets)		

12.7　**-hon, -pon, -bon**: Counters for Long and Slender Objects

Long and slender objects such as pens, pencils, trees, fingers, bottles, etc., are counted by adding the counter **-hon** to the number words. The counter **-hon** has variants **-pon** and **-bon** which occur in combination with certain numerals. These combination rules might require additional memorization efforts from the student learning Japanese as a foreign language.

ippon	[ichi + hon]	(one slender piece)
nihon		(two slender pieces)
sambon	[san + hon]	(three slender pieces)
yonhon		(four slender pieces)
gohon		(five slender pieces)
roppon	[roku + hon]	(six slender pieces)
nanahon		(seven slender pieces)
happon	[hachi + hon]	(eight slender pieces)
kyuuhon		(nine slender pieces)
juppon	[juu + hon]	(ten slender pieces)
nambon	[nani + hon]	(how many slender pieces)

12.8   -tsu, -ko: Counters for Small Objects

The counter -tsu is used to count small objects such as oranges, apples, candies, erasers, and so forth that are not characterized by any specific shapes. It is also used as a kind of 'general counter' when one is not quite sure of the appropriate counter to use. This counter is one of the most basic counters which Japanese children acquire in their very early childhood.

hitotsu	(one object)	muttsu	(six objects)
futatsu	(two objets)	nanatsu	(seven objects)
mittsu	(three objects)	yattsu	(eight objects)
yottsu	(four objects)	kokonotsu	(nine objects)
itsutsu	(five objects)	too	(ten objects)
ikutsu	(how many objects)		

The numerals hi-, fu-, mi-, yo-, itsu-, mu-, nana-, ya-, kokono-, and too are the original native Japanese words. The other set of numerals ichi, ni, san, etc., are words originally borrowed from Chinese. The two sets of numerals have been mixed in the course of time and both are used indiscriminately in modern Japanese.

Another counter for small objects is -ko added to the numerals.

ikko	(one object)	rokko	(six objects)
niko	(two objects)	nanako	(seven objects)
sanko	(three objects)	hakko	(eight objects)
yonko	(four objects)	kyuuko	(nine objects)
goko	(five objects)	jukko	(ten objects)
nanko	(how many objects)		

Both counters are used by many people, while some prefers one over the others.

12.9   -satsu: Counter for Bound Objects

In counting books, magazines, dictionaries, notebooks, etc., the counter **-satsu** is added to numerals. When the two elements, a numeral and a counter, are combined into a compound word, certain sound changes may occur.

issatsu	[ichi + satsu]	(one volume)
nisatsu		(two volumes)
sansatsu		(three volumes)
yonsatsu		(four volumes)
gosatsu		(five volumes)
rokusatsu		(six volumes)
nanasatsu		(seven volumes)
hassatsu	[hachi + satsu]	(eight volumes)
kyuusatsu		(nine volumes)
jussatsu	[juu + satsu]	(ten volumes)
nansatsu	[nani + satsu]	(how many volumes)

12.10   mikan

mikan is usually translated into English as 'tangerine,' but the student should be aware that the word refers to something more than the canned product most Americans are familiar with. The **mikan** is a winter fruit--most plentiful during the cold winter months. The fresh **mikan** is about the size and color of a tangerine, but in flavor and texture is more like a sweet, juicy orange.

EXERCISES

12E.1   Repetition Drill: The instructor brings ten sheets of paper, ten pens or pencils, several books and some small objects such as fruit, erasers or paper cups. As the instructor counts the objects using the correct counters the students repeat after. Continue the drill until the students can count different objects with ease.

1. (counting sheets of paper)

ichimai	(one)	rokumai	(six)
nimai	(two)	nanamai	(seven)
sammai	(three)	hachimai	(eight)
yommai	(four)	kyuumai	(nine)
gomai	(five)	juumai	(ten)

2. (counting pens or pencils)

ippon	(one)	roppon	(six)
nihon	(two)	nanahon	(seven)
sambon	(three)	happon	(eight)
yonhon	(four)	kyuuhon	(nine)
gohon	(five)	juppon	(ten)

3. (counting books)

issatsu	(one)	rokusatsu	(six)
nisatsu	(two)	nanasatsu	(seven)
sansatsu	(three)	hassatsu	(eight)
yonsatsu	(four)	kyuusatsu	(nine)
gosatsu	(five)	jussatsu	(ten)

4. (counting small objects)

hitotsu	(one)	muttsu	(six)
futatsu	(two)	nanatsu	(seven)
mittsu	(three)	yattsu	(eight)
yottsu	(four)	kokonotsu	(nine)
itsutsu	(five)	too	(ten)

12E.2 Repetition Drill: The instructor picks up different numbers of different objects and says the following sentences. The students repeat each sentence after the instructor. The second time, the instructor shows the objects, and the students say the sentences without looking at their books.

1.	(one book)	hon ga issatsu arimasu.
2.	(two sheets of paper)	kami ga nimai arimasu.
3.	(three pencils)	empitsu ga sambon arimasu.
4.	(four pieces of fruit)	kudamono ga yottsu arimasu.
5.	(five [paper] cups)	koppu ga itsutsu arimasu.
6.	(six pens)	pen ga roppon arimasu.
7.	(seven sheets of paper)	kami ga nanamai arimasu.
8.	(eight pencils)	empitsu ga happon arimasu.
9.	(nine [paper] cups)	koppu ga kokonotsu arimasu.
10.	(ten books)	hon ga jussatsu arimasu.

12E.3   Say the following sentences in Japanese using the most natural word order and the correct counters.

1. There are three pens on the desk.
2. There are six apples in the box.
3. There is one large dictionary on the desk.
4. There are three small oranges on the table.
5. There are three bananas on the plate.
6. There are four Japanese magazines in the briefcase.
7. There are four large windows in this room.
8. There are five small chairs in this room.

12E.4   Answer the following questions.

1. kyoo Buraun-san no uchi de paatii ga arimasu ka?
2. anata wa kyoo nan no kurasu ga arimasu ka?
3. getsuyoobi ni nihongo no kurasu ga arimasu ka?
4. nichiyoobi ni mo kurasu ga arimasu ka?
5. tokidoki nihongo no kurasu de shiken ga arimasu ka?
6. kyoo rekishi no kurasu ga arimasu ka?
7. konsaato wa taitei naniyoobi ni   arimasu ka?
8. itsu kurisumasu-paatii ga arimasu ka?
9. konshuu deeto ga arimasu ka?
10. ashita donna yotei ga arimasu ka?

12E.5   Practice the following short dialogues in pairs.

1. A: kyoo wa kyampasu de nani ga arimasu ka?
   B: konsaato ga arimasu.
   A: nanji kara desu ka?
   B: juuniji kara desu. issho ni ikimasen ka?
   A: kyoo wa ichiji kara shiken ga arimasu.
   B: zannen desu ne... ja, watakushi wa hitori de ikimasu.

2. A: juuichigatsu muika ni tomodachi no risaitaru ga arimasu.
   B: nan no risaitaru desu ka?
   A: piano desu.
   B: ii desu ne! watakushi wa piano ga daisuki desu.
   A: koko ni kippu ga nimai arimasu. issho ni ikimasu ka?
   B: ee, zehi! sore wa ureshii desu. arigatoo!

VOCABULARY

VERBS

arimasu	(something is located; there is; there are: -masu form of aru, 12.2)
aru	(to exist; to be; to be located at such and such place)
kimasu	(someone comes; someone is coming: -masu form of kuru)
kuru	(to come; one of the irregular verbs)
tetsudaimashoo ka?	(Shall I assist [you]? Shall I help [you]?: -mashoo form of tetsuda[w]u + ka)
tetsuda[w]u	(to assist someone's work; to help)
kazoete kudasai	(please count: -te form of kazoeru + kudasai)
kazoeru	(to count)
dashite kudasai	(please take [something] out: -te form of dasu + kudasai)
dasu	(to take [something] out)

ADJECTIVES

tanoshii	(enjoyable; fun)
ureshii	(happy; delighted)

NOUNS

teeburu	(table)
ue	(on; on top of: a noun of location, 12.1)
iroiro (na)	(various: a copula noun, 11.8)
mono	(tangible thing[s])
koto	(abstract thing[s]; activity; event; happening)
paatii	(party; gathering)
(o)kyaku(san)	(guest; visitor; customer)
oozei	(many people)
sara	(plate[s]; dish[es])
bin	(bottle)
nambon	(how many long (or tall) and slender object, 12.7)
shita	(under; below; beneath; a noun of location, 12.1)
hako	(box)
naka	(inside; in; a noun of location, 12.1)
mikan	(tangerine oranges; mikan, 12.10))

OTHERS

ga	(particle denoting the subject of the verb aru, 12.2)
ni	(particle marking location of existance, 12.3)
de	(particle denoting the location of activity or event, 12.4)
yo	(emphasis marker, 12.5)
-mai	(counter for thin and flat objects such as paper, plates, towels and sheets, 12.6)
-hon, -bon, -pon	(counter for slender and long objects, 12.7)
nambon	(how many bottles; how many long and slender objects, 12.7)

153

-tsu	(the general counter for small objects, 12.8)
-satsu	(counter for books and other bound volumes, 12.9)
nansatsu	(how many volumes, 12.9)
minna de	(all together; in all)
ikutsu	(how many: a bound interrogative word iku [how many] + -tsu, the general counter for small objects, 12.8)
hodo	(about; roughly as many as...)
juubun	(enough; sufficient)
sore kara	(and after that)
eeto...	(well, let me see...)

ADDITIONAL VOCABULARY

soba	(near; near-by, 12.1)
mae	(in front of, 12.1)
itsu	(when: interrogative word)
koppu	(cup)
napukin	(napkin)
shiken	(exam; test; quiz)
konsaato	(concert)
itsu	(at which time; when)
kurisumasu paatii	(Christmas party)
konshuu	(this week)
deeto	(date)
yotei	(plan)
kyampasu	(campus)
risaitaru	(recital)
piano	(piano)
kippu	(ticket)

READING AND WRITING

Exercise 1: Practice writing the following kanji, using correct stroke order, until you can comfortably write each from memory.

19. 火 (fire; Tuesday)　　火曜日　　丶 ⺌ ⺌ 少 火

20. 水 (water; Wednesday)　水曜日　　丿 刁 水 水

21. 木 (tree; Thursday)　　木曜日　　一 十 才 木

22. 金 (gold; Friday)　　　金曜日　　丿 人 ⼈ 全 全 全

　　　　　　　　　　　　　　　　　　　余 金

23. 土 (earth; Saturday)　　土曜日　　丨 十 土

24. 曜 (day of week)　　　日曜日　　丨 冂 冃 日 日' 日ㄱ

　　　　　　　　　　　　　　　　　日' 日ㄱ 日ㄱㄱ 日ㄱㄱ 日ㄱㄱ 曜

　　　　　　　　　　　　　　　　　曜 曜 曜 曜 曜 曜

155

Exercise 2: Read the following words and expressions and give their meanings in English.

1. 日曜日。月曜日。火曜日。水曜日。木曜日。金曜日。
   土曜日。

2. きょうは、何月何日、何曜日ですか。

3. きょうは、三月三日、土曜日です。

4. 月曜日と、水曜日と、金曜日には、日本語のクラスが、
   あります。

5. 火曜日と、木曜日には、クラスが、ありません。

6. 土曜日と、日曜日には、がっこうに、いきません。

7. きのうは、日曜日でした。 ぎんざのデパートで、
   いろいろなものを、かいました。

8. 本やで、日本語の本と、英語のざっしを、かいました。

9. わたくしは、水曜日より、金曜日のほうが、すきです。

10. ブラウンさんは、日曜日のあさ、たいてい、英語の
    しんぶんを、よみます。

11. 水は、英語で、何といいますか。

    水は、英語で、"water" といいます。

12. 木は、英語で、何といいますか。

    木は、英語で、"tree" といいます。

13. 土曜日のよる八時から、ブラウンさんのうちで、
    パーティーがあります。 いっしょに、いきましょう。

Exercise 3: Activity: Read the following dialogue in pairs.

やまだ：　つくえのうえに、いろいろなものがありますね！

チェン：　ほんとですね！　本や、えんぴつや、かみや、
　　　　　くだものなどが　ありますね！

やまだ：　本が、何さつありますか。

チェン：　一さつ、二さつ、三さつ、四さつ、五さつ、
　　　　　六さつ、七さつ、八さつ、九さつ、十さつ、
　　　　　みんなで、十さつ　あります。

やまだ：　えんぴつは、何本ありますか。

チェン：　一本、二本、三本・・・　三本あります。

やまだ：　かみは、何まいありますか。

チェン：　五まいあります。

やまだ：　つくえのしたに、どんなものがありますか。

チェン：　はこが、あります。

やまだ：　はこのなかに、なにがありますか。

チェン：　みかんが、あります。一つ、二つ、三つ、四つ、
　　　　　五つ、六つ、七つ、八つ、九つ、十 あります。

やまだ：　これは、だれのつくえでしょうか。

チェン：　そうですねえ。たぶん、ブラウンさんの
　　　　　つくえでしょう。ブラウンさんは、みかんが、
　　　　　だいすきです。

Exercise 4: Fill in the blanks in each sentence with the correct **hiragana**. Read the resulting sentences aloud.

1. 日本しょく＿＿＿、すきです＿＿＿。
   はい、だいすきです。

2. どんなもの＿＿＿、すきです＿＿＿。
   すきやき＿＿＿、おすし＿＿＿、すきです。

3. ときどき、日本のおちゃ＿＿＿、のみます＿＿＿。
   はい、まい日、おちゃ＿＿＿、のみます。

4. コーヒー＿＿＿、日本のおちゃ＿＿＿、どちらのほう＿＿＿、
   すきです＿＿＿。
   りょうほう＿＿＿ ＿＿＿、だいすきです。

5. なんだか、おなか＿＿＿、すきました＿＿＿。
   そうですね。じゃ、おすし＿＿＿ ＿＿＿、たべましょう。

6. あなたは、おかあさん＿＿＿、日本語＿＿＿、話します
   ＿＿＿、英語＿＿＿、話しますか。

7. ブラウンさん＿＿＿、ときどき、アメリカ人＿＿＿ とも
   だち＿＿＿、英語＿＿＿、てがみ＿＿＿、かきますね。

Exercise 5. Say the best Japanese equivalent of the following sentences, and write them using **hiragana**, **katakana** and **kanji** correctly.

1. There will be a party on December 20th.
2. Please come to my house on October 15th.
3. There is going to be a Japanese test on Friday. Let's study together.
4. Let's meet at Tokyo Station on Sunday at three o'clock.
5. Are you busy on Friday night?
6. Would you like to go shopping with me on Saturday afternoon?

13

Tanaka:	kore wa watakushi no kazoku no shashin desu.
Brown:	aa, chotto misete kudasai.
Tanaka:	hai, doozo.
Brown:	hitori, futari, sannin, yonin, gonin, rokunin, (s)hichinin...
	Tanaka-san no kazoku wa minna de (s)hichinin desu ka?
Tanaka:	hai, soo desu.
Brown:	kono kata ga otoosan desu ka?
Tanaka:	hai, sore ga chichi desu.
Brown:	rippa na kata desu ne!
Tanaka:	arigatoo. chichi wa futsuu no sarariiman desu.
Brown:	kono kata ga okaasan desu ka?
Tanaka:	hai, sore ga haha desu.
Brown:	kirei na kata desu ne!
Tanaka:	arigatoo. haha wa ikebana no sensei desu.
Brown:	Tanaka-san wa gonin-kyoodai desu ka?
Tanaka:	ee. ani to ane to otooto to imooto to watakushi desu.
Brown:	ii gokazoku desu ne!
Tanaka:	okagesamade.
Brown:	otaku ni wa petto ga imasu ka?
Tanaka:	hai, uchi ni wa inu ga ippiki imasu.
Brown:	zuibun ookikute rippa na otaku desu ne!
Tanaka:	iie... sore hodo de mo arimasen.
	moo kanari furui uchi desu.

159

ENGLISH EQUIVALENT

Tanaka: This is a photograph of my family.

Brown: Oh, please let me just see it!

Tanaka: Here you are.

Brown: One, two, three, four, five, six, seven...
          Are there altogether seven people in your family?

Tanaka: Yes, that's right.

Brown: Is this person your father?

Tanaka: Yes, that's my father.

Brown: [He] is a distinguished-looking person!

Tanaka: Thank you. My father is an ordinary salaried worker.

Brown: Is this person your mother?

Tanaka: Yes, that's my mother.

Brown: She's beautiful.

Tanaka: Thank you. My mother teaches flower-arrangement.

Brown: Are you five brothers and sisters?

Tanaka: Yes. My older brother, my older sister, my younger brother, my younger
          sister, and myself.

Brown: You have a nice family!

Tanaka: Fortunately.

Brown: Do you have a pet at your house?

Tanaka: Yes, we have a dog.

Brown: [Your home] is really a large, good-looking house!

Tanaka: Oh, no... Not that way. It's a rather old house.

GRAMMATICAL AND CULTURAL NOTES

13.1   Family Members

There are two sets of family words in Japanese: one is a set used to refer to someone else's family
and has added meaning of respect. This set is called the **exalted forms** in this book. The other
set is used to refer to one's own family and has the added meaning of humility. This set is called
the **humble forms** in this book. An adult native speaker distinguishes these sets and selects
correct forms each time he or she talks about someone's family or his or her own family.
However, when he or she directly addresses or calls a member of his or her own family the exalted
forms are spoken.

The Exalted Forms

otoosan	(your father; someone's father; Father!)
okaasan	(your mother; someone's mother; Mother!)

oniisan	(your older brother; someone's older brother)
oneesan	(your older sister; someone's older sister)
otooto-san	(your younger brother; someone's younger brother)
imooto-san	(your younger sister; someone's younger sister)
goshujin or goshujinsama	(your husband; someone's husband)
okusan or okusama	(your wife; someone's wife)

The Humble Forms

chichi	(my father)
haha	(my mother)
ani	(my older brother)
ane	(my older sister)
otooto	(my younger brother)
imooto	(my younger sister)
shujin	(my husband)
kanai or tsuma	(my wife)

There are no words in Japanese which correspond exactly to the English words 'sister' or 'brother.' One must designate either 'older' or 'younger.'

kono kata ga **otoosan** desu ka?	(Is this person [**your**] **father**?
sore ga **chichi** desu.	(That is [**my**] **father**.)
kono kata ga **okaasan** desu ka?	(Is this person [**your**] **mother**?)
sore ga **haha** desu.	(That's [**my**] **mother**.)
otoosan, ohayoo gozaimasu!	(Good morning, **Father**!)
okaasan, oyasuminasai!	(Good night, **Mother**!)
oniisan! oniisan! chotto kite kudasai.	(**Brother! Brother!** Please come over here.)
oneesan, kore o yonde kudasai.	(**Sister**, please read this.)

13.2 **ga** denoting Subject in Emphasis

When there are more than two items and you want to select one of them to talk about, this selected word is called the subject in emphasis or in contrast. In the dialogue of this lesson Mr. Brown is looking at seven people in the picture. He, then, points to one of them and asks the question, 'Is this person your father?' In this sentence 'this person' implies 'this particular person and not any other persons in the picture.' In this case, the word 'this person' is grammatically the subject in emphasis and is marked by **ga**, not **wa**, in Japanese. To answer the question, the particle **ga** is used as well to mark the subject.

kono kata ga otoosan desu ka?	(Is **this person** your father?).
hai, **sore ga** chichi desu.	(Yes, **that** is my father.)

When you look at one particular person and ask a question about that person, the emphasis in the sentence falls on the predicate. In that case the subject is marked by **wa**, not **ga**.

kono kata wa   **otoosan desu ka?**   (Is this person **your father [not your uncle or friend]**?)

hai, sore wa   **chichi desu.**   (Yes, that's **my father [not my uncle or friend].**)

13.3   -nin: Counter for People

The counter **-nin** is used to count people. This counter is irregular in a sense that the native number words **hi-** and **fu-** are combined with the native word **-tari** (people), to make the first two words in the sequence. Beyond the first two words, the compounds are made of Sino-Japanese numbers and the counter **-nin** (person).

hitori	(one person)	rokunin	(six people)
futari	(two people)	(s)hichinin	(seven people)
sannin	(three people)	hachinin	(eight people)
yonin	(four people)	kyuunin	(nine people)
gonin	(five people)	juunin	(ten people)

nannin   (how many people)

13.4   to meaning 'and' in Complete Enumeration

The particle **to** connecting two or more nouns or phrases means 'and' in **complete** enumeration. **A to B to C** means '**A and B and C [and no more].**' In English you do not repeat the word 'and' after each word, but in Japanese it is more common to repeat the particle **to** after each noun included in the enumeration.

ani **to**   ane **to**   otooto **to**   imooto **to**   watakushi desu.
(My older brother, my older sister, my younger brother, my younger sister, **and** myself.)
tsukue no shita ni   hako **to** kaban ga   arimasu.
(Under the desk are [two things]: a box **and** a briefcase.)
hon ga   sansatsu **to**   kami ga   nimai   arimasu.
(There are three books **and** two sheets of paper.)

There is another particle **ya** meanig 'and.' As noted in 8.3, **ya** linking two or more nouns means 'and' in **incomplete** enumeration. That is to say, **A ya B ya C** means '**A and B and C and so forth**'; the speaker suggests that he or she is not completing the enumeration and more is implied. The word **nado** which means 'et cetera' or 'so forth' is often added to the sequence.

hon **ya** empitsu **ya** kami **ya** kudamono **nado** ga arimasu.
(There are books, pencils, paper, fruit, **and such things.**)
Buraun-san wa nihongo **ya** chuugokugo **ya** kankokugo **nado** ga joozu desu.
(Mr. Brown is fluent in Japanese, Chinese, **and** Korean **[and maybe more].**)

13.5   rippa na: a Copula Noun

The descriptive word **rippa na** (distinguished-looking, fine) belongs to the class of copula nouns. As noted in 11.8, copula nouns are grammatically different from adjectives in that adjective endings such as **-i**, **-ku**, and **-kute** do not combine with these words. Copula nouns are more like adjectives in meanings but they are more like nouns in grammar. In the pre-noun position they take **na** to act as modifiers of the nouns that follow. **na** is a variant of the copula **da** which is the plain version of **desu**. That is why grammarians call these words copula nouns.

In addition to the above, **kirei na** (pretty, clean), **shinsetsu na** (kind), **shizuka na** (quiet), and **benri na** (convenient) are some of the frequently used copula nouns.

When Japanese has adopted English words such as 'handsome' or 'charming' in describing a person, the loan words **hansamu na** and **chaamingu na** are borrowed as copula nouns.

otoosan wa **rippa na** kata desu ne!. (Your father is a **distinguished-looking** person!) or
(Your father **looks distinguished!**)

okaasan wa **kirei na** kata desu ne! (Your mother is a **beautiful [pretty]** person!) or (Your mother **looks beautiful [pretty]!**)

rippa na uchi desu ne! (The house **looks gorgeous!**.)

Tanaka-san wa **chaamingu na** hito desu.
(Tanaka-san is a **charming** person.)

Copula nouns are small in number, but are an important part of the modern Japanese vocabulary. In this book, they are listed in the noun section of the vocabulary along with **na.**

13.6   ...ga imasu

imasu is the **-masu form** of the verb **iru** which means 'to exist,' or 'being located,' with reference to animate objects like people, animals, birds and insects. Plants do not belong to this group: **arimasu** is used when talking about the existence or location of trees and flowers. The particle **ga** denotes the subject of **imasu**, as with **arimasu**.

otaku ni wa petto **ga imasu** ka? (**Do you have** a pet at your house?)
uchi ni wa chiisai inu **ga** ippiki **imasu**. (**We have** a small dog at our house.)
asoko ni inu **ga imasu**. (**There is** a dog over there.)
neko **ga imasu**. (**There is** a cat.)
hito **ga** nannin **imasu** ka? (How many people **are there?**)

13.7   uchi, otaku

The system of humble and exalted words extends to the words expressing 'home' or 'house hold.' The exalted word **otaku** is used to refer to 'your home' or 'someone else's home' while the humble form **uchi** is selected to refer to the speaker's own home or house hold.

otaku ni wa petto ga imasu ka? (Do you have a pet at **your house?**)
uchi ni wa inu ga imasu. (We have a dog at **our house.**)
ookikute rippa na **otaku** desu ne! (**Your house** is large and good-looking!)

13.8   -hiki: Counter for Animals

The counter **-hiki**, in combination with number words, is applied to count small animals and other pets such as dogs, cats, mice, fish, and insects. This counter has alternants **-piki** and **-biki** when compounding with certain number words.

ippiki	[ichi + hiki]	(one animal)
nihiki		(two animals)
sambiki	[san + hiki]	(three animals)
yonhiki		(four animals)
gohiki		(five animals)
roppiki	[roku + hiki]	(six animals)
nanahiki		(seven animals)
happiki	[hachi + hiki]	(eight animals)
kyuuhiki		(nine animals)
juppiki	[juu + hiki]	(ten animals)
nambiki	[nani + hiki]	(how many animals)

13.9   Giving and Receiving Compliments

In English, when someone offers you a compliment, you acknowledge it by saying 'Thank you.' In Japanese it is customary to be humble in receiving compliments. So, people often deny compliments saying 'Oh, no.' or 'That's not exactly true.' Young people may be more frank and accept compliments by saying '**arigatoo**' but older people may be more traditional and deny your compliments. This cultural difference is reflected in the dialogue in this lesson: when Mr. Brown compliments on Tanaka-san's home being large and good-looking, she denies it by saying it is rather old. She is not contradicting Mr. Brown but rather being humble about her own home.

ookikute rippa na uchi desu ne!	(You certainly have a large, gook-looking house!)
iie... sore hodo demo arimasen. kanari furui uchi desu yo.	
	(No, it's not that good. It's a rather old house.)

13.10   -kute

-kute is an inflectional ending of adjectives which indicates a 'non-final' use of the word. For example, the adjective **ookii** (large) in its **-kute** ending usually appears in an expression where two or more descriptive words modify the noun head, as in 'a big gorgeous house,' or 'a tall and slender tree.' When the first member of these modifiers ('big' and 'tall' in the above examples) is an adjective, it is usually marked by the **-kute** ending.

ookikute rippa na uchi desu.	(It's a **big and** gorgeoust house.)
furukute kitanai uchi desu.	(It's an **old and** poor-looking house.)
chiisakute kawaii inu ga imasu.	(There is a **small and** cute dog.) or (There is a cute little dog.)

There is no grammatical rule as to the order of the two modifiers. If there is cause and effect, the word expressing the cause should come first; but other than that, word order is not fixed.

164

EXERCISES

13E.1 Response Drill: The instructor brings a photo or drawing of a family or draws a picture on the board, and asks the following questions while pointing to the different animate or inanimate objects. The students respond choosing **imasu** or **arimasu** correctly.

1. koko ni shashin ga arimasu ka?
2. koko ni e ga arimasu ka?
3. koko ni hito ga imasu ka?
4. koko ni inu ga imasu ka?
5. koko ni uchi ga arimasu ka?
6. koko ni anata no kazoku ga imasu ka?
7. koko ni dare no kazoku ga imasu ka?
8. koko ni ki ga arimasu ka?
9. koko ni hana ga arimasu ka?
10. koko ni neko ga imasu ka?
11. koko ni donna mono ga arimasu ka?
12. koko ni dare ga imasu ka?

13E.2 Repetition Drill: The instructor brings a photo or drawing of people, or draws a picture of stick figures on the board. As the instructor counts the people, the students repeat after.

1. (one) hitori
2. (two) futari
3. (three) sannin
4. (four) yonin
5. (five) gonin
6. (six) rokunin
7. (seven) (s)hichinin
8. (eight) hachinin
9. (nine) kyuunin
10. (ten) juunin

11. hito ga (juunin) imasu.
12. otoko no hito ga (yonin) imasu.
13. onna no hito ga (rokunin) imasu.
14. kono kurasu ni gakusei ga (nijuunin) imasu.
15. kono kurasu ni sensei ga (hitori) imasu.

13E.3   Response Drill: Answer the following questions according to the content of the dialogue of this lesson.

1. Tanaka-san no kazoku no shashin ga arimasu ka?
2. kono shashin no naka ni hito ga nannin imasu ka?
3. otoko no hito wa   nannin imasu ka?
4. onna no hito wa   nannin imasu ka?
5. shashin no naka ni Tanaka-san no otoosan ga imasu ka?
6. okaasan mo imasu ka?
7. oniisan mo imasu ka?
8. oneesan mo imasu ka?
9. otooto-san mo imasu ka?
10. imooto-san mo imasu ka?
11. inu mo imasu ka?
12. neko mo imasu ka?

13E.4   Response Drill: The instructor asks the following questions and the students give appropriate responses, using the adjective -kute forms correctly.

1. anata no uchi wa ookikute rippa na uchi desu ka?
2. anata no uchi wa furukute chiisai uchi desu ka?
3. Tanaka-san no uchi ni wa chiisakute kawaii inu ga imasu ka?
4. kurokute ookii neko mo imasu ka?
5. uchi no mae ni hosokute takai ki ga arimasu ka?
6. nihon ni wa amakute oishii mikan ga arimasu ka?
7. ookikute akai ringo wa taitei amakute oishii desu ka?

13E.5   Response Drill: The instructor places the following objects in a box and asks the corresponding questions. The students respond using the number words and the counters correctly.

1. (a pen and a book)
      hako no naka ni pen to hon ga arimasu ka?
      pen ga ippon to hon ga issatsu arimasu ka?
2. (two pens and a sheet of paper)
      hako no naka ni pen to kami ga arimasu ka?
      pen ga nihon to kami ga ichimai arimasu ka?
3. (three pencils and two erasers)
      hako no naka ni empitsu to keshigomu ga arimasu ka?
      empitsu ga nambon to keshigomu ga ikutsu arimasu ka?

4. (an apple and a banana)

    hako no naka ni ringo to banana ga arimasu ka?

    ringo ga ikutsu to banana ga nambon arimasu ka?

5. (two magazines and three keys)

    hako no naka ni zasshi to kagi ga arimasu ka?

    zasshi ga nansatsu to kagi ga ikutsu arimasu ka?

13E.6   Short dialogues for practice. Work in pairs.

1. A: anata no kazoku wa minna de nannin desu ka?
     B: yoninn desu.
     A: otoosan to okaasan to sore kara dare desu ka?
     B: chichi to haha to ani to watakushi desu.
     A: oniisan wa gakusei desu ka?
     B: hai, ani mo kono daigaku no gakusei desu.

2. A: anata ni wa kyoodai ga arimasu (imasu) ka?
     B: hai, ane ga hitori to imooto ga hitori imasu.
     A: sannin-kyoodai desu ka?
     B: ee, soo desu. anata wa nannin-kyoodai desu ka?
     A: watakushi wa hitorikko desu.
     B: aa, soo desu ka.

3. A: otaku ni wa petto ga imasu ka?
     B: hai, neko ga ippiki imasu.
     A: donna neko desu ka?
     B: shirokute chiisai neko desu.
     A: watakushi wa neko ga daisuki desu.
     B: watakushi mo inu yori neko no hoo ga suki desu.

13E.7   Activity: Classmates' families. Interview three classmates and find out about their families: how many people are in his or her family and who they are, and also find out as much as possible about each member. Find out if they have any pets. If yes, find out what they are and how they look. Make a list of findings and report to your instructor.

VOCABULARY

VERBS

imasu	(is located [referring to animate object or objects]: -masu form of iru, 13.6)
iru	(to exist; to be located at ...)

ADJECTIVES

ookikute	(large and ...: -kute form of ookii, 13.10)
furukute	(old and ...: -kute form of furui, 13.10)
furui	(old)

NOUNS

shashin	(photograph; picture)
kazoku	(family)
gokazoku	(your family; honorable family: exalted prefix go- + kazoku)
hitori, futari, sannin ...	(one, two, three ... : number + -tari or -nin [counters for people], 13.3)
otoosan	(your father, 13.1)
chichi	(my father, 13.1)
rippa (na)	(distinguished looking; impressive: a copula noun, 13.5)
sararii-man	(salaried worker)
okaasan	(your mother, 13.1)
haha	(my mother, 13.1))
kirei (na)	(pretty; beautiful: a copula noun, 13.5)
ikebana	(flower arrangement)
kyoodai	(brothers and sisters; siblings)
gonin-kyoodai	(five brothers and sisters [including myself])
ani	(my older brother, 13.1)
ane	(my older sister, 13.1)
otooto	(my younger brother, 13.1)
imooto	(my younger sister, 13.1)
otaku	(your house hold: exalted word, 13.7)
petto	(pet)
inu	(dog)
ippiki	(one animal; ichi + -hiki [a counter for animals], 13.8)
sore hodo demo arimasen	(not really so; not exactlly as you say: a humble response to a compliment given)

OTHERS

ga	(a particle marking the subject in emphasis)
to	('and' in complete enumeration, 13.4)
-hiki, -piki, -biki	(counter for animals, 13.8)
nannin	(how many persons; nan(i) + -nin [a counter for human beings], 13.3)

ADDITIONAL VOCABULARY

shujin	(my husband, 13.1)
goshujin	(your husband, 13.1)
kanai	(my wife, 13.1)
tsuma	(my wife [formal use], 13.1)
okusan; okusama	(your wife, 13.1)
shizuka (na)	(quiet; peaceful: a copula noun, 13.5)
benri (na)	(convenient: a copula noun, 13.5)
oniisan	(older brother, 13.1)
oneesan	(older sister, 13.1)
ki	(tree)
hana	(flower)
neko	(cat)
chiisakute	(small and ...: -kute form of chiisai, 13.10)
kawaii	(loveable; cute)
mae	(in front of)
hosoi	(slender; thin)
amakute	(tasting sweet and ...: -kute form of amai)
amai	(sweet tasting)
suppai	(sour)
oishii	(delicious; good tasting)
takai	(high; tall)
tori	(bird)
hitorikko	(the only child)

READING AND WRITING

Exercise 1: Practice writing the following **kanji**, using correct stroke order, until you can comfortably write each from memory.

25. 男 (male; man)　男　 丨 冂 冎 田 田 罗 男

26. 女 (female; woman) 女　 く 女 女

27. 先 (ahead)　先生　 ′ ⺧ 牛 生 步 先

28. 生 (to be born; life) 先生　 ′ ⺧ 牛 牛 生

29. 時 (time; o'clock) 六時　 丨 冂 日 日 日⁻ 日⁺ 昨 昨
時 時

30. 分 (minute)　五分　 ′ 八 分 分

Exercise 2: Read the following sentences and give their meanings in English.

1. ブラウンさんは、男の人です。

2. たなかさんは、女の人です。

3. ささき先生は、女の先生です。

4. 英語のクラスは、何時に、はじまりますか。
ごぜん十時に、はじまります。

5. いま、何時ですか。

   いま、九時十五分^{じゅうごふん}すぎです。

6. 金曜日にも、英語のクラスが、ありますか。

   はい、まい日^{にち}、あります。

7. わたくしは、火曜日の一時に、れきしのクラスが、

   あります。二時には、すうがくが、あります。

8. 一分^{いっぷん}。二分^{にふん}。三分^{さんぷん}。四分^{よんぷん}。五分^{ごふん}。六分^{ろっぷん}。七分^{ななふん}。八分^{はっぷん}。

   九分^{きゅうふん}。十分^{じゅっぷん}。

Exercise 3: As a homework assignment, write answers to the following questions using complete sentences and the **kanji** already introduced.

1. きのうは、何月何日でしたか。

2. きのうは、何曜日でしたか。

3. あなたは、まいあさ、何時ごろに、おきますか。

4. わたくしたちの日本語のクラスは、何時何分に、

   おわりますか。

6. あなたの日本語の先生は、男の先生ですか、女の先生

   ですか。

7. 水曜日と、金曜日と、どちらのほうが、すきですか。

8. きのう、英語のしんぶんを、よみましたか。

9. あなたは、スペイン語が、わかりますか。

10. あなたは、まいばん、何時ごろに、ねますか。

Exercise 4: Fill in the blanks with appropriate **hiragana**. Read the passage aloud.

　あそこ＿＿＿、ちいさ＿＿＿　＿＿＿　かわい＿＿＿　いぬ＿＿＿、
います。あのいぬ＿＿＿、たなかさん＿＿＿ペットです。いぬ
＿＿＿　なまえ＿＿＿、ぽち＿＿＿　いいます。

　うち＿＿＿　まえ＿＿＿、ほそ＿＿＿　＿＿＿　たかい木＿＿＿、
あります。木のした＿＿＿、あか＿＿＿　＿＿＿きれい＿＿＿はな
＿＿＿あります。たなかさん＿＿＿うち＿＿＿、おおき＿＿＿　＿＿＿
りっぱ＿＿＿うちです。

　たなかさん＿＿＿かぞく＿＿＿、みんなで、七人です。
男＿＿＿人＿＿＿、三人います。おとうさん＿＿＿、おにいさん
＿＿＿、おとうとさんです。女＿＿＿人＿＿＿、四人います。
おかあさん＿＿＿、おねえさん＿＿＿、いもうとさん＿＿＿、
たなか・まさこさんです。とても、いいかぞくです。

　たなかさん＿＿＿つくえ＿＿＿うえ＿＿＿、いろいろ＿＿＿
もの＿＿＿　あります。おおき＿＿＿　＿＿＿りっぱ＿＿＿とけい
＿＿＿、コンピューター＿＿＿、でんわなど＿＿＿、あります。
日本語＿＿＿本＿＿＿、三＿＿＿　＿＿＿　あります。英語＿＿＿
本＿＿＿、ありません。

14

Salesperson:	irasshaimase!
Tanaka:	ano ... onna mono no kasa ga hoshii n desu ga...
Salesperson:	hai, iroiro gozaimasu. donna iro ga yoroshii desu ka?
Tanaka:	aka ka ao ga ii n desu ga ...
Salesperson:	kochira no akai no wa ikaga desu ka?
Tanaka:	aa, kirei desu ne! chotto misete kudasai.
Salesperson:	hai, doozo. sore wa kinu hyaku-paasento desu.
Tanaka:	nedan wa ikura desu ka?
Salesperson:	ichiman-gosen en desu.
Tanaka:	naruhodo. ja, moo sukoshi yasui no wa arimasen ka?
Salesperson:	hai, gozaimasu. sochira no kiiroi no wa gosen en de, achira no aoi no wa rokusen-happyaku en desu.
Tanaka:	ja, ano aoi no o misete kudasai.
Salesperson:	hai, doozo. kore wa itaria-sei desu.
Tanaka:	ii dezain desu ne. poriesuteru desu ka?
Salesperson:	men to nairon desu.
Tanaka:	nakanaka ii desu ne... ja, kore o ippon kudasai.
Salesperson:	hai, arigatoo gozaimasu. ichiman en oazukari itashimasu.
	......
	omatase itashimashita.
	sanzen-nihyaku en no otsuri desu.
	doomo arigatoo gozaimashita.

ENGLISH EQUIVALENT

Salesperson:	Hello. May I help you?
Tanaka:	Ummm... I want [to find] an umbrellas for women...
Salesperson:	Yes. We have a variety. What color would you like?
Tanaka:	Either red or blue would be good, I suppose.
Salesperson:	How about this red one?
Tanaka:	Oh, that's pretty! May I see it?
Salesperson:	Here you are. That one is 100% silk.
Tanaka:	How much is the price?
Salesperson:	It's 15,000 yen.
Tanaka:	I see. Umm, do you have one that's less expensive?
Salesperson:	Yes, we do. That yellow one is 5,000 yen, and that blue one over there is 6,800 yen.
Tanaka:	Okay...well...let me take a look at the blue one, please. (All right, show me that blue one over there, please.)
Salesperson:	Here you are. It's made in Italy.
Tanaka:	It has a nice design. Is it [made of] polyester?
Salesperson:	It's [made of] cotton and nylon.
Tanaka:	This looks pretty good. I'll take one of these. (Fine. Please give me one of these.)
Salesperson:	All right, thank you. And that's out of 10,000 yen... (I'll take your ¥10,000 bill [and return with the change.]) ..... Thank you for waiting. Here is 3,200 yen change. Thank you very much.

GRAMMATICAL AND CULTURAL NOTES

14.1   irasshaimase

irasshaimase is the expression with which salespersons in Japan greet customers as they enter the stores. The word **irasshai** literally means 'Please come in' or 'You are welcome here,' and the ending **-mase** adds politeness to the greeting.

> **irasshaimase!**   (**Hello!** May I help you?)

14.2   ano ...

ano... spoken with sustained intonation (marked by three dots '...') means that the speaker is getting his or her thoughts together to say something. In a similar situation, we often say 'well ...' or 'umm ...' or some such expression in English.

14.3   mono

mono, as in **onna mono**, means 'clothing designed for' and is used to categorize clothing and accessories for men and women.

onna mono no kasa	(umbrella(s) **for women**)
otoko mono no kasa	(umbrella(s) **for men**)

14.4   (hoshii) **n desu ga...**

In colloquial Japanese the predicate construction ending in **desu** is often replaced by **... n desu ga...** This **n** is a short form of **no** meaning 'fact,' and, when it is combined with **ga** (but) and spoken with sustained intonation it adds a friendly and relaxed tone to the meaning of the sentence. **...n desu ga** simply makes the speech more conversational.

hoshii is an adjective expressing 'a strong desire to obtain something' or 'a wish to get something.' The word **hoshii** is commonly used by young children when they want to get something. When adult speakers use the word **hoshii** they restrain the tone of wish by adding **...n desu ga...** and speak it with sustainging intonation. The word **hoshii** is quite natural and appropriate when someone is shopping as in the dialogue of this lesson. In other situations adult speakers may use some other words to express their desire which will be introduced later. The negative of **hoshii** is **hoshiku arimasen**, the ending **-i** changed to **-ku** as with other adjectives.

kasa ga **hoshii n desu ga...**	(**I'd like to obtain** an umbrella, **but** [I wonder if you can show me some]).
aka ka ao ga **ii n desu ga...**	(**I suppose** red or blue **would be good...**)

14.5   **gozaimasu**: Honorific Style

gozaimasu means the same as **arimasu** (there is or I have) but it has the added meaning of 'being spoken with extra politeness.' This style of speaking is called the **honorific** style of speech. Salespersons usually speak to the customers in this style. The honorific style is chosen also in formal speeches and when an adult speaker is speaking to superiors. In the honorific style exalted forms and humble forms are used, and the sentence final **desu** and **arimasu** are replaced by **gozaimasu**. This style is also referred to as the **gozaimasu** style as opposed to the **desu-masu** style.

hai, iroiro **gozaimasu.**	(**Yes, we have** a variety.)
arigatoo gozaimashita.	(**Thank you very much.**)

The adjective **yoroshii** means 'good' and is the honorific counterpart of **ii** (good). The salesperson is speaking in the honorific style in this dialogue.

donna iro ga **yoroshii desu ka?**	(What color **would be good ?**)

The verb **itashimasu** means 'I humbly do' and is the humble counterpart of the verb **shimasu** (I do). The salesperson is speaking politely in the honorific style in this dialogue.

ichiman-en oazukari **itashimasu.**	(**I am humbly taking** ten-thousand yen [from you] now.)

14.6   Color Words

The following list indicates the names of the basic colors.   Grammatically, they are nouns.

aka	(the color **red**)
ao	(the color **blue**)
kiiro	(the color **yellow**)
shiro	(the color **white**)
kuro	(the color **black**)

When the basic color words modify nouns they are made into adjectives by adding the adjective ending **-i**.

akai kasa	(a **red** umbrella)
aoi kasa	(a **blue** umbrella)
kiiroi kasa	(a **yellow** umbrella)
shiroi kasa	(a **white** umbrella)
kuroi kasa	(a **black** umbrella)

The basic color words can be used both nominally or adjectivally, depending upon the speaker's intent.   Grammatical rules apply accordingly.

kono iro wa   **aka desu ka?**   (**Is** this color **red** [color]?)
iie, sore wa   **aka ja arimasen**.   (No, that is **not red**.)

kono kasa wa   **akai desu ka?**   (**Is** this umbrella **red**?)
iie, sono kasa wa   **akaku arimasen**.(No, it is **not red**.)

kasa no   iro wa   **aka de**, seetaa no   iro wa   **shiro desu**.
(The color of the umbrella is **red and** that of the sweater is **white**.)
kono ringo wa   **akakute** amai desu. (This apple is **red and** sweet.)

Non-basic color words   are mostly nouns.   The following nouns are often used in describing clothings.

midori iro (or guriin) **no** seetaa	(a green sweater)
murasaki iro no seetaa	(a purple sweater)
chairo no (or **chairoi**) seetaa	(a brown sweater)
kon iro no seetaa	(a navy blue sweater)

14.7   (A) **ka** (B)

The particle **ka** linking two words or phrases as in   (A) **ka** (B)   means 'either or' as in '**either (A) or (B).**'

aka **ka**   ao ga   ii n desu ga...   (**Either** red **or** blue would be good.)
Tanaka-san no   otoosan **ka**   okaasan o   shitte imasu ka?
(Do you know Tanaka-san's father **or** mother?)
aisukuriimu **ka**   keeki o   tabemashoo. (Let's eat some icecream **or** cake.)

176

14.8   no

no following an adjective, as in **akai no** or **yasui no**, is a noun meaning 'one.' This substitute noun is used when the word is repeated in a conversation and the meaning is clear to both parties.

kochira no **akai no** wa ikaga desu ka?   (How about the **red one** over here?)
yasui no wa arimasen ka?   (Don't you have **one that is less expensive?**)
achira no **aoi no** wa   ikura desu ka?   (How much is that **blue one** over there?)

14.9   ikura

ikura is an interrogative word meaning 'how much' with reference to the prices of merchandise.

nedan wa   **ikura** desu ka?   (**How much** is the price?)

14.10   Numbers 100 - 100,000,000

The following list indicates the numbers larger than 100 which are frequently used in daily conversations in Japan.

100	hyaku	30,000	samman
200	nihyaku	40,000	yomman
300	sambyaku	50,000	goman
400	yonhyaku	60,000	rokuman
500	gohyaku	70,000	nanaman
600	roppyaku	80,000	hachiman
700	nanahyaku	90,000	kyuuman
800	happyaku	100,000	juuman
900	kyuuhyaku	200,000	nijuuman
1,000	sen (or issen)	300,000	sanjuuman
2,000	nisen	400,000	yonjuuman
3,000	sanzen	500,000	gojuuman
4,000	yonsen	600,000	rokujuuman
5,000	gosen	700,000	nanajuuman
6,000	rokusen	800,000	hachijuuman
7,000	nanasen	900,000	kyuujuuman
8,000	hassen	1,000,000	hyakuman
9,000	kyuusen	10,000,000	issenman
10,000	ichiman	100,000,000	ichioku
20,000	niman		

14.11   ...o   kudasai

...o   kudasai means 'please give me ...' and is one of the commonest expressions used by the person buying a merchandise at a store. The merchandise is marked by the particle **o** and the expression **kudasai** expresses 'please give me such and such,' or 'I'll buy....'

ja, **kore o** ippon **kudasai**.   (Well, **I'll take** one of these.) or
                                          (**Please give me** one of these.)

mikan to ringo o **kudasai**.   (**I'll take** some tangerines and apples.)

14.12   en

en is the Japanese word for the name of the Japanese currency 'yen.' **ichiman-en** (¥10,000) bills, **gosen-en** (¥5,000) bills, and **sen-en** (¥1,000) bills are commonly used in shopping and banking; and **hyaku-en** (¥100), **gojuu-en** (¥50) and **juu-en** (¥10) coins are used for transportation fares and public telephones.

> **ichiman-gosen en** desu.   (It costs **15,000 yen**.)
> kiiroi no wa **gosen en** desu.   (That yellow is **5,000 yen**.)
> are wa **rokusen-happyaku en** desu. (That one over there is priced **6,800 yen**.)

14.13   (o)tsuri

(o)tsuri means 'change' or the difference between the price of the merchandise and the amount of money the customer gives to the salesperson. When a person buys merchandise priced at ¥7,000 and hands the salesperson a ¥10,000 bill to pay for the purchase, he or she receives **otsuri** (change) of ¥3,000. If a person wants change for a ¥1,000 bill, however, he or she asks for **ryoogae** (equal amount of change for paper money) and not for **otsuri**.

> rokusen-nihyaku en no **otsuri** desu.   (Here is your **change** of 6,200 yen.)
> ichiman en de **otsuri** ga arimasu ka?   (Do you have **change** for 10,000 yen?)
> (The implication is that the speaker wants to pay for the
> merchandise and has a 10,000 yen bill.)

Japanese salespersons count out the amount of change when returning it to a customer rather than adding the amount of change to the price of purchase and then counting it out as we do in the U.S.

EXERCISES

14E.1   Short dialogues for practice, first as a repetition drill and next in pairs.

1. A: otoko mono no kasa ga hoshii n desu ga...
   B: hai, iroiro gozaimasu. donna iro ga yoroshii desu ka?
   A: kuro ka ao ga ii n desu ga...
   B: dewa, kochira no kuroi no wa ikaga desu ka?
   A: ii desu ne... ja, chotto misete kudasai.
   B: hai, doozo. sore wa kinu hyaku-paasento desu.

2. A: onna mono no seetaa ga hoshii n desu ga...
   B: hai, iroiro gozaimasu. donna iro ga yoroshii desu ka?
   A: soo desu ne... ao ka midori ga ii n desu ga...
   B: kono aoi no wa ikaga desu ka? itaria-sei desu.
   A: ii dezain desu ne! L-saizu ga arimasu ka?
   B: hai, gozaimasu.

3. A: otoko mono no kaban ga hoshii n desu ga...
   B: hai, iroiro gozaimasu. donna iro ga yoroshii desu ka?
   A: soo desu ne... chairo ga ii n desu ga...
   B: dewa, kono itaria-sei no wa ikaga desu ka?
   A: nedan wa ikura desu ka?
   B: goman-gosen en desu.

4. A: onna mono no tokei ga hoshii n desu ga...
   B: hai, iroiro gozaimasu. amerika-sei ga yoroshii desu ka?
   A: soo desu ne... suisu-sei de mo ii n desu ga...
   B: kochira wa amerika-sei de nanaman-hassen en desu.
   A: sochira no suisu-sei no wa ikura desu ka?
   B: juuman en desu.
   A: ryoohoo to mo ii desu ne... sukoshi kangaemasu.
   B: doozo goyukkuri.

14E.2 Drill on color words: The instructor brings several objects in different colors, and asks questions. The students respond, using color words correctly.

1. (a red pen)   kore wa akai pen desu ka?
2. (a blue pen)   kore wa aoi pen desu ka?
3. (a black pen)   kore wa kuroi pen desu ka?
4. (a white paper)   kore wa shiroi kami desu ka?
5. (a yellow pencil) kore wa kiiroi empitsui desu ka?
6. (a green paper)   kore wa midori iro no kami desu ka?
7. (purple paper)   kore wa murasaki iro no kami desu ka?
8. (navy blue paper) kore wa kon iro no kami desu ka?

The instructor changes the sentence pattern, and the students respond correctly.

9. kono pen wa akai desu ka?
10. kono kami wa midori iro desu ka?
11. kono empitsu wa kiiroi desu ka?
12. kono pen wa aoi desu ka?
13. kono pen wa kuroi desu ka?
14. kono pen wa akakute nagai desu ka?
15. kono empitsu wa kiirokute mijikai desu ka?
16. kono empitsu wa kurokute hosoi desu ka?

Answer the following questions negatively.

17. kono kami wa   kon iro desu ka?
18. kono pen wa   murasaki iro desu ka?
19. kono empitsu wa   chairo desu ka?
20. kono kami wa   aoi desu ka?
21. kono pen wa   kuroi desu ka?
22. kono pen wa   midori iro desu ka?

14E.3   Response Drill: Answer the following questions according to the main dialogue of this lesson.

1. Tanaka-san wa   hajime ni   donna kasa o   mimashita ka?
2. akai kasa wa   kinu no   kasa deshita ka,   poriesuteru no   kasa deshita ka?
3. akai   kinu no   kasa wa   takai   kasa deshita ka?
4. sono kasa wa   kirei na   kasa deshita ka?
5. sono kasa no   nedan wa   ikura deshita ka?
6. sono mise ni   moo sukoshi   yasui kasa ga   arimashita ka?
7. kiiroi kasa no   nedan wa   ikura deshita ka?
8. aoi kasa no   nedan wa   ikura deshita ka?
9. sono kasa wa   men to   poriesuteru deshita ka?
10. kinu no   kasa wa   poriesuteru no   kasa yori   takai desu ka?
11. Tanaka-san wa   ikura no   kasa o   kaimashita ka?
12. otsuri wa   ikura deshita ka?

14E.4   Say the following numbers in Japanese.

1. 24, 73, 69
2. 85, 37, 99
3. 108, 862
4. 623, 777
5. 339, 486
6. 521, 673
7. 884, 105
8. 1000, 1235
9. 2523, 3765
10. 4762, 5090
11. 6989, 7002
12. 9999, 8723
13. 13,246
14. 33,333
15. 90,098
16. 40,541
17. 99,856
18. 123,675
19. 765,210
20. 1,696,345

14E.5 Role Play: Shopping. Student A plays the role of a customer and Student B plays the role of a salesperson. The customer wants to buy the following items. The salesperson shows available merchandise and tells all the nice things about the item. They discuss the prices. When the customer decides to buy the item the sales person receives the payment politely and hand over correct changes, if any. Reverse the roles, if time allows.

1. a black, silk umbrella
2. a large Japanese dictionary
3. a white T-shirt
4. a leather wallet for men
6. a briefcase for men
8. a camera

14E.6 Say the following sentences in Japanese.

1. I'd like to buy a silk shirt.
2. I want one made in China or in France.
3. What is the price of this green one made in Korea?
4. How much is this purple one made in Italy?
5. Do you have one that's less expensive?
6. I'll take that white and navy blue one made in Japan.

VOCABULARY

VERBS

gozaimasu	(there is; there are; we have: -masu form of the archaic verb gozaru used by salespersons to add politeness to arimasu, 14.5)
misete kudasai	(please show me: -te form of miseru + kudasai)
miseru	(to show)
oazukari itashimasu	(I humbly take [your money] in my custody)
omatase itashimashita	(Thank you very much for waiting)

ADJECTIVES

hoshii	(wish to obtain, 14.4)
yoroshii	(good; desirable: honorific equivalent of ii)
yasui	(inexpensive; cheap)
akai	(red, 14.6)
kiiroi	(yellow, 14.6)
aoi	(blue, 14.6)
kuroi	(black, 14.6)
shiroi	(white, 14.6)

NOUNS

onna mono	(clothing or accessories made for women; ladies', 14.3)
kasa	(umbrella)
iro	(color)
aka	(red color, 14.6)
ao	(blue color, 14.6)
kinu	(silk)
hyaku	(one hundred, 14.10)
paasento	(percent; %)
nedan	(price)
ichiman-gosen	(fifteen thousand, 14.10)
en	(yen: the Japanese currency, 14.12)
itaria-sei	(made in Italy)
dezain	(design)
poriesuteru	(polyester)
men	(cotton)
nairon	(nylon)
otsuri	(change, 14.13)

OTHERS

irasshaimase	(Hello!; May I help you? , 14.1)
ano ...	(well; umm ..., 14.2)
iroiro	(in a wide selection; various)
(A) ka (B)	([A] or [B], 14.7)
...n desu ga	(it's a fact that..., 14.4)
kochira	(over here; this way)
(akai) no	(the [red] one, 14.8)
ikaga desu ka?	(How about ...? How would you like ....?)
aa	(oh)
ikura	(how much, 14.9)
naruhodo	(indeed; I see)
moo sukoshi (yasui)	(a little bit [cheaper])
sochira	(over there; that way)
sore kara	(and then)
achira	(over yonder; that way over there)
... o kudasai	(please give me ...)
ga	(a particle marking the subject of the question which begins with an interrogative word)
nakanaka	(quite; pretty [good])

ADDITIONAL VOCABULARY

otoko mono	(for men; men's, 14.3)
mise	(store)
kangaemasu	(I'll think [about it]: -masu form of kangaeru)
kangaeru	(to think; to contemplate)

midori iro	(green, 14.6)
murasaki iro	(purple; violet, 14.6)
chairo	(brown, 14.6)
kon iro	(navy blue, 14.6)
hosoi	(slender; thin)
hajime ni	(at first)
takai	(high; expensive)
L-saizu	(large size: L, M, S are used to stand for large, medium, and small sizes)
kamera	(camera)
kawa	(leather)
suisu	(Switzerland)
goyukkuri	(please take time; [do] slowly and leisurely: the honorific prefix -go + yukkuri meaning slowly))
shatsu	(shirt)
sukaafu	(scarf)

READING AND WRITING

Exercise 1: Practice writing the following **kanji**, using correct stroke order, until you can comfortably write each from memory.

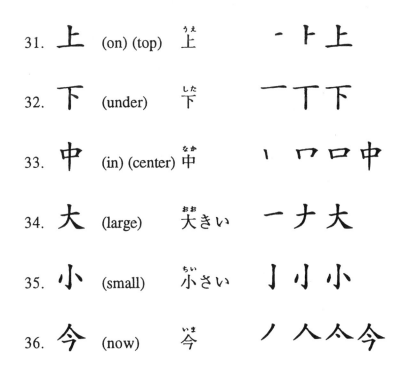

31. 上 (on) (top) 上(うえ)   一 ├ 上

32. 下 (under) 下(した)   一 丁 下

33. 中 (in) (center) 中(なか)   丨 冂 口 中

34. 大 (large) 大(おお)きい   一 ナ 大

35. 小 (small) 小(ちい)さい   亅 小 小

36. 今 (now) 今(いま)   丿 人 亽 今

Exercise 2: Read the following sentences and give their meanings in English.

1. つくえの上に、ノートや、かぎや、さいふが、あります。

2. つくえの下に、大きいかばんが、あります。

3. かばんの中に、本が、三さつあります。

4. 大きい本は、日本語のじしょで、小さい本は、英語の
   きょうかしょです。

5. まどのそばに、とけいが、あります。今、四時です。

6. このしゃしんの中に、女の人が、四人います。
   わたくしの先生と、ともだちです。

7. あの大きくてりっぱなうちは、たなかさんのうちです。

8. たなかさんのうちに、小さいいぬがいます。いぬの
   なまえは、「ポチ」と、いいます。

9. 今日は、何時に、でかけましょうか。
   九時十五分すぎごろに、でかけましょう。

10. あの大きい木の下で、おすしをたべましょう。

11. 今日は、何月何日ですか。月がきれいですね。

12. きむら先生は、本を、十五さつ、かきました。

13. 「金」は、英語で、何と、いいますか。

14. はこの中に、みかんがあります。一つ、二つ、三つ、
    四つ、五つ、六つ、七つ、八つ、九つ、十、みんなで、
    十あります。

Exercise 3: Practice reading the following dialogue in pairs.

てんいん　いらっしゃいませ！

たなか　　あの・・・。女もののかさが、ほしいんですが。

てんいん　はい、いろいろ、ございます。

　　　　　どんないろが、よろしいですか。

たなか　　あかか、あおが、いいんですが。

てんいん　こちらのあかいのは、いかがですか。

たなか　　ああ、きれいですね！ちょっとみせてください。

てんいん　はい、どうぞ。これは、きぬ 100 パーセントです。

たなか　　ねだんは、いくらですか。

てんいん　15000えんです。

たなか　　なるほど。じゃ、もうすこし、やすいのは、

　　　　　ありませんか。

てんいん　はい、ございます。そちらのきいろいのは、

　　　　　5000えんで、あちらのあおいのは、6800えんです。

たなか　　じゃ、あのあおいのを、みせてください。

てんいん　はい、どうぞ。これは、イタリアせいです。

たなか　　いいデザインですね。ポリエステルですか。

てんいん　めんと、ナイロンです。

たなか　　なかなか、いいですね。じゃ、これを 1 本ください。

てんいん　はい、ありがとうございます。

　　　　　1 まんえん、おあずかりいたします。

　　　　　・・・

　　　　　おまたせいたしました。3200えんのおつりです。

　　　　　どうも、ありがとうございました。

Exercise 4: As a homework assignment, write answers to the following questions using complete sentences and the **kanji** you already know.

1. あなたのつくえは、大きいですか、小さいですか。

2. つくえの上に、どんなものがありますか。

3. 今日は、どんなてんきですか。

4. 今、何時何分ですか。

5. あなたのつくえの上に、日本語の本がありますか。

6. あなたは、うちで、何語を話しますか。

7. 大きいみかんと、小さいみかんと、どちらのほうが
   すきですか。

Exercise 5: Write the Japanese equivalent of the following words in **katakana**.

1. design
2. shirt
3. scarf
4. pet
5. camera
6. department store
7. nylon
8. size M
9. polyester
10. computer

Exercise 6: Write the following words in **kanji**.

1. Monday
2. Tuesday
3. Wednesday
4. Thursday
5. Friday
6. Saturday
7. Sunday
8. March 15th
9. April 24th
10. August 8th

15

Yamada: shuumatsu wa   doo deshita ka?

Brown: totemo   tanoshikatta desu.

Yamada: dokoka e   ikimashita ka?

Brown: hai,   nichiyoobi ni   tomodachi to issho ni   Tookyoo no

            kankoo o   shimashita.

Yamada: sore wa   yokatta desu ne!   basu de   ikimashita ka?

Brown: hai,   kankoo basu de   ikimashita.

Yamada: donna   tokoro e   ikimashita ka?

Brown: hajime ni   Tookyoo-tawaa ni   noborimashita.

Yamada: Tookyoo-tawaa kara   Fujisan ga   miemashita ka?

Brown: iie,   kinoo wa   Fujisan ga   miemasen deshita.

Yamada: sore wa   zannen deshita ne!

            ja,   sono hoka   donna tokoro o   mimashita ka?

Brown: kookyo o   mimashita.   taihen   utsukushikatta desu.

            sore kara,   Ueno ya   Asakusa ni mo   ikimashita.

Yamada: zuibun   iroiro na   tokoro e   ikimashita ne!

Brown: hai,   dakara   kanari   isogashikatta desu.

Yamada: kinoo wa   samukatta deshoo?

Brown: hai,   soto wa   kanari   samukatta desu ga,   basu no

            naka wa   chittomo   samuku arimasen deshita.

            Tookyoo wa   hontoo ni   subarashii tokoro desu.

ENGLISH EQUIVALENT

Yamada: How was your weekend?

Brown: I had a good time.

Yamada: Did you go anywhere?

Brown: Yes. On Sunday I went sightseeing in Tokyo with my friends.

Yamada: Oh, that's good! Did you go on the bus?

Brown: Yes, we went on a sightseeing bus.

Yamada: What sort of places did you go to?

Brown: First we went up Tokyo Tower.

Yamada: Were you able to see Mt. Fuji from Tokyo Tower?

Brown: No, we couldn't see Mt. Fuji yesterday.

Yamada: That's too bad. Well, besides that, what other places did you see?

Brown: We saw the Imperial Palace. It was really beautiful.
After that, we also went to Ueno and Asakusa [and places like that].

Yamada: You went to a lot of different places, didn't you?

Brown: Yes, so we were quite busy.

Yamada: Wasn't it cold yesterday?

Brown: Yes, it was pretty cold outside, but inside the bus wasn't cold at all.
Tokyo really is a wonderful place.

GRAMMATICAL AND CULTURAL NOTES

15.1   -katta

Japanese adjectives have an inflectional ending **-katta** which indicates that the condition or quality expressed by the adjective has passed or is completed. ADJECTIVE + **-katta desu**, the past form, corresponds in function to VERB + **-mashita** or NOUN + **deshita**. Some people use ADJECTIVE + **-i deshita** to express the same idea, but it is more common and colloquial to say **-katta desu**.

<blockquote>

totemo **tanoshikatta desu**. (It **was** very **enjoyable**.)

kanari **isogashikatta desu**. (I **was** quite **busy**.)

kinoo wa **samukatta deshoo?** (**Wasn't** it **cold** yesterday?)

</blockquote>

15.2   -ku arimasen deshita

-ku arimasen deshita makes the past form of the adjective 'negative.' **arimasen** carries the idea of 'negation' and **deshita** marks the predicate 'past.'

<blockquote>

basu no naka wa   chittomo **samuku arimasen deshita**.

(Inside the bus **wasn't cold** at all.)

(o)tenki wa **yoku arimasen deshita**.

(The weather **wasn't good**.)

</blockquote>

15.3   Review of Predicate Types

The predicate, the most important element in a Japanese sentence, can be one of three types: a verb construction, an adjective construction, or a noun construction. In the polite conversational style, or the **desu-masu** style of speech, **-masu** is added to a verb stem and **desu** is added to an adjective or a noun (including copula noun) to form the predicate of a sentence. With regard to time, there are two distinctions made in the predicate, non-past (present and future) and past. Each predicate type has its affirmative and negative forms. The following is a summary of the predicate constructions presented so far.

AFFIRMATIVE   **NEGATIVE**

Non-Past   **Past**   **Non-Past**   **Past**

Verb Construction   **Verb Construction**

wakari**masu.**   wakari**mashita.**   wakari**masen.**   wakari**masen deshita** .
(I understand.) (I understood.)   (I don't understand.)   (I didn't understand.)

tabe**masu.**   tabe**mashita.**   tabe**masen.**   tabe**masen deshita** .
(I eat.)   (I ate.)   (I don't eat.)   (I didn't eat.)

Adjective Construction   **Adjective Construction**

samui **desu** .   samu**katta desu** .   samuku **arimasen** .   samuku **arimasen deshita** .
(It's cold.)   (It was cold.)   (It isn't cold.)   (It wasn't cold.)

ii **desu** .   yokatta **desu** .   yoku **arimasen** .   yoku **arimasen deshita** .
(It's good.)   (It was good.)   (It isn't good.)   (It wasn't good.)

Noun Construction   **Noun Construction**

hon **desu** .   hon **deshita** .   hon **de wa arimasen.** hon **de wa arimasen deshita** .
(It's a book.)   (It was a book.)   (It's not a book.)   (It wasn't a book.)

kirei **desu** .   kirei **deshit** a.   kirei **de wa arimasen** . kirei **de wa arimasen deshita** .
(It's pretty.)   (It was pretty.)   (It isn't pretty.)   (It wasn't pretty.)

15.4   ...ga miemashita

miemashita is the **-mashita** (past) form of the verb **mieru** which means 'something is visible' or 'can be seen.' **mieru** is an intransitive predicate verb which takes the particle **ga** to mark its subject. In English, the similar idea is expressed by the sentence 'I can see ...' in which the predicate verb 'see' (which is a transitive verb) takes a direct object.

> Tookyoo-tawaa kara Fujisan ga **miemashita** ka?
> > (**Was** Mt. Fuji **visible** from Tokyo Tower?) or
> > (**Were** you **able to see** Mt. Fuji from Tokyo Tower?)

kinoo wa Fujisan ga **miemasen deshita** .

(Mt. Fuji **was not visible** yesterday.)

15.5   chittomo + negation

chittomo   is usually spoken with a negative sentence to give the idea of complete negation which is expressed in English by 'not at all.' **chitto**   is a variant of **chotto**   (a little) or **sukoshi**   (a small amount); **mo** followed by a negative expression conveys the meaning of 'not any.' This has a meaning similar to that of **nani mo shimasen   deshita** (I didn't do anything), which was introduced earlier. **chittomo**   + negation can be used in any predicate construction to express the idea of complete negation.

basu no naka wa **chittomo**   samuku arimasen deshita.

(The inside of the bus was **not** cold **at all** .)

chittomo   wakarimasen.   (I don't understand[it] **at all** .)

chittomo   kirei ja arimasen.   (That's **not** pretty **at all** .)

15.6   yokatta desu ne!

yokatta , the past form of the adjective **ii** (good), is often spoken to express the hearer's reaction to good news. It is spoken in a sense that 'what I have heard is good,' or 'what has been done is excellent.'

sore wa **yokatta desu ne!**   (**Oh, I'm glad to hear** that!) or (That**'s good** !)

15.7   Tookyoo-tawaa

Tokyo, one of the largest cities in the world, has a number of famous places which tourists make sure to visit.   **Tokyo Tower** is one such place and is the highest building standing in the middle of Tokyo, and boasts the technological accomplishment of contemporary Japan. From the top of the tower one can enjoy a panoramic view of the entire city of Tokyo and its surrounding areas. On a clear day, even Mt. Fuji can be seen.

15.8   kookyo

kookyo   or **The Imperial   Palace**   is a graceful, traditional Japanese castle surrounded by green pine trees and a moat. In contrast to the tall and square modern office buildings and freeways which characterize most of the inner city, the palace marks one section of Central Tokyo with traditional serenity and dignity. It is one of the most beautiful places to visit.

15.9   Ueno

Ueno in downtown Tokyo is a cultural center where several science and art museums are located. **Ueno Park** is also famous for its cherry blossoms and for being the home of Japan's largest zoo.

15.10   Asakusa

Asakusa , also in the downtown section, is the merchants' center where entertainment and food are relatively inexpensive. The famous **Kannonji Temple** daily attracts thousands of people who come to visit the temple and make wishes for good fortune.

EXERCISES

15E.1   Grammar Drill: Change the time words in the following sentences to 'kinoo ' (yesterday) and make other necessary changes to convert the sentences to past tense. Next, with your book closed, make the same changes in each sentence as your instructor reads them aloud.

1. Buraun-san wa shuumatsu ni kankoo o shimasu.
2. kankoo kyaku wa taitei basu de iroiro na tokoro ni ikimasu.
3. gakusei wa shuumatsu ni paatii o shimasu.
4. nihongo no kurasu de wa kin'yoobi ni shiken ga arimasu.
5. Tookyoo no kankoo basu wa mainichi kookyo e ikimasu.
6. kankoo kyaku wa mainichi Tookyoo-tawaa ni noborimasu.
7. Tookyoo-tawaa kara tokidoki Fujisan ga miemasu.
8. Sasaki-sensei wa mainichi totemo isogashii desu.
9. kyoo wa tenki ga ii desu.
10. kyoo wa sukoshi samui desu.
11. maiasa nihon no ocha o nomimasu. totemo oishii desu.
12. tokidoki nihongo no zasshi o yomimasu ga, muzukashii desu.
13. nihongo no kurasu wa mainichi omoshiroi desu.
14. kyoo wa juunigatsu tsuitachi, getsuyoobi desu.
15. kyoo wa sora ga kirei desu.

15E.2   Response Drill: Answer the following questions negatively.

1. kinoo Tookyoo-tawaa kara Fujisan ga miemashita ka?
2. kinoo Buraun-san wa gakkoo ni ikimashita ka?
3. kinoo Yamada-san wa Tookyoo-tawaa ni noborimashita ka?
4. kinoo Buraun-san wa Fujisan ni noborimashita ka?
5. kinoo anata wa Tookyoo no kankoo o shimashita ka?
6. kinoo anata wa Asakusa ni ikimashita ka?
7. kinoo kankoo basu no naka wa samukatta desu ka?
8. kinoo soto wa atsukatta desu ka?
9. kinoo sora wa aokatta desu ka?
10. kinoo tenki wa yokatta desu ka?
11. kinoo anata wa isogashikatta desu ka?
12. kinoo no nihongo no shiken wa yasashikatta desu ka?

15E.3   First, read the following questions and check their meanings in English. Next, Student A asks the questions and Student B answers the questions without looking at the book.

1. kono heya no mado kara yama ga miemasu ka?
2. kono heya no mado kara sora ga miemasu ka?
3. kono heya no mado kara hito ga miemasu ka?
4. anata no seki kara soto ga miemasu ka?
5. anata no seki kara kokuban no ji ga miemasu ka?
6. Tookyoo-tawaa kara yama ya kawa ga miemasu ka?
7. kono heya no mado kara kawa ga miemasu ka?
8. anata no seki kara donna mono ga miemasu ka?

15E.4   Activity: What did you do yesterday? Student A asks Students B if he or she did the following things as indicated in (a). If the answer is positive, continue to ask (b). If the answer is negative, give an appropriate response.

1. (a)   if he or she went shopping yesterday
   (b)   if it was cold
2. (a)   if he or she watched T.V. on Sunday
   (b)   if he or she saw anything good
3. (a)   if he or she ate Japanese food yesterday
   (b)   if it tasted good
4. (a)   if he or she saw a movie over the weekend
   (b)   if it was interesting
5. (a)   if he or she did various things yesterday
   (b)   if he or she was busy
6. (a)   if he or she ate an apple yesterday
   (b)   if it was sweet

15E.5   Say in Japanese.

1. How was your weekend?
2. It was very enjoyable.
3. Did you go anywhere?
4. Yes, I went sightseeing in Los Angeles.
5. With whom did you go?
6. I went with my Japanese friends.

VOCABULARY

VERBS

noborimashita	(I have climbed; I climbed: -mashita form of noboru)
noboru	(to climb; to go up to the top of [some place])
miemashita	(It has been visible; it was visible; I could see: -mashita form of mieru, 15.4)
mieru	(to be visible; to be seen)

ADJECTIVES

tanoshikatta	(it was enjoyable: -katta form of tanoshii, 15.1)
isogashikatta	(I was busy: -katta from of isogashii, 15.1)
samukatta	(it was cold: -katta form of samui, 15.1)
yokatta	(that's good; it was good: -katta form of ii, yoi, 15.1, 15.3)
utsukushikatta	(it was beautiful: -katta form of utsukushii, 15.1)
utsukushii	(beautiful)
subarashii	(wonderful)

NOUNS

shuumatsu	(weekend)
kankoo	(tour; sight-seeing)
kankoo-basu	(tour bus; sightseeing bus)
tokoro	(place)
Tookyoo-tawaa	(Tokyo Tower, 15.7)
Fujisan	(Mt. Fuji, 15.7)
kookyo	(the Imperial Palace, 15.8)
Ueno	(the cultural center in downtown Tokyo, 15.9)
Asakusa	(the merchants' center in downtown Tokyo, 15.10)
soto	(outdoors; outside)

OTHERS

-katta desu	(the affirmative past form in an adjective construction, 15.1, 15.3)
-ku arimasen deshita	(the negative past form in an adjective construction, 15.2, 15.3)
sono hoka	(apart from that; other than that)
taihen	(extremly; exceedingly; very much)
dakara	(therefore; and so; that's why)
chittomo ...-masen	(not ... at all, 15.5)
kanari	(quite; considerably)
yokatta desu ne!	(I'm glad to hear that! 15.6)

ADDITIONAL VOCABULARY

kankoo kyaku	(tourist)
heya	(room)

yama   (mountain)
sora   (sky)
seki   (seat)
kawa   (river)

READING AND WRITING

Exercise 1: Practice writing the following **kanji**, using correct stroke order, until you can comfortably write each from memory.

37. 田 (rice field) 田^{たなか}中   丨 冂 冂 冊 田

38. 父 (father) 父^{ちち}   ノ 丷 父 父

39. 母 (mother) 母^{はは}   乚 乃 母 母 母

40. 毎 (every) 毎^{まいにち}日   ノ 厶 仁 ケ 毎 毎

41. 学 (learning) 学^{がっこう}校   丶 ゛ ゛゙ ゛゙ 丷 学 学

42. 校 (institution) 学^{がっこう}校   一 十 才 木 杧 杧 校 校

杧 校

Exercise 2: Read the following words and expressions and give their meanings in English.

1. 田^{たなか}中さんのお父^{とう}さんは、先生です。

2. お父さんは、毎^{まいにち}日、学^{がっこう}校で、英語をおしえます。

3. 田中先生は、クラスの中では、英語だけ話します。

4. その大学^{だいがく}は、かなり、大きい大学です。

5. 大学のキャンパスには、木が、たくさんあります。

6. 学生^{がくせい}は、よく、木の下で、本をよみます。

7. 田中先生は、毎あさ、八時ごろ、学校に、でかけます。

8. 田中先生の英語のクラスには、男の学生が、十五人と、
   女の学生が、十八人います。かなり大きいクラスです。

9. クラスは、毎日、九時から、十一時までです。

10. きのうは、日曜日でした。田中先生は、うちで、英語
    の本をかきました。

Exercise 3: Inside each set of parentheses above the following words and phrases, write the correct **yomigana/furigana** for the corresponding **kanji**.

   (   ) (   )(   ) (   )
1. 今日は、五月五日、金曜日です。

   (   )   (   )   (   )
2. 田中さんのお母さんは、いけばなの先生です。

      (   ) (   ) (   )   (   )
3. あなたの日本語の先生は、男のかたですか、女のかた
   ですか。

   (   )   ( ) (   ) ( )( )
4. お父さんのかばんの中に、大きい英語の本があります。

  ( )( )(   )   (   )
5. 今、四時十分すぎです。日本語のテレビをみましょう。

  (   )(   ) (   )
8. 十一月二十日、水曜日に、コンサートがありますよ。

Exercise 4: Practice reading Dialogue 15 in pairs.

やまだ	しゅうまつは、どうでしたか。
ブラウン	とても、たのしかったです。
やまだ	どこかへ、いきましたか。
ブラウン	はい、日曜日に、ともだちといっしょに、 とうきょうのかんこうを、しました。
やまだ	それは、よかったですね。バスで、いきましたか。
ブラウン	はい、かんこうバスで、いきました。
やまだ	どんなところへ、いきましたか。
ブラウン	はじめに、とうきょうタワーに、のぼりました。
やまだ	とうきょうタワーから、ふじさんが、みえましたか。
ブラウン	いいえ、きのうは、ふじさんが、みえませんでした。
やまだ	それは、ざんねんでしたね！ じゃ、そのほか、どんなところを、みましたか。
ブラウン	こうきょをみました。とても、うつくしかった です。それから、うえのや、あさくさにも、 いきました。
やまだ	ずいぶん、いろいろなところへ、いきましたね！
ブラウン	はい、だから、かなり、いそがしかったです。
やまだ	きのうは、さむかったでしょう。
ブラウン	はい、そとは、かなりさむかったですが、バス の中は、ちっとも、さむくありませんでした。 とうきょうは、ほんとうに、すばらしいところ です。

Exercise 5: As a homework assignment, write answers to the following questions using complete sentences and the **kanji** already introduced.

1. ブラウンさんは、日曜日に、何をしましたか。

2. だれといっしょに、いきましたか。

3. のりものは、何で、いきましたか。

4. はじめに、どこに、のぼりましたか。

5. とうきょうタワーから、ふじさんが、みえましたか。

6. こうきょは、どんなところでしたか。

7. きのうは、どんなてんきでしたか。

8. あなたも、とうきょうのかんこうを、しましたか。

Exercise 6: Write the following words in **katakana**.

1. piano
2. party
3. table
4. concert
5. test

6. taxi
7. bus
8. video
9. ice cream
10. pineapple

Tokyo Tower

The Imperial Palace

16

Instructor:	*(Showing the back of a picture,)* saa, minai de atete kudasai.
	Buraun-san wa ima nani o shite imasu ka?
	watakushi wa shitsumon ni 'hai' ka 'iie' de kotaemasu.
Student 1:	Buraun-san wa ima terebi o mite imasu ka?
Instructor:	iie, Buraun-san wa ima terebi o mite imasen.
Student 2:	nanika tabete imasu ka?
Instructor:	iie, nanni mo tabete imasen.
Student 2:	ja, asagohan ka nanika tsukutte imasu ka?
Instructor:	iie, tsukutte mo imasen.
Student 2:	ja, koohii ka nanika nonde imasu ka?
Instructor:	iie, nanni mo nonde imasen.
Student 2:	ja, ongaku o kiite imasu ka?
Instructor:	iie, chigaimasu. ongaku o kiite imasen.
Student 3:	nanika yonde imasu ka? shimbun toka, zasshi toka...
Instructor:	iie, nanni mo yonde imasen.
Student 3:	uu...n. ja, nanika kaite imasu ka?
Instructor:	hai, kaite imasu. saa... nani o kaite imasu ka?
Student 3:	uu...n. pen de tegami o kaite imasu ka?
Instructor:	iie, Buraun-san wa pen o tsukatte imasen.
Student 3:	aa! ja, fude o tsukatte imasu ka?
	Buraun-san wa (o)shuuji no renshuu o shite imasu ka?
Instructor:	hai, soo desu. atarimashita!
	Buraun-san wa ima (o)shuuji no renshuu o shite imasu.

ENGLISH EQUIVALENT

Instructor:	(Showing the back of a picture), OK, please come up with the correct answer without looking. (Please guess what the correct answer is.) What is Mr. Brown doing now? I'll answer [your] questions with 'yes' or 'no.'
Student 1:	Is Mr. Brown watching TV now?
Instructor:	No, Mr. Brown is not watching TV.
Student 2:	Is he eating something?
Instructor:	No, he is not eating anything.
Student 2:	Then, is he making [his] breakfast or something?
Instructor:	No, he is not making anything either.
Student 2:	Then, is he drinking coffee or something?
Instructor:	No, he is not drnking anything.
Student 2:	Well, then, is he listening to the music?
Instructor:	No, that's wrong. He is not listening to the music.
Student 3:	Is he reading something, say, a newspaper or a magazine...?
Instructor:	He's not reading anything.
Student 3:	humm... Then, is he writing something?
Instructor:	Yes, he's writing. OK, what is he writing?
Student 3:	humm... He is writing a letter with a pen.
Instructor:	No, he is not using a pen.
Student 3:	Oh! I see. Is he using a brush? Is he doing his calligraphy practice?
Instructor:	Yes! That's right. You guessed it correctly! Mr. Brown is doing his calligraphy practice now.

GRAMMATICAL AND CULTURAL NOTES

16.1   minai de

minai means 'not looking' and is composed of **mi-** (verb stem of miru) + **nai** (the plain negative form). The particle **de** following marks the word **minai** as adverbial, i.e. 'in that manner.' The phrase **minai de**, therefore, means 'without looking.'

> **minai de**   atete kudasai.   (Please guess **without looking**.)
> mada **kakanai de kudasai**. (Please **don't write** [it] yet.)

16.2   -te imasu: Descriptive Present

-te imasu is called the **descriptive present** form. The same idea is expressed in English through the present progressive tense of verbs, as in 'He is reading a newspaper.' or 'He is drinking coffee.' **-te** is more like the '-ing' form in English. **-te** is one of the inflectional endings which all Japanese verbs may take. The **-te form** characteristically ends in either **-te** or **-de**.

The **-te form** may combine with several other words to make idiomatic expressions. Previously, **-te kudasai** (please do [such and such]) was introduced. The **-te + imasu** is also an idiom which describes (1) activities in progress or (2) the present state of being.

shite is the **-te form** of the irregular verb **suru** (to do). **shite imasu** means '[Someone] is doing [such and such].'

Most verbs may occur in both the **-masu** and the **-te imasu** forms, but some verbs, due to their meanings, occur more often in **-te imasu** and rarely in **-masu**. One of such verbs in **shiru** (to know). We have already studied the expression, **...o shitte imasu ka?** (Do you know ...?)

Another such verb is **... o motte imasu** (I own ... ; I have ... ; I'm holding ...).

Also verbs describing the weather conditions, **hareru** (the sky to clear), **kumoru** (to get cloudy), and others, appear more often in the descriptive present form. In English, some of these verb forms are translated into 'to be' + adjective, as in 'The sky is clear.' or 'It's cloudy.'

> Buraun-san wa ima nani o **shite imasu** ka?
> (What i s Mr. Brown **doing** now?)
> ima terebi o **mite imasu** ka? (**Is** [he] **watching** TV?)
> nanika **tabete imasu** ka? (**Is** [he] **eating** anything?)
> Buraun-san wa ongaku o **kiite imasen.**
> (Mr. Brown **is not listening** to the music.)
> tokei o **motte imasu** ka? (Do you **have** a watch?)
> sora ga **harete imasu.** (The sky **is clear.**)
> sora ga **kumotte imasu.** (The sky **is cloudy.**)
> Tanaka-san wa **okite imasu.** (Miss Tanaka **is up.**)

16.3 Major Verb Classes

There are three major classes of verbs in Japanese: the **vowel verbs**, the **consonant verbs**, and the **irregular verbs**. The verbs like **tabe-ru** (to eat) and **mi-ru** (to see) that take the ending **-ru** in their dictionary forms are vowel verbs, as their stems **tabe-** and **mi-** end with a vowel. To make the **-masu forms** of vowel verbs, simply replace **-ru** with **-masu**, as in **tabe-masu** and **mi-masu**. To make the **-te form**, replae **-ru** with **-te**: **tabe-te** and **mi-te**.

The verbs like **kik-u** (to hear) or **yom-u** (to read) that take the ending **-u** in their dictionary forms are consonant verbs, as their stems characteristically end with a consonant. As the Japanese language does not normally allow two or more consonants to cluster, the stem of a consonant verb takes a filler **-i-** before connecting to **-masu**, as in **kik-i-masu** and **yom-i-masu**. Depending upon the consonant sound at the end of the stem there are several ways to make the **-te forms** of consonant verbs. These will be explained in detail in the next section.

There are three irregular verbs in Japanese: **suru** (to do), **iku** (to go), and **kuru** (to come). Only with these three verbs do the vowel sounds in the stem change (suru becomes shimasu, for example) when different endings are attached. With regular verbs, the stem remains unchanged.

16.4   -te Form Formation Rules

As explained above, the -te forms of the vowel verbs are formed by replacing the **-ru** ending of the verb in dictionary form by **-te.**

Formation of the **-te** forms of the consonant verbs depends upon the type of consonant at the end of the stem. **tsukurimasu** (to make [something]) is an example of the consonant verbs whose stems end in the consonant '**r**.' The student of Japanese who knows only the dictionary form **tsukuru** (to make) cannot classify this verb, as '**r**' might conceivably be the last sound of the stem or the first of the ending **-ru**. But as soon as the student learns **tsukur-i-masu**, it becomes clear that this verb belongs to the consonant verb group, since it does **not** become *tsuku-masu as it would if it were a vowel verb. And when the **-te** form **tsukutte** is introduced, the student is confirmed in his knowing that **tsukuru** is not a vowel verb (it doesn't become *tsuku<u>te</u>); that, instead, it is a consonant verb whose stem ends with '**r**.'

The following list summarises different ways the **-te** fomrs are made with the vowel verbs, the consonant verbs with several sub-groups, and the irregular verbs.

Dictionary Form	(Meaning)	**-masu** Form	-te Form + **imasu**
Vowel Verbs:			
taberu	(to eat)	tabemasu	tabete imasu
miru	(to see)	mimasu	mite imasu
Consonant Verbs:			
Group 1: the 'r' verbs			
tsukuru	(to make)	tsukurimasu	tsukutte imasu
kaeru	(to return)	kaerimasu	kaette imasu
noboru	(to climb)	noborimasu	nobotte imasu
hajimaru	(something begins)	hajimarimasu	hajimatte imasu
owaru	(something ends)	owarimasu	owatte imasu
Group 2: the 'k' (and 'g') verbs			
kiku	(to hear)	kikimasu	kiite imasu
naku	(to cry)	nakimasu	naite imasu
aruku	(to walk)	arukimasu	aruite imasu
suku	(to become hungry)	sukimasu	suite imasu
isogu	(to hurry)	isogimasu	isoide imasu
Group 3: the 't' verbs			
matsu	(to wait)	machimasu	matte imasu
tatsu	(to stand up)	tachimasu	tatte imasu
motsu	(to have; to hold)	mochimasu	motte imasu

Group 4: the 's' verbs

hanasu   (to speak)   hanashimasu   hanashite imasu

Group 5: the 'm' (and 'b') verbs

yomu	(to read)	yomimasu	yonde imasu
nomu	(to drink)	nomimasu	nonde imasu
asobu	(to play)	asobimasu	asonde imasu

Group 6: the 'w' verbs

[The 'w' sound before 'u' is silent, but 'w' is pronounced before 'a,' which occurs in a form that will be introduced later. For this reason this hidden [w] is marked. It is easier if the student learns the verbs with [w] in the stem.]

i[w]u	(to say)	iimasu	itte imasu
a[w]u	(to meet)	aimasu	atte imasu
ara[w]u	(to wash)	araimasu	aratte imasu
tsuka[w]u	(to use)	tsukaimasu	tsukatte imasu

Irregular verbs

suru	(to do)	shimasu	shite imasu
iku ~ yuku	(to go)	ikimasu ~ yukimasu	itte imasu
kuru	(to come)	kimasu	kite imasu

There are other inflectional endings, namely **-ta,-tara** and **-tari**, which are derived from the **-te form**. If the students master the correct **-te forms** these other endings will be much easier to formulate. Each time the students learn a new verb, its three basic forms--**the dictionary form, the -masu form,** and **the -te form**--should be memorized so that students will be comfortable in using them in new sentences.

16.5   ...ka nanika

...ka nanika means '... or something.' It is used very much like the expression **...demo**. It can be applied to other interrogative words to make the similar phrases; **...ka dareka** (... or someone); **...ka dokoka** (... or somewhere) and so forth.

koohii ka nanika nonde imasu ka?
> (Is he drinking **coffee or something?**)

osushi ka nanika tabemasen ka?
> (Wouldn't you like to eat **sushi or something?**)

Tanaka-san ka dareka imasu ka?
> (Is **Tanaka-san or someone** available?)

Ginza ka dokoka ni ikimasen ka?
> (Wouldn't you like to go **to the Ginza or somewhere?**)

16.6   mo + negation

When you give a negative answer twice the second is marked by the particle **mo**. This second negation is usually marked by 'not ... either' in English.

> **tsukutte mo imasen.**   (He is **not** making [anything] **either**.)
> **tabete mo imasen.**   (He is **not** eating [anything] **either**.)
> **watakushi mo** wakarimasen.   (**I don't** understand it, **either**.)

16.7   nani mo, nanni mo

When the expression **nani mo + masen** is emphasized, **nani mo** may add an extra syllable and be pronounced **na<u>n</u>ni mo**. This device of adding a syllable for emphasis, either a vowel or a moraic consonant, may be a similar device used in English to give emphasis by adding stronger stress or higher pitch. The use of emphatic form is common in conversation, but in writing the regular form is preferred.

> Buraun-san wa **nanni mo tabete imasen.**
> (Mr. Brown **isn't eating anything at all**.)
> iie, **nanni mo yonde imasen.**   (No, he is **not** reading **anything at all**.)

16.8   ...toka ...toka

...toka means 'such things as ...' When **...toka** is repeated as in **shimbun toka zasshi toka** the meaning is very much like **...ka ...ka** (... or ... or). This expression is colloquial and used often in a casual conversation.

> **nanika yonde imasu ka?   shimbun toka zasshi toka...**
> (Is he reading? Something like a newspaper or a magazine?)

16.8   fude

A **fude** is a Japanese style writing brush used for the calligraphy art. In calligraphy practice the student uses **suzuri** (ink plate) and **sumi** (ink-making charcoal cake) or prepared ink. One dips the **fude** into the ink and shape it on the **suzuri** before writing.

> **fude** o tsukatte imasu ka?   (Is he using a **calligraphy brush**?)

EXERCISES

16E.1 Grammar Drill: Fill in the blanks with correct meanings and verb forms.

Dictionary Form	Meaning	-masu Form	-te Form + imasu
1. taberu	(to eat)	tabemasu	tabete imasu
2. oshieru	_____	_____	_____
3. miru	_____	_____	_____
4. neru	_____	_____	_____
5. mieru	_____	_____	_____
6. okiru	_____	_____	_____
7. dekakeru	_____	_____	_____
8. tsukuru	(to make)	tsukurimasu	tsukutte imasu
9. noboru	_____	_____	_____
10. shiru	_____	_____	_____
11. hajimaru	_____	_____	_____
12. owaru	_____	_____	_____
13. kaeru	_____	_____	_____
14. hanasu	(to speak)	hanashimasu	hanashite imasu
15. kaku	(to write)	kakimasu	kaite imasu
16. aruku	_____	_____	_____
17. kiku	_____	_____	_____
18. yomu	(to read)	yomimasu	yonde imasu
19. nomu	_____	_____	_____
20. matsu	_____	_____	_____
21. i[w]u	_____	_____	_____
22. a[w]u	_____	_____	_____
23. ara[w]u	_____	_____	_____
24. suru	_____	_____	_____
25. iku	_____	_____	_____
26. kuru	_____	_____	_____

The instructor and the students double-check the answers and review the rules governing the formation of the **-te** forms.

16E.2   Here are some new verbs. The dictionary forms, the meanings, and the **-masu** forms are given. Figure out their **-te** forms.

1.	suwaru	(to sit down)	suwarimasu	_____
2.	akeru	(to open)	akemasu	_____
3.	hashiru	(to run)	hashirimasu	_____
4.	noru	(to ride)	norimasu	_____
5.	ikeru	(to arrange flowers)	ikemasu	_____
6.	kiru	(to wear)	kimasu	_____
7.	kiru	(to cut)	kirimasu	_____
8.	kotaeru	(to answer)	kotaemasu	_____
9.	magaru	(to turn)	magarimasu	_____
10.	shimeru	(to close)	shimemasu	_____

16E.3   Say the best Japanese equivalent of the following sentences.

1. The teacher is standing but all the students are sitting.
2. Mr. Brown is opening a big box.
3. A white car is running fast.
4. Tanaka-san's mother is arranging beautiful flowers.
5. Tanaka-san's older sister is wearing a pretty kimono.
6. Please cut this paper.
7. Please close the door.
8. Please turn right.
9. Please go to Tokyo Tower this afternoon.
10. Please be at Tokyo Tower at three o'clock.

16E.4   The following is a list of common verbs that occur often in their **-te** forms. Figure out the missing parts and fill in the blanks correctly.

1.	_____	( )	_____	shitte imasu
2.	_____	( )	_____	kekkon shite imasu
3.	_____	(to have)	mochimasu	motte imasu
4.	_____	( )	_____	kitte imasu
5.	_____	( )	_____	kite imasu
6.	_____	(to laugh)	_____	waratte imasu
7.	_____	(to swim)	oyogimasu	oyoide imasu

16E.5   Answer the following questions according to the main text of the lesson.

1. kono kaiwa no naka de dare to dare ga hanashite imasu ka?
2. Buraun-san wa ima gakkoo ni imasu ka, uchi ni imasu ka?
3. Buraun-san wa uchi no naka ni imasu ka, soto ni imasu ka?
4. nete imasu ka, okite imasu ka?
5. uchi no naka de terebi o mite imasu ka?
6. nani ka tabete imasu ka?
7. nani ka nonde imasu ka?
8. Buraun-san wa benkyoo shite imasu ka?
9. nihongo no kyookasho o yonde imasu ka?
10. tegami o kaite imasu ka?
11. Buraun-san wa pen o tsukatte imasu ka?
12. fude o tsukatte imasu ka?
13. fude de nani o shite imasu ka?

16E.6   Grammar Drill: Change the time words in the following sentences to **ima** (right now) and convert the verbs to the descriptive present forms, **-te imasu**.

1. Tanaka-san no kazoku wa (s)hichiji ni asagohan o tabemasu.
2. otoosan wa maiasa shimbun o yomimasu.
3. okaasan wa maiasa asagohan o tsukurimasu.
4. oniisan wa maiasa ongaku o kikimasu.
5. oneesan wa maiasa kudamono o kirimasu.
6. Tanaka-san wa maiasa miruku o nomimasu.
7. okaasan wa mainichi (o)sara o araimasu.
8. oneesan wa tokidoki yuugohan o tsukurimasu.
9. Tanaka-san wa tokidoki dezaato o tsukurimasu.
10. otooto-san to imooto-san wa mainichi gakkoo ni ikimasu.
11. Tanaka-san no otoosan wa mainichi daigaku de oshiemasu.
12. okaasan wa maishuu ikebana o oshiemasu.

16E.7   Answer the following questions.

1. watakushitachi wa ima nanigo o hanashite imasu ka?
2. watakushitachi wa ima nanigo o benkyoo shite imasu ka?
3. ima kyooshitsu de nanika kaite imasu ka?
4. ima dareka shimbun o yonde imasu ka?
5. watakushitachi wa ima nanika nonde imasu ka?

6. anata wa   ima   onaka ga   suite imasu ka?
7. nodo ga   kawaite imasu ka?
8. ima   okane o   motte imasu ka?
9. Tanaka-san no   denwa-bangoo o   shitte imasu ka?

16E.8   Activity: Guessing game. Each student prepares a picture of either Miss Tanaka or Mr. Brown doing something. (Make sure that the writer knows all the words to describe the activity represented in the picture.) He or she asks the class to pose questions, and answers only by 'yes' or 'no' in Japanese. The party who guesses with fewer questions wins.

VOCABULARY

VERBS

minai de	(without looking, 16.1)
shite imasu	(he is doing: -te form of suru + imasu, 16.2, 16.4)
atete kudasai	(please guess; please come up with a right answer: -te form of ateru + kudasai)
ateru	(to guess or to come up with a correct answer)
mite imasu	(he is watching; he is looking at: -te form of miru + imasu, 16.2, 16.4)
mite imasen	(he is not watching: the negative of mite imasu)
tabete imasu	(he is eating, 16.2, 16.4)
nonde imasu	(he is drinking, 16.2, 16.3, 16.4)
kiite imasu	(he is listening; he is hearing: -te form of kiku + imasu)
yonde imasu	(he is reading: -te form of yomu + imasu, 16.2, 16.3, 16.4)
kaite imasu	(he is writing: -te form of kaku + imasu)
tsukatte imasu	(he is using: -te form of tsuka[w]u + imasu, 16.4)
tsuka[w]u	(to use, 16.4)
tsukuru	(to make, 16.4)
renshuu suru	(to practice: compound verb made up of renshuu (practice) + suru)
atarimashita	(you have hit the target; you have given the right answer: -mashita form of atarimasu, ataru)
ataru	(to be correct in guessing)
ataru	(to strike the target; to guess [something] right)
matsu	(to wait)
kuru	(to come)
aruite	(-te form of aruku, 16.2, 16.3, 16.4)
hanashite	(-te form of hanasu, 16.2, 16.3, 16.4)
nete imasu	(I am sleeping: -te form of neru + imasu, 16.2)
neru	(to go to bed; to sleep)
suite imasu	(I am hungry: -te form of suku + imasu, 16.2, 16.3, 16.4)
kawaite imasu	(I am thirsty; something is dry: -te form of kawaku + imasu, 16.2, 16.3)
kawaku	(to get dry; to be thirsty [nodo ga] kawaku)
itte	(-te form of i[w]u (to say), 16.2, 16.3, 16.4)
i[w]u	(to say)

| kite | (-te form of kuru (to come), 16.3, 16.4) |
| kuru | (to come; irregular verb, 16.3, 16.4) |

ADJECTIVES   (- - -)

NOUNS

ongaku	(music)
fude	(writing brush, 16.8)
renshuu	(practice; exercise)
suzuri	(ink plate for calligraphy art, 16.8)
sumi	(charcoal ink for calligraphy art, 16.8)
okane	(money)

READING AND WRITING

Exercise 1: Practice writing the following **kanji**, using correct stroke order, until you can comfortably write each from memory.

43. 口 (mouth)   口（くち）   丨 冂 口

44. 食 (to eat)   食（た）べる   ノ 人 人 今 今 今 食 食 食

45. 目 (eye)   目（め）   丨 冂 冂 冃 目

46. 見 (to see)   見（み）る   丨 冂 冂 冃 目 貝 見

47. 手 (hand)   手（て）   一 二 三 手

48. 読 (to read)   読（よ）む   丶 二 二 三 言 言 言 計 計 計 誌 読 読

209

Exercise 2: Read the following sentences and give their meanings in English.

1. 口で、何をしますか。

   口で、食べます。それから、話します。

2. 目で、何をしますか。

   目で、見ます。

3. ブラウンさんは、日本食が大すきです。ときどき、

   すきやきや、おすしを食べます。すきやきは、

   おはしで食べますが、おすしは、手で食べます。

4. あなたは、てんぷらを、手で食べますか、おはしで

   食べますか。

5. 田中さんのお母さんは、今、テレビを見ています。

6. お父さんは、毎あさ、しんぶんを読みます。

   今、しんぶんを、読んでいます。

7 ブラウンさんは、毎ばん、日本語のしんぶんを、読み

   ます。それから、テレビを見ます。学校で、ともだち

   と、日本語を、話します。毎日、とてもたのしいです。

8. 今日は、何月何日ですか。

   今日は、十二月二十日です。もうすぐクリスマスです。

   クリスマス・プレゼントを、かいましょう。

Exercise 3: Read Dialogue 16 in pairs.

先生	さあ、見ないで、あててください。
	ブラウンさんは、今、何をしていますか。
	わたくしは、「はい」か「いいえ」でこたえます。
学生 1	ブラウンさんは、今、テレビを、見ていますか。
先生	いいえ、ブラウンさんは、今、テレビを、見ていません。
学生 2	何か、食べていますか。
先生	いいえ、何も、食べていません。
学生 2	あさごはんか、何か、つくっていますか。
先生	いいえ、つくっても、いません。
学生 2	じゃ、コーヒーか、何か、のんでいますか。
先生	いいえ、何も、のんでいません。
学生 2	じゃ、おんがくを、きいていますか。
先生	いいえ、ちがいます。おんがくを、きいていません。
学生 3	何か、読んでいますか。しんぶんとか、ざっしとか。
先生	いいえ、何も、読んでいません。
学生 3	うーん、じゃ、何か、かいていますか。
先生	はい！　かいています。さあ、何をかいていますか。
学生 3	うーん、ペンで、手がみを、かいていますか。
先生	いいえ、ブラウンさんは、ペンを、つかっていません。
学生 3	ああ！じゃ、ふでをつかっていますか。ブラウンさんは、しゅうじのれんしゅうを、していますか。
先生	はい、そうです。　あたりました。ブラウンさんは、今、しゅうじのれんしゅうを、しています。

Exercise 4: Read the following letter, and give the meaning in English.

　ひろしさん、おげんきですか。お父さんやお母さんも、おげんき
ですか。わたくしもげんきです。こちらは、今、かなりさむいです
が、そちらは、どうですか。

　今、わたくしは、日本の学校で、日本語をべんきょうしています。
毎日、いそがしいですが、とてもたのしいです。学校は、ごぜん九
時からごご三時までです。先生は、女のかたで、ささき先生といい
ます。とてもいい先生です。学生は、いろいろな人がいます。アメ
リカ人や、中国人や、かんこく人の学生がいます。みんな、日本語
がじょうずです。毎日、日本語だけで、話します。ときどき、とも
だちと、レストランにいきます。たいてい、日本食を食べます。日
本のそばは、とても、おいしいですよ。でも、ときどき、ピザや、
ハンバーガーを食べます。

　きのうは、日曜日でした。ともだちと、いっしょに、とうきょう
のかんこうをしました。はじめに、とうきょうタワーに、のぼりま
した。きのうは、とうきょうタワーの上から、ふじさんが見えまし
た。とてもきれいでした。

　では、また、かきます。みなさんに、よろしく。

　　　　　　　　　　　　　　　　　　さようなら

二月五日　　　　　　　　　　　　　　ブラウン

Exercise 5: Fill in the blanks with the correct **hiragana**.

　田中さん＿＿＿、日曜日＿＿＿しんじゅく＿＿＿デパート＿＿＿、
きれい＿＿＿かさ＿＿＿かいました。それ＿＿＿、めん＿＿＿ポリ
エステル＿＿＿、かさでした。ねだん＿＿＿かなり、やすかっ
たです。それから、きっさてん＿＿＿、コーヒー＿＿＿のみま
した。とても、おいし＿＿＿＿＿＿＿です。

17

山田　　　　ブラウンさん、学期しけんは、どうでしたか。

ブラウン　おかげさまで、かなり、よくできました。

山田　　　　それは、よかったですね。わたくしは、こんど、
　　　　　　ぜんぜん、だめでした。

ブラウン　そうですか。ざんねんでしたね。

山田　　　　しかたがありません。勉強しませんでしたから。

ブラウン　あなたのせんこうは、何ですか。

山田　　　　わたくしのせんこうは、化学です。

ブラウン　化学のクラスでは、しけんが、たくさんありま
　　　　　　すか。

山田　　　　はい、ほとんど毎しゅう、あります。

ブラウン　しゅくだいも、ありますか。

山田　　　　はい、もちろん、あります。毎日、午後には、
　　　　　　じっけんも、あります。

ブラウン　日本語のクラスも、おなじようです。毎しゅう、
　　　　　　ぶんぽうや、たん語のしけんがありますし、
　　　　　　午後には、ラボもあります。

山田　　　　毎日、何時間ぐらい、勉強しますか。

ブラウン　クラスがおわってから、ラボに行って、一時間
　　　　　　ぐらい、テープをききます。それから、としょ
　　　　　　かんに行って、二時間ぐらい勉強します。

Yamada: Buraun-san, gakki-shiken wa doo deshita ka?

Buraun: okagesamade, kanari yoku dekimashita.

Yamada: sore wa yokatta desu ne. watakushi wa kondo

            zenzen dame deshita.

Buraun: soo desu ka. zannen deshita ne.

Yamada: shikata ga arimasen. benkyoo shimasen deshita kara.

Buraun: anata no senkoo wa nan desuka?

Yamada: watakushi no senkoo wa kagaku desu.

Buraun: kagaku no kurasu de wa shiken ga takusan

            arimasu ka?

Yamada: hai, hotondo maishuu arimasu.

Buraun: shukudai mo arimasu ka?

Yamada: hai, mochiron arimasu.

Buraun: mainichi gogo ni wa jikken mo arimasu.

Yamada: nihongo no kurasu mo onaji yoo desu. maishuu

            bumpoo ya tango no shiken ga arimasu shi,

            gogo ni wa rabo mo arimasu.

Buraun: mainichi nanjikan gurai benkyoo shimasu ka?

Yamada: kurasu ga owatte kara rabo ni itte, ichi-jikan gurai

            teepu o kikimasu. sore kara toshokan ni itte

            ni-jikan gurai benkyoo shimasu.

ENGLISH EQUIVALENT

Yamada: How did your finals go, Mr. Brown?

Brown: Quite well, thank you.

Yamada: That's good. I did't do well at all this time.

Brown: Really? That's too bad.

Yamada: There is no other way [things could have turned out], because I didn't study.

Brown: What's your major?

Yamada: My major is chemistry.

Brown: Do you have a lot of tests in [your] chemistry class?

Yamada: Yes, almost every week.

Brown: Do you also have homework?

Yamada: Yes, of course, there is homework. We also have an experiment every afternoon.

Brown: [My] Japanese class seems to be the same, [too]. We have grammar and vocabulary tests every week, and we have labs in the afternoon.

Yamada: About how many hours do you study every day?

Brown: After class is over, I go to the lab and listen to tapes for about an hour. Then I go to the library and study for about two hours.

GRAMMATICAL AND CULTURAL NOTES

17.1   gakki-shiken

gakki means the academic period 'semester,' 'quarter,' or 'session,' depending upon the school. The word **gakki** is composed of **gaku** (study) and **ki** (period). **shiken** is 'examination.' **gakki-matsu-shiken** with **matsu** (end) between **gakki** and **shiken** is the formal way to say 'the semester-end-examination,' or 'the final examination.' Japanese students often shorten the word to **gakki-shiken** or **ki-matsu-shiken** just like American students call it a 'final.'

> **gakki-shiken** wa   doo deshita ka?   (How was [your] **final**?)
> moo sugu   **kimatsu-shiken** desu ne...   (The **finals** are coming soon...)

17.2   kondo

kondo literally means 'this time,' and usually indicates an event in the near past or immediate future. As the Japanese verb has two basic time dimensions, past and non-past, **kondo** spoken with the past form of a verb usually refers to the most immediate of 'past events.' In English, the same idea is expressed by 'this [past] time' or 'the last time.' When **kondo** is spoken with a non-past form of a verb, the English equivalent is more likely to be 'this [coming] time,' 'the next time,' or 'sometime.'

watakushi wa **kondo** zenzen dame deshita.

(I didn't do well at all **this time**.)

kondo wa yoku dekimashita. (I did pretty well **this time**.)

kondo issho ni osushi o tabemasen ka?

(Would you like to eat sushi with me **sometime**?)

kondo wa Shinjuku ni ikimashoo. (Let's go to Shinjuku **next time**.)

17.3 zenzen

zenzen is an adverb expressing intenseness of degree or condition and is most often used in sentences with negative connotations. The words, 'absolutely' or 'completely' may be some of the English equivalents.

zenzen dame deshita. ([It] was **absolutely** terrible.) or (I **blew** it.)

zenzen wakarimasen. (I do **not** understand **a word**.)

17.4 dame

dame is a very frequently spoken colloquial word meaning 'no good.' Although it sounds somewhat informal, it does not sound vulgar. A mother scolds a child by saying '**dame desu yo**' to express disapproval of his or her conduct. Adult speakers use **dame** to express disappointment as well as disapproval. **dame** is a copula noun.

kondo wa zenzen **dame deshita.** (This time I totally **blew it**.)

dame na hito desu. ([He] is a **rotten** person.)

ii desu ka, **dame** desu ka? (Is [it] good or **no good**?)

17.5 shikata ga arimasen

shikata means 'way of managing' and **ga arimasen** means 'not existing.' The phrase **shikata ga arimasen** (often spoken as **shikata ga nai**) expresses the feeling of resignation which English speakers usually express by saying 'It couldn't be helped,' 'What do you expect,' 'I couldn't expect much else,' or 'There's not much choice.'

shikata ga arimasen. benkyoo shimasen deshita kara.

(**I couldn't expect much else.** It's because I didn't study.)

17.6 kara meaning 'because'

kara added at the end of a clause or a sentence means 'because' and states a reason or cause for the results or the events being discussed. The clause stating a reason may follow the clause stating an event, or it may precede.

kondo wa zenzen dame deshita. benkyoo shimasen deshita **kara.**

(This time I didn't do well at all. **It's because** I did not study.)

yoku   benkyoo shimashita **kara**   kanari   yoku   dekimashita.

> (**Because** I studied a lot, I did fairly well this time.)

onaka ga   sukimashita **kara**   hayaku   tabemashoo.

> (**Because** we are hungry, let's hurry up and eat.)

kara normally follows the predicate in the polite form marked by **desu** or **-masu**.   There is another word **node** (because) which follows the plain form **da,** or verb in the dictionary form **-ru** or **-u**.   The use of **node** will be explained later.

The word **kara** meaning 'because' is different from the particle **kara** meaning 'from' which was introduced earlier.

17.7   yoo

yoo means 'appearance' or 'looks,' and is often spoken when the speaker wants to describe something as being 'just like' something else.   **yoo** is a copula noun.   In the pre-noun position it takes **na** as in ...**no yoo na...** , and when used as an adverb it takes **ni** as in ...**no yoo ni...**

onaji **yoo** desu.   (It's **just about the same**.)
sore to   **onaji yoo na**   kasa o   kaimashita.

> ([I] bought an umbrella **just like** that one.)

Buraun-san wa   nihongo o   nihonjin **no yoo ni**   hanashimasu.

> (Mr. Brown speaks Japanese **just like** a native speaker.)

17.8   ...shi

shi is a conjunctive particle, usually added at the end of a clause to mean 'and,' 'moreover,' or 'and in addition.'   In using **shi** at the end of a clause, the speaker indicates that he or she has additional things to add to the same line of thought.

maishuu   shiken ga   arimasu **shi**,   gogo ni wa   rabo mo   arimasu.

> (Every week, there is a quiz, **and on top of that** we have a lab in the afternoon.)

Buraun-san wa   nihongo ga   dekimasu **shi**,   kankokugo ya   chuugokugo mo   wakarimasu.

> (Mr. Brown can speak Japanese, **and moreover**, he can understand Korean and Chinese.)

17.9   jikan

The idea of duration or interval in time is expressed by **jikan**.   The word **jikan** means 'hour' when used with numerals, e.g. **ni-jikan** (two hours).

mainichi   **nanjikan** gurai   benkyoo shimasu ka?

> (About **how many hours** do you study every day?)

217

nijikan gurai benkyoo shimasu.   ([I] study for about **two hours**.)
kyoo wa   isogashikute **jikan** ga   arimasen.
                                    ([I] am busy today and have no **time** [for it].)

17.10   gurai

gurai expresses approximation in time duration or quantity which English speakers express by 'approximately' or 'about.'

nijikan **gurai** benkyoo shimasu.   ([I] study for **about** two hours.)
Buraun-san wa   mikan o   mittsu **gurai** tabemashita.
                              (Mr. Brown ate **about** three tangerines.)

17.11   -te kara

A verb in **-te form + kara** (point of departure) means 'after doing such and such,' and specifies that the activity or event expressed by the main predicate takes place after the one described by the first verb in **-te form**.

kurasu ga **owatte kara** rabo ni ikimasu.
                              (**After** class **i s over** [I] go to the lab.)
gohan o **tabete kara** gakkoo ni dekakemasu.
                              (**After eating** breakfast [I] leave for school.)
Buraun-san wa terebi o **mite kara** sukoshi benkyoo shimsu.
                              (Mr. Brown studies a little **after watching** TV.)

17.12   -te meaning 'and'

When two or more activities in sequence are mentioned as in 'Mr. Brown gets up, eats breakfast, and goes to school,' the verbs in non-final positions (gets up and eats) are marked in their **-te forms** in Japanese to indicate that the speaker has in mind using some other verb to complete the sentence. In English, a corresponding construction is produced by using commas or by using 'and' to link a series of verbs. The use of **-te form** meaning 'and' is particularly appropriate when there is one actor designated in the sentence and he or she performs two or more activities one after another in a time sequence.

rabo ni **itte** ichi-jikan gurai teepu o kikimasu.
                              ([I] **g o** to the lab **and** listen to the tape for
                              about an hour.)
asagohan o **tabete** gakkoo ni ikimasu.
                              ([I] **eat** breakfast **and** go to school.)

EXERCISES

17E.1   Activity: Talking about the tests.   Student A asks Student B how he or she did in the following tests or examinations.   Student B must give different responses to each question asked.

Example: A: kagaku no shiken wa   doo deshita ka?
            B: okagesamade,   yoku   dekimashita.

1. Japanese final examination
2. grammar test
3. vocabulary test
4. katakana test
5. hiragana test
6. kanji quiz
7. math examination
8. history examination
9. chemistry examination

17E.2   Student B asks Student A how he or she did in the final examinations of the subject below.   In each case Student A reports a complete disaster, and gives reasons (suggested below in English) for his or her failure.   Student B expresses regrets.

Subject	Reason
1. history	did not study at all
2. math	did not understand at all
3. Chinese	did not have time
4. Korean	did not get up early
5. French	did not listen to the tape
6. German	did not go to the lab
7. chemistry	did not do the experiments
8. Spanish	did not study the grammar
9. Japanese	did not study the vocabulary

17E.3   Grammar Drill: Fill in the blanks with correct meanings and verb forms.

Dictionary form	(meaning)	-masu form	-te form + imasu
1. okiru	( )	_____	_____
2. _____	(to read)	_____	yonde imasu
3. _____	( )	_____	motte imasu
4. _____	(to come)	kimasu	_____
5. _____	( )	iimasu	_____
6. _____	(to teach)	_____	_____
7. _____	( )	arukimasu	_____
8. omo[w]u	(to think)	_____	_____
9. oyogu	(to swim)	_____	_____
10. asobu	(to play)	_____	_____
11. ka[w]u	( )	_____	_____
12. _____	( )	kikimasu	_____

17E.4   Grammar Drill: Mr. Brown did the following paired activities (listed in the dictionary forms) yesterday. Each time he did the second activity after doing the first. Compose a sentence stating Mr. Brown's activities in a sequence.

Example: hon o yomu / terebi o miru
--> Buraun-san wa hon o yonde kara terebi o mimashita.

1. zasshi o yomu / gohan o taberu
2. rabo de teepu o kiku / shukudai o suru
3. kagaku no jikken o suru / uchi ni kaeru
4. yuugohan o tsukuru / terebi o miru
5. yuugohan o taberu / osara o ara[w]u
6. ocha o nomu / shuuji no renshuu o suru
7. tegami o kaku / shinbun o yomu
8. doitsugo o benkyoo suru / kagaku no shukudai o suru
9. toshokan ni iku / rabo ni iku
10. depaato de seetaa o ka[w]u / koohii o nomu

17E.5 Oral Response Drill: First the instructor asks individual students, next Student A and Student B ask each other.

1. anata no senkoo wa nan desu ka?
2. mainichi nanjikan gurai benkyoo shimasu ka?
3. taitei uchi de benkyoo shimasu ka, toshokan de benkyoo shimasu ka?
4. tokidoki nihongo no teepu o kikimasu ka?
5. taitei nanjikan gurai teepu o kikimasu ka?
6. doko de shukudai o shimasu ka?
7. shukudai wa omoshiroi desu ka, tsumaranai desu ka?
8. bumpoo to tango to dochira no hoo ga muzukashii desu ka?
9. moo nihongo no kanji o ikutsu gurai shitte imasu ka?
10. nihongo no tango o ikutsu gurai shitte imasu ka?
11. kagaku no kurasu de wa taitei jikken ga arimasu ka?
12. anata mo kongakki kagaku o benkyoo shite imasu ka?

17E.6 Oral Composition: Complete the following sentences supplying appropriate words so that each statement makes a cause-and-effect relationship.

1. watakushi wa kondo nihongo no shiken ga yoku dekimashita.
   _____ kara.
2. onaka ga sukimashita. kesa asagohan o _____
   _____ kara.
3. kyoo wa totemo isogashii desu. ashita kagaku no _____
   _____ kara.
4. kinoo depaato ni ikimashita ga, nanimo kaimasen deshita.
   _____ kara.
5. watakushi wa Buraun-san to onajiyoo desu. _____
   _____ kara.
6. watakushi wa Tanaka-san to onajiyoo desu. _____
   _____ kara.

17E.7 つぎのかんじを、ただしくかいて、おぼえなさい。(Practice writing the following **kanji** using correct stroke order until you can write them from memory.)

49. 山 (mountain) 山田 (やまだ)　　｜ 山 山

50. 勉 (effort) 勉強 (べんきょう)　　ノ ケ ケ 凸 岙 免 免

勉 勉

51. 強 (strong) 勉強 (べんきょう)　　フ フ 弓 弓 弘 弘 弦 弦

強 強 強

52. 午 (noon) 午後 (ごご)　　ノ ヒ 二 午

53. 後 (after) 午後 (ごご)　　ノ ク イ 彳 彳 後 後 後

後

54. 間 (interval) 時間 (じかん)　　｜ ｜ ｜ ｜ 門 門 門

門 門 間 間

55. 行 (to go) 行く (い)　　ノ ク 彳 彳 行 行

17E.8　かんじに読みがな／ふりがなをつけて、こえをだして読みなさい。英語でいみをいいなさい。(Assign correct **yomigana/furigana** to the **kanji** below and read the sentences aloud. Give the meaning of each sentence orally in English .)

1. 　（　　　）　　（　　　）　　　（　　　　　）
山田さんと山下さんは、大学生です。

2. 　（　　　）　　（　　）（　　）　　　　　　（　　　）
山田さんは、毎日、午後、としょかんで、勉強します。

3. 　（　　　）　　（　　　）
山下さんは、英語のクラスがおわってから、ラボに
　（　）　（　　　　）
行って、一時間ぐらい、テープをききます。

4. 　（　　）（　　　）（　　　）　　　　（　　　）
今日は、金曜日です。学校がおわってから、山田さん
　　（　　　）　　　　　　　　　　　（　）
と山下さんは、いっしょにえいがに、行きます。

5. 　（　　）　　（　　）　　（　　）　　　　（　）
山田さんのお父さんは、毎日、ゆうごはんを、食べて
　　（　　　　）　　　　　　（　）
から、二時間ぐらい、テレビを見ます。

6. 　（　　）　　　　　（　）（　）
田中さんは、きのう、午後八時ごろ、ブラウンさんと、
　　　　　　　　　　　　　（　　　）
いっしょに、としょかんで、勉強していました。

7. （　　）　　　　　（　　）（　）
勉強がおわってから、二人は、きっさてんに、行って、
　　　　　　　　（　）
アイスクリームを食べました。

8. 　（　　）　　　　　（　）（　）
山田さんのつくえの下で、小さいねこが、ねています。

17E.9 本文について、つぎのしつもんに、こたえてごらんなさい。

(Answer the following questions according to the information presented in the main dialogue of this lesson.)

1. ブラウンさんは、こんどの学期しけんが、よくできましたか。

2. 山田さんは、どうでしたか。

3. 山田さんは、たくさん、勉強しましたか。

4. ブラウンさんは、たくさん、勉強しましたか。

5. 山田さんのせんこうは、何ですか。

6. 山田さんの化学のクラスでは、しけんが、たくさん、ありますか。

7. しゅくだいも、たくさん、ありますか。

8. 午後には、じっけんも、ありますね。

9. ブラウンさんの、日本語のクラスでは、午後、何が、ありますか。

10. 日本語のクラスでは、毎しゅう、どんなしけんが、ありますか。

11. ブラウンさんは、毎日、クラスがおわってから、何をしますか。

12. 何時間ぐらい、テープをききますか。

13. それから、としょかんに行って、どのぐらい勉強しますか。

14. あなたも、ブラウンさんとおなじように、勉強しますか。

17E.10 かきとりをしてみましょう。(Write the following passage as a dictation practice.)

　日本語のクラスの学生は、毎日、クラスがおわってから、ラボに行って、テープをききます。それから、午後、三時間ぐらい、日本語の本を読みます。勉強がおわってから、日本人のともだちや、先生といっしょに、日本語で、話します。金曜日には、よく、いっしょに、日本食を食べます。

17E.11 Activity: Meeting new classmates. (This activity assumes that the students are now in the second semester of Japanese study, and probably find new classmates. If the situation is different the activity should be modified by the instructor.) Each student is asked to meet three new classmates and do the following to exchange information about each other.

1. Introduce oneself and exchange each other's name
2. Find out each other's home language
3. Where he or she is from
4. Where he or she took Japanese I, and who the teacher was
5. What his or her academic major is
6. How many hours he or she studies every day
7. How many classes he or she is taking this semester

17E.12 Write the following words in **katakana.**

1. notebook
2. class
3. printer
4. pen
5. sweater
6. chocolate
7. hamburger
8. sandwich
9. salad
10. soup

VOCABULARY

VERBS

owatte [kara]	([after something] is over: -te form of owaru)
owaru	(to be over; something ends: intransitive verb)
itte	(I go and ...: -te form of iku)

225

iku   (to go: irregular verb, 16.2)

ADJECTIVES   (---)

NOUNS

gakki   (school term; session; semester)
shiken   (examination; test; quiz)
gakki-shiken   (final examination, 17.1)
senkoo   (major field of study)
kagaku   (chemistry)
shukudai   (homework assignment)
jikken   (experiment)
onaji   (same)
bumpoo   (grammar)
tango   (vocabulary word)
rabo   (laboratory)
teepu   (tape)
toshokan   (library)

OTHERS

kondo   (this time; the next time; some time, 17.2)
zenzen   (absolutely; completely: adverb expressing intense degree, 17.3)
dame   (no good: a copula noun, 17.4)
shikata ga arimasen   (it couldn't be helped; it can't be helped, 17.5)
kara   (because; a particle denoting a reason or cause, 17.6)
hotondo   (almost; for the most part)
maishuu   (every week)
yoo   (appearance; looks: a bound copula noun, 17.7)
shi   (and; moreover; and in addition: a conjunctive particle, 17.8)
nanjikan   (how many hours, 17.9)
gurai   (approximately; about, 17.10)
-te kara   (after doing such and such, 17.11)
-te...   (doing such and such and..., 17.12)

ADDITIONAL VOCABULARY

toru   (to take)
dono gurai   (about how long; how much)
kon-gakki   (this semester)
moo   (already; by now)
kesa   (this morning)

18

山田	ブラウンさん、あなたが日本に来てから、もう、どのくらいに、なりますか。
ブラウン	そうですね・・・ きょ年の七月に来ましたから、もう、そろそろ、六か月になります。
山田	もう、日本のせいかつに、なれましたか。
ブラウン	はい、もう、すっかり、なれました。
山田	それはそうと、今、どのへんに、すんでいますか。
ブラウン	「よつや」の、えきのそばに、すんでいます。
山田	アパートですか、ホームステイですか。
ブラウン	ホームステイです。とてもしずかないい家です。
山田	学校まで、どのぐらい、かかりますか。
ブラウン	バスで十分、歩いて三十分ぐらい、かかります。
山田	じゃ、わりと、近いですね。
ブラウン	ええ、そんなに、遠くありません。山田さんの家は、どのへんですか。
山田	わたくしの家は、「みたか」です。しんじゅくから、でんしゃで、十分ぐらいですから、こんど、あそびに来てください。
ブラウン	ありがとうございます。じゃ、いつか、うかがいます。

Yamada: Buraun-san, anata ga nihon ni kite kara, moo,

     dono gurai ni narimasu ka?

Brown: soo desu ne... kyonen no shichigatsu ni kimashita kara,

     moo sorosoro rokkagetsu ni narimasu.

Yamada: moo, nihon no seikatsu ni naremashita ka?

Brown: hai, moo sukkari naremashita.

Yamada: sore wa soo to, ima, dono hen ni sunde imasu ka?

Brown: yotsuya no eki no soba ni sunde imasu.

Yamada: apaato desu ka, hoomusutei desu ka?

Brown: hoomusutei desu. totemo shizuka na ii uchi desu.

Yamada: gakkoo made dono gurai kakarimasu ka?

Brown: basu de juppun, aruite sanjuppun gurai kakarimasu.

Yamada: ja, warito chikai desu ne.

Brown: ee, sonna ni tooku arimasen.

     yamada-san no uchi wa dono hen desu ka?

Yamada: watakushi no uchi wa Mitaka desu.

     Shinjuku kara densha de juppun gurai desu kara,

     kondo asobi ni kite kudasai.

Brown: arigatoo gozaimasu.

     ja, itsuka ukagaimasu.

ENGLISH EQUIVALENT

Yamada	Mr. Brown, about how long has it been since you came to Japan?
Brown	Let's see... I came last July, so it'll be six months pretty soon.
Yamada	Have you gotten used to life in Japan?
Brown	Yes, I'm completely used to it.
Yamada	By the way, where are you living now?
Brown	I'm living near the Yotsuya station.
Yamada	Is it an apartment, or are you staying with a family?
Brown	I am staying with a family. It's a very quiet, nice home.
Yamada	About how long does it take to get to school?
Brown	It takes about ten minutes by bus or thirty minutes on foot.
Yamada	Then it's pretty close, isn't it?
Brown	Yes, It isn't very far. What neighborhood do you live in? (In what area is your home?)
Yamada	I live in Mitaka. (My home is in Mitaka.) It's only about ten minutes by train from Shinjuku, so please come by to visit some time.
Brown	Thank you. I 'll drop in some time, then.

GRAMMATICAL AND CULTURAL NOTES

18.1   -te kara moo . . . ni naru

In order to describe how long it has been or how much time has elapsed since a certain event took place in the past, Japanese use the idiomatic expression **-te kara   moo ...ni naru**. The phrase **-te kara** means 'after doing such and such,' or 'since such and such event took place'; the word **moo** means 'already,' or 'by now'; **...ni naru** means 'it has been (...amount of time).' In English one normally says 'it has been so many months (or days or years) since such and such took place.' Japanese does not have a specific verb tense equivalent to the English present perfect tense, and the ideas described by the present perfect tense in English are expressed in various ways in Japanese. One of these is **-te kara moo ... ni naru**.

> anata ga   nihon ni **kite kara moo dono gurai ni narimasu** ka?
> **(How long has it been since you came** to Japan?) or
> **(How long have you been in** Japan?)
> Buraun-san ga   Tanaka-san ni **atte kara moo dono gurai ni narimasu** ka?
> **(How long has it been since** Mr. Brown **met** Miss Tanaka?)

18.2   dono gurai

dono gurai is the expression Japanese use to ask about approximate quantity, cost, or length of time. When more specific infomation is desired, **dono** (which ---) can be replaced by **nanjikan** (how many hours), **nannichi** (how many days), **nanshuukan** (how many weeks), **nankagetsu**

(how many months) or **nannen** (how many years). When talking about quantity, one can use such words as **ikutsu** (how many) or **nammai** (how many sheets) to replace **dono**. Also, one can say **ikura gurai** to ask 'about how much.' The word **dono gurai** is vague in a sense, but it is sometimes more polite to be somewhat vague in asking certain questions--just as it is in English.

> anata ga nihon ni kite kara moo **dono gurai** ni narimasu ka?
>> (**How long** has it been since you came to Japan?)
> moo **dono gurai** nihongo o benkyoo shite imasu ka?
>> (**How long** have you been studying Japanese?)

18.3   ga marking the Subject of a Subordinate Clause

In a simple sentence, the particle **wa** normally marks the subject or topic of the sentence as in '**Buraun-san wa shichigatsu ni nihon e kimashita**' (Mr. Brown came to Japan in July). When such a sentence or clause is embedded within another sentence (and grammatically reduced to a subordinate clause), the particle **wa** is normally replaced by the particle **ga** to mark the subject or topic of the subordinate clause.

> **Buraun-san ga** nihon ni kite kara rokkagetsu ni narimasu.
>> (It's been six months since **Mr. Brown** came to Japan.)
> **anata ga** nihon ni kite kara moo dono gurai ni narimasu ka?
>> (How long has it been since **you** came to Japan?)

18.4   -kagetsu: Counter for Months

The counter **-kagetsu** is used to count months. The student should remember that when a counter begins with a voiceless consonant such as 'p,' 't,' or 'k,' some of the number words undergo modifications, as with the counters for slender objects or for animals.

ikkagetsu	[ichi + kagetsu]	(one month)
nikagetsu		(two months)
sankagetsu		(three months)
yonkagetsu		(four months)
gokagetsu		(five months)
rokkagetsu	[roku + kagetsu]	(six months)
nanakagesu		(seven months)
hakkagetsu	[hachi + kagetsu]	(eight months)
kyuukagetsu		(nine months)
jukkagetsu	[juu + kagetsu]	(ten months)
juuikkagetsu	[juuichi + kagetsu]	(eleven months)
juunikagetsu		(twelve months)

The writing of **-kagetsu** has recently undergone various changes: the syllable **-ka** of -kagetsu used to be written with a small **katakana** 'ケ' (ke). Then it was changed to a small 'カ' (ka) in **katakana**. Most recentlly, it has been changed to a regular-sized 'か' (ka) in **hiragana**. Native speakers may continue to write **-kagetsu** in the ways they originally learned, and the transcriptions of previously printed **-kagetsu** in books may also remain unchanged. The students of Japanese are thus advised to recognize these variations in transcribing **-kagetsu** as they read Japanese, while writing it correctly in the new way.

18.5   ni nareru

nareru is a verb meaning 'to get used to.' It takes the particle **ni** to mark the thing that someone is getting used to, such as 'life in Japan,' 'people in Japan,' or 'Japanese food.'

> moo   nihon no **seikatsu ni   naremashita** ka?
> > (Have you **gotten used to life** in Japan now?)
>
> Buraun-san wa   moo   **nihon-shoku ni   naremashita**.
> > (Mr. Brown **has gotten used to Japanese food**.)

18.6   sore wa soo to

sore wa soo to literally means to 'leave that [subject] as is.' This is the expression a Japanese speaker uses when he or she wishes to change the subject without offending his or her partner in a conversation. In English, such expressions as 'by the way,' or 'anyway' may be close equivalents.

> **sore wa soo to**, ima   dono hen ni   sunde imasu ka?
> > (**By the way**, which part of town are you living in now?)
>
> **sore wa soo to**, kyoo wa   nangatsu   nannichi desu ka?
> > (**By the way**, what is the date today?)

18.7   hoomusutei

hoomusutei (home stay) or **geshuku** is a word describing a special housing arrangement between a single person and the landlord who rents a room in his or her house. The arrangement is usually made by a mutual friend who believes the rental situation will be beneficial to both landlord and tenant. The landlord usually makes a 'room-and-board' arrangement with the prospective tenant, setting up monthly rent payments. After the tenant moves in, the landlord treats him or her as though he or she were a family member, and extends personal care and homelike housing accomodations.

18.8   aruite ... kakaru

aruite is the **-te form** of the verb **aruku** (walk), and **kakaru** is the verb meaning 'to take (in terms of time or cost).' **aruite ... kakaru** literally means 'by walking it takes such and such.' In English, we normally say 'it takes such and such (time) on foot.'

> basu de   juppun,   **aruite** sanjuppun gurai   **kakarimasu**.
> > (It **takes** ten minutes by bus and thirty minutes **on foot**.)

18.9   asobi ni kuru

asobi is related to the verb **asobu**, 'to enjoy oneself' or 'to play.' **ni** expresses purpose. **asobi**

231

ni kuru is the expression used in Japanese to refer to friendly visits by close friends or relatives. **asobi ni iku** (to go for a friendly visit) is also a common expression.

> kondo **asobi ni kite kudasai**.
>> (Please **come by to visit** some time.)
>
> kondo Buraun-san no uchi e **asobi ni ikimashoo**.
>> (Let's **go visit** Mr. Brown some time.)

18.10   Additional notes on the innovative use of katakana

In recent years, Japanese people have adopted a large number of loan words from foreign languages, especially from English. Along with the words innovative speakers borrowed some sounds that are not used in the native vocabulary. The sounds [f] and [v] as in 'fork' and 'violin' are written in **katakana** and innovative speakers use new devices to write [f] and [v].

> [fa, fi, fe, fo] are written ファ、フィ、フェ、フォ
>
> [va, vi, ve, vo] are written ヴァ、ヴィ、ヴェ、ヴォ
>
> |ti, di] are written ティ、ディ、

There are considerable variations in the use of **katakana**, particularly when writing personal and place names. It is wise to observe first how foreign words are adopted and how they are written by the majority of the speakers.

> ヴァイオリン   (violin)
> フィルム   (film)
> フォーク   (fork)

EXERCISES

18E.1   Oral translation: Say the following sentences in Japanese.

Example: How long has it been since you came to Japan?
    --> anata ga nihon ni kite kara moo dono gurai ni narimasu ka?

1. How long has it been since you came to Tokyo?
2. How long has it been since you came to California?
3. How long has it been since you came to this school?
4. How long has it been since you came to the United States?
5. How long has it been since you met Mr. Brown?
6. How long has it been since Mr. Brown met Miss Tanaka?

Example: How long have you been living in Japan?
    --> (anata wa) moo dono gurai nihon ni sunde imasu ka?

7. How long have you been living in Tokyo?

8. How long have you been living in this house??
9. How long have you been studying Japanese?
10. How long have you been studying Spanish?
11. How long have you been waiting here?
12. How long have you been watching TV?
13. How long has Mr. Brown been studying Japanese calligraphy?

18E.2 Response Drill: Student A and Student B take turn to ask qustions about Mr. Brown and his friend Mr. Yamada. Respond to each other's questions. (Review the information presented in Dialogues 17 and 18.)
Ask:

1. where Mr. Brown lives now
2. if Mr. Brown lives in an apartment or with a family
3. what kind of house Mr. Brown lives in
4. where Mr. Yamada lives
5. how far from Shinjuku Mr. Yamada's house is
6. if Mr. Brown is going to visit Mr. Yamada sometime
7. if Mr. Brown studies in the library everyday
8. how many hours he listens to the tape
9. what he does after getting home in the afternoon
10. what he did after eating dinner yesterday

18E.3 Activity: Asking questions. Work in pairs. Student A asks Student B the following questions in Japanese. Student B gives appropriate answers. Reverse the roles.
Ask:

1. where (in which part of town) he or she lives
2. if his or her residence is far from school or relatively near
3. if he or she comes to school on foot or by car
4. how long it takes to come to school
5. what his or her major is
6. which one of the two he or she likes better, chemistry or math

18E.4 Fill in the blanks with correct forms of the verbs suggested in the parentheses.

1. Buraun-san wa ima nihon ni (kuru)_____ imasu.

tookyoo de nihongo o benkyoo (suru) _____ imasu. getsuyoobi kara kin'yoobi made gakkoo ni (iku) _____ ,   benkyoo (suru) _____

____ . doyoobi to nichiyoobi ni wa ikimasen. kurasu ga (aru) _____

____ kara. taitei kaimono ni (dekakeru) _____ .

   2. ima gozen hachiji desu. Buraun-san wa asagohan o (taberu)

_____ imasu. Buraun-san wa koohii o (nomu) _____ imasu.

asa no shimbun o (yomu) _____ imasu. maiasa hachiji-han ni

gakkoo ni (dekakeru) _____ ,   kuji ni sensei ya tomodachi ni

(a[w]u) _____ . sorekara go-jikan gurai (benkyoo suru) _____

_____ . kurasu ga (owaru) _____ kara toshokan ni (iku)

_____ , shukudai o (suru) _____ .

18E.5 つぎのかんじを、ただしくかいて、おぼえなさい。

56. 来 (to come) 来る   一 ㄷ ㄇ ㅍ 平 来 来

57. 年 (year)   きょ年   丿 ㇉ 二 午 仁 年

58. 家 (house) 家・家   ` ㇔ 宀 宀 宁 宁 字 字

     字 家

59. 歩 (to walk) 歩く   丨 ㇉ 卜 止 歩 歩 歩 歩

60. 近 (near)   近い   ` 厂 ㇏ 斤 斤 近 近

61. 遠 (far)　　遠い　　一 十 土 吉 吉 吉 声 声

声 袁 袁 速 遠

62. 朝 (morning)　毎朝　　一 十 ㄈ 古 古 古 直 卓

朝 朝 朝 朝

18E.6　つぎのかんじに、読みがな／ふりがなをつけなさい。
(Assign correct **yomigana/furigana** to the **kanji** below.)

　　（　　）（　　）（　　）（　　　）（　　）
1. 勉強。　学校。　英語。　日本語。　毎朝。
　（　）（　）（　）（　）　（　）（　）　（　）（　　）
2. 本の上。　木の下。　水の中。　女の先生。
　　（　　　　）（　　　）（　　　）（　　　　）
3. 九月七日。　十月四日。　金曜日。　午後四時。
　　（　）（　）（　）（　）（　　）　　（　）
4. 話す。　読む。　男の人。　田中さんのお父さん。
　（　）（　）（　）（　）　　（　）（　）（　）
5. 大きい家。　今、何時ですか。　遠い。来る。時間。
　（　）（　）　　　（　）（　）（　）（　）　（　）
6. 山田。　お母さん。　手。目。口。　食べる。見る。

18E.7　つぎの文を、こえをだして、読んでごらんなさい。(Read the
following sentences aloud.)

1. ブラウンさんは、きょ年の七月に、日本に来ました。

日本へ来てから、もう、そろそろ六か月になります。
もう、日本のせいかつに、すっかり、なれました。

2. ブラウンさんの家は、学校から、そんなに遠くありません。

    せんから、毎朝、歩いて、学校に行きます。

3. 山田さんの家は、みたかのえきから、近いです。歩いて、三分ぐらいかかります。

4. 田中さんの家は、かなり遠いです。学校まで、一時間ぐらいかかります。毎朝、六時におきて、七時ごろ、朝ごはんを食べて、いそいで、学校にでかけます。

5. わたくしの家は、大学の近くです。歩いて五分ぐらいですから、こんど、あそびに来てください。

6. 今朝、朝ごはんに、コーヒーをのんで、トーストを三まい食べました。

7. ヴィクターさんが、カリフォルニア大学に来てから、もう、一年になります。

8. フォードさんが、ハワイ大学に来てから、もう、一年三か月になります。

19. ニューヨークから、サンフランシスコまで、ジェットで、六時間ぐらいかかります。

10. ハワイは、遠いです。ロサンゼルスから、ジェットで、五時間ぐらいかかります。いつか、行きましょう。

11. ワシントン D.C.から、ボストンまで、くるまで、何時間ぐらいかかりますか。

18E.8　こたえをかいてごらんなさい。(Write the answers to the following questions using as many **kanji** as you know.)

1. あなたは、毎朝、何時におきますか。
2. 朝ごはんに何を食べますか。
3. あなたは、今、どのへんに、すんでいますか。
4. あなたの家は、学校から近いですか、遠いですか。
5. それは、りょうですか、アパートですか。
6. 学校まで、歩きますか、くるまで、行きますか。
7. 何分ぐらい、かかりますか。
8. あなたは、毎日、何時間ぐらい、勉強しますか。
9. たいてい、どこで、勉強しますか。
10. しゅくだいは、一人でしますか、だれかといっしょに、しますか。

VOCABULARY

VERBS

kite (kara)	([after] coming: -te form of kuru + kara, 18.1)
kuru	(to come: irregular verb, 16.3, 16.4)
kimashita	(to have come; I came: -mashita form of kuru)
(ni) narimasu	(it comes to; it amounts to, 18.1)
naremashita	(I have become familiar with ...: -mashita form of nareru)
nareru	(to get used to [a situation]; to become familiar with such and such)
sunde imasu	(I am living: -te form of sumu + imasu)
sumu	(to live in or at; to reside at ...)
kakarimasu	(it takes such and such length of time: -masu form of kakaru, 18.8)
kakaru	(to take a certain length of time or amount of money, 18.8)
aruite	(on foot; to go by walking: -te form of aruku, 18.8)
aruku	(to walk, 18.8)
asobi ni kite kudasai	(Please come and visit, 18.9)
ukagaimasu	(I will visit; I'll drop in: -masu form of ukaga[w]u)
ukaga[w]u	(to visit; to go: humble verb)

237

ADJECTIVES

chikai	(near)
tooku arimasen	(not far: negative of tooi desu)
tooi	(far away; distant)

NOUNS

kyonen	(last year)
seikatsu	(life; living)
(dono) hen	(whereabout; in what neighborhood)
hen	(approximate point in space)
Yotsuya	(a place in central Tokyo) .
apaato	(apartment)
hoomusutei	(home-stay; a Japanese style room and board arrangement, 18.7)
Mitaka	(a residential section in the western part of Tokyo)
daigaku	(university; college)

OTHERS

-te kara moo ... ni naru	(it has been .... since I did such and such, 18.1)
dono gurai	(how long, 18.2)
ga	(a particle marking the subject of a subordinate clause)
-kagetsu	(month[s]: a counter for months, 18.4)
sore wa soo to	(by the way, 18.6)
shizuka (na)	(quiet: a copula noun)
soro soro	(nearly; gradually or slowly approaching)
sukkari	(completely; really; terribly)
warito	(relatively)
itsuka	(sometime)

ADDITIONAL VOCABULARY

Vikutaa	(the personal name 'Victor' as pronounced in Japanese)
Foodo	(the personal name 'Ford' as pronounced in Japanese)
Kariforunia	(the state name 'California' as pronounced in Japanese)
Hawai	(the state name 'Hawaii' as pronounced in Japanese)
Sanfuranshisuko	(the city name 'San Francisco' as pronounced in Japanese)
Rosanzerusu	(the city name 'Los Angeles' as pronounced in Japanese)
Nyuuyooku	(the city name 'New York' as pronounced in Japanese)
Washinton D.C.	('Washington D.C.' as pronounced in Japanese)
Bosuton	(the city name 'Boston' as pronounced in Japanese)
jetto	(jet: a loan word from English)
ryoo	(dormitory; student housing offered by the school)

19

田中　　　今度の日曜日に、何をするつもりですか。

ブラウン　かまくらに、行くつもりです。

田中　　　かまくらで、どんな所を見るつもりですか。

ブラウン　まず、大ぶつを見てから、ふるいおてらを、
　　　　　見るつもりです。

田中　　　それは、おもしろそうですね。

ブラウン　いっしょに、行きませんか。

田中　　　ええ、ありがとう。何時ごろに、出かける
　　　　　つもりですか。

ブラウン　なるべく、はやく、出かけたいんですが・・・

田中　　　そうですね。東京から、かまくらまで、一時間
　　　　　ぐらい、かかりますから。

ブラウン　そして、おてらを見てから、かいがんにも、
　　　　　行きたいんですが・・・

田中　　　それは、いいですね。じゃ、わたくしが、
　　　　　おべんとうに、おすしでも作りましょう。

ブラウン　じゃ、わたくしが、のみものを買って行きます。

田中　　　カメラを、もっていますか。

ブラウン　はい、もっています。じゃ、あたらしいカメラ
　　　　　をもって行きます。

Tanaka	kondo no nichiyoobi ni nani o suru tsumori desu ka?
Brown	kamakura ni iku tsumori desu.
Tanaka	kamakura de donna tokoro o miru tsumori desu ka?
Brown	mazu, Daibutsu o mite kara, furui otera o miru tsumori desu.
Tanaka	sore wa omoshirosoo desu ne.
Brown	issho ni ikimasen ka?
Tanaka	ee, arigatoo. nanji goro ni dekakeru tsumori desu ka?
Brown	narubeku hayaku dekaketai n desu ga...
Tanaka	soo desu ne. Tookyoo kara Kamakura made, ichi-jikan gurai kakari masu kara.
Brown	soshite, otera o mite kara, kaigan ni mo ikitai n desu ga...
Tanaka	sore wa ii desu ne. ja, watakushi ga obentoo ni osushi demo tsukurimashoo.
Brown	ja, watakushi ga nomimono o katte ikimasu.
Tanaka	kamera o motte imasu ka?
Brown	hai, motte imasu. ja, atarashii kamera o motte ikimasu.

ENGLISH EQUIVALENT

Tanaka: What are you planning to do this Sunday?

Brown: I'm planning to go to Kamakura.

Tanaka: What kind of places are you planning to see in Kamakura?

Brown: First, after seeing the Daibutsu, I plan to go see some historic [old] temples.

Tanaka: That sounds interesting.

Brown: How about going with me?

Tanaka: All right, thanks. What time are you planning to leave?

Brown: I'd like to leave as early as possible...

Tanaka: Right. Let's see. It takes about an hour from Tokyo to Kamakura.

Brown: And after seeing the temples, I also want to go to the beach.

Tanaka: That sounds good. Listen, I 'll make some sushi or something for lunch.

Brown: Okay. I'll buy some drinks.

Tanaka: Do you have a camera?

Brown: Yes, I do. I've got a new camera that I'll bring along.

GRAMMATICAL AND CULTURAL NOTES

19.1   tsumori

tsumori is a noun meaning 'intention' or 'a definite plan.' The word **tsumori** is usually preceded by a verb in its dictionary form to specify what one intends to do. In this construction, the verb is grammatically a clause modifier of the noun **tsumori**.

> nani o **suru**   **tsumori** desu ka?   (What do you **intend to do**?) or
> (What do you **plan to do**?)
> Kamakura ni **iku**   **tsumori** desu. (I **plan to go** to Kamakura.)
> donna tokoro o **miru**   **tsumori** desu ka?
> (What sort of places do **you plan to see**?)

19.2   Kamakura

The city of **Kamakura** is located southwest of Tokyo, and is a historical site famous for its temples and its huge bronze statue of Buddha which attracts many tourists and visitors, domestic and international. Because of its relative proximity to metropolitan Tokyo and to the Enoshima beaches, it is perhaps one of the most popular tourist sites near Tokyo. Educated visitors also enjoy visiting its old temples to recall events in the Kamakura period of Japanese history.

19.3   (omoshiro)soo

-soo is a bound copula noun which means 'to look like' or 'to sound like.' It is usually attached to the stem of an adjective to form a compound word. **omoshiro-** is the stem of the adjective **omoshiroi; omoshirosoo** is a compound word meaning 'it looks interesting.' **-soo** is a productive bound word which may be used in generating many expressions by following the above word formation rule.

> sore wa **omoshirosoo** desu ne.   (That **sounds interesting**.)
> sore wa **omoshirosoo na**   hon desu ne.
> > (That **looks like an interesting** book.)
>
> **oishisoo na**   keeki ga   arimasu.   (There's a cake that **looks delicious**.)

19.4   narubeku (hayaku)

narubeku means 'as ... as possible' and, when used with **hayaku** means 'as early (soon, quickly) as possible.' **narubeku** can be used with many other adjectives or adverbs of quantity or manner to form a number of useful expressions.

> **narubeku hayaku**   dekakemashoo. (Let's leave **as early (soon) as possible**.)
> **narubeku yasui**   mono o kaimashoo.
> > ([**As much as possible**] let's buy **inexpensive** things.)
>
> **narubeku yukkuri**   itte kudasai.   (Please say it **as slowly as you can**.)

19.5   -tai

-tai is a bound adjective meaning 'a strong desire' and is usually attached to the bound form of a verb to express the speaker's desire to perform the action indicated by the verb. The bound form of a verb is the portion of the verb to which the **-masu form** is attached: i.e. **tabe-** of **tabemasu**, **kiki-** of **kikimasu**, and **shi-** of **shimasu**. The bound form and the stem of a verb are the same in vowel verbs, but they are different in consonant verbs and irregular verbs: the filler **-i-** is added to the stem of a consonant verb before **-masu** or **-tai** can be attached, as in **yomimasu** and **yomitai** (the **-masu** and **-tai** forms of **yomu**).

Like **-soo**, **-tai** is a productive bound word which, in combination with many verbs, produces a number of useful expressions. However, adult speakers normally restrain their expressions of strong desire or modify such expressions by adding **-n desu ga** (the fact is ..., but) to make the expression gentle and more adult-like.

> narubeku   hayaku   **dekaketai n desu ga.**
> > (**I'd like to leave** as early as possible [**if you don't mind**].)
>
> otera o   mite kara   kaigan ni mo   **ikitai n desu ga.**
> > (After seeing temples, **I'd like to go** to the beach [**if it's okay with you**].)
>
> watakushi wa   **ikitaku   arimasen.**
> > (**I don't want to go**.)

19.6 motte (iru, iku, kuru)

motte is the **-te form** of the verb **motsu** (to have, to hold) and is often followed by the verbs **iru**, **iku**, or **kuru** to form three useful compound verbs. **motte iru** means 'to have' or 'to own,' and **motte iku** means 'to take,' 'to bring' or 'to carry something with oneself.' The third of these compound verbs, **motte kuru**, is a common expression meaning 'to bring.'

kamera o **motte imasu** ka?   (Do you **have** a camera?)
atarashii kamera o **motte ikimasu**.
                                              (I'll **take along** a new camera **with me**.)
okashi to   kudamono o   **motte kite** kudasai.
                                              (Please **bring [me]** some cookies and fruit.)

19.7   Additional katakana rules

The following lists shows additional rules to use katakana for innovated speech.

The 'th' sounds [θ] and [ð] do not occur in Japanese. They are usually replaced by [s] and [z], thus represented by ス or ズ.

スミスさんですか。   (Are you Ms. Smith?)
はい、キャシー・スミスです。   (Yes, I'm Cathy Smith.)

ブラザーミシン   (Brother Sewing machine)

The [w] sound occurs only before [a]. So, the syllables 'wi, we, wo' do not occur in Japanese. When Japanese people want to write English words containing these sound combinations, they normally combine ウ with small size symbols イ、エ、オ, as in ウィ、ウェ、ウォ.

ウェンディー   (Wendy)
ウェイトレス   (Waitress)
ウィンストン   (Winston)
ウォック   (Wok)

EXERCISES

19E.1 Grammar Drill: The instructor reads the following statements, and the student responds by saying that he or she also plans to do the same.

Example:

Instructor: Buraun-san wa ashita Kamakura ni ikimasu.
Student: watakushi mo ashita kamakura ni iku tsumori desu.

1. Buraun-san wa Kamakura de daibutsu o mimasu.
2. Tanaka-san wa Kamakura de furui otera o mimasu.

3. Buraun-san wa ashita no asa hayaku dekakemasu.

4. Tanaka-san wa ashita obentoo ni osushi o tsukurimasu.

5. Tanaka-san wa ashita kaigan de obentoo o tabemasu.

6. Buraun-san wa nomimono o katte ikimasu.

7. Buraun-san wa ashita kamera o motte ikimasu.

8. Buraun-san wa kondo no doyoobi ni kaimono ni ikimasu.

9. Yamada-san wa kondo no shuumatsu ni Tookyoo-tawaa ni noborimasu.

10. Chen-san wa kondo tomodachi to isshoni Fujisan ni noborimasu.

19E.2 Oral Translation: Say the following sentences in Japanese.

Example: What are you planning to do this Sunday?

--> kondo no nichiyoobi ni nani o suru tsumori desu ka?

1. What are you planning to do this weekend?
2. What are you planning to do this evening?
3. What are you planning to do tomorrow?
4. What are you planning to do after eating dinner tonight?
5. Where are you planning to go shopping?
6. Where are you planning to study this evening?
7. With whom are you planning to go to Kamakura?
8. At what time are you planning to leave home?

19E.3 Response Drill: Answer the questions according to the main dialogue.

1. Buraun-san wa kondo no nichiyoobi ni doko ni iku tsumori desu ka?
2. kamakura de daibutsu o miru tsumori desu ka, kaimono o suru tsumori desu ka?
3. daibutsu o mite kara nani o suru tsumori desu ka?
4. Buraun-san wa dare to isshoni iku tsumori desu ka?
5. nanji goro ni dekakeru tsumori desu ka?
6. Tanaka-san wa obentoo ni nani o tsukuru tsumori desu ka?
7. Buraun-san wa nani o katte iku tsumori desu ka?
8. Buraun-san wa atarashii kamera o motte iku tsumori desu ka?

9. Buraun-san to Tanaka-san wa doko de obentoo o taberu tsumori desu ka?

10. anata wa kondo no nichiyoobi ni nani o suru tsumori desu ka?

19E.4 Oral Translation: Say the following sentences in Japanese.

Example 1: I want to leave as soon as possible.
--> narubeku hayaku dekaketai n desu ga...

1. I want to go to Kamakura as soon as possible.
2. I want to see the Great Buddha as soon as possible.
3. I want to buy a new camera as soon as possible.
4. I want to go to Japan as soon possible.
5. I want to meet my calligraphy teacher as soon as possible.
6. I want to know the results of the exam as soon as possible.

Example 2: I want to go to the beach after seeing the temples.
--> otera o mite kara kaigan ni ikitai n desu ga...

7. I want to go to the beach after seeing the Great Buddha.
8. I want to see some historic (old) temples after eating our lunch.
9. I want to live in an apartment after getting used to life in Tokyo.
10. I want to go shopping after the final examinations are finished.
11. I want to go to the library after doing my chemistry homework.

19E.5 Number Review: Say the following numbers in Japanese.

1. 5; 13; 26; 38; 49; 52.
2. 63; 71; 88; 95; 100.
3. 300; 400; 500; 600; 700; 800; 900.
4. 1,200; 5,600; 3,562; 7,945; 2,306; 4,114.
5. 13,600; 33,200; 65,840; 99,357; 63,220.
6. 100,000; 200,000; 300,000; 450,000; 765,000.

Review the counters, and say the following senences in Japanese.

1. There are twenty students in this class.
2. There are twenty-five desks in this classroom.
3. We have three dogs at our house.
4. Please bring me three plates and six napkins.
5. Please bring me five pencils and five erasers.
6. I read two books yesterday.
7. My older brother has three cars.

19E.5　つぎのかんじをただしくかいて、おぼえなさい。

63. 度 (occasion)　今度　　　丶　亠　广　广　庐　庐　庐　庐

度

64. 所 (place)　所　　　丶　ヲ　ヺ　戸　戸　所　所　所

65. 出 (to go out)　出かける　丨　屮　屮　出　出

66. 東 (east)　東京　　一　亅　冂　㒼　百　車　東　東

67. 京 (capital)　東京　　丶　亠　六　古　古　亨　京　京

68. 作 (to make)　作る　　ノ　イ　仁　仁　作　作　作

69. 買 (to buy)　買う　　丶　冂　罒　罒　四　罒　罒　罒

罒　罒　買　買

19E.6 こえをだして、読んでごらんなさい。つぎに、かきとりをしてみましょう。(Read the following expressions aloud. Then prepare the material for dictation.)

1. 今度_{こんど}の木曜日。
2. 東京_{とうきょう}へ行く。
3. 遠い所_{ところ}。
4. 出_でかける。
5. 東京えきの出口_{でぐち}。
6. 朝ごはんを作_{つく}る。
7. カメラを買_かう。
8. 今度、山田さんと、勉強する。
9. 午後、英語のクラスへ、行く。
10. 田中さんの家まで、歩いて行く。

19E.7 つぎのかいわを、れんしゅうしてごらんなさい。
(Practice the following conversations.)

1. A: かまくらまで行きたいんですが、今度のバスは、何時ですか。
   B: 午後一時十分です。
   A: かまくらまで、どのぐらいかかりますか。
   B: 四十五分ぐらいです。
   A: かまくらまで、いくらですか。
   B: 二千五百六十えんです。

2. A: このしゃしんの中の女の人は、だれですか。

B: わたくしたちのフランス語の先生です。

A: やさしそうな先生ですね。

B: ええ、でも、この先生のクラスでは、毎日のように、しけんがありますから、わたくしは、毎ばん十二時まで、勉強します。

A: それは、いそがしそうですね。

19E.8 かんじに、読みがな／ふりがなをつけて、英語で、いみをいってごらんなさい。(Assign correct **yomigana/furigana** to the **kanji** below. Give the English equivalent of each sentence orally.)

    (   )   (   )

1. 東京からロサンゼルスまで、九時間かかります。

   (   )(   )(   )   (   )   (   )

2. 今度の金曜日の午後かまくらの大ぶつを見るつもりです。

               (   )   (   )(   )

3. なるべくはやく出かけて、いろいろな所へ行きましょう。

   (   )   (   )

4. 今度のしけんは、だめでした。勉強しませんでしたら。

             ( )(   )   (   )( )

5. わたくしは、きょ年の九月に、東京に来ましたから、

               ( )( )

もうそろそろ、八か月になります。

         (   )   (   )   (   )

6. ここから東京えきの出口まで、三分ぐらいかかります。

        (   )   (   )

そんなに遠くありません。わりと、近いです。

（　　）　　　　　　（　　）　　　（　　）

7. 今度いっしょに、買いものに行きませんか。

　　　　　　（　　）　　　　（　　）　（　　）

8. かまくらは、遠いですから、朝はやく出かけましょう。

19E.9　つぎのしつもんに、こたえてごらんなさい。ノートに、こたえをかきなさい。(Answer the following questions, writing the responses in your notebook.)

1. 今度の日曜日に、田中さんとブラウンさんは、どこに行くつもりですか。

2. 田中さんは、おべんとうに、何を作るつもりですか。

3. ブラウンさんは、何を買うつもりですか。

4. かまくらで、何を見るつもりですか。

5. あなたは、今度の日曜日に、何をするつもりですか。

19E.10　カタカナのふくしゅう。(**Katakana** review: Read and write the following personal names written in **katakana**.)

1. キャサリン
2. ヴィクター
3. ティファニー
4. ディック
5. デイビッド
6. クリストファー
7. ヴィンセント
8. ウィリアム
9. マイケル
10. ジョセフ
11. フィリップ
12. ベス

VOCABULARY

VERBS

mite (kara)	([after] seeing: -te form of miru)
ikitai	(I want to go: bound form of iku + tai, 19.5)
kaimashoo	(I will buy; let's buy: -mashoo form of ka[w]u)
ka[w]u	(to buy)
motte imasu ka?	(Do you have ...?: -te form of motsu + imasu + ka, 19.6)
motsu	(to have; to own; to possess)
motte iku	(to take along; to bring along, 19.6)
motte kuru	(to bring, 19.6)

ADJECTIVES

furui	(old; ancient; historical)
atarashii	(new)

NOUNS

Kamakura	(a famous historical site located southwest of Tokyo, 19.2)
daibutsu	(the Great Buddha, 19.2)
(o)tera	(Buddhist temple)
kaigan	(beach; seashore)
(o)bentoo	(boxed or sack lunch; picnic lunch)
kamera	(camera)

OTHERS

tsumori	(intention; plan: a noun usually preceded by a verb in its dictionary form, 19.1)
omoshirosoo	(looks like or sounds like fun: the stem of the adjective omoshiroi + soo, 19.3)
-soo	(to look like; to sound like: a bound copula noun, 19.3)
narubeku hayaku	(as early as possible; as soon as or as quickly as possible, 19.4)
narubeku	(as ... as possible, 19.4)
-tai	(want to; would like to: a bound adjective, 19.5)

ADDITIONAL VOCABULARY

kekka	(results)
fukushuu	(review of previous lesson)
yoshuu	(preparation for the next lesson)
-dai	(counter for machinery)

20

ブラウン　　　　あのう … すみませんが、このへんに、
　　　　　　　　くすり屋が、ありますか。

つうこう人　　　くすり屋ですか。ええと … えきのそばに、
　　　　　　　　一けんあります。

ブラウン　　　　えきは、どちらの方ですか。

つうこう人　　　あちらの方です。あそこに、くだもの屋が、
　　　　　　　　ありますね。あのかどを、右にまがって、
　　　　　　　　五十メートルほど、行ってください。二つ目
　　　　　　　　のしんごうで、今度は、左にまがります。
　　　　　　　　そうすると、えきの前に出ます。

ブラウン　　　　えきは、すぐわかりますか。

つうこう人　　　ええ、すぐわかります。前に、大きい銀行が
　　　　　　　　ありますから。

ブラウン　　　　くすり屋は、その近くですか。

つうこう人　　　そうです。銀行のとなりが、本屋です。
　　　　　　　　本屋のそばに、ゆうびんきょくがあって、
　　　　　　　　そのとなりが、くすり屋です。

ブラウン　　　　わかりました。どうも、ありがとうござい
　　　　　　　　ました。

つうこう人　　　いいえ、どういたしまして。

Brown: anoo... sumimasen ga, kono hen ni

            kusuriya ga arimasu ka?

Passerby: kusuriya desu ka? eeto... eki no soba ni

            ikken arimasu.

Brown: eki wa dochira no hoo desu ka?

Passerby: achira no hoo desu. asoko ni kudamonoya ga

            arimasu ne? ano kado o migi ni magatte,

            gojuu-meetoru hodo itte kudasai. futatsu me no

            shingoo de kondo wa hidari ni magarimasu.

            soo suru to eki no mae ni demasu.

Brown: eki wa sugu wakarimasu ka?

Passerby: ee, sugu wakarimasu. mae ni ookii ginkoo ga

            arimasu kara.

Brown: kusuriya wa sono chikaku desu ka?

Passerby: soo desu. ginkoo no tonari ga hon'ya desu.

            hon'ya no soba ni yuubinkyoku ga atte,

            sono tonari ga kusuriya desu.

Brown: wakarimashita. doomo arigatoo gozai

            mashita.

Passerby: iie, doo itashimashite.

ENGLISH EQUIVALENT

Brown: Umm... Excuse me, but is there a pharmacy around
            here?
Passerby: A pharmacy? Let me see... There's one near the train
            station.
Brown: Which way is the train station?
Passerby: It's over that way. See that fruit shop over there?
            Turn right at that corner and go about
            fifty meters. Then turn left at the second light, and
            you'll end up right in front of the station.
Brown: Will I be able to recognize the train station right away?
Passerby: Yes, you should. There's a big bank across
            the street.
Brown: Is the pharamcy near the bank?
Passerby: Right. Next to the bank is a bookstore. Near the bookstore
            is the post office, and next to the post office
            is the pharmacy.
Brown: All right, I've got it. Thank you very much.
Passerby: You're welcome.

GRAMMATICAL AND CULTURAL NOTES

20.1   -ya

The bound noun **-ya** means 'store,' and it is attached to other nouns to form the compound nouns comprising store names. As **-ya** is a bound word it cannot be used independently to mean 'a store.' The following store names are commonly used in daily conversations.

kusuriya	(pharmacy)
kudamonoya	(fruit shop)
hon'ya	(bookstore)
okashiya	(confectionary)
nikuya	(meat market)
sakanaya	(fish market)
pan'ya	(bakery)
hanaya	(florist)
yaoya	(green grocer)

20.2   -ken: Counter for Small Buildings

-ken is a counter used to count houses, stores and small buildings. The following list shows the sound changes involved when **-ken** is attached to numbers one through ten.

253

ikken	[ichi + ken]	(one house)
niken		(two houses)
sangen	[san + ken]	(three houses)
yonken		(four houses)
goken		(five houses)
rokken	[roku + ken]	(six houses)
nanaken		(seven houses)
hakken	[hachi + ken]	(eight houses)
kyuuken		(nine houses)
jukken	[juu + ken]	(ten houses)
nangen	(nani + ken)	(how many houses)

20.3   hoo

hoo means 'direction' or 'way to.'   When one wants to ask his or her way, he or she uses the phrase **dochira no hoo** (which way). In answering the question '**dochira no hoo desu ka?**' most people would point the way and say '**kochira no hoo**' (this way), '**sochira no hoo**' (that way), or '**achira no hoo**' (over that way).   When one wants to have more specific information as to the location of a place, he or she might use the word **doko** (where); in response to a question with **doko**, the words **koko**, **soko** or **asoko** are commonly used, as well as more detailed descriptions of places.

eki wa **dochira no hoo** desu ka?   (**Which way** is the station?)
achira no hoo desu.   (It's **over that way**.)

20.4   kado

kado is a noun meaning 'corner,' and it specifically refers to the outside corner of an enclosure, an object, or a defined rectangular space, such as a street corner or the outside corner of a bulding. There is another word, **sumi**, which refers to inside corners, such as the corner of a room.   Another example: **tsukue no kado** is a corner of a desk where one might accidentally hit oneself; **tsukue no sumi** is a corner on the desk top where one might leave a tray or a telephone.

ano **kado** o migi ni magatte kudasai.   (Please turn right at that **corner** over there.)
kado ni ginkoo ga arimasu.   (There is a bank at the **corner**.)

20.5   meetoru

meetoru is the Japanese word for the metric unit of length, the 'meter.'   In Japan--which has adopted the metric system--the 'meter' is the basic unit of length, and the 'gram' is the basic unit of weight.   The following words for units of length and weight are commonly heard in daily conversations.

meetoru	(meter[s])
senchi-meetoru	(centimeter[s])
miri-meetoru	(millimeter[s])
kiro-meetoru	(kilometer[s])
guramu	(gram[s])

kiroguramu   (kilogram[s])
gojuu-meetoru hodo   itte kudasai. (Please go about **50 meters**.)
kono niku o   **gohyaku guramu** kudasai.

(Please give me **500 grams** of this meat.)

20.6   hodo

hodo means 'approximately' and is used with reference to number, quantity, or distance. **hodo** and **gurai**, both meaning 'approximately,' can be used interchangeably in most cases. However, **hodo** sounds slightly more sophisticated

gojuu meetoru **hodo**   itte kudasai.   (Please go **about** 50 meters.)
mikan o   muttsu **hodo**   kudasai.   (Please give me **about** six tangerines **or so**.)

20.7   futatsume

-me, as in **futatsume** (the second), designates ordinal numbers, such as 'the first,' 'the second,' and 'the third' in English. In Japanese one must remember the correct counter for objects being counted in order to correctly form the appropriate ordinal numbers.

hitotsume no shingoo   (the first traffic signal)
futatsume no shingoo   (the second traffic signal)
mittsume no shingoo   (the third traffic signal)

hitorime no kodomo   (the first-born child)
futarime no kodomo   (the second-born child)
sannimme no kodomo   (the third-born child)

ikkemme no uchi   (the first house)
nikkemme no uchi   (the second house)
sangemme no uchi   (the third house)

issatsume no hon   (the first volume of a set of books)
nisatsume no hon   (the second volume of a set of books)
sansatsume no hon   (the third volume of a set of books)

20.8   soo suru to

The particle **to** added to a clause ending in the dictionary form means 'when' or 'if,' marking the preceding clause as a subordinate clause and limiting the time or the 'condition' of the event expressed by the main predicate verb. In English, one normally expresses a similar idea by saying, 'when such and such takes place, something happens,' or 'if you do this, that will happen.'

soo suru to eki no   mae ni   demasu.

(If you do that, you will end up right in front of the train station.)

migi ni magaru to ginkoo ga   arimasu.

(When you turn right you will see a bank.)

20.9   ni deru

deru is a verb meaning 'to appear,' 'to turn up,' or 'come to.' The place where one 'comes to' or 'ends up' is marked by the particle **ni**.

> eki no   **mae ni**   demasu.   ([You] end up **in front of** the station.)
> shingoo no   tokoro de   hidari ni   magatte, sakanaya no **soba ni**   demashita.
> ([I] turned left at the signal, and ended up **near** the fish market.)

20.10   tonari, soba

tonari refers to someone or something which is immediately next to the object in question. With reference to stores or houses, **tonari** is used to signify the immediate neighbor.

> **ginkoo no   tonari** ga   honya desu.
> (**Next door to the bank** is a bookstore.)
> honya no   soba ni   yuubinkyoku ga   atte,   **sono tonari** ga kusuriya desu.
> (There is a post office near the bookstore, and **next to tha**t is the pharmacy.)

20.11   Abbreviation in katakana words

Japanese people often abbreviate or shorten foreign loan words. The word 'television' is shortened to become **terebi** in Japanese. In stead of shortening it to T.V. the Japanese tends to take a beginning part of a word.

> デパート   (department store)
> ラボ   (laboratory)
> ハンカチ   (handkerchief)
> ノート   (notebook)

When an original foreign word ends in a consonant, Japanese loan word tends to have an added vowel.

> サラダ   (salad)
> ミルク   (milk)
> コップ   (cup)
> ボール   (ball)
> ビーフ   (beef)
> ケーキ   (cake)

The above examples are more or less standardized in the current use, but there are many words, especially personal names and place names, considerable variations can be observed in newspapers and magazines. It takes many years for any new words to settle in a language, and the use of **katakana** in current Japanese is no exception. One should be aware of these variations and select the most commonly used ones for writing. On this point it is better to consult your instructor or your Japanese friends.

> ロサンジェルス   or   ロスアンゼルス   (Los Angeles)

EXERCISES

20E.1   Activity: Finding the stores. Work in pairs. Student A is looking for the following places and asks Student B if he or she knows one nearby. Students B gives, each time, a different answer.

Example.   A: kono hen ni sushiya ga arimasu ka?
            B: eeto... eki no soba ni ikken arimasu.

1. bookstore
2. fruit shop
3. bakery
4. bank
5. post office
6. meat market
7. florist
8. pharmacy
9. train station
10. coffee shop

20E.2   Activity: Study the following map, and find out what merchandise or service each place offers. Then tell how to get to each place from the station.

本屋	銀行	カメラ屋	レストラン
にく屋	かばん屋	さかな屋	すし屋
パン屋	とけい屋	そば屋	やお屋
くすり屋	くだもの屋	はな屋	ベーカリー
本屋	きっさてん	くつ屋	スーパー
おかし屋	銀行	マクドナルド	ゆうびんきょく

えき

20E.3 Oral Translation: Say the following sentences in Japanese.

1. I want to buy some fish. Is there a fish market near here?
2. Please go about 50 meters and turn left.
3. Turn right at the third traffic signal.
4. There is a large florist and a bakery next to the bank.
5. The fish market is across the street from the bank. You can't miss it.
6. Please go about 100 meters and turn right at the corner.
7. I want to catch a taxi. Is there a taxi stand near here?
8. There is a taxi stand right in front of the train station.

20E.4 Number Review.

1. This camera was 55,000 yen.
2. This dictionary is 2,400 yen.
3. This raincoat is 36,000 yen.
4. Please go about 300 meters.
5. Mr. Kimura's telephone number is (310) 659-4577.
6. The bank opens at 10:00 A.M. and closes at 3:00 P.M.
7. The bakery opens from 9:00 A.M. to 6:00 P.M.
8. Today is Friday, February 24th.
9. There will be meeting on Wednesday, March 10th, from 2:30 P.M.
10. There are 19 students in this class.
11. I have three little dogs at home.
12. Please give me four bananas and three apples.

20E.5 Role Play: Bargain hunting. Work in pairs or small groups. Each student brings to class a flyer of supermarket sales. Each makes a shopping list and compare the prices of cheese, ham, bread, coke, fruits and vegetables with your partner. Find out the best prices for the items and decide which store to go. Then find out how to get to that place, how long it takes to get there.

20E.6 つぎのかんじを、ただしくかいて、おぼえなさい。

70. 屋 (store) くすり屋 　　ア ゴ 尸 尸 尸 居 居

屋 屋

71. 方 (direction) …の方 　　、 一 宁 方

72. 右 (right) 右 　　ノ ナ ナ 右 右

73. 左 (left) 左 　　一 ナ ナ ナ 左

74. 前 (in front) 前 　　、 ソ ソ 亡 芹 芹 芹

前 前

75. 銀 (silver) 銀行 　　ノ ノ ヒ ヒ 牟 牟 余

金 釒 釘 釘 鈤 鈤 銀

76. 百 (hundred) 百 　　一 ア ア 百 百 百

77. 千 (thousand) 千 　　ケ 二 千

78. 万 (ten thousand) 万 　　一 ア 万

79. 円 (yen) 円 　　｜ 冂 冂 円

20E.7 こえをだして、読んでごらんなさい。

1. 本屋。パン屋。どちらの方ですか。あちらの方です。
2. 右の方。左の方。前の方。銀行の前。大きい銀行。
3. 午前十時五分前。午後三時十分前。
4. 百円。三百円。六百円。八百円。千円。三千円。
5. 一万円。十万円。百万円。三百万円。

20E.8 つぎのかいわを、れんしゅうしてごらんなさい。

1. A: いらっしゃいませ。

   B: アスピリンを買いたいんですが... ありますか。

   A: はい、ございます。五百五十円でございます。

   B: それから、せっけんと、はブラシもありますか。

   A: はい、あちらにございます。

   B: じゃ、これで、いくらですか。

   A: 千三百円でございます。五千円おあずかりいたします。
      おまたせいたしました。 三千七百円のおつりです。
      ありがとうございました。

2. A: レインコートを見たいんですが、どこにありますか。

   B: レインコートは、三がいの左手にございます。

   A: じゃ、ほうせきうりばは、どこですか。

   B: 七かいの右手で、ございます。

   A: エスカレーターは、七かいまで行きますか。

   B: はい、まいります。あちらに、エレベーターもございます。

20E.9　かんじに、読みがな／ふりがなをつけなさい。つぎに、あいているところに、ただしいひらがなをいれなさい。

1．A:　レモン____買いたいんですが、このへん____、
　　　　くだもの屋____ありますか。
　　B:　ええと...　学校の近く____、一____ ____あります。
　　　　学校のもんの前____、本屋が____ ____ ____、
　　　　そのとなり____ 、くだもの屋です。

2．A:　東京大学は、どちら____ 方ですか。
　　B:　あちら____方です。あそこのかど____ 、左____
　　　　まがって、百メートル____ ____ 、行ってください。
　　　　かどに大きい銀行____ あります。その銀行の
　　　　かど____ 、今度は、右____ まがります。そうする
　　　　____ 、東京大学のもんの前____ 出ます。そんなに
　　　　遠____ ありません。

VOCABULARY

VERBS

magatte	(I turn and ...: -te form of magaru)
magaru	(to turn; to change course of direction)
(ni) demasu	(you turn up [at]...; I come to [the place of]: -masu form of deru)
atte	(there is ... and ...; I'll see ... and ...: -te form of aru)
itte kudasai	(please go: -te form of iku + kudasai)

ADJECTIVES　　(---)

NOUNS

kusuriya	(pharmacy; drugstore, 20.1)
tsuukoonin	(passerby)
hoo	(direction, 20.3)
kudamonoya	(fruit shop, 20.1)
kado	(corner; street corner, 20.4)

migi	(right; right-hand side)
shingoo	(traffic signal)
hidari	(left; left-hand side)
ginkoo	(bank, 20.1)
tonari	(next-door neighbor)
hon'ya	(bookstore)
yuubinkyoku	(post office)

OTHERS

-ya	(store: a bound noun usually suffixed to a noun indicationg a specific merchandise, 20.1)
ee to...	(let me see...)
(ik)ken	(one store: ichi + ken, 20.2)
-ken	(counter for stores and buildings, 20.1)
dochira no hoo	(which way to ..., 20.3)
futatsume	(the second object, 20.7)
-me	(a bound noun designating ordinal numbers, 20.7)
meetoru	(meter[s], 20.5)
hodo	(approximately, 20.6)
soo suru to	(if you do that, 20.8)
sugu	(immediately; right away)
sugu wakarimasu ka?	(Will I recognize it right away?)
chikaku	(nearby)
de gozaimasu	(it is: salesperson's honorific style of saying desu)

ADDITIONAL VOCABULARY

pan'ya	(bakery, 20.1)
pan	(bread)
hanaya	(florist, 20.1)
yaoya	(green grocer)
sumi	(inside corner)
senchi-meetoru	(centimeter, 20.5)
miri-meetoru	(millimeter, 20.5)
kiro-meetoru	(kilometer, 20.5)
guramu	(gram, 20.5)
kiroguramu	(kilogram, 20.5)
asupirin	(aspirin)
sekken	(soap)
haburashi	(tooth brush)
reinkooto	(raincoat)
sangai	(third floor)
hidarite	(on [your] left)
hooseki	(jewelry)
uriba	(department or section of a store; sales counter)
esukareetaa	(escalator)
erebeetaa	(elevator)
remon	(lemon)

21

ブラウン　田中さんは、音楽がすきですか。

田中　　　はい、大すきです。

ブラウン　何か、楽器をひくことが、できますか。

田中　　　すこし、ピアノをひくことが、できます。

ブラウン　もう、どのぐらい、ピアノをならっていますか。

田中　　　もう、五年ぐらい、ならっています。

ブラウン　じゃ、ずいぶん、じょうずでしょうね。

田中　　　いいえ、まだまだ、へたです。

　　　　　あんまり、れんしゅうしませんから。

ブラウン　わたくしは、楽器をひくことは、できませんが、
　　　　　音楽を聞くことや、歌を歌うことが、大すき
　　　　　です。

田中　　　どんな歌が、すきですか。

ブラウン　日本の歌が、一番すきです。「さくら、さくら」
　　　　　とか、「こうじょうの月」は、ほんとうに、
　　　　　いいですね。

田中　　　そうですか。わたくしは、クラシックの音楽が
　　　　　一番すきです。ベートーヴェンとか、モーツァルト
　　　　　などは、ほんとうに、すばらしいと思います。

ブラウン　わたくしの耳には、日本の「こと」や「しゃく
　　　　　八」の音が、一番美しく聞こえます。

Brown: Tanaka-san wa ongaku ga suki desu ka?

Tanaka: hai, daisuki desu.

Brown: nanika gakki o hiku koto ga dekimasu ka ?

Tanaka: sukoshi piano o hiku koto ga dekimasu.

Brown: moo dono gurai naratte imasuka?

Tanaka: moo gonen gurai naratte imasu.

Brown: ja, zuibun joozu deshoo ne.

Tanaka: iie, mada mada heta desu.

            ammari renshuu shimasen kara.

Brown: watakushi wa gakki o hiku koto wa dekimasen ga,

            ongaku o kiku koto ya, uta o utau kooto ga daisuki

            desu.

Tanaka: donna uta ga suki desu ka?

Brown: nihon no uta ga ichiban suki desu.

            'sakura, sakura' toka 'koojoo no tsuki' wa

            hontoo ni ii desu ne.

Tanaka: soo desu ka. watakushi wa kurashikku no ongaku ga

            ichiban suki desu. Beetooven toka Mootsuaruto nado wa

            hontoo ni subarashii to omoimasu.

Brown: watakushi no mimi ni wa nihon no 'koto' ya

            'shakuhachi' no oto ga ichiban utsukushiku kikoemasu.

ENGLISH EQUIVALENT

Brown: Do you like music?

Tanaka: Yes, very much.

Brown: Can you play any instruments?

Tanaka: I play the piano a little.

Brown: How long have you been taking piano lessons?

Tanaka: For about five years now.

Brown: Then you must be really good!

Tanaka: Oh, no, I'm still not very good because I don't practice much.

Brown: I can't play any instruments, but I love listening to music and singing songs.

Tanaka: What kind of songs do you like?

Brown: I like Japanese songs best. Songs like 'Cherry Blossoms' and 'The Moon Over the Ruined Castle' are really good, aren't they?

Tanaka: Are they? I like classical music best. I think [composers like] Beethoven and Mozart are really wonderful.

Brown: To my ears, the sounds of the koto and shakuhachi are the most beautiful.

GRAMMATICAL AND CULTURAL NOTES

21.1   (hiku) **koto ga dekiru**

koto is an abstract noun meaning 'fact,' and when it follows a verb in its dictionary (the plain, non-past) form, it functions similarly to the English infinitive 'to do [something]' as in 'I am able to (or can) play the piano,' or 'I am able to read Chinese.'

Grammatically, the verb preceding **koto** is a clause modifier of the noun **koto**. In Japanese, a subordinate clause is characterized by having its predicate in its plain form. The polite form, on the other hand, marked by **desu** or **-masu** or their variants, usually designates the main predicate of a sentence.

> nanika gakki o **hiku koto ga dekimasu** ka?
>> (Are you **able to play** any musical instruments?) or
>> (**Can** you **play** any musical instruments?)
>
> piano o **hiku koto ga dekimasu**.
>> (I am **able to play** the piano.) or
>> (I **can play** the piano.)
>
> Buraun-san wa nihongo o **hanasu koto ga dekimasu**.
>> (Mr. Brown **is able to speak** Japanese.) or
>> (Mr. Brown **can speak** Japanese.)

21.2   moo dono gurai . . . -te iru

moo dono gurai (how long by now) followed by a verb in its descriptive present (the **-te iru form**) gives the meaning, 'how long [you] have been doing [certain things].' This is one of the Japanese equivalents of the English present perfect tense. The **-te iru** implies that the activity started sometime in the past has continued until the present time and is still going on.

> **moo dono gurai** piano o **naratte imasu** ka?
> > (**How long have you been taking** piano lessons?)
>
> **moo gonen gurai naratte imasu**.
> > (**I've been learning for about five years.**)
>
> **moo dono gurai** nihongo o **benkyoo shite imasu** ka?
> > (**How long have you been studying** Japanese?)

21.3   Receiving Compliments

In English, when someone gives you a compliment you normally say 'thank you' to show appreciation or friendliness. As mentioned earlier (13.9), Japanese people try to be humble about receiving compliments and normally 'deny the words of a compliment' or say something to show their humility rather than 'accepting' a compliment by saying 'thank you.'

> ja **zuibun joozu deshoo ne!**   (Then, **you must be pretty good at it!**)
> **iie, mada mada heta desu**.   (**Oh, no. I'm still clumsy at it.**)

21.4   . . . koto ga suki

The grammatical construction of ... **koto ga suki** is basically the same as ... **koto ga dekiru** (21.1). The plain, non-past verb which precedes **koto** is the clause modifier of **koto** (fact or act). **uta[w]u koto** means the 'act of singing' or 'to sing,' and **suru koto** means 'act of doing or 'to do [such and such].' ... **ga suki** (introduced earlier) means 'pleasing' or '[I] like [something].' ... **suru koto ga suki** means '[I] like to do such and such.'

> uta o **uta(w)u koto** ga daisuki desu.
> > (I love **to sing** songs.)
>
> ongaku o **kiku koto** ga suki desu. (I like **to listen** to music.)

In English the same form of the verb 'listen' is used in the sentence 'I **listen** to music every day' (where 'listen' is the main verb) and in the sentence 'I love **to listen** to music every day' (where 'listen' is the predicate of a subordinate clause). In Japanese, the two sentences above must be expressed using different verb forms:

> watakushi wa mainichi ongaku o **kikimasu**.
> > (I **listen** to music every day.)
>
> watakushi wa mainichi ongaku o **kiku koto** ga suki desu
> > (I like **to listen** to music every day.)

21.5   ichiban suki

ichiban literally means 'number one' and expresses the idea of 'superlative' which English speakers would express by 'the best' or 'the [pretti]est.' **ichiban suki** means that someone 'likes something the best.' **ichiban** can be added to a word expressing quality to make up a number of expressions, such as **ichiban ookii** (the largest), **ichiban ii** (the best), **ichiban utsukushii** (the most beautiful). Copula nouns and other words often combine with **ichiban.**

> nihon no uta ga **ichiban suki** desu.
>> (I **like** Japanese songs **the best**.)
>
> watakushi wa kurashikku no ongaku ga **ichiban suki** desu.
>> (I **like** classical music **the best**.)
>
> nihon no shakuhachi no oto ga **ichiban utsukushiku** kikoemasu.
>> (The sounds of the Japanese shakuhachi are **the most beautiful**.)
>
> Buraun-san ga kurasu de **ichiban joozu** desu.
>> (Mr. Brown is **the best [most skillful]** in the class.)
>
> Fujisan ga nihon de **ichiban kirei na** yama desu.
>> (Mt. Fuji is **the prettiest** mountain in Japan.)

21.6   toka

As explained earlier (16.6), **toka** is a conjunctive particle meaning 'and.' **toka** is very similar to **ya** in meaning, and can be used interchangeably with **ya** in many cases. However, **toka** can be added to nouns, phrases, and clauses, while **ya** is usually added only to nouns.

> 'sakura sakura' **toka** 'koojoo no tsuki' wa hontoo ni ii desu.
>> ([Songs **such as**] "Cherry Blossoms" **and** "The Moon Over the Ruined Castle" are really good.)
>
> Beetooven **toka** Mootsuaruto nado wa   honto ni subarashii to omoimasu.
>> (I think [composers **like**] Beethoven **and** Mozart are really wonderful.)

21.7   to omo[w]u

omo[w]u is a verb meaning 'to think' or 'to hold in mind.' The particle **to** is used to mark the preceding clause as the content of someone's thought. Thus, **to** and **omo[w]u** usually go together. When a clause is followed by **to omo[w]u**, its predicate in the subordinate clause takes the **plain** form. The plain form construction has three types: the adjective construction, the noun construction and the verb construction.

Adjective Construction:
(Plain and Polite, Non-past)

The **plain non-past** form of a predicate adjective ends with the ending **-i**. This form is the same as its dictionary form. The **polite non-past** form of the predicate adjective, on the other hand, takes **desu** or its variants at the end.

(Plain)	sore wa **subarashii** to omoimasu.	(I think [**that**] it **is excellent**.)
(Polite)	sore wa **subarashii desu**.	(It **is excellent**.)

(Plain)	kanji wa **muzukashii** to omaimasu.	(I think [**that**] kanjis **are difficult**.)
(Polite)	kanji wa **muzukashii desu**.	(kanjis **are difficult**.)

Noun Construction:
(Plain and Polite, Non-past)

The plain non-past form of **desu** is **da**. The nouns take the plain non-past copula **da** when it is used as the predicate in the subordinate clause. As the main predicate of a sentence the nouns take **desu** after the nouns. In this position both the copula nouns and other regular nouns behave the same way. The copula nouns are more like adjectives in meaning but they behave just like the nouns in grammatical constructions.

Copula Nouns

(Plain)	Tanaka-san wa **kirei da** to omoimasu.	(I think [**that**] Tanaka-san **is pretty**.)
(Polite)	Tanaka-san wa **kirei desu**.	(Tanaka-san **is pretty**.)

(Plain)	Buraun-san wa **shinsetsu da** to omoimasu.	
		(I think [**that**] Mr Brown **is kind**.)
(Polite)	Buraun-san wa **shinsetsu desu**.	(Mr. Brown **is kind**.)

Nouns

(Plain)	Tanaka-san wa **nihonjin da** to omoimasu.	
		(I think [**that**] Tanaka-san **is Japanese**.)
(Polite)	Tanaka-san wa **nihonjin desu**.	(Tanaka-san **is Japanese**.)

(Plain)	sore wa **hon da** to omoimasu.	(I think [**that**] that **is a book**.)
(Polite)	sore wa **hon desu**.	(That **is a book**.)

Verb Construction:
(Plain and Polite, Non-past)

The plain non-past form of a verb is the same as the dictionary form. **to omo[w]u** is also added to the plain form of a verb. In the polite non-past form, a predicate verb ends with **-masu**.

(Plain)	ashita shiken ga **aru** to omoimasu.	(I think [**that**] there **will be** a test tomorrow.)
(Polite)	ashita shiken ga **arimasu**.	(There **will be** a test tomorrow.)

(Plain)	Buraun-san wa mainichi **benkyoo suru** to omoimasu.	
		(I think [**that**] Mr. Brown **studies** every day.)
(Polite)	Buraun-san wa mainichi **benkyoo shimasu**.	
		(Mr. Brown **studies** every day.)

The above examples are all in the non-past forms. They can be changed to their corresponding past forms, and also into the negative forms. These other forms will be presented later. It is important that the students master the plain non-past forms first.

21.8   ga kikoeru: an Intransitive Verb

kikoeru is an intransitive verb meaning ['to be audible' or to sound to [one's] ear.' The particle **ga** marks the subject of an intransitive verb, if no additional grammatical rules are applied.

shakuhachi no oto ga ichiban utsukushiku **kikoemasu**.

(The sounds of the shakuhachi **sound** the most beautiful.)

piano no oto ga **kikoemasu**.   (The sounds of the piano **are audible**.) or

(I **can hear** the piano sounds.)

EXERCISES

21E.1 Oral Translation: Say the Japanese equivalent of the following sentences.

Example 1. Can you play any musical instruments?

--> nanika gakki o hiku koto ga dekimasu ka?

1. Can you sing some Japanese songs?
2. Can you play the piano?
3. Can you write kanji?
4. Can you speak Spanish?
5. Can you read the Japanese newspaper?

Example 2. I like to sing songs.

--> (watakushi wa) uta o uta[w]u koto ga daisuki desu.

6. Mr. Brown likes to get up early every morning.
7. Mr. Brown likes to watch (see) T.V.
8. I like to listen to classical music.
9. I like to study Japanese in the library.
10. I like to walk to school every day.

Example 3. I like Japanese songs the best.

--> nihon no uta ga ichiban suki desu.

11. I like classical music the best.
12. I think that koto music is the most beautiful.
13. I think that Mr. Brown is the kindest person.

21E.2 つぎのかんじをただしくかいて、おぼえなさい。

80. 音 (sound) 音楽(おんがく)   ` 二 亠 立 产 音 音

音

81. 楽 (to enjoy) 音楽(おんがく)   ′ ′ 自 白 白 白 泊 泊

泊 楽 楽 楽 楽

82. 聞 (to hear) 聞(き)く   丨 丨 ſ ſ ſ 門 門 門

門 門 門 閂 聞 聞

83. 歌 (song) 歌(うた)   一 ſ 可 可 可 哥 哥

哥 哥 哥 歌 歌 歌

84. 番 (order) 一番(いちばん)   一 ′ 亠 立 平 平 采 采

番 番 番 番

85. 思 (to think) 思(おも)う   丶 口 日 田 田 思 思

思

86. 耳 (ear)　耳（みみ）　一 丁 丁 丐 臣 耳

87. 書 (to write)　書（か）く　フ ユ ユ ヨ ヨ 事 書 書
書 書

88. 美 (beautiful)　美（うつく）しい　丶 丷 丷 半 羊 美 美 美
美

21E.2 こえをだして、読んでごらんなさい。つぎに、書きとりをしてみましょう。(Pay special attention to the **kanji** that are read differently in different context. The different readings are called **yomikae**.)

1. 音楽（おんがく）を聞（き）く。　ピアノの音（おと）が聞こえる。

2. 耳（みみ）で、音楽を聞く。　目で本を読む。

3. ふじ山（さん）は、日本で一番美（うつく）しい山（やま）です。

4. ペンでかんじを書（か）く。　大きく書いてください。

5. 日本の歌（うた）を歌（うた）う。　日本の歌は、美しいと思（おも）う。

6. 銀行に行く。　大きい大学に行く。

7. 大学の前に、大きい本屋があると思います。

8. 銀行のかどを右にまがって、五十メートル行ってください。二つ目のしんごうで、今度は、左にまがります。

21E.4　つぎのしつもんに、こたえてごらんなさい。

1. 田中さんは、音楽がすきですか。

2. 田中さんは、ピアノをひくことができますか。

3. ブラウンさんは、何か楽器をひくことができますか。

4. ブラウンさんは、日本語を話すことができますか。

5. 田中さんは、もうどのぐらい、ピアノをならっていますか。

6. 田中さんは、よく、ピアノのれんしゅうをしますか。

7. ブラウンさんは、歌を歌うことがすきですか。

8. ブラウンさんは、どんな歌が一番すきですか。

9. あなたは、「さくら、さくら」をしっていますか。

10. あなたは、「こうじょうの月」をしっていますか。

11. 田中さんは、ベートーヴェンとか、モーツァルトが、すきですか。

12. あなたは、クラシックの音楽が、すばらしいと、思いますか。

13. ブラウンさんは、日本の「こと」や「しゃく八」がすきですね。

14. あなたの耳にも、「こと」や「しゃく八」の音楽が、美しく聞こえますか。

15. あなたは、歌を歌うことが、じょうずですか、へたですか。

21E.5　つぎのしつもんのこたえを、書いてごらんなさい。

1. 田中さんは、何か、楽器をひくことができますか。

2. ブラウンさんは、どんな音楽が一番すきですか。

3. あなたは、どんな音楽が一番すきですか。

4. あなたは、クラシックとジャズと、どちらの方が、
　すきですか。

5. 音楽とスポーツと、どちらの方が、すきですか。

6. どんなスポーツが、一番すきですか。

7. 歌を歌うことと聞くことと、どちらの方がすきですか。

8. 「こと」や「しゃく八」の音が、美しいと思いますか。

9. あなたは、もうどのぐらい、日本語を勉強していますか。

10. 田中さんは、もうどのぐらい、ピアノをならっている
　　と思いますか。

11. ブラウンさんは、もうどのぐらい、日本にすんでいる
　　と思いますか。

12. あなたの家から一番近い銀行まで、どのぐらいかかる
　　と思いますか。

13. 日本で一番美しい山は、どの山だと思いますか。

VOCABULARY

VERBS

hiku	(to play a musical instrument)
naratte imasu	(I am learning; I am taking lessons: -te form of nara[w]u + imasu)
nara[w]u	(to learn; to take lessons)
uta[w]u	(to sing a song)
kikoemasu	(I can hear; [something] is audible: -masu form of kikoeru, 21.8)
kikoeru	(to be audible: an intransitive verb, 21.8)

ADJECTIVES

subarashii	(excellent; wonderful)
utsukushiku	([something looks or sounds] beautiful: -ku form of utsukushii)

NOUNS

ongaku	(music)
gakki	(musical instrument)
piano	(piano)
nen	(year)
joozu (na)	(to be skillful at; to be good at)
heta (na)	(to be unskillful at; to be not good at)
uta	(song)
Sakura, Sakura	(the title of a famous Japanese song praising the beauty of cherry blossoms)
sakura	(cherry tree; cherry blossoms)
Koojoo no Tsuki	(the title of a famous Japanese song about the moon over a ruined castle)
kurashikku	(classical [music])
Beetooven	(Beethoven, a famous composer)
Mootsaruto	(Mozart, a famous composer)
mimi	(ear[s])
koto	(a Japanese string instrument [place an accent on the first syllable])
shakuhachi	(a Japanese-style flute)
oto	(sound)

OTHERS

koto ga dekiru	(to be able to do ..., 21.1)
moo donogurai ... -te iru	(how long have [you] been [do]ing ..., 21.2)
(go)nen	([five] years: a counter for years)
mada mada	(still; not yet: 'mada' repeated for emphasis, 21.3)
koto ga suki	(to like to [do such and such], 21.4)
ichiban (suki)	(the best; the most; I [like] ... the best, 21.5)
(A) toka (B) toka	([A] and [B] and such things, 21.6)

ADDITIONAL VOCABULARY

jazu	(jazz)
supootsu	(sports)

22

山田	ブラウンさん、あなたは、日光（にっこう）へ行ったことが、ありますか。
ブラウン	いいえ、まだ、行ったことが、ありません。
山田	日光について、聞いたことが、ありますか。
ブラウン	はい、聞いたことは、あります。日光は、大変（たいへん）美しい所でしょう。
山田	そうです。たきや、みずうみで、有名（ゆうめい）です。
ブラウン	それから、有名なとうしょうぐうもありますね。しゃしんで、見たことが、あります。
山田	じゃ、はこねには、行ったことが、ありますか。
ブラウン	はい、先月（せんげつ）、かまくらに行った時、はこねにも、行ってみました。
山田	はこねに行った時、おんせんに、入（はい）りましたか。
ブラウン	いいえ、おんせんには、入りませんでした。
山田	はこねは、高（たか）い山や、ふかいたにで、有名です。
ブラウン	そうでしょうね。バスで山を下（くだ）った時、何（なん）だか、少（すこ）し、こわかったです。でも、天気（てんき）がよくて、けしきがすばらしかったので、たくさん、しゃしんをとりました。
山田	日光は、もっと美しいですよ。
ブラウン	そうですか。それは、楽（たの）しみです。

Yamada: Buraun-san, anata wa Nikkoo e itta koto ga arimasu ka?

Brown: iie, mada itta koto ga arimasen.

Yamada: Nikkoo ni tsuite kiita koto ga arimasu ka?

Brown: hai, kiita koto wa arimasu. Nikkoo wa taihen utsukushii tokoro deshoo?

Yamada: soo desu. taki ya mizuumi de yuumei desu.

Brown: sore kara yuumei na tooshooguu mo arimasu ne? shashin de mita koto ga arimasu.

Yamada: ja, Hakone ni wa itta koto ga arimasu ka?

Brown: hai, sengetsu kamakura ni itta toki, Hakone ni mo itte mimashita.

Yamada: Hakone ni itta toki onsen ni hairimashita ka?

Brown: iie, onsen ni wa hairimasen deshita.

Yamada: Hakone wa takai yama ya fukai tani de yuumei desu.

Brown: soo deshoo ne. basu de yama o kudatta toki, nandaka sukoshi kowakatta desu. demo tenki ga yokute keshiki ga subarashikatta node, takusan shashin o torimashita.

Yamada: Nikkoo wa motto utsukushii desu yo.

Brown: soo desu ka. sore wa tanoshimi desu.

ENGLISH EQUIVALENT

Yamada: Mr. Brown, have you ever been to Nikko?

Brown: No, I haven't been there yet.

Yamada: Have you heard of Nikko?

Brown: Yes, I have heard of it. Nikko is a very beautiful place, isn't it?

Yamada: That's right. It's famous for its waterfalls and its lake.

Brown: And there's also the famed Toshogu, isn't there?
        I have seen pictures of it.

Yamada: Let's see, have you ever been to Hakone?

Brown: Yes, when I went to Kamakura last month, I also went there.

Yamada: When you were in Hakone, did you go in a hot spring?

Brown: No, I didn't go in a hotspring.

Yamada: Hakone is famous for its high mountains and deep gorges.

Brown: I am sure it is. I was a little scared when we were descending from the
        mountain by bus. But the scenery was fantastic, so I took a lot of
        pictures.

Yamada: Nikko is even more beautiful.

Brown: Really? I am looking forward to [seeing] it.

GRAMMATICAL AND CULTURAL NOTES

22.1   **itta:** the -ta form or the Plain Past Form

itta is the **-ta** form of the verb **iku** (to go). **-ta** is an inflectional verb ending which marks a verb as being in the **plain past** form. The **polite past** equivalent of the same verb, **iku**, is **ikimashita**. The main predicate verb of a sentence in past tense will be in the **-mashita** form in the **desu -masu** style of standard usage. But when a past tense verb is used in a subordinate clause, it is marked by the **plain past** form or the **-ta** form. The adjective, the noun, and the verb constructions follow different rules to form the **plain past** forms just like the non-past forms are made.

**Verb Construction:
(Plain and Polite, Past)**

The **-ta** form of a verb is formed by changing the vowel sound [**e**] of the **-te** form to [**a**]: **tabete** changes to **tabeta**, **itte** to **itta**, **yonde** to **yonda**, and so forth.

(Plain)	Nikkoo ni **itta** toki...	(When I **went** to Nikko...)
(Polite)	Nikkoo ni **ikimashita.**	(I **went** to Nikko.)
(Plain)	Sushi o **tabeta** toki...	(When I **ate** sushi...)
(Polite)	Sushi o **tabemashita.**	(I **ate** sushi.)

Adjective Construction:
(Plain and Polite, Past)

(Plain)   yama ga **utsukushikatta** node...   (Because the mountains **were beautiful** ...)
(Polite)   yama ga **utsukushikatta desu**.   (The mountains **were beautiful**.)

(Plain)   tenki ga **yokatta** node...   (Because the weather **was good**...)
(Polite   tenki ga **yokatta desu**.   (The weather **was good**.)

(Plain)   **kowakatta** node...   (Because it **was scary**...)
(Polite)   **kowakatta desu**.   (It **was scary**.)

Noun Construction:
(Plain and Polite, Past)

Copula Nouns

(Plain)   yama wa **kirei datta** node...   (Because the mountain **was pretty**...)
(Polite)   yama wa **kirei deshita**.   (The mountain **was pretty**.)

(Plain)   Tooshooguu wa **rippa datta**. node...
                                   (Because Toshogu **was magnificent**...)
(Polite)   Tooshooguu wa **rippa deshita**.   (Toshogu **was magnificent**.)

Nouns

(Plain)   kinoo wa **nichiyoobi datta** node...
                                     (Because yesterday **was Sunday**...)
(Polite)   kinoo wa **nichiyoobi deshita**.   (Yesterday **was Sunday**.)

(Plain)   **getsuyoobi datta** to omoimasu
                                     (I think [that] it **was Monday**.)
(Polite)   **getsuyoobi deshita**.   (It **was Monday**.)

22.2   -ta koto ga aru

-ta koto ga aru is an idiomatic expression which literally means 'the fact of having done certain things exists in one's life experience,' or 'someone has done something.' In English one would normally use the present perfect tense to express the same idea: 'Have you ever been to Japan?' or 'I have never seen such a thing.'

    Nikkoo ni **itta koto ga arimasu** ka?
                    (**Have you ever gone [been]** to Nikko?)
    iie, mada **itta koto ga arimasen**.
                    (No, **I have never gone [been]** there before.)
    Nikkoo ni tsuite **kiita koto ga arimasu** ka?
                    (**Have you ever heard** about Nikko?)

22.3 . . . de yuumei

yuumei is a copula noun meaning 'famous.' The thing something or someone is famous for is marked by the particle **de**. When **yuumei** is used to modify a noun it is followed by **na**.

> Nikkoo wa taki ya mizuumi **de yuumei** desu.
> > (Nikko is **famous for** its waterfalls and its lake.)
>
> **yuumei na Tooshooguu** mo arimasu.
> > (There is also **the famous Toshogu Shrine.**)
>
> Hakone wa **nan de yuumei** desu ka?
> > (**What** is Hakone **famous for?**)

22.4 Nikkoo, Hakone

Nikkoo is a famous tourist site located north of Tokyo, separated from the city by a two-hour ride by train or car. **Nikkoo** is located in one of the most beautiful mountainous areas in Japan, with breathtaking waterfalls, a tranquil lake, and several scenic drives. The most important attraction of Nikko (the word is spelled with one o in English but this long vowel is written **o o** in Japanese) is the famous Toshogu Shrine which displays many architectural splendors: its exquisite wall carvings and abundant sculptural masterpieces are a 'must' for anyone to see. The Japanese say, 'Don't say kekkoo (I'm okay) until after you've seen Nikkoo.'

Hakone is a famous resort area located southwest of Tokyo, again separated from the city by a two-hour drive. **Hakone** is famous for its hot springs and its scenic drives along steep mountain roads and deep gorges. Volcanic activities in the past created many beautiful lakes in the **Hakone** area. Volcanic activities still continue in some places where one can see white steam and hot water bubbling out from cracks on the ground or from between rocks. It is possible for a visitor to visit both **Kamakura** and **Hakone** in a single day, since many well-planned tours are available for this famous sight-seeing 'package.' Mt. Fuji is fairly close to **Hakone**, so some people extend the tour an additional day to cover Mt. Fuji and its five lakes.

22.5 shashin de miru

shashin de miru means that the speaker has seen the object or person in a photograph, but not in real contact. Here, **de** means 'by means of,' and is essentially the same 'agency' particle introduced earlier. In English, the idea of [shashin] **de** [miru] is expressed using 'in' or 'on.'

> **shashin de** mita koto ga arimasu. (I've seen it **in a photograph.**)
> **terebi de** mita koto ga arimasu.   (I've seen that **on T.V.**)
> **rajio de** kiita koto ga arimasu.   (I've heard about it **on the radio.**)

22.6 sengetsu and other Time Words

sen- of **sengetsu** means 'the past,' and **-getsu** means 'month': the word **sengetsu**, then, refers to 'last month.' The following list explains similar compound words that are useful in daily conversations. Some of these have already been introduced.

kongetsu	(this month)	konshuu	(this week)
sengetsu	(last month)	senshuu	(last week)
raigetsu	(next month)	raishuu	(next week)
kotoshi	(this year)	kyoo	(today)
kyonen	(last year)	kinoo	(yesterday)
rainen	(next year)	ashita	(tomorrow)

22.7 toki

toki is a noun meaning 'point in time,' and it can be preceded by a verb in its plain form to make a subordinate clause meaning 'when such and such happen(ed) ...' **toki**, together with a clause modifier, specifies the point in time of the event or condition in the main predicate. Thus, in the sentence '**Kamakura ni itta toki, Hakone ni mo itte mimashita,**' the time of the main predicate, '**Hakone ni mo itte mimashita** (I also visited Hakone) is specified by the subordinate clause '**Kamakura ni itta toki**' (when I went to Kamakura).

> sengetsu Kamakura ni **itta toki**, Hakone ni mo itte mimashita.
> > (**When I went** to Kamakura last month, I also visited Hakone.)
>
> Hakone ni **itta toki** onsen ni hairimashita ka?
> > (Did you take a dip in the hot springs **when you went** to Hakone?)
>
> basu de yama o **kudatta toki**, sukoshi kowakatta desu.
> > (**When we drove down** the mountains, I was a bit scared.)

22.8 -te miru

A verb in its **-te** form followed by **miru** (to see) is an idiom meaning 'to try to do such and such,' or 'to do such and such to find out how [something] is.' In daily conversations, Japanese speakers use this expression quite often.

> Kamakura ni itta toki Hakone ni mo **itte mimashita**.
> > (When I went to Kamakura, I also **went** to Hakone [**to see how it was**].)
>
> kondo Hakone ni **itte mimashoo**.
> > (**Let's go and see** Hakone sometime [**to find out how it is**].)
>
> kanji de **kaite mimashoo**.   (**Let's try to write** [that word] in kanji.)

22.9 node

node means 'because,' and is used to mark a subordinate clause indicating the reason or cause for the event reported in the main predicate of the sentence. The subordinate clause marked by **node** usually precedes the main clause. The meanings of **kara** (meaning 'because' introduced earlier) and **node** are the same, but they differ slightly in their grammatical positions. **kara** is usually added to polite forms (**desu** or **-masu** and their variants), while **node** usually follows plain forms to mark a subordinate clause. (The plain past form of an adjective is marked by the ending **-katta**, while the polite past form is marked by **-katta desu**.)

keshiki ga **subarashikatta node** takusan shashin o torimashita.

(**Because** the scenery **was superb**, I took many pictures.)

kinoo wa otenki ga **yokatta node** Fujisan ga miemashita.

(**Because** the weather **was good** yesterday, Mt.Fuji could be seen.)

Buraun-san wa takusan **benkyoo shita node** gakki-shiken ga yoku dekimashita.

(Mr. Brown did pretty well at the final examinations **because** he **studied** a lot.)

22.10 yo

The particle **y o** is usually added at the end of an utterance to indicate that the speaker is placing emphasis on or confidence in what he or she is saying. In spoken English, emphatic intonation or a short expression such as 'I tell you' or 'believe me' are used to convey the same message. In written English, an exclamation point may be used.

Nikkoo wa motto utsukushii desu **y o**.

(Nikko is more beautiful [than that], **I'm telling you**.)

Buraun-san wa subarashii hito desu **y o**.

(**I tell you**, Mr. Brown is really a wonderful person.)

dame desu **y o**!

(Oh, no. Don't do that!)

EXERCISES

22E.1 First, change each of the following verbs (listed here in the dictionary forms) to the "**-te + imasu**" and "**-ta koto ga arimasu**" forms. Write these forms correctly in the spaces provided.

1. 食べる。 食べています。 食べたことがあります。
2. 見る。 _____ _____
3. 聞く。 _____ _____
4. 行く。 _____ _____
5. 来る。 _____ _____
6. 下る。 _____ _____
7. とる。 _____ _____
8. 作る。 _____ _____
9. 歩く。 _____ _____
10. 買う。 _____ _____

Second, compose a short sentence using each of the above verb forms correctly supplying other necessary words.

22E.2 Activity: Wonderful Trips. Work in pairs. Student A asks Student B about the following questions about a foreign trip. Student B tells about his or her experiences and asks Student A similar questions.

Ask: 1. if he/she has been to any foreign countries
2. where he/she went
3. what sort of place it was
4. what he/she did when he/she went there
5. if he/she bought anything there
6. if he/she wants to go there again

22E.3 Read 1~6 and a~f. Select a plausible reason for each statement, connect the two with the word ので and write the resulting sentences.

Statements:

1. 今、日本語の勉強をしています。
2. もう一度日光へ行って、しゃしんをとるつもりです。
3. 今、ケーキを作っています。
4. 今度、はこねに行くつもりです。
5. よくねることができませんでした。.
6. 買いませんでした。

Reasons:

a. ブラウンさんのおたんじょうパーティーがあります。
b. みずうみが、大変、きれいでした。
c. おんせんに、入ってみたいです。
d. ゆうべ、コーヒーをたくさんのみました。
e. きぬのかさは、とても高かったです。
f. あした、かんじのしけんがあります。

22E.4　つぎのかんじをただしく書いて、おぼえなさい。

89.　光　(to shine)　日光　　ノ ⺌ ⺌ 业 业 光

90.　変　(to change)　大変　　ヽ 亠 亠 古 亦 亦 亦 変

変

91.　有　(to have)　有名　　ノ ナ オ 有 有 有

92.　名　(name)　有名　　ノ ク タ タ 名 名

93.　入　(to enter)　入る　　ノ 入

94.　高　(high)　高い　　ヽ 亠 亠 古 古 戸 高 高

高高

95.　少　(a little)　少し　　亅 小 小 少

96.　天　(heaven)　天気　　一 二 チ 天

97.　気　(feeling)　天気　　ノ ⺈ 仁 气 気 気

22E.5 こえをだして、読んでごらんなさい。つぎに、書きとりをしてみましょう。

1. 日光（にっこう）は、大変（たいへん）美しい所です。たきで有名（ゆうめい）な所です。
2. 先月、はこねに行った時、おんせんに入（はい）りました。
3. 高（たか）い山を下（くだ）った時、少（すこ）しこわかったです。
4. 天気が大変よかったので、高い山の上で、歌を歌いました。とても美しく、聞こえました。
5. 東京タワーは、大変高いです。天気のいい日には、タワーの上から、遠い所が見えます。

22E.6 つぎのしつもんに、こたえてごらんなさい。

1. あなたは、日光に行ったことがありますか。
2. 日光について、聞いたことがありますか。
3. あなたは、日光のしゃしんを見たことがありますか。
4. 日光は、どんな所ですか。何で有名ですか。
5. 日光は、東京から、何時間ぐらい、かかりますか。
6. はこねは、どんな所ですか。行ってみたいですか。
7. あなたは、おんせんに入ったことがありますか。
8. 日本には、高い山や、美しいみずうみが、たくさん、ありますね。

22E.7   Fill in the blanks with correct particles.

　東京＿＿ ＿＿日光＿＿ ＿＿ 二時間ぐらいかかります。

日光＿＿ たき＿＿ みずうみ＿＿ 有名です。

それから、有名＿＿ とうしょうぐう＿＿ あります。

　先月、はこね＿＿ 行った時、天気＿＿ よくて、けしき＿＿

すばらしかった＿＿ ＿＿、山の上＿＿ しゃしん＿＿ とり

ました。はこね＿＿ おんせん＿＿ 入りました。大変たのし

かったですが、バス＿＿ 山＿＿ 下った時は、少し、こわかっ

たです。今度、もう一度、行ってみたい＿＿ 思います。

22E.8   Write the best Japanese equivalent of the following sentences, using **kanji** for underlined words.

1. <u>When</u> I <u>went</u> to <u>Nikko</u> <u>last</u> <u>month</u>, I took many pictures.
2. <u>Japan</u> is <u>famous</u> for its hot springs and <u>beautiful</u> <u>mountains</u>.
3. Have you ever <u>seen</u> the Great Buddha in photos?
4. Since the <u>weather</u> was so good yesterday, we took lots of pictures.
5. Have you ever <u>listened</u> to koto <u>music</u> on the radio?

VOCABULARY

VERBS

itta (koto ga arimasu)	(I have been [there]; I have gone [there] before: -ta form of iku, 22.2)
kiita	(I have heard: -ta form of kiku, 22.2)
mita	(I have seen: -ta form of miru)
itte miru	(to go and see [how it is], 22.8)
hairimashita	(I went into; I took a dip in: -mashita form of hairu)
hairu	(to enter; to go in)
kudatta	(I descended; I went down [the hill]: -ta form of kudaru)
kudaru	(to descend; to go down)
torimashita	(I took; I have taken: -mashita form of toru)
toru	(to take)
haitta	(I have entered: -ta form of hairu, 22.1)

ADJECTIVES

fukai	(deep)

kowakatta	(I was scared: -katta form of kowai, 22.1)
kowai	(scary; frightening)
subarashikatta	([it] was wonderful: -katta from of subarashii)
warukatta	([it] was bad: -katta from of warui)
warui	(bad)

NOUNS

Nikkoo	(a famous cultural site north of Tokyo, 22.4)
taki	(waterfall)
mizuumi	(lake)
Tooshooguu	(a famous shrine in Nikko, 22.4)
shashin	(photograph; picture)
Hakone	(a scenic national park southwest of Tokyo, 22.4)
sengetsu	(last month, 22.6)
toki	(time; when [something happened], 22.7)
onsen	(hotspring)
yama	(mountain)
tani	(valley; gorge)
keshiki	(scenery)
tanoshimi	(something to look forward to)

OTHERS

-ta koto ga aru	(I have done [such and such], 22.2)
ni tsuite	(concerning; about; on the subject of)
taihen	(extremely; very)
yuumei (na)	(famous: a copula noun, 22.3)
de (yuumei)	([famous] for [such and such], 22.3)
(shashin) de miru	(to see [something] in [photographs], 22.5)
-te miru	(to do [such and such] and see [how it is], 22.8)
nandaka	(somehow; rather)
node	(because, 22.9)
yo	(emphasis, 22.10)

ADDITIONAL VOCABULARY

kongetsu	(this month, 22.6)
konshuu	(this week, 22.6)
senshuu	(last week, 22.6)
raigetsu	(next month, 22.6)
raishuu	(next week, 22.6)
kotoshi	(this year, 22.6)
kyonen	(last year, 22.6)
rainen	(next year, 22.6)

23

田中　春、夏、秋、冬の中で、どのきせつが、一番
　　　すきですか。

ブラウン　わたくしは、夏が、一番すきです。

田中　どうしてですか。

ブラウン　夏には、夏休みがあって、海に行ったり、山に
　　　行ったり、できるからです。

田中　わたくしは、夏より、冬の方がすきです。

ブラウン　どうしてですか。

田中　冬には、クリスマスやお正月があって、パーティー
　　　に行ったり、友だちとあそんだりできるからです。

ブラウン　それもそうですね。わたくしは、日本の春も、
　　　大すきです。春には、ひなまつりもあるし、
　　　さくらの花もさきますから。

田中　それはそうと、今日は、何月何日ですか。

ブラウン　今日は、二月二十日です。

田中　じゃ、もうすぐ、ひなまつりですね。うちでも、
　　　おひなさまをかざりますから、よかったら、見
　　　に来てください。

ブラウン　それは、ありがとうございます。おひなさまは、
　　　まだ、しゃしんでしか見たことがないので、ぜひ
　　　一度、見たいと思っていました。

田中　じゃ、ちょうどよかったですね。

ENGLISH EQUIVALENT

Tanaka: Out of spring, summer, fall, and winter, which season do you like the best?

Brown: I like summer the best.

Tanaka: Why?

Brown: Because in the summer you have summer vacation, and you can go to the beach and the mountains.

Tanaka: I like winter better than summer.

Brown: Why?

Tanaka: Because Christmas and New Year's come during the winter, and you can go to parties and have fun with friends.

Brown: That's true. I also like spring in Japan very much because the Doll Festival comes in the spring and the cherry blossoms bloom, too.

Tanaka: By the way, what's the date today?

Brown: Today is February 20th.

Tanaka: Then the Doll Festival is coming pretty soon, isn't it? We'll have a Hina doll display at home, so if you like, please come by to see it.

Brown: Thank you. I've only seen Hina dolls in pictures, so I was really hoping to see them once.

Brown: Well, then, this will be the perfect opportunity, won't it?
(Then, this is just right, isn't it?)

GRAMMATICAL AND CULTURAL NOTES

23.1 ... no naka de ichiban (suki)

When a Japanese speaker wants to talk about a choice among several alternatives A, B, and C, the boundary of choice is marked by the phrase, 'A, B, C **no naka de**.' This phrase means 'within the choices A, B, and C.'

haru, natsu, aki, fuyu **no naka de,** dono kisetsu ga ichiban suki desu ka?
(**Out of** spring, summer, fall and winter, which season do you like the best?)

kudamono **no naka de,** nani ga ichiban suki desu ka?
(**Among [various kinds of]** fruits, what do you like the best?)

nihongo no benkyoo **no naka de,** nani ga ichiban muzukashii desu ka?
(**Among the [various] tasks** involved in studying Japanese, what is the most difficult one?)

23.2   -tari (... -tari suru)

-tari is an inflectional ending which has the basic meaning of 'alternation' in activities. The **-tari** form of a verb is formed by adding the syllable **-ri** onto its **-ta** form. For example, **itta** becomes **ittari** and **yonda** becomes **yondari**. The **-tari** form is somewhat more restricted in usage than other verb endings in that it appears, in most cases, in an idiomatic expression, **-tari** . .. **-tari suru**. This idiomatic expression--involving two or more verbs marked by **-tari** and followed by either **suru** (to do) or **dekiru** (be able to handle) as the main predicate--is used in reference to two or more activities performed in no fixed order or sequence.

The **-tari ... -tari** forms also occur in several fixed expressions, such as '**ittari kitari suru**' (to go back and forth) or '**futtari yandari suru**,' (it rains off and on).

> umi ni **ittari**, yama ni **ittari dekiru** kara desu.
>> (It's because I **can g o** to the beach [sea] or [I **can g o**] to the mountains.)
>
> paatii ni **ittari**, tomodachi to **asondari dekiru** kara desu.
>> (Because I **can g o** to parties or [I **can] have a good** time with my friends.)
>
> Buraun-san wa nichiyoobi ni wa hon o **yondari** tegami o **kaitari** shimasu.
>> (On Sunday, Mr. Brown [usually] **reads** books **and writes** letters.)

23.3   ... yori ... no hoo ga suki

When one says, '**A yori B** no hoo ga suki,' one means that he or she likes **B better than A**. The speaker's preference or choice is marked by **no hoo ga** and the less preferable item is marked by **yori**, which is similar to 'than' in the English sentence, 'I like **B** better than **A**.' The word order in English is opposite to the Japanese word order.

> watakushi wa **natsu yori** fuyu no hoo ga suki desu.
>> (I like winter better **than summer**.)
>
> **doitsugo yori** nihongo no hoo ga muzukashii desu.
>> (Japanese is harder **than German**.)

23.4   (o)shoogatsu, hinamatsuri

(o)shoogatsu (New Year's Day) is the most important holiday in Japan. Japanese people clean their homes spic-and-span before the arrival of the first of January, and prepare an elaborate feast to celebrate the occasion. The New Year's celebration lasts several days: all stores, banks and offices are closed for at least three days, and the schools are closed for one week. **mochi** is the traditional staple food of the New Year's Day celebration, and houses are decorated with pine tree branches and citrus fruit. Many people visit temples and shrines to make their wishes for the new year.

hinamatsuri (The Doll Festival) falls on the third of March, and is the traditional celebration for Japanese girls. A display in the home of a special set of dolls called **ohinasama**, or the Hina dolls, highlights the occasion. Young girls enjoy the beauty of these dolls which symbolize an ancient imperial court. In making the display, three, five, or seven steps are covered with red **moosen** carpet: on the top step sit the emperor and the empress dolls, on the second step are three ladies in waiting dressed in white **kimonos** and red skirts, and on the third step are five musicians. Other dolls are added for additional steps in the display. An exquisite set of Hina dolls is something which has no American equivalent; one must actually see a display to appreciate its beauty. This festival is also called **Momo no sekku** (Peach Blossom Festival) because peach blossoms bloom during the month of March.

The boy's counterpart of **Hinamatsuri** is **Tango no sekku** which falls on May 5th is now designated as the holiday **Kodomo no Hi** (Children's Day). **koinobori** (carp-shaped kites) are hoisted in the blue sky of May in Japan to symbolize the vitality of young males.

The romantic **Tanabata** (Star Festival) falls on the seventh day of the seventh month. Culturally, Japanese seem to view the numbers one, three, five and seven as lucky numbers. At least, many cultural events seem to fall on days corresponding to these numbers.

23.5   -tara

-tara and **-kattara** are inflectional endings of verbs and adjectives, respectively, having the basic meaning of 'if' or 'when (referring to future time).' These endings are called 'conditional' endings by many grammarians and other textbook writers in Japanese. The major use of the **-tara forms** is to mark the subordinate clause as setting a condition or supposition for the main clause or to designate the future time for the main predicate. English words 'if' or 'when' are the best translations of the **-tara forms**. The **-tara form** of a verb is made simply by adding the syllable **-ra** to the **-ta form** of a verb or the **-katta form** of an adjective.

> **yokattara** mi ni kite kudasai.   **(If you like [if it's good or convenient for you]**, please come and see [it].)
>
> **atsukattara** mado o akete kudasai. **(If it's warm**, please open the window.)
>
> shiken ga **owattara** asobimashoo.   **(When** the exam **is over**, let's get together for some fun.)
>
> natsuyasumi ni **nattara**, yama ni noborimashoo.
> **(When** summer vacation **comes**, let's go mountain climbing.)

23.6   (mi) **ni** (iku, kuru)

The particle **ni** added to the bound form of a verb expresses 'purpose.' This **ni** is basically the same as the **ni** introduced earlier with the phrase **kaimono ni iku** (to go shopping), where the word **kaimono** is a noun. However, **ni** may also be added to the bound form of certain verbs to mark the purpose of the main predicate verb, especially when the main predicate verb is a verb of motion, such as **iku** or **kuru**. In other words, the expression **mi + ni iku** literally means 'to go for the purpose of seeing,' or 'to go to see'--or simply 'to go and see.'

> **mi ni** kite kudasai.   (Please come **to see** [it].)
>
> ohinasama o **mi ni** ikimashoo.   (Let's **go see** the Hina dolls.)
>
> kinoo sushi o **tabe ni** ikimashita.
> ([We] went **to eat** sushi yesterday.)

23.7 shika ... nai

shika means 'only,' and normally occurs only with a negative predicate to mean 'not ... except,' or 'only.' The sentence, '**ringo ga hitotsu shika arimasen**' conveys basically the same message as '**ringo ga hitotsu dake arimasu,**' meaning 'There is only one apple.' The difference is that in the former, **shika** goes with a negative predicate--in this case, **arimasen** (there is not)--to literally mean 'there are not any apples excepting one.' In the latter case, **dake** (only) occurs with positive predicates--**arimasu,** in this case--to literally mean 'there is only one apple.' The literal meaning of the first sentence may sound cumbersome to English speakers, but Japanese use **shika nai** frequently in their daily conversations. **nai** is a negation sign, and it is also the plain counterpart of **arimasen**.

The negative form of the expression ... **-ta koto ga aru** is ...**-ta koto ga nai**. When this particular negative form is used with **shika**, the resulting meaning is, '[I] have done such and such only in such and such a way.'

> shashin de **shika** mita koto ga **nai** node ...
> > (Because I have seen [it] **only** in pictures ...)
> > or (Because I have **not** seen [it] **except** in pictures ...)
>
> Buraun-san ni ichido **shika** atta koto ga **arimasen**.
> > (I have met Mr. Brown **just once**.) or (I have **not** met Mr. Brown **but** once.)

EXERCISES

23E.1 つぎのしつもんに、こたえてごらんなさい。

1. 春、夏、秋、冬の中で、どのきせつが、一番すきですか。

2. りんご、バナナ、みかん、パイナップルの中で、どのくだものが、一番すきですか。

3. すきやき、てんぷら、すし、うどんの中で、どの日本食が一番すきですか。

5. コーヒー、ミルク、オレンジジュース、コーラの中で、どののみものが一番すきですか。

6. ロック、ジャズ、クラシックの中で、どの音楽が、一番すきですか。

6. テニス、スキー、ゴルフ、バスケットボールの中で、どのスポーツが、一番すきですか。

7. ロサンゼルス、シカゴ、ボストン、サンフランシスコの中で、どのとしが、一番大きいですか。

8. ケーキ、アイスクリーム、パイ、フルーツの中で、どのデザートが、一番食べたいですか。

9. 日本語、スペイン語、ドイツ語、フランス語の中で、どのことばが、一番むずかしいですか。

10. すうがく、化学、れきし、日本語の中で、どの学かが一番むずかしいですか。

11. ひらがな、かたかな、かんじの中で、どのじが一番むずかしいと思いますか。

12. 日本語を聞くこと、話すこと、読むこと、書くこと、の中で、どれが一番むずかしいと思いますか。

23E.2　「... たり... たり　する」をつかって、つぎのしつもんに、こたえなさい。

1. パーティーのまえに、どんなことをしますか。
2. パーティーでは、どんなことをしますか。
3. 日本語のクラスでは、何をしますか。
4. としょかんで、学生は、何をしますか。
5. 今度のしゅうまつに、何をするつもりですか。
6. 夏休みには、何をするつもりですか。
7. お正月には、何をするつもりですか。

23E.3   Activity: Planning for this week. Work in pairs. You'll have to do the following things this week. Each day plan to do two things. First, make your own plans. Next, talk with your partner and find out his or her plans.

1. 本屋に行って、日本語のじしょを買う。
2. としょかんに行って、英語のレポートを書く。
3. くるまをあらう。
4. 母のたんじょう日のプレゼントを買う。
5. すしを作ってみる。
6. 銀行に、行く。
7. 友だちと、テニスをする。
8. 母に、てがみを書く。
9. 日本の歌をならう。
10. しゅうじのれんしゅうをする。
11. 日本食のマーケットに、行く。
12. ゆうびんきょくに、行く。
13. 花屋に行って、花を買う。
14. シャツとくつしたをあらう。

	わたくし	あなた
月曜日		
火曜日		
水曜日		
木曜日		
金曜日		
土曜日		
日曜日		

23E.4　つぎのかんじを正^{ただ}しく書いて、おぼえなさい。

98.　春 (spring)　春^{はる}　　一 二 三 丯 夫 耒 春 春

　　　　　　　　　　　　　春

99.　夏 (summer)　夏^{なつ}　　一 丆 厂 石 百 百 頁

　　　　　　　　　　　　　頁 夏

100.　秋 (autumn)　秋^{あき}　　一 二 千 千 禾 禾 禾 秋

　　　　　　　　　　　　　秋

101.　冬 (winter)　冬^{ふゆ}　　ノ ク 夂 冬 冬

102.　休 (vacation)　休^{やす}み　　ノ イ 亻 什 什 休

103.　海 (sea)　海^{うみ}　　丶 丶 氵 氵 汇 汒 海 海

　　　　　　　　　　　　　海

104.　正 (correct)　正^{しょうがつ}月　　一 丁 下 正 正

105.　友 (friend)　友^{とも}だち　　一 ナ 方 友

106.　花 (flower)　花^{はな}　　一 艹 艹 苎 芀 花 花

23E.5 こえをだして、読んでごらんなさい。つぎに、書きとりをしてみましょう。

1. 春には、花がさいて、美しいです。夏には、夏休みがあって、楽しいです。

2. 秋には、勉強します。冬には、お正月があります。

3. 冬休みには、友だちと、山へ、スキーに行きます。

4. 今度の夏休みには、海に行きたいと、思っています。

5. 友だちといっしょに音楽を聞くことは、楽しいです。

6. 日光は、大変美しい所ですから、ぜひ一度、行ってみたいと思います。

7. 日曜日には、本を読んだり、日本語の勉強をしたりします。

8. 今度の土曜日に、天気がよかったら、東京タワーにのぼってみましょう。

23E.6 かんじに、読みがな／ふりがなをつけて、英語で、いみをいってごらんなさい。

（　　）　　　（　　）（　　）　　　（　　）（　　）　　　　　（　　）
1. 夏休みには、海へ行ったり、山へ行ったりして、楽しいです。

　　　　　　　　　　（　　）（　　）　　　（　　）（　　）
2. パーティーで、歌を歌ったり、音楽を聞いたりして、あそびました。

（　　）（　　）　　　（　　）　　　（　　）
3. 日本語を読んだり、書いたり、話したりすることができますか。

4. 小さいくすり屋を（　）さがして、銀行の前（　）を、（　）（　）行（　）ったり
（　）来たりしました。

5. 日曜日には、（　）音楽を（　）聞いたり（　）、テレビ（　）を見たりします。

6. 大学のもんを、（　）学生が（　）、（　）出（　）たり入（　）ったりしています。

7. 春、（　）夏、（　）秋、（　）冬（　）の中（　）で、どのきせつに、スキーを
したり、スケートをしたりしますか。

8. あなたは、おひなさまを見た（　）ことが、ありますか。

9. 田中さんの家では、（　）ひなまつり（　）に、おひなさまを
かざりますか。

10. クリスマスや、お正月には、（　）たいていどんなことを
しますか。

11. あなたは、日曜日に、（　）たいてい、どんなことをしま
すか。

12. 毎日、家に（　）かえ（　）ってから、どんなことをしますか。

23E.7   Rewrite the following sentences using "... shika ...nai."

1. ブラウンさんは、毎朝、ミルクだけのみます。

2. 田中さんに、一度だけあったことがあります。

3. 日本語の先生は、クラスで日本語だけ話します。

4. うちのねこは、さかなだけ食べます。

5. 田中さんのお父さんは、日曜日にだけ、家にいます。

6. ひるまは、お母さんだけ、家にいます。

7. 日光の美しい山を、しゃしんでだけ、見たことが、
   あります。

8. おひなさまは、三月のひなまつりのころにだけ、
   かざります。

23E.8 Reading: Read the following passage aloud and translate it into English.

　春、夏、秋、冬の、四つのきせつの中で、秋が一番すき
です。日本では、秋は、毎日天気がよくて、きもちがいい
からです。それから、秋には、いろいろなおいしい食べも
のがあります。秋のくだものの中で、「かき」が一番おい
しいと思います。でも、日本で、秋に一番おいしいものは、
たぶん、さかなでしょう。日本人は、秋に、よく「さんま」
を食べます。わたくしも「まつたけ」のごはんといっしょ
に、「さんま」を食べることが、大すきです。

VOCABULARY

VERBS

atte	(there is … and: -te form of aru)
(A) ni ittari (B) ni ittari dekiru	(I can go to either [A] or [B]: -tari form of iku in an idiomatic expression -tari -tari suru, 23.2)
asondari	(I [can] play or …: -tari form of asobu)
asobu	(to play; to enjoy oneself; to have fun)
sakimasu	([flowers] bloom: -masu form of saku)
saku	(to bloom: intransitive verb)
kazarimasu	(I decorate; I put out a display of …: -masu form of kazaru)
kazaru	(to decorate; to display)

mi ni kite kudasai	(please come and see, 23.6)
sukii o suru	(to ski)
sukeeto o suru	(to skate)

ADJECTIVES

yokattara	(if it's good [for you]; if you'd like: -tara form of ii, 23.5)

NOUNS

haru	(spring)
natsu	(summer)
aki	(fall; autumn)
fuyu	(winter)
kisetsu	(season)
natsu-yasumi	(summer vacation)
yasumi	(holiday; vacation)
umi	(sea; ocean; beach)
(o)shoogatsu	(New Year's, 23.4)
paatii	(party)
hinamatsuri	(the Doll Festival, 23.4)
hana	(flower; blossom)
ohinasama	(Hina dolls, 23.4)

OTHERS

no naka de	(out of; within the choices of ..., 23.1)
dooshite	(why)
... -tari ... -tari suru	(to do [such and such] alternating with [such and such], 23.2)
(A) yori (B) no hoo ga	([choosing] (B) over (A); I [like] (B) better than (A), 23.3)
-tara	(when; if: an inflectional ending denoting a 'condition,' 23.5)
sore mo soo desu ne	(that's true; you have a point)
moo sugu	(pretty soon)
shika ... nai	(only; nothing but ..., 23.7)
zehi	(for sure; please make sure to [do such and such])
ichido	(once; one time)
... -tai to omo[w]u	(I'd like to [do such and such])
choodo	(just; it so happens that ...)

ADDITIONAL VOCABULARY

toshi	(city)
kaki	(persimmon; native Japanese fruit ripe and sweet in autumn)
samma	(a kind of fish plentiful and delicious in autumn)
matsutake	(a kind of mushroom very fragrant and delicious in autumn)

24

　東京では、お正月がすぎて、二月になると、うめの花が咲きます。うめの花が咲くと、春は、もうすぐです。

　三月の、ひなまつりのころになると、ぽかぽかと、あたたかくなります。そして、あちらこちらに、ももの花が咲きます。

　四月には、学校の新学年が、始まります。かわいい子供たちが、新しいようふくを着て、新しいぼうしをかぶって、新しいくつをはいて、学校にかよいます。そのころ、さくらの花が、一度に、ぱっと、開きます。

　さくらの花が咲くと、人々は、近くのこうえんに、お花見に出かけます。人々は、さくらの花を見ながら、和歌や、俳句を作ります。また、ある人たちは、おさけをのみながら、歌を歌ったり、おどったりします。若い人たちは、おべんとうを食べながら、おしゃべりをします。

　風がふくと、さくらの花が、ちらちらと、ちって、ゆきのように、きれいです。日本の春は、ほんとうに、美しいです。

ENGLISH EQUIVALENT

In Tokyo, when January (the new year's month) is past and February is just beginning, the plum blossoms bloom. When the plum blossoms bloom, spring has nearly arrived.

About the time of the Doll Festival in March, it becomes comfortably warm. And the peach blossoms begin blooming here and there.

In April, a new school year begins. The small children go to school wearing their new clothes, their new caps, and their new shoes. Around that time, the cherry blossoms suddenly burst open all at once.

When the cherry blossoms bloom, people go to nearby parks for 'flower viewing.' Some people write *waka* and *haiku* while they gaze at the blossoms. And some people sing songs or dance as they drink *sake*. Young people chat while they eat box-lunches.

When the breeze blows, the cherry blossoms flicker and fall, and they look as lovely as snow. Spring in Japan is very beautiful.

GRAMMATICAL AND CULTURAL NOTES

24.1   ni naru / -ku naru

naru is a verb which basically expresses 'change from one state to another.' In English, such phases as 'to become' or 'to turn into' may express the similar idea. **naru** normally follows a **noun + ni** construction or an **adjective** in its **-ku** ending, and indicates the state into which something or someone changes.

> nigatsu **ni naru** to hana ga sakimasu.
> > (**When February comes,** flowers bloom.) or
> > (**When it becomes February,** flowers bloom.)
>
> hinamatsuri no koro **ni naru** to atatakaku narimasu.
> > (**When** the Doll Festival **approaches** it **becomes warm.**)
>
> **atatakaku naru** to hana ga sakimasu.
> > (**When·it becomes warm** flowers bloom.)
>
> **samuku naru** to yuki ga furimasu. (**When it becomes cold** it snows.)

24.2   (Verb, plain non-past) + to

The particle **to** following a verb in the plain, non-past form--such as '**... ni naru to**'--marks a subordinate clause meaning 'when,' 'whenever,' or 'if.'

> sakura no hana ga **saku to** hitobito wa ohanami ni dekakemasu.
> > (**When** cherry blossoms **bloom** people go out for flower viewing.)

kaze ga fuku t o sakura no hana ga chirimasu.

> (**When wind blows** cherry blossoms fall.)

osake o **nomu t o** odoritaku narimasu.

> (**When I drink** sake I feel like dancing.)

gakkoo ga **hajimaru t o** gakusei wa isogashiku narimasu.

> (**When** school **begins** students get busy.)

24.3   pokapoka to

There is, in Japanese, a large class of 'reduplicated, onomatopoetic adverbs' which describe the manners or feelings of certain things. As there are no English equivalents of many of these words, the student of Japanese must learn the underlying concept of each of these words, along with specific contexts in which each word is used.

pokapoka to is one of these adverbs. It expresses the comfortable, cozy warmth of the spring sun, as Japanese people enjoy and appreciate this warmth as a sign of approaching springtime.

> hinamatsuri no koro ni naru to **pokapoka t o** atatakaku narimasu.
>
> > (When the Doll Festival approaches, it becomes **comfortably and cozily** warm.)

The following includes some of the commonly used reduplicated words.

> Tanaka-san ga **nikoniko waratte imasu.**
>
> > (Tanaka-san **is smiling happily**.)
>
> haru kaze ga **soyosoyo fuite imasu.**
>
> > (Spring breeze **is blowing gently**.)
>
> ame ga **zaazaa** futte imasu.   (Rain **is pouring heavily**.)
>
> yuki ga **chirachira** futte imasu.   (Snow is **falling lightly**.)

24.4   shin-gakunen

gakunen means 'an academic year,' and the prefix **shin-** indicates the idea of 'newness'; **shin-gakunen**, therefore, means 'a new academic year.' In Japan, a school year begins in April and ends in March of the following year. The students of elementary schools through colleges and universities enter new schools or begin their new academic grades during the early part of April. As Japanese people place a great deal of emphasis on education or scholastic competition, Japanese mothers normally encourage their young children to achieve their very best. Mothers provide brand new clothing and school supplies to show their support.

24.5   Verbs meaning 'To Wear'

In Japanese there are several verbs meaning 'to wear,' and different verbs are selected depending upon the part of the body where the clothing is worn. **kiru** means 'to wear on the upper part of the body'; **haku**, 'to wear on the lower part of the body or on the legs or feet'; and **kaburu**, 'to wear on one's head.' When one puts on a jacket, sweater or shirt the verb **kiru** is selected. When one wears pants, socks, shoes or a skirt, the verb **haku** is used. When a hat or a scarf is worn the verb **kaburu** must be employed. Eye glasses take the verb **kakeru**, and a wrist watch or accessaries, **tsukeru**.

kodomotachi ga atarashii **yoofuku** o **kite**, atarashii **booshi** o **kabutte**,
atarashii **kutsu** o **haite** gakkoo ni kayoimasu.

> (Children go to school **wearing** brand new
> **clothes**, **putting** new **hats** on and **wearing**
> new **shoes** on their feet.)

Tanaka-san wa atarashii **burausu** o **kite imasu**.

> (Tanaka-san **is wearing** a new **blouse**.)

Buraun-san wa kuroi **zubon** o **haite imasu**.

> (Mr. Brown **is wearing** black **pants**.)

Yamada-san wa **megane** o **kakete imasu**.

> (Mr. Yamada **is wearing glasses**.)

24.6   (o)hanami

Japanese people love nature, and often bring an appreciation of nature into their everyday lives. As Japan has distinct seasons with specific beauties and natural spectacles accompanying each seasonal change, cultured Japanese often combine their social activities with an appreciation of nature. **(o)hanami**, or the 'flower viewing,' is one such event: people plan a social get-together under cherry trees in full bloom.   Traditionally, educated people entertain themselves by improvising witty poems on this occasion. Such poems take either the form of the **waka** (the 31-syllable poem) or **haiku** (the 17-syllable poem). It is only natural, however, that even highly cultured persons would rather drink, eat and dance than improvise poetic masterpieces . Many **(o)hanami** parties, therefore, end up skipping the poetry competition and go right into the enjoyment of food and conversation.

24.7   -nagara

The bound word **-nagara** may be added to the bound form of a verb (**tabe-**, **iki-**, or **nomi-**) to form a compound word meaning 'while ... -ing.' When one person performs two activities at the same time (as in 'reading a newspaper while drinking coffee' or 'carrying on a conversation while eating lunch'),' the activity marked by 'while ...-ing' is secondary to the main activity. In a Japanese sentence, **-nagara** indicates this secondary activity.

> aru hito wa (o)sake o **nominagara** uta o utaimasu.
>
> > (Some people sing songs **while drinking**
> > sake.)
>
> wakai hitotachi wa obentoo o **tabenagara** oshaberi o shimasu.
>
> > (Young people chat [with their friends] **while**
> > **eating** their box-lunches.)
>
> Tanaka-san wa uta o **utainagara** osara o aratte imasu.
>
> > (Tanaka-san is washing dishes **while singing**
> > a song.)

24.8   chirachira to

chirachira to is another 'reduplicated onomatopoetic word'; it describes the way flower petals or snowflakes or similar small and light things float or fall from a higher place. Cherry blossoms are short-lived; and as soon as they reach the state of full bloom, their petals are sensitive to winds. Even with the slightest breeze, cherry blossoms flicker down like snow. 'Full-bloom' cherry blossoms have been compared to snow, clouds or mists in many poetic masterpieces in Japanese literature.

EXERCISES

24E.1 Read the following words of clothig and write English equivalent in the parenthesis. Choose the correct verb of wearing for each word.

Question: つぎのものは、着ますか、かぶりますか、はきますか。

1. シャツ 　　(　　　　　)は、＿＿＿＿＿ます。
2. サンドレス (　　　) 　　＿＿＿＿＿。
3. ハイヒール (　　　) 　　＿＿＿＿＿。
4. Tシャツ 　(　　　) 　　＿＿＿＿＿。
5. スカーフ 　(　　　) 　　＿＿＿＿＿。
6. ジャケット (　　　) 　　＿＿＿＿＿。
7. スラックス (　　　) 　　＿＿＿＿＿。
8. ジーパン 　(　　　) 　　＿＿＿＿＿。
9. ショートパンツ(　　　) 　＿＿＿＿＿。
10. ワンピース (　　　) 　　＿＿＿＿＿。
11. ぼうし 　　(　　　) 　　＿＿＿＿＿。
12. サンダル 　(　　　) 　　＿＿＿＿＿。

Fill in the blanks with appropriate words.

1. 春になると、わたくしは、＿＿＿＿を着て、＿＿＿＿
   をはいて、＿＿＿＿をします。
2. 夏が来ると、田中さんは、＿＿＿＿を着て、＿＿＿を
   かぶって、＿＿＿＿をはいて、ビーチに行きます。

3. 秋になると、ブラウンさんは、＿＿＿＿を着て、＿＿＿＿
   をかぶって、＿＿＿＿＿をはいて、ゴルフをします。

4. クリスマスが来ると、田中さんは、＿＿＿＿＿を着て、
   ＿＿＿＿＿をはいて、＿＿＿＿＿をつけて、パーティーに
   行きます。

5. 一学期がおわると、ブラウンさんは、＿＿＿＿＿を着て、
   ＿＿＿＿＿をはいて、＿＿＿＿＿をかぶって、へやの大そ
   うじをします。

24E.2 Oral Translation: Say the best Japanese equivalent of the following sentences.

1. When I sing songs, I feel (become) very happy.

2. When I study Japanese, I get hungry.

3. When I see cherry blossoms, I feel like composing a haiku.

4. When I study in the library, I feel like chatting with my friend.

5. When I hear some good music, I feel like dancing.

6. When I see a movie, I feel like eating potato chips.

7. When I eat potato chips, I get thirsty.

24E.3 Complete the following sentences.

1. 春休みになると、＿＿＿＿＿＿＿＿＿＿＿＿＿＿＿＿＿＿＿＿＿。

2. 学期がおわると、＿＿＿＿＿＿＿＿＿＿＿＿＿＿＿＿＿＿＿＿。

3. おさけをたくさんのむと、＿＿＿＿＿＿＿＿＿＿＿＿＿＿＿＿。

4. 夏休みがおわると、＿＿＿＿＿＿＿＿＿＿＿＿＿＿＿＿＿＿＿。

5. いいえいがを見ると、＿＿＿＿＿＿＿＿＿＿＿＿＿＿＿＿＿＿。

6. あまいケーキを食べると、＿＿＿＿＿＿＿＿＿＿＿＿＿＿＿＿＿。

7. 日本語のテープを聞くと、＿＿＿＿＿＿＿＿＿＿＿＿＿＿＿＿。

24E.4 Read the following sentences aloud and give their meanings in English.

1. ブラウンさんは、テレビを見ながら、勉強しています。

2. 田中さんは、音楽を聞きながら、本を読んでいます。

3. 山田さんは、ごはんを食べながら、しゅくだいをしています。

4. 日本人は、よく、おさけをのみながら、歌を歌います。

5. マークさんは、ピアノをひきながら、歌を歌っています。

6. わたくしは、たいてい、音楽を聞きながら、くるまをドライブします。

7. トムさんは、今、コーヒーをのみながら、新聞を読んでいます。

8. さくらの木の下で、若い人たちが、おべんとうを食べながら、おしゃべりをしています。

9. かわいい子供たちが、新しいようふくを着て、歌を歌いながら、歩いています。

10. 山田さんは、りんごを食べながら、化学のじっけんをしています。

24E.5 つぎのかんじを正しく書いて、おぼえなさい。

107. 咲 (to bloom) 咲く 　　 ⎸ 口 口 口 口 咲 咲 咲

　　　　　　　　　　　　　咲

108. 新 (new) 新しい 　　 ⎸ 亠 宀 六 立 立 辛 亲

　　　　　　　　　　　　　亲 新 新 新 新

109. 始 (to begin) 始まる 　 く 女 女 女 如 始 始 始

110. 子 (child) 子供 　　　 フ 了 子

111. 供 (follower) 子供 　　 ノ イ 仁 什 仕 供 供 供

112. 着 (to wear) 着る 　　 ⎸ ⎈ 二 兰 羊 羊 羊

　　　　　　　　　　　　　着 着 着 着

113. 開 (to open) 開く 　　 ⎸ 冂 冂 冂 門 門 門

　　　　　　　　　　　　　門 門 開 開

114. 々 (repetition sign) 人々 　 ノ 夕 夂

115. 若 (young)　若い　一十艹艹芊芋若若

116. 風 (wind)　嵐　丿几几凡凨凨凨風

風

24E.6　かんじに読みがなをつけて、英語でいみをいってごらんなさい。しつもんの、こたえを、書きなさい。

（　　）（　　）　　　　（　）（　）（　）
1. 東京では、二月になると、何の花が咲きますか。
（　　）（　　）（　　　）（　　）（　）
2. 日本の学校の新学年は、何月に始まりますか。
　　　　　　　（　　）　　　　　　　（　　）
3. さくらの花は、どんなふうに開きますか。
　　　　　　（　）（　）　　（　　）（　）
4. さくらの花が咲くと、人々は、何をしますか。
（　）（　）　　　　（　　）（　）
5. 若い人たちは、お花見に行ってどんなことをしますか。
　　　　　（　　）　　　　　　　　（　　）
6. 風がふくと、さくらの花は、どうなりますか。
　　　　　　　　　　　　（　）（　）
7. ブラウンさんは、さくらの花を見ながら、和歌や
　　（　）
俳句を作りますか。
　　　　（　）　　　　　　　　　　（　）（　）
8. ある人は、おさけをのみながら、歌を歌いますか。
（　）（　）（　）（　）（　）　　　　　（　）（　）　（　）
9. 春、夏、秋、冬の中で、どのきせつが一番美しいと思
いますか。

　　　　　　　　（　　）（　　　）　　　（　　）
10. アメリカの大学の新学年は、いつ始まりますか。

24E.7　あいているところを、正しいことばでうめてごらんなさい。

1. 三月に（　　　　）と、（　　　　　　　）とあたたかく
　なって、（　　　　　　　）に、ももの花が（　　　　　）
　ます。ひなまつりが来ると、（　　　　　　）を、かざ
　ります。

2. 新学年が（　　　　　）と、かわいい（　　　　　）が
　新しいようふくを（　　　）て、新しいくつを（　　　　）
　て、（　　　　　　）にかよいます。

3. さくらの花が咲くと、人々は、（　　　　　　　）に、
　出かけます。さくらの花を見ながら、（　　　　　）や、
　（　　　　　　）を作ります。

4. 風が（　　　　　）と、さくらの花が（　　　　　　）と
　ちって、（　　　　　）のようにきれいです。

24E.8 Write the best Japanese equivalent of the sentences below, using **kanji** for the underlined words.

1. When a <u>new</u> <u>academic</u> <u>year</u> <u>begins</u>, <u>college</u> <u>students</u> <u>buy</u> lots of <u>books</u>.

2. When the <u>summer</u> <u>vacation</u> <u>comes</u>, <u>young</u> <u>people</u> <u>go</u> to the <u>beaches</u> and <u>mountains</u> with their <u>friends</u>.

3. Whenever Mr. Brown <u>sees</u> <u>beautiful</u> scenery, he takes a lot of pictures.

4. Mr. Brown is <u>composing</u> a haiku while <u>looking</u> at the cherry <u>blossoms</u>.

5. Mr. Brown is <u>reading</u> a <u>Japanese</u> <u>book</u> while <u>listening</u> to the <u>music</u>.

6. Miss Tanaka is <u>making</u> her <u>breakfast</u> while <u>singing</u> a <u>song</u>.

7. <u>Children</u> are talking happily while <u>eating</u> their lunches.

VOCABULARY

VERBS

sugite	([it] is past and ...: -te form of sugiru)
sugiru	([for time] to elapse; to be over)
(ni) naru	(to become; to turn into, 24.1)
kite	(I wear and ...: -te form of kiru, 24.5)
kiru	(to wear on the upper part of the body, 24.5)
kabutte	(I wear on my head and ...: -te form of kaburu, 24.5)
kaburu	(to wear on one's head, 24.5)
haite	(I wear on my feet: -te form of haku, 24.5)
haku	(to wear on one's legs or feet, 24.5)
kayoimasu	(I commute; I go to: masu form of kayo[w]u)
kayo[w]u	(to commute; to go to [school])
hirakimasu	([it] opens: -masu form of hiraku)
hiraku	(to open; to blossom)
minagara	(while looking; while gazing [at]: the bound form of miru + nagara, 24.7)
nominagara	(while drinking: the bound form of nomu + nagara, 24.7)
utattari	(I sing or ...: -tari form of uta[w]u)
uta[w]u	(to sing)
odottari	(I dance or ...: -tari form of odoru)
odoru	(to dance)
tabenagara	(while eating: the bound form of taberu + nagara, 24.7)
fuku	([the wind] blows)
chitte	(fall from trees and ...: -te form of chiru)
chiru	(to fall: an intransitive verb used for flowers or leaves to fall from trees)

ADJECTIVES

atatakaku	(warm: -ku form of atatakai)
atatakai	([comfortably] warm; nice and warm)
wakai	(young)

NOUNS

ume	(plum)
koro	(approximate time or season)
momo	(peach)
shin-gakunen	(new academic year, 24.4)
kodomotachi	(children)
yoofuku	(Western-style clothing; dress)
booshi	(hat; cap)

kutsu	(shoe)
hitobito	(people; many people)
kooen	(park)
(o)hanami	(flower-viewing, 24.6)
waka	(31-syllable Japanese poem, 24.6)
haiku	(17-syllable Japanese poem, 24.6)
(o)sake	(Japanese style liquor; sake)
oshaberi	(chatting; talking; friendly conversation)
kaze	(wind; breeze)
yuki	(snow)

OTHERS

...(naru) to	(when; whenever; if: a particle marking a subordinate clause, 24.1, 24.2)
pokapoka to	(comfortably or cozily [warm]: a reduplicated onomatopoetic adverb, 24.3)
achira kochira ni	(here and there)
shin-	(new--: a prefix indicating newness, 24.4)
ichido ni	(all at once)
patto	(suddenly [open])
-nagara	(while ...ing: a bound word, 24.7)
mata	(or; and on the other hand)
aru	(a certain; some)
-tachi	(a suffix expressing plurality of people)
chirachira to	(flickering down: a reduplicated onomatopoetic word, 24.3, 24.8)
hontoo ni	(truly; indeed: more formal or written style variant of honto ni)

ADDITIONAL VOCABULARY

megane	(eye glasses)
kakeru	(to wear [glasses])
tsukeru	(to wear accessories; to attach on clothing)
oosooji o suru	(to do a big cleaning; to clean up the room)
potetochippusu	(potato chips)

25

山田	おや、ブラウンさん、どうかしたんですか。
ブラウン	ちょっと、風邪をひいてしまったんです。
山田	それは、いけませんね。おだいじに。
ブラウン	ありがとう。昨日は頭がいたかったので、学校を休みましたが、今日は、もう大じょうぶです。
山田	雨にでも、ぬれたんですか。
ブラウン	そうなんです。昨日電車をおりた時、雨がざあざあふっていましたが、かさを持っていなかったので、びっしょりぬれてしまいました。
山田	それは、お気のどくでしたね。つゆの間は、天気が変わりやすいので、毎日、かさを持って、出た方がいいですよ。
ブラウン	昨日家を出た時は、天気がよくて、空がはれていたので、つゆのことを、すっかり、わすれてしまったんです。
山田	つゆになると、にわか雨が多いので、よく気をつけた方がいいですよ。
ブラウン	ところで、つゆは、どのくらい続くんですか。
山田	大体六月のなかばから、七月の十日ごろまでです。
ブラウン	三週間も続くんですか。日本のつゆだけは、あんまり、いいものじゃありませんね。

ENGLISH EQUIVALENT

Yamada: Hey, Mr. Brown, what's the matter?

Brown: I've caught a slight cold.

Yamada: That's not good. Please, take care of yourself.

Brown: Thanks. I was absent from school yesterday because I had a headache, but I'm already okay today.

Yamada: Did you get wet in the rain or something?

Brown: That's right. When I got off the train yesterday, it was raining cats and dogs, but I didn't have an umbrella, and so I got soaked.

Yamada: That's too bad. During the rainy season the weather is changeable, so you had better carry around an umbrella with you every day.

Brown: Yesterday when I left my house, the weather was fine and the sky was clear, so I completely forgot about the rainy season.

Yamada: During the rainy season there are a lot of cloudbursts, so you had better be careful.

Brown: Hmm... About how long does the rainy season last?

Yamada: Generally from mid-June till around the 10th of July.

Brown: You mean it lasts for whole three weeks? Well, the Japanese rainy season is the only thing [in Japan] that isn't particularly nice.

GRAMMATICAL AND CULTURAL NOTES

25.1   oya, dooka shita n desu ka?

When a Japanese speaker notices something unusual or unexpected, he or she may say **'oya?'** to express such a feeling. It often accompanies such an expression as **'dooka shita n desu ka?'** which means 'Did anything happen [to you]?' In this present lesson, Mr. Brown, who is always healthy and cheerful looked a bit different this morning, and his friend Yamada noticed it. In English, one may say, 'What happened?' or 'Is anything wrong?'

> **oya**, Buraun-san, **dooka shita n desu ka?**
> > **(Is anything wrong**, Mr. Brown?)
>
> **oya**, Buraun-san wa doko ni itta n desu ka?
> > **(Well**, where did Mr. Brown go? [I thought
> > he should be here.])

25.2   -te shima[w]u

shima[w]u is a verb meaning 'to complete' or 'to put something away,' and when it is added to the **-te form** of a verb it emphasizes or signifies the 'completion' of the activity or state expressed by the verb in **-te form**. In English, this idea is expressed by the phrase '[something is] completely [done],' or--in order to draw attention to the significance of an event--by the phrase, '[someone] ended up doing [something].' The expression **-te shima[w]u** may make the sentence more 'conversational' in the sense that this type of emphasis is more likely to be signaled by intonation in English. The **-ta form** of **shima[w]u** is **shimatta**.

chotto kaze o **hiite shimatta** n desu.
(**I ended up catching** a cold.) or
(**I unfortunately caught** a cold.)

bisshori **nurete shimaimashita.** (**I got soaking wet.**) or (**I was completely wet.**)

sukkari **wasurete shimatta** n desu. (**I completely forgot** [about it].)

25.3 (atama) ga itai

itai is an adjective meaning 'painful' or '[somewhere] hurts.' When a Japanese speaker wants to report a headache or sore throat or similar discomfort or pain, he or she normally chooses the expression **... ga itai.** The following expressions are commonly heard in daily conversations.

atama ga itai.	([I] **have a headache.**)
onaka ga itai.	([I] **have a stomach ache.**)
ha ga itai.	([I] **have a toothache.**)
nodo ga itai.	([I] **have a sore throat.**)
ashi ga itai.	([My] **foot hurts.**)

kinoo wa **atama ga itakatta** node gakkoo o yasumimashita.
(I missed school yesterday because I **had a headache.**)

onaka ga itai n desu ka? (Do you **have a stomach ache?**)

iie, moo **itaku arimasen.** (No it **doesn't hurt** anymore.)

25.4 (soo) na n desu.

na is a copula which basically means the same as **desu**, except that two grammatical rules have been applied to change **desu** to **da** and then to **na**. As has been discussed, the copula **desu** is spoken in the final position of the sentence to express the main predicate in polite conversational style: in a subordinate clause the polite copula **desu** is changed to its plain counterpart, which is **da**. The plain copula **da** further changes to **na** when the following word begins with a nasal sound as with **n (desu)**, **no**, or **node**. Therefore, when the phrase **soo desu** (that's right) is spoken before **...n desu** (it's a fact that ...) **desu** changes into **da** (because it occurs in a subordinate clause) and then to **na** as explained above. The final result is **soo na n desu**, to mean 'that's right.'

25.5 -nai, -nakatta

inakatta is the **-katta form** or the past form of the word **inai** which means 'not existing'--the opposite of **iru** (to be or to exist). The word **inai** is also the negative form of the verb **iru**: the negation sign **-nai** replaces the ending **-ru**. The **i-** of **iru** and the **i-** of **inai** are the same verb stem. The meaning of **inai** is the same as **imasen** except that **inai** is in the plain (non-past) form and **imasen** is in the polite (non-past) form. **inakatta**, the plain past form, corresponds in meaning to its polite past counterpart **imasen deshita** (was not).

The negation sign **-nai** can be added to the stem of vowel verbs such as **taberu, miru** or **dekiru** to make their negative forms **tabenai, minai** and **dekinai**. These are the negative plain non-past forms of the verbs. To the consonant verbs such as **kaku** or **yomu**, **-anai** is added to form the negative plain non-past forms. The syllable **-a-** has no meaning, but it acts as a filler to connect the stem-ending consonant onto the negation sign **-nai**. The **-i** of **-nai** is grammatically the adjective ending **-i** which can be changed to **-ku**, **-kute**, or **-katta**. The expression **motte inakatta** is the negative plain past form of the compound verb **motte iru** (to have [something] with oneself): it is in the plain form because the expression is followed by **node** (because) which normally requires the subordinate clause construction.

> kasa o **motte inakatta node** bisshori nurete shimaimashita.
> > (**Because I did not have** an umbrella, I got soaking wet.)
>
> asagohan o **tabenakatta node** moo onaka ga sukimashita.
> > (**Because I did not eat** breakfast, I'm already hungry.)
>
> benkyoo **shinakatta node** kondo no shiken wa zenzen dame deshita.
> > (**Because I didn't study**, I completely blew the last test.)

25.6 Summary of Predicate Types

One of the most complicated parts of Japanese grammar is to grasp the rules governing the correct forms of three predicate types--verb, adjective and noun constructions--in two time dimensions, non-past and past. Each of the predicate forms has its plain forms which are used in subordinate clause constructions. Most of these forms have already been introduced, but a summary is presented below to confirm understandings or to fill in the gaps, if any.

	AFFIRMATIVE		**NEGATIVE**	
	ADJECTIVE CONSTRUCTION			
	Polite Form	**Plain Form**	**Polite Form**	**Plain Form**
	(Regular Adjectives)			
Non-Past	samui desu	samui	samuku arimasen	samuku nai
Past	samukatta desu	samukatta	samuku arimasen deshita	samuku nakatta
	(Irregular Adjectives)			
Non-Past	ii desu	ii	yoku arimasen	yoku nai
Past	yokatta desu	yokatta	yoku nakatta desu ~ yoku arimasen deshita	yoku nakatta

NOUN CONSTRUCTION

	Polite Form	Plain Form	Polite Form	Plain Form
(Regular Nouns)				
Non-Past	hon desu	hon da	hon de wa arimasen	hon de wa nai
Past	hon deshita	hon datta	hon de wa arimasen deshita	hon de wa nakatta
(Copula Nouns)				
Non-Past	kirei desu	kirei da (~na)	kirei de wa arimasen	kirei de wa nai
Past	kirei deshita	kirei datta	kirei de wa arimasen deshita	kirei de wa nakatta

VERB CONSTRUCTION

	Polite Form	Plain Form	Polite Form	Plain Form
(Vowel Verbs)				
Non-Past	tabemasu	taberu	tabemasen	tabenai
Past	tabemashita	tabeta	tabemasen deshita	tabenakatta
Non-Past	mimasu	miru	mimasen	minai
Past	mimashita	mita	mimasen deshita	minakatta
(Consonant Verbs)				
Non-Past	kakimasu	kaku	kakimasen	kakanai
Past	kakimashita	kaita	kakimasen deshita	kakanakatta
Non-Past	yomimasu	yomu	yomimasen	yomanai
Past	yomimashita	yonda	yomimasen deshita	yomanakatta
(Irregular Verbs)				
Non-Past	shimasu	suru	shimasen	shinai
Past	shimashita	shita	shimasen deshita	shinakatta
Non-Past	ikimasu	iku	ikimasen	ikanai
Past	ikimashita	itta	ikimasen deshita	ikanakatta

315

| Non-Past | kimasu | kuru | kimasen | konai |
| Past | kimashiata | kita | kimasen deshita | konakatta |

(Special Verbs)

| Non-Past | arimasu | aru | arimasen | nai |
| Past | arimashita | atta | arimasen deshita | nakatta |

| Non-Past | imasu | iru | imasen | inai |
| Past | imashita | ita | imasen deshita | inakatta |

25.7 (kawari)**yasui**

kawariyasui is a compound word made up of **kawari**, which is the bound form of the verb **kawaru** (to change), and an adjective **yasui** (easy [to do]). **kawariyasui** meaning 'easy to change' or 'changeable.' **yasui** can be combined with certain additional verbs to form other useful expressions. Some of the more common expressions are listed below.

> **kawariyasui**   **(changeable)**
> **wakariyasui**   **(easy to understand)**
> **oboeyasui**   **(easy to memorize)**

25.8 -ta hoo ga ii

The **-ta form** of a verb followed by **hoo ga ii** is an idiomatic expression meaning '[someone] had better do such and such.' This expression is spoken when giving advice or offering opinions or counsel to someone.

> mainichi kasa o **motte deta hoo ga ii** desu yo.
> > (You **had better take** an umbrella **with you** as you leave home every day.)
>
> yoku **ki o tsuketa hoo ga ii** desu yo.
> > (You'd **beter be careful** about, I tell you.)
>
> motto **benkyoo shita hoo ga ii** desu yo.
> > (You'd **better study** harder!)

25.9 tsuyu

tsuyu literally means 'dew drops' or 'moisture drops,' but it also refers to the season of much rain and humidity caused by the low pressure system that wraps up the islands of Japan during June and July. It normally starts in mid-June and lasts for three or more weeks. During this **tsuyu** season the weather is changeable and it rains off and on all the time. The temperature is relatively high, which makes the excessive humidity even more uncomfortable. Moisture gets into everything, and mold and mildew grow on shoes, walls, and clothing. One must keep everything clean to stay healthy. However, the rain and water which are brought by this low pressure system are considered very important to Japanese agriculture. So the Japanese people don't mind the **tsuyu** too much. In fact, they become worried if it doesn't rain enough during the **tsuyu** period.

25.10   (san-shuukan) mo

mo added to a word of time duration or quantity gives an added meaning of 'as much as ...!' or 'that many!' to express the speaker's feeling about a very long time period or a very large quantity.

san-shuukan   tsuzukimasu.   (It lasts for three weeks.)
san-shuukan **mo**   tsuzuku n desu ka?
                                    (Do you mean that it lasts **as long as** three weeks?)
uchi kara   gakkoo made   ichijikan **mo**   kakaru n desu ka?
                                    (Do you mean it takes a **whole** hour to come to school from home?)

EXERCISES

25E.1   つぎの文を、ひていけいに、書きなおしなさい。(Make the following sentences negative. The underlined parts are in the plain past forms.)

1. わたくしは、昨日、頭がいたかった。

2. 昨日は、天気がわるかった。

3. 昨日は、さむかった。

4. 日本語のクラスは、よかった。

5. 昨日は、木曜日だった。

6. 昨日は、ひなまつりだった。

7. ももの花が、きれいだった。

8. こうえんは、しずかだった。

9. わたくしは、昨日、あさごはんにトーストを食べた。

10 学校に、かさを持って行った。

11 田中さんは、学校を休んだ。

12 山田さんは、お母さんに、てがみを書いた。

13. 電車の中に、学生がおおぜいいた。

14 パーティーに、ブラウンさんが、来ていた。

15. つくえの上に、大きい本が、あった。

317

25E.2 「ので」をつかって、AとBを、正しくつなぎなさい。
(Connect A and B correctly using **node** as the conjunction.)

1. A: 田中さんは、昨日、かさを持っていませんでした。

   B: 雨にぬれてしまいました。

2. A: わたくしは、かさを持っていました。

   B: 雨にぬれませんでした。

3. A: 昨日は、天気がよくて、空がはれていました。

   B: つゆのことを、すっかりわすれてしまいました。

4. A: つゆは、三週間も続きます。

   B: 新しいかさを買った方がいいです。

5. A: ここから大学まで、三十分ぐらいかかります。

   B: 電車で行った方がいいです。

6. A: 日本のつゆだけは、いいものではありません。

   B: つゆの間は、日本に行かない方がいいです。

7. A: 夏には、海に行ったり、山に行ったりできます。

   B: 夏が一番すきです。

8. A: 日光は、大変有名な所です。

   B: ぜひ、一度行って見た方がいいです。

9. A: クリスマスには、パーティーに行ったり、お正月
      には、友だちとあそんだりできます。

   B: 冬が、一番楽しいです。

10. A: かまくらの大ぶつは、しゃしんでしか、見たこと
       がありません。

    B: 今度、ぜひ一度見たいと思っています。

25E.3　つぎのかんじを、正しく書いて、おぼえなさい。

117. 昨 (previous)　昨日(きのう)　　｜ 冂 円 日 日ˊ 旿 昨 昨

　　　　　　　　　　　　　昨

118. 頭 (head)　頭(あたま)　　一 ㄱ 戸 듸 戸 豆 豆 豆

　　　　　　　　豆ˊ 豇 頭 頭 頭 頭 頭 頭

119. 雨 (rain)　雨(あめ)　　一 厂 冂 币 币 雨 雨 雨

120. 電 (electric)　電車(でんしゃ)　　一 ㄷ 币 币 雨 雷 雷

　　　　　　　　雷 雷 雷 雷 電

121. 車 (car)　電車(でんしゃ)　　一 厂 币 币 百 亘 車

122. 持 (to hold)　持(も)つ　　一 扌 扌 扩 扩 拌 持

　　　　　　　　持

123. 空 (sky)　空(そら)　　丶 丷 宀 宀 空 空 空

124. 多 (numerous)　多(おお)い　　ノ ク タ タ 多 多

125. 続 (to continue) 続く　　　ㄥ ㄠ ㄠ ㅑ 糸 糸 紀 紀

紀 紲 絟 絓 続

126. 週 (week)　週間　　　丿 冂 冃 冄 冄 用 周 周

冑 凋 週

25E.4　こえをだして、読んでごらんなさい。つぎに、書きとりを
してみましょう。

1. 電車にのる。電車をおりる。電車で学校にかよう。
2. 電話で話す。電話をかける。電話ばんごうを書く。
3. 車で行く。新しい車を買う。車で五分かかる。
4. かさを持って出る。持って行く。持って来る。
5. つゆの間。三週間の間。夏休みの間。
6. 雨が続く。天気のわるい日が続く。三週間も続く。
7. 気持ちがわるい。頭がいたい。
8. 空がはれる。空がくもる。空にくもが多い。
9. 昨日学校を休んだ。昨日は雨だった。昨日家にいた。
10. 気をつける。電気をつける。風がふく。かぜをひく。

25E.5　つぎのしつもんに、こたえてごらんなさい。ノートに、こ
たえを書きなさい。

1. ブラウンさんは、どうして、昨日学校を休みましたか。

320

2. 今日は、もう大じょうぶですか。

3. 昨日 ブラウンさんが家を出た時、雨がふっていましたか。

4. 電車をおりた時、どんなお天気でしたか。

5. つゆの間は、天気がかわりやすいですか。

6. 日本のつゆは、だいたい、どのくらい続きますか。

7. それは、いつごろから、いつごろまでですか。

8. つゆになると、にわか雨が多いですか。

9. つゆの間は、毎日、何を持って出た方がいいですか。

10. 日本では、つゆがあけると、夏になりますか。

VOCABULARY

VERBS

hiite shimatta	(I ended up catching [a cold]: -te form of hiku + -ta form of shima[w]u, 25.2)
hiku	(to catch; to pull; to draw in)
shima[w]u	(to completely do ...; to put something away)
yasumimashita	(I was absent from work or school: -mashita form of yasumu)
yasumu	(to take a rest from ...; to be absent from regular work)
nureta	(I got wet: -ta form of nureru)
nureru	(to get wet)
orita	(I got off [the vehicle]: -ta form of oriru)
(... o) oriru	(to get off [the vehicle]; to descend [the slope])
futte imashita	(it was raining: -te form of furu + imashita)
furu	(to storm; to fall: rain, snow, or hail to fall from the clouds)
motte inakatta	(I did not have: -te form of motsu + inakatta, 25.5)
kawariyasui	([something] is changeable: the bound form of kawaru + yasui, 25.7)
kawaru	(to change)
wasurete shimatta	(I have completely forgotten about ...: -te form of wasureru + shimatta, 25.2)
wasureru	(to forget)
ki o tsukeru	(to take particular note of; to be careful about ...)
tsuzuku	(to continue; something continues)
denwa o kakeru	(to call [someone] on [the telephone])
denki o tsukeru	(to turn on [the light])

tsuyu ga akeru   ([the rainy season] ends: clouds lift or break up)

ADJECTIVES

itakatta	(I had pain; it hurt: -katta from of itai, 25.3)
itai	(something hurts; to have pain, 25.3)
yokute	(it [was] good and ...: -kute form of ii)
ooi	(numerous; many; lots; frequent)

NOUNS

kaze	(a common cold [that people catch in cold weather])
atama	(head)
ame	(rain)
tsuyu	(the rainy season in Japan during June and July, 25.9)
niwaka ame	(sudden shower; cloudburst)
nakaba	(the middle part of a month)
shuukan	(week)
mono	(thing; object; idea)
denwa	(telephone)
kumo	(cloud)
denki	(electricity; electric light)

OTHERS

oya	(hey; well, 25.1)
dooka shita	(has anything happened, 25.1)
-te shima[w]u	([something] is completely done; [someone] ended up doing [something], 25.2)
ikemasen ne	(that's too bad; I'm sorry to hear that)
(o)daiji ni	(take care)
daijoobu	(I'm fine; I'm all right)
soo na n desu	(that's right, 25.4)
-ta toki	(when [I] did such and such)
zaazaa	(pouring; [raining] cats and dogs)
nai	(a negation sign, 25.5)
nakatta	(past negation sign, 25.5)
bisshori	(soaking wet)
kinodoku	([I] feel sorry for [you])
no aida	(during the time ...)
-yasui	(easy to ..., 25.7)
-ta hoo ga ii	(I had better do [such and such], 25.8)
no koto	(with reference to; concerning)
sukkari	(completely)
tokoro de	(by the way)
daitai	(in general)
mo	(as much as, 25.10)
datta	(the past form of da, the plain form of deshita, 25.6)

26

山田　　　ブラウンさん、日本には、島がいくつあるか、知っていますか。

ブラウン　さあ・・・大きい島は、四つだと思いますが、小さい島は、いくつあるか知りません。

山田　　　じゃ、その四つの大きい島の名前を、知っていますか。

ブラウン　もちろん、知っていますよ。一番北にある島が、北海道です。まん中にある一番大きい島が本州で、本州の南にあるのが、四国と九州です。

山田　　　そのとおりです。じゃ、日本で一番高い山は、どれだか、わかりますか。

ブラウン　それは、たぶん、富士山でしょうが、富士山は、一番高いというよりは、むしろ、一番美しいといった方が、いいですね。

山田　　　まあ、そうですね。じゃ、富士山の西の方にある都市の名前を、いくつか、知っていますか。

ブラウン　ええと、まず、京都、大阪、奈良、神戸・・・

山田　　　ずいぶん、よく知っていますね。

ブラウン　夏休みになったら、りょこうをしようと思って、ちずを買って、しらべていたところなんです。

山田　　　そうだったんですか。

ENGLISH EQUIVALENT

Yamada: Mr. Brown, do you know how many islands there are in Japan?

Brown: Hmm... I think there are four large islands, but I don't know how many small ones there are. (I think the large islands are four in number, but I don't know how many small islands there are.)

Yamada: All right, do you know the names of those four large islands?

Brown: Of course I do. The northernmost island is Hokkaido. The largest island in the middle is Honshu, and the ones south of Honshu are Shikoku and Kyushu.

Yamada: That's exactly right. Let's see, can you tell me which is the highest mountain in Japan?

Brown: That's probably Mt. Fuji, but rather than saying it's the highest, it's more accurate (more appropriate) to say it's the most beautiful.

Yamada: Yeah, I guess so... Well, do you know the names of some of the cities to the west of Mt. Fuji?

Brown: Ummm... To begin with, Kyoto, Osaka, Nara, Kobe...

Yamada: Gosh, you know quite a few.

Brown: I thought I'd go on a trip when summer vacation comes, so I bought a map and had just been studying it [before you came].

Yamada: Oh, I see. (Oh, so that's the case.)

GRAMMATICAL AND CULTURAL NOTES

26.1   ikutsu aru ka

When a subordinate clause is led by an interrogative word such as **ikutsu** (how many), **dore** (which one) or **nani** (what), it is necessary to mark the end of the subordinate clause by **ka**. As was explained earlier, the predicate of the subordinate clause takes the plain form.

> nihon ni wa shima ga **ikutsu aru ka** shitte imasu ka?
> > (Do you know **how many** islands **there are** in Japan?)
>
> chiisai shima wa **ikutsu aru ka** shirimasen.
> > (I don't know **how many** small islands **there are** [in Japan].)
>
> nihon de ichiban takai yama wa **dore da ka** wakarimasu ka?
> > (Can you tell me **which is** the highest mountain in Japan?)
>
> **nani ga tabetai ka** itte kudasai. (Please tell me **what you'd like to eat**.)
> **dare ga kita ka** oshiete kudasai. (Please tell me **who came**.)

26.2   da to omo[w]u

da is the plain, counterpart of the copula **desu**. **to omo[w]u** means 'I think [that] ...' The object of one's thought is placed in a subordinate clause preceding **to omo[w]u**; grammatically, the subordinate clause **...da** is a noun construction. Both nouns and copula nouns may be used in this structure.

> ookii shima wa **yottsu da to** omoimasu.
> > (I think [that] the large islands **are four** [in number].)
>
> nihon wa **kirei da to** omoimasu. (I think [that] Japan **is pretty**.)

26.3   kita ni aru shima

A subordinate clause can act as a modifier of a noun head. When a subordinate clause modifies a noun, the entire **relative clause** is placed immediately before the noun head. There is no relative pronoun in Japanese. The plain ending of a predicate immediately followed by a noun indicates the syntactic relationship equivalent to the noun head + a relative pronoun + a relative clause in English.

> **ichiban kita ni aru** shima ga Hokkaidoo desu.
> > (The island **that is farthest north** is Hokkaido.)
>
> **mannaka ni aru** ichiban ookii shima ga Honshuu desu.
> > (The largest island **that is located in the middle** is Honshu.)
>
> **Honshuu no minami ni aru** no ga Shikoku to Kyuushuu desu.
> > (The ones **which are located south of Honshu** are Shikoku and Kyushu.)
>
> **osushi o tabete iru** hito wa Buraun-san desu.
> > (The person **who is eating sushi** is Mr. Brown.)
>
> **Ginza de katta** kasa wa takakatta desu.
> > (The umbrella **that I bought at the Ginza** was expensive.)

26.4   Hokkaidoo, Honshuu, Shikoku, Kyuushuu

Japan is an island country and its territory consists of many islands. The largest one is called **Honshuu** (which means 'the main or central states'); the second largest **Hokkaidoo** ('the northern sea way') lies in the north; the third largest, **Kyuushuu** ('the nine states') is located south of **Honshuu**; and the fourth, **Shikoku** ('the four countries'), is separated from **Honshuu** and **Kyushuu** by an inland sea named **Setonaikai**. There are numerous islands surrounding these four major islands. The student of Japanese is encouraged to review the geography of Japan.

26.5   ikutsuka

ikutsu (how many) and the following **ka** make up a new compound word meaning 'some [indefinite number]' or several.'

toshi no namae o **ikutsuka** shitte imasu ka?

> (Do you know **some** city names?)

kudamono o **ikutsuka** katte kite kudasai.

> (Would you please buy me **some pieces of** fruit?)

Previously, several words of the same composition--such as **dareka** (someone) **dokoka** (somewhere) and **itsuka** (sometime)--were introduced. Other number words can also combine with **ka** in a similar way to make related compound words.

nangen**ka**	(**some number of** houses)
nammai**ka**	(**some number of** sheets)
nannin**ka**	(**some number of** persons)

26.6 (shi)**yoo to omo[w]u**

-yoo is an inflectional verb ending which is usually called 'the plain tentative,' or 'the **-yoo form**.' The basic meaning of the **-yoo form** (as in **shiyoo**) corresponds roughly to **shimashoo** (let's do) except that the **-yoo form** is in plain form and **shimashoo** is in polite form. In a subordinate clause construction, the **-yoo** or plain form is selected.

To make the **-yoo form**, add **-yoo** to the stem of a vowel verb or **-oo** to the stem of a consonant verb.

tabe<u>ru</u>	-->	tabe<u>yoo</u>
mi<u>ru</u>	-->	mi<u>yoo</u>
kak<u>u</u>	-->	kak<u>oo</u>
nom<u>u</u>	-->	nom<u>oo</u>
su<u>ru</u>	-->	shi<u>yoo</u>
ku<u>ru</u>	-->	ko<u>yoo</u>
ik<u>u</u>	-->	ik<u>oo</u> ~ yuk<u>oo</u>

-to omo[w]u (I think that ...) is a predicate construction the Japanese people use very often in conversation. When **-to omo[w]u** immediately follows a verb in **-yoo form**, the construction expresses an intention similar to that of the English phrase, 'I'm thinking of doing such and such.'

natsuyasumi ni nattara ryokoo o **shiyoo to omotte** ...

> (I **was thinking of making** a trip when summer vacation comes ...)

nihon ni **ikoo to omotte** imasu. (I'm **thinking of going** to Japan.)

kondo ohanami ni ittara haiku o **tsukuroo to omoimasu**.

> (I'm **going to compose** a haiku when I go flower-viewing next time.)

26.7 **-ta tokoro**

tokoro is a noun which means 'point in space' as well as 'point in time.' **tokoro**, when it is used in the sense of a point in space, is usually translated into English as 'place.' When **tokoro** follows a verb in **-ta form** it may mean 'a point in time when some activity has been completed,' or 'something has just happened.'

chizu o katte **shirabete ita tokoro** na n desu.

> (I bought a map and **was just at the point of checking** it.)

ima choodo kurasu ga **owatta tokoro** desu.

> (The class **has just ended** now.)

26.8 soo datta n desu ka?

datta, as mentioned previously, is the **plain past copula**, or the plain counterpart of **deshita**. **datta** is used in subordinate clauses involving a noun or a copula noun construction. When the emphasis marker **'n desu ka?'** is added to a clause, its predicate (**soo deshita**) changes to plain form (**soo datta**).

soo **datta n** desu ka?　　(Oh, **was that the case?**) or
　　　　　　　　　　　　(I see. So **that's what it was.**)

dame **datta n** desu ka?　　(You mean it **was no good?**) or
　　　　　　　　　　　　(You mean it **didn't work out?**)

EXERCISES

26E.1 Oral Composition: Student A asks Student B if he or she **knows** the following.

Example: how many islands there are in Japan

---> 日本には、島がいくつあるか、知っていますか。

1. how many large islands there are in Japan
2. how many islands there are in Hawaii
3. how many states there are in the United States
4. how many students there are in this school
5. which mountain is the most beautiful one in Japan
6. which mountain is the tallest one in Japan
7. which island is the largest one in Japan
8. which state is the largest one in the United States
9. in what month cherry blossoms bloom in Japan
10. when Mr. Brown came to Japan
11. why Mr. Brown likes summer best among the four seasons
12. why Mr. Brown caught a cold yesterday
13. who went to the Ginza with Mr. Brown last month
14. what is the name of the largest city west of Mt. Fuji
15. what is the name of the island located in the south of Honshu

26E.2 Oral Translation: Say the best Japanese equivalent of the following sentences.

Example: The island that is located northernmost is Hokkaido.

--> 一番北にある島が、北海道です。

1. The island that is located in the middle is Honshu.
2. The island that is located in the south is Kyushu.
3. The city that is located west of Mt. Fuji is Kyoto.
4. The city that is located west of Kyoto is Kobe.
5. The tree that is in front of the house is a cherry tree.
6. The person who is reading a book is Mr. Brown.
7. The person who is playing the piano is Miss Tanaka.
8. The person who got wet in the rain yesterday was Mr. Brown.
9. The month when Japanese schools begin a new academic year is April.
10. The place where we went to see cherry blossoms was a nearby park.

26E.3 つぎのしつもんに、こたえてごらんなさい。

1. 今夜は、何時にねようと思いますか。
2. あしたは、何時におきようと思いますか。
3. 今度の週末は、どこに行こうと思いますか。
4. 夏休みになったら、りょこうをしようと思いますか。
5. 冬休みになったら、何をしようと思いますか。
6. そつぎょうしたら、何になろうと思いますか。

26E.4 Combine Sentence A and Sentence B and make one complex sentence.

Example: A: 昨日、ぎんざでおすしを食べました。
B: そのおすしは、とてもおいしかったです。
--> 昨日ぎんざで食べたおすしは、とてもおいしかったです。

1. A: 昨日、本屋で、日本語のじしょを買いました。
B: そのじしょは、二千円でした。

2. A: 昨日ぎんざのデパートで、セーターを買いました。

    B: そのセーターは、やすかったと思います。

3. A: わたくしは、日本語を勉強しています。

    B: わたくしは、大学生です。

4. A: ミラーさんは、アメリカから来ました。

    B: ミラーさんは、英語の先生です。

5. A: 先月、日光で、しゃしんをとりました。

    B: これは、そのしゃしんです。

6. A: それは、京都にあります。

    B: それは、ふるいおてらの名前です。

26E.5 つぎのかんじを正しく書いて、おぼえなさい。

127. 島 (island) 島(しま)　　´ ⺊ ⼾ ⼾ ⾃ ⾃ 鸟 島

               島 島

128. 知 (to know) 知(し)る　　ノ ⼂ ⼓ 矢 矢 知 知

129. 北 (north) 北(きた)　　⼀ ⼅ ⼟ ⼟ 北

130. 道 (road) 北海道 `丶丷丷꜀ꜛ产首首首 首道道道

131. 州 (state) 州 `ꜜ丿少少州州州

132. 南 (south) 南 一十十冇冇南南南 南

133. 国 (country) 四国 丨冂冂冂困国国国

134. 西 (west) 西 一丅丏丏西西

135. 都 (capital) 京都 一十土耂耂者者者 者都都

136. 市 (city) 都市 `丶亠亣亣市

137. 阪 ([O]saka) 大阪 ꜕阝阝阝阪阪

26E.6　こえをだして読んで、英語でいみをいいなさい。

1. 本州は、北海道や九州より、大きい島です。

2. 一番北にある島は、北海道で、まん中にある一番大きい島が本州です。

3. 九州と四国は、本州の南にあります。

4. 京都や大阪は、富士山の西にある大きい都市です。

5. 富士山は、日本で一番美しい山です。

6. 東京は、富士山の東にある一番大きい都市の名前です。

7. 日光は、東京の北にある美しい所です。

8. かまくらは、東京の近くにある有名な所です。

9. 夏休みになったら、三週間ぐらい、九州にりょこうしようと思っています。

10. 秋になったら、もっと勉強しようと思って、新しい本をたくさん買いました。

26E.7　「...と思います」をくわえて、こたえてごらんなさい。
(Answer the following questions in Japanese, adding the clause 'I think that...')

1. 日本の一番北にある大きい島は、北海道ですか。

2. 富士山は、一番高い山というより、むしろ、一番美しい山、といった方がいいですか。

3. 京都には、ふるいおてらが、たくさんありますか。

4. 東京から大阪まで、何時間ぐらい、かかりますか。

5. 奈良にある大仏は、日本で一番大きい大仏ですか。

6. 箱根は、高い山や、ふかい谷で、有名ですか。

7. ブラウンさんは、日本のちずを、持っていますか。

8. 風がふくと、さくらの花がちらちらとちって、ゆきの
   ようにきれいですか。

9. 京都や大阪は、東京の西の方に、ありますか。

10. 日本では、四月に、新学年が、始まりますか。

26E.8 あいている所を、正しいことばで、うめなさい。

島田　キムさん、春、夏、秋、冬の中＿＿＿、どのきせつ
　　　＿＿＿一番すきですか。

キム　春＿＿＿、一番すきです。

島田　どうしてですか。

キム　春＿＿＿なる＿＿＿、ぽかぽか＿＿＿　あたたかく
　　　なる＿＿＿＿＿、お花見＿＿＿、行く＿＿＿＿＿が、
　　　できますから。わたくしは、さくら＿＿＿花＿＿＿
　　　見＿＿＿＿＿、おべんとうを食べる＿＿＿＿＿が、
　　　大すきです。

島田　わたくしも、春が大すきです。四つのきせつの
　　　中＿＿＿、春＿＿＿、一番美しい＿＿＿　思います。
　　　春休みになったら、りょこうをし＿＿＿＿＿と、思っ
　　　ています。

キム　　　どこへ行く_____ですか。

島田　　　日本の一番北___ある北海道に、行き_____ん

　　　　　ですが、三月は、まだ、とてもさむい_____、

　　　　　南の方にある九州___行_____と思っています。

キム　　　いいですね！

26E.9 Reading: Read the following passage aloud and translate it into English.

　日本では、六月のなかばになると、天気がわるくなって、毎日、雨の日が続きます。このきせつは、「梅雨」といって、大体、七月の十日ごろまで続きます。この三週間の間は、天気が変わりやすいので、朝、天気がよくても、かさを持って出た方がいいです。「梅雨」の間は、しっけが強くて、あまり気持ちがよくありません。でも、この雨は、日本の農作物には、とても大切なものです。「梅雨」があけると、あつい夏が来ます。学校は、七月二十日ごろから、夏休みになります。夏休みになると、日本の人たちは、いろいろな所へ、りょこうに出かけることが、大すきです。

VOCABULARY

VERBS

(to) omoimasu	(I think that ..., 26.2)
nattara	(when [it] becomes that way; when such and such happens: -tara form of naru)
naru	(to change to; to become)
shiyoo	(I'm thinking of doing such and such: -yoo form of suru, 26.6)
omotte	(I am thinking ... and ...: -te form of omo[w]u)
omo[w]u	(to think; to hold in mind)

katte   (I bought [something] and ...: -te form of ka[w]u)

shirabete ita   (I was checking [it]: -te form of shiraberu + ita, the plain form of imashita)

shiraberu   (to check; to investigate)

ADJECTIVES   (---)

NOUNS

shima   (island)

Hokkaidoo   (one of the major islands of Japan, located north of Honshu, 26.4)

mannaka   (center; middle)

Honshuu   (the largest island of Japan, located in the center of the island chain, 26.4)

Shikoku   (one of the major islands of Japan, located south of Honshu, 26.4)

Kyuushuu   (one of the major islands of Japan, located southwest of Honshu, 26.4)

toshi   (city)

Kyooto   (Kyoto, the former capital of Japan)

Oosaka   (Osaka, the second largest city in Japan)

Nara   (the quaint ancient capital of Japan located south of Kyoto)

Koobe   (one of the major seaports in western Japan)

ryokoo   (traveling; touring)

chizu   (map)

shuu   (state)

OTHERS

ikutsu aru ka   ([Do you know] how many there are?, 26.1)

saa   (well, let me see ...)

mochiron   (of course)

sono toori   (exactly [as you said]; I agree)

tabun ... deshoo   (probably is ...)

mushiro   (rather than [saying that])

maa soo desu ne   (I guess so ...)

ikutsuka   (some [indefinite number]; several, 26.5)

eeto   (ummm ...)

-yoo to omo[w]u   (I'm thinking of doing such and such, 26.6)

-ta tokoro   (such and such has just happened; [I have] just been doing [such and such]; [I was] just now doing [such and such], 26.7)

soo datta n desu ka?   (Is that what it was?, 26.8)

ADDITIONAL VOCABULARY

yokute mo   (even if it is good)

shikke   (humidity)

tsuyoi   (to be strong; intense)

noosakubutsu   (agricultural products)

taisetsu (na)   (important)

akeru   (to open; something lifts off; [rainy season] ends)

27

田中夫人　ブラウンさんは、日本にいらっしゃってから、
もう、どのくらいになりますか。

ブラウン　去年の七月に、まいりましたから、もう、
そろそろ、一年近くになります。

田中夫人　それにしては、ずいぶん日本語がお上手ですね。

ブラウン　いいえ、まだまだ、わからないことばかりです。

田中夫人　こちらの生活には、おなれになりましたか。

ブラウン　はい、もう、すっかりなれました。

田中夫人　ご家族の皆さまは、お元気でいらっしゃいますか。

ブラウン　はい、おかげさまで、父も母も、みんな元気で
おります。

田中夫人　ブラウンさんには、ご兄弟がいらっしゃいますか。

ブラウン　はい、姉が一人と、弟が一人おります。姉は、
もうけっこんしていますが、弟はまだ高校生です。

田中夫人　そうですか。ところで、ブラウンさんは、日本
食をめしあがりますか。

ブラウン　はい、もちろん、いただきます。

田中夫人　それでは、今日は、すきやきでも作りますから、
よろしかったら、お夕食を、めしあがって、
いらっしゃってください。

ブラウン　それは、すみません。どうぞ、おかまいなく。

田中夫人　まあ、ごえんりょなく。どうぞ、ごゆっくり。

ENGLISH EQUIVALENT

Mrs. Tanaka:	Mr. Brown, how long has it been since you came to Japan?
Brown:	I came last July, so it'll be almost a year pretty soon.
Mrs. Tanaka:	Taking that into consideration, your Japanese is very good.
Brown:	Oh, no. I still don't understand much of anything. (There's nothing but things I don't understand yet.)
Mrs. Tanaka:	Have you gotten used to life here (in Japan)?
Brown:	Yes, I've gotten completely used to it.
Mrs. Tanaka:	Is everyone in your family in good health?
Brown:	Yes, thank you for asking. Both my father and mother and everyone else is fine.
Mrs. Tanaka:	Do you have brothers and sisters?
Brown:	Yes, I have an older sister and a younger brother. My sister is married already, but my brother is still a high school student.
Mrs. Tanaka:	Is that so? By the way, do you eat Japanese food?
Brown:	Yes, of course I do.
Mrs. Tanaka:	Well, then, I'll make Sukiyaki or something today, and if you would like, please have dinner [with us] before you go.
Brown:	Oh, [I would like that, but] I don't want to cause you any extra trouble. So please don't do anything special.
Mrs. Tanaka:	Now, don't worry about a thing. Just make yourself at home.

GRAMMATICAL AND CULTURAL NOTES

27.1   Exalted and Humble Family Words

Certain words in Japanese have built-in 'exalted' meanings while others have inherent 'humble' meanings. There are also a great many words that have no such dimensions. Proper use of exalted words and humble words makes a person's Japanese more sophisticated--more characteristic of the educated adult.   Exalted words are used particularly when two speakers talk about each others' families, possessions or activities. The speaker, or the first person, selects exalted forms to refer to the second person's family or activities while choosing humble forms to refer to his own or his family's affairs. The following list presents some of the basic exalted and humble words frequently spoken in daily conversations among educated adults.

Humble Words		Exalted Words	
kazoku	([my] family)	gokazoku	([your honorable] family)
kyoodai	(siblings)	gokyoodai	([your] siblings)
chichi	([my] father)	otoosan~otoosama	([your honorable] father)
haha	([my] mother)	okaasan~okaasama	([your honorable] mother)
ani	([my] older brother)	oniisan	([your] older brother)

ane	([my] older sister)	oneesan	([your] older sister)
otooto	([my] younger brother)	otootosan	([your] younger brother)
imooto	([my] younger sister)	imootosan	([your] younger sister)
kanai	([my] wife)	okusan	([your honorable] wife
shujin	([my] husband)	goshujin	([your honorable] husband)
genki	(good health)	ogenki	([your] good health)
joozu	(skillful)	ojoozu	([your] good skillfulness)

27.2   irassharu and Other Exalted and Humble Verbs

The verb **irassharu** is one of the most frequently used exalted verbs. **irassharu** may be spoken in place of **iru, iku,** or **kuru** when such verbs refer to another's activities. Because **irassharu** is inherently exalted, it is not to be used to refer to the speaker's own (or his family members') being, going, or coming.

There are two methods by which a verb is made exalted or humble. The first is simply to replace a neutral verb with its exalted or humble counterparts. There are several neutral verbs used in daily conversations which have specific exalted and humble counterparts; some of the most important examples are listed below.

Meaning	Humble Verbs	Neutral Verbs	Exalted Verbs
(to be)	oru	iru	irassharu
(to go)	mairu	iku	irassharu
(to come)	mairu	kuru	irassharu
(to eat)	itadaku	taberu	meshiagaru
(to do)	itasu	suru	nasaru
(to say)	moosu	i[w]u	ossharu
(to see)	haiken suru	miru	goran ni naru

The second method applies to verbs which have no 'ready-made' exalted or humble counterparts--the method by which must neutral verbs are made exalted. To make the exalted form of a verb such as **wakaru,** for example: 1) identify the bound form of the verb (**wakari-**) and 2) add the polite prefix **o -** in front of the bound form and **ni naru** at the end. In this case, **owakari ni naru** is the exalted counterpart of the verb **wakaru.** The neutral form, or non-exalted form, **wakaru** is used for both 'neutral' and 'humble' meanings.

(to understand)	wakaru	wakaru	o wakari ni naru
(to speak)	hanasu	hanasu	o hanashi ni naru
(to go out)	dekakeru	dekakeru	o dekake ni naru
(to get used to)	nareru	nareru	o nare ni naru
(to return)	kaeru	kaeru	o kaeri ni naru
(to write)	kaku	kaku	o kaki ni naru

nihon ni **irasshatte kara** moo dono gurai ni narimasu ka?

(How long has it been since you came to Japan?)

kyonen no shichigatsu ni **mairimashita kara** moo sorosoro ichinen chikaku ni narimasu.

> (**Because I came** [here] last July, it's going to be almost a year pretty soon.)

kochira no seikatsu ni **onare ni narimashita** ka?

> (**Have you gotten used to** life in this country?)

hai, moo sukkari **naremashita**. (Yes, **I've** completely **gotten used to** it by now.)

nihon-shoku o **meshiagarimasu** ka?

> (Do **you eat** Japanese food?)

hai, mochiron **itadakimasu**. (Yes, of course, **I do** [eat it].)

oyuushoku o **meshiagatte irasshatte** kudasai.

> (Please **stay for** dinner.) or
> (Please **eat** dinner **and then go**.)

27.3 joozu

joozu refers to someone else's good skill, especially some learned skills like speaking a foreign language, drawing pictures, and swimming. The opposite of **joozu** is **heta**, which means 'being unskillful at such and such' or 'not good at such and such.'

zuibun nihongo ga **ojoozu desu ne**!

> (Oh, you are **so good at** [speaking] Japanese!)

iie, mada mada **heta desu**. (No, I'm **not good at all** yet.)

Buraun-san wa totemo **ji ga joozu desu**.

> (Mr. Brown **has beautiful handwriting**.) or
> (Mr. Brown is quite **good at** [**writing**] **characters**.)

27.4 wakaranai koto bakari

wakaranai is the negative plain form of **wakaru** and acts here as the modifier of the noun, **koto** (thing). **bakari** means 'nothing but.' This phrase literally means '[I have] nothing but the things [which] I don't understand.'

As noted before, Japanese people like to be humble about accepting compliments. In this dialogue, Mr. Brown demonstrates his mastery of Japanese culture and behavior, and humbles himself by denying the acceptance of compliments spoken by Mrs. Tanaka, just like any educated speaker might do in Japan.

27.5 kekkon shite iru

kekkon means 'marriage' and **kekkon suru** means 'to get married.' When a person is married, since such is a present state of being, it is expressed in the descriptive present form, **-te iru**.

ane wa moo **kekkon shite imasu** ga ...

> (My older sister **is** already **married**, but ...)

Buraun-san wa mada **kekkon shite imasen**.

(Mr. Brown **is not married** yet.)

27.6 kookoosei

Students in high schools are called **kookoosei** in Japanese. This word is an abbreviation composed of the following elements: **koo** of **kootoo** (higher level) and **koo** of **gakkoo** (school) and **sei** of **gakusei** (student). The following are similar words naming some other types of students.

daigakusei	(college students)
kookoosei	(high school students)
chuugakusei	(junior high students)
shoogakusei	(elementary school students)

27.7 yoroshikattara

yoroshii is an adjective meaning 'good' and is more polite than **ii**. **yoroshikatara**, therefore, sounds a little more polite than **yokattara** which is the **-tara form** of the adjective **ii**. In this dialogue, Mrs. Tanaka, an educated lady and the mother of Masako Tanaka, naturally chooses more polite language when speaking to Mr. Brown, a foreigner. Mr. Brown also speaks politely to her.

27.8 sumimasen, okamainaku

sumimasen (or **suimasen**) is spoken occasionally to express someone's humble acceptance of what is spoken to him or to her. In such a case, 'thank you' may be an appropriate English translation. The speaker really wants to say that he or she is sorry for causing extra trouble. **doozo okamainaku** means 'please do not do or make anything special,' or 'please do not pay too much attention to my presence.' This expression means in essence that the speaker is 'humbly staying'; that he is accepting an invitation.

27.9 goenryo naku, doozo goyukkuri

enryo is a word which expresses a concept of modesty and humbleness as a cultural virtue. In Japan, it is considered to be a mark of good manners and a sign of personal good taste to be modest and reserved about accepting offers, especially of food. Due to this cultural habit, most Japanese will show hesitation in accepting an offer at first, and will instead say something which demonstrates their awareness of **enryo**. The hostess, in turn, recognizes this awareness and insists on 'not bothering to behave so formally in accordance with the concept of **enryo**.' The **go-** of **goenryo** is an exalted prefix, similar in meanig to **o-** of **ogenki** (your good health). In this case, it indicates that Mrs. Tanaka recognizes Mr. Brown's good manners, or his conformance with **enryo**. **naku** is the adverbial form of **nai** (not existing) which means 'without.' **goenryo naku**, consequently, means something similar to 'please do not act so formally as to recognize **enryo**.'

When a hostess invites a guest to stay on in a comfortable way, he or she says **doozo** (please) **goyukkuri** ([your honorable] relaxed mood), which means something similar to 'please make yourself at home' in English.

EXERCISES

27E.1 Oral translation: Using the correct exalted and humble words, say the following expressions in Japanese.

Example: How is your family? --> ご家族は、いかがですか。

1. A: How is your mother?
   B: My mother is fine.

2. A: Is your father a math teacher?
   B: No, my father is not a math teacher.

3. A: Do you have brothers and sisters?
   B: Yes, I have an older sister.

4. A: Is your husband busy?
   B: Yes, my husband is very busy every day.

5. A: Is your wife at home now?
   B: No, my wife is not at home this afternoon.

6. A: Is your younger sister a high school student?
   B: Yes, my sister is a high school student.

7. A: Is your younger brother studying Japanese?
   B: Yes, my younger brother is studying Japanese at a junior high school.

8. A: What is your father's name?
   B: My father's name is William Brown.

9. A: Where is your mother living now?
   B: My mother is living in Tokyo now.

10. A: What is your older brother doing in Japan?
    B: He is teaching English at a high school in Osaka.

27E.2 Politely, using the exalted words properly, ask your teacher the following questions.

1. how long he or she has been living in this city
2. if his or her family lives here
3. if he or she has any brothers or sisters
4. if his or her father is well
5. if his or her mother speaks English
6. if his or her mother sometimes eats American food

7. if his or her family watch T.V. very often
8. if he or she can speak Spanish
9 if he or she has ever climbed Mt. Fuji
10. what his or her father's name is
11. if he or she ate breakfast this morning
12. if he or she would like to have something to eat (to eat something)
13. if he or she has ever seen the famous Buddha in Nara
14. if he or she would like to stay for dinner
15. if he or she is married

27E.3 Activity: Polite Talk. Work in Pairs. Assume that both A and B are sophisticated adults. They are new acquaintances, and as such, talking politely using exalted and humble words.   First, A reads the questions and B answers. Second time, reverse the roles.

1. おなまえは、何と、おっしゃいますか。

2. どちらから、いらっしゃいましたか。

3. もう、どのくらい、日本語を、勉強なさいましたか。

4. スペイン語が、おできになりますか。

5. 家で、何語を、お話しになりますか。

6. ご家族の皆さまは、どちらに、すんでいらっしゃいますか。

7. ご兄弟が、いらっしゃいますか。

8. お母さまは、お元気でいらっしゃいますか。

9. お父さまは、おいそがしいですか。

10. 日本食が、おすきですか。

11. 時々、日本食をめしあがりますか。

12. 今度の週末に、何をなさりたいですか。

13. 東京に、いらっしゃったことが、ありますか。

27E.4　つぎのかんじを、正しく書いて、おぼえなさい。

138.　夫　(spouse)　夫人 (ふじん)　一 二 夫 夫

139.　去　(past)　去年 (きょねん)　一 十 土 去 去

140.　活　(active)　生活 (せいかつ)　丶 丶 丶 氵 汁 汗 汗

活 活

141.　族　(clan)　家族 (かぞく)　丶 二 亐 方 方 方

族 族 族 族

142.　皆　(all)　皆さま (みな)　一 ヒ ヒ 比 比 比 皆

皆 皆

143.　元　(origin)　元気 (げんき)　一 二 テ 元

144.　兄　(older brother)　兄弟・兄 (きょうだい・あに)　丶 口 口 尸 兄

145.　弟　(younger brother)　弟 (おとうと)　丶 丷 丷 当 当 弟 弟

146. 姉 (older sister)　姉　　く 女 女 女` 妒 妒 姉
　　　　　　　　　　　　姉

147. 妹 (younger sister)　妹　　く 女 女 女` 妒 妹 妹
　　　　　　　　　　　　妹

148. 夕 (evening)　夕食　　ノ ク 夕

27E.5　つぎのしつもんに、こたえてごらんなさい。ノートに、こたえを書きなさい。

1. ご家族は、今、どこにすんでいらっしゃいますか。
2. ご家族の皆さまは、お元気でいらしゃいますか。
3. あなたには、お姉さまが、いらっしゃいますか。
4. 妹さんが、いらっしゃいますか。
5. ゆうべ、お夕食に、何をめしあがりましたか。
6. 毎晩、何時間ぐらい、勉強なさいますか。
7. 春、夏、秋、冬の中で、どのきせつが一番おすきですか。
8. 夏休みになったら、どんなことをなさりたいですか。
9. 京都にいらっしゃったことが、ありますか。
10. 富士山の東の方にある、大きい都市の名前を、知っていらっしゃいますか。

27E.6 Place Sentence A within Sentence B, so that they will form one complex sentence without changing its meaning.

1. A: 今日は、日曜日です。

   B: _____ ので、学校に行きません。

2. A: 昨日、かさを持っていませんでした。

   B: わたくしは、_____ ので、雨にぬれてしまいました。

3. A: つゆは、大体、三週間続きます。

   B: _____ と思います。

4. A: 夏休みは、何月何日から、何月何日までですか。

   B: _____知っていますか。

5. A: 新学年は、いつ、始まりますか。

   B: あなたは、_____知っていますか。

6. A: すきやきを作っています。

   B: あの_____人は、田中さんのお母さんです。

7. A: 本州の南にあります。

   B: _____島は、四国と九州です。

27E.7 かんじに、読みがな／ふりがなをつけて、英語で、いみを
いってごらんなさい。つぎに、書きとりをしてみましょう。
(Provide **yomigana/furigana** for all **kanji** below, then say the meaning of each
word in English. Finally, be prepared for a dictation.)

( )	( )	( )	( )
1. 去年	2. 今年	3. 来年	4. 昨年
( )	( )	( )	( )
5. 高校生	6. 中学生	7. 小学生	8. 大学生
( )	( )	( )	( )
9. 家族	10. 兄弟	11. 元気	12. 天気
( )	( )	( )	( )
13. 父	14. お父さん	15. 母	16. お母さん
( )	( )	( )	( )
17. 兄	18. お兄さん	19. 姉	20. お姉さん
( )	( )	( )	( )
21. 弟	22. 妹	23. 頭	24. 耳
( )	( )	( )	( )
25. 夕食	26. 朝食	27. 上手	28. 下手
( )	( )	( )	( )
29. 音楽	30. 電車	31. 銀行	32. 新聞
( )	( )	( )	( )
33. 南	34. 秋	35. 朝	36. 歌
( )	( )	( )	( )
37. 高い	38. 遠い	39. 新しい	40. 美しい
( )	( )	( )	( )
41. 若い	42. 左	43. 入る	44. 買う
( )	( )	( )	( )
45. 歩く	46. 聞く	47. 書く	48. 思う
( )	( )	( )	( )
49. 来る	50. 読む	51. 話す	52. 知る
( )	( )	( )	( )
53. 花屋	54. 今日	55. 昨日	56. 生活

VOCABULARY

VERBS

irasshatte (kara)	([since] you came: -te form of irassharu)
irassharu	(to come; to go; to be: an exalted verb, 27.2)
mairimashita	(I came: -mashita form of mairu)
mairu	(to come: a humble verb, 27.2)
onare ni narimashita	(you have become accustomed to; you have gotten used to: -mashita form of the exalted construction of nareru)
orimasu	(there is; there are; I have: -masu form of oru)
oru	(to be: a humble verb, 27.2)
kekkon shite iru	([someone] is married, 27.5)
meshiagarimasu	(you eat: -masu form of meshiagaru, 27.2)
meshiagaru	(to eat: an exalted verb, 27.2)
itadakimasu	(I eat: -masu form of itadaku, 27.2)
itadaku	(to eat; to receive: a humble verb, 27.2)

ADJECTIVES

yoroshikattara	(if it's good; if it's convenient for you: -tara form of yoroshii, 27.7)
yoroshii	(good: an exalted adjective)

NOUNS

kyonen	(last year)
joozu	(to be good at ...; skillful, 27.3)
gokazoku	(your family: exalted form of kazoku, 27.1)
minasama	(everyone in your family)
chichi	([my] father, 27.1)
haha	([my] mother, 27.1)
gokyoodai	(your brothers and sisters, 27.1)
ane	([my] older sister, 27.1)
otooto	([my] younger brother, 27.1)
kekkon	(marriage, 27.5)
kookoosei	(high school student, 27.6)
enryo	(the virtue of modesty and humility, 27.9)

OTHERS

sore ni shite wa	(taking that into consideration)
wakaranai koto bakari	(nothing but things I don't understand, 27.4)
bakari	(nothing but; only)
o (verb) ni naru	(an exalted verb construction, 27.2)
tokoro de	(by the way)
doozo okamai naku	(Please don't do anything special, 27.8)
goenryo naku	(Please don't worry about a thing, 27.9)
goyukkuri	(in a relaxed way or leisurely manner, 27.9)

28

ブラウン	山田さん、あなたは、大学をそつぎょうしたら、しょうらい、何をするつもりですか。
山田	まだ、はっきり、わかりませんが、できたら、医学の研究をしたいと思っています。
ブラウン	じゃ、生物や化学や数学など、むずかしい学科を、たくさん、勉強しなければなりませんね。
山田	そうなんです。ところで、ブラウンさんは、どんなきぼうを、持っていますか。
ブラウン	きぼうは、山のようにありますよ。 まず、もっと日本語を勉強して、日本の本や新聞を、どんどん読んでみたいと思います。
山田	たとえば、どんな本に、きょうみがありますか。
ブラウン	日本の文化をよくりかいするために、歴史の本や文学書を読まなければなりません。そして、いつかほんやくで読んだ夏目漱石の小説などを、原書で読んでみたいなあと思いますよ。
山田	それなら、漢字を、たくさん、おぼえなければ、なりませんね。
ブラウン	それが大変です。
山田	おたがいに、きぼうが大きいから、いっしょうけんめいに、勉強しなければなりませんね。
ブラウン	そうですね。しっかり、がんばりましょう。

347

ENGLISH EQUIVALENT

Brown: Mr. Yamada, what do you intend to do [in the future] after you graduate?

Yamada: I have not really decided yet (I don't know yet), but I think I'd like to do medical research, if possible.

Brown: Then you will have to study a lot of difficult subjects like biology, chemistry, and math, won't you?

Yamada: Exactly. And you, what kind of ambitions do you have?

Brown: I've got a million things I'd like to do. (I have a mountain of ambitions.) To start with, I think I'd like to study Japanese more so that I can read Japanese books and newspapers [one after another].

Yamada: What sort of books are you interested in, for example?

Brown: In order to truly understand [and appreciate] the culture of Japan, it's necessary to read [Japanese] history books and literature. And someday, I'd really like to read the original texts of Natsume Soseki's novels which I've read sometime before in [English] translation.

Yamada: In that case, you'll have to memorize a lot of kanji, won't you?

Brown: That's the hard part.

Yamada: We've both got high ambitions, so we'll have to study as hard as we can.

Brown: Right. Let's give it our best. [Let's keep up the good work.]

GRAMMATICAL AND CULTURAL NOTES

28.1   (shi)nakereba naranai

The idiomatic expression, **(shi)nakereba naranai**, means [one] 'must or has to do such and such.' The first element **(shi)nakereba** is composed of the stem **shi-** of the irregular verb **suru** (to do) followed by the negation sign **-nai** whose **-i** ending is replaced by another ending, **-kereba**. The ending **-kereba** is an inflectional ending usually referred to as the 'provisional ending' by grammarians and textbook writers, because it has the basic meaning of 'provided that ...' The following summarizes the composition of the word **(shi)nakereba**.

su-ru	(to do)
shi-na-i	(not do)
shi-na-kereba	(provided that [someone]does not do; if [someone] does not do)

The provisional ending which is also called the **-reba form** (it may appear as **-kereba** or **-reba** or **-eba** depending upon the stem to which it is added), has a relatively restricted usage--especialy in conversational Japanese, where it is often replaced by the **-tara form** or the particle **to**. The provisional ending is very important, however, because of its occurrence in several very useful expressions such as the one introduced in this lesson.

The word **naranai** is the negative plain form of the verb **naru** which means 'to become [acceptable] or 'to work out [all right].' The double negative **-nakereba naranai** literally means 'if [someone] does not [do something], it is not [acceptable]'--in other words, that one 'must' do or 'has to' do a certain thing. At first, the composition of this idiom may seem cumbersome to the learner, but as it is one of the most frequently used expressions in daily conversation in Japan, its use will likely become more natural to the learner as he or she practices the expression.

The negative answer to the question **shinakereba narimasen ka?** (Do I have to [do such and such]?) is **(shi)nakute mo ii desu**, which literally means 'it is all right not to do such and such.'

> muzukashii gakka o takusan **benkyoo shinakereba narimasen** ne.
> > (You'll **have to study** a lot of difficult subjects won't you?)
>
> rekishi no hon ya bungakusho o **yomanakereba narimasen**.
> > (I'll **have to read** history books and literature.)
>
> kanji o takusan **oboenakereba narimasen** ne.
> > (You'll **have to memorize** lots of kanji then.)
>
> kono kanji wa **oboenakute mo ii** desu.
> > (You **don't have to memorize** this kanji.)

28.2   ...ni kyoomi ga aru

kyoomi is a noun meaning 'interest.' In English we say that 'someone is interested in something.' To express a similar idea, Japanese people say '[someone] **wa** [something] **ni kyoomi ga aru**.'

> donna hon **ni kyoomi ga arimasu** ka?
> > (What sort of books **are [you] interested in?**)
>
> Buraun-san wa **nihon-bungaku ni kyoomi ga arimasu**.
> > (Mr. Brown **is interested in Japanese literature.**)
>
> Tanaka-san wa **ongaku ni kyoomi ga arimasu**.
> > (Miss Tanaka **is interested in music.**)

28.3   tame ni

tame is a noun meaning 'sake' or 'benefit.' When **tame + ni** is immediately added to a verb in its plain non-past form, it has the meaning 'in order to ...'

> nihon no bunka o yoku **rikai suru tame ni** rekishi no hon o yomanakereba narimasen.
> > (**In order to understand** Japanese culture well, you have to read history books.)
>
> bungakusho o **yomu tame ni** takusan kanji o oboemashoo.
> > (Let's memorize lots of kanji **in order to read** literature books.)
>
> nihon e **iku tame ni** nihongo o naraimashita.
> > (I learned Japanese **to go** to Japan.)

28.4   Natsume Sooseki

Natsume Sooseki (1867-1916) is one of the most widely read authors in Japan, ranking among the foremost writers of modern Japanese literature. Having studied English literature and having spent some of his early years in England, **Soseki** (often written with one 'o' in English) wrote with a crisp style and an intellectual appeal that are savored by many readers who are bilingual in Japanese and English. Among his many novels, **Wagahai wa Neko de aru** (I Am a Cat) and **Botchan** (Young Master) are the most popular among young people and are now considered Japanese literary classics. Other notable works such as the novel **Kokoro**--as well as those mentioned above--have been translated into English. Those who read these works in both translation and original Japanese unanimously agree that the works must be read in the originals to appreciate their true value.

28.5   honyaku de, gensho de (yomu)

honyaku means 'translation' and **gensho** means 'original.' The particle **de** in **honyaku de** (in translation) or **gensho de** (in the originals) is the 'agency' particle introduced earlier. Here, **de** denotes the means by which (or the form in which) someone reads works of literature.

Some of the masterpieces of Japanese literature have been translated into English, but there are many more works that still have not been translated. Interestingly enough, however, most works of foreign literature have been translated into Japanese.

> itsuka **honyaku de** yonda Natsume Sooseki no shoosetsu nado **gensho de** yonde mitai naa to omoimasu.   (Someday I'd really like to read **in the original texts** some of Natsume Soseki's novels which I've already read **in translation**.)
> watakushi wa waka ya haiku o **gensho de** yomitai desu.
> (I want to read some waka and haiku poems **in the original text**.)
> nihongo no shoosetsu o **honyaku de** yonda koto ga arimasu ka?
> (Have you ever read Japanese novels **in translation**?)

28.6   -tai naa to omo[w]u

naa is basically an interjection which expresses strong emotion. As has been noted, **-tai** is a bound word expressing 'desire.' When someone has a very strong desire or a wish, **-tai** may be followed by **naa!** or **naa to omo[w]u** (I think) to make the expression of such wishes more adult-like or sophisticated.

> Natsume Sooseki no shoosetsu o gensho de **yomitai naa** to omoimasu yo.
> (**I really want to read** Natsume Sooseki's novels in the original text.)
> hayaku nihon ni **ikitai naa** to omoimasu.
> (**I wish I could go** to Japan soon.)
> itsuka Buraun-san ni **aitai naa** to omoimasu.
> (**I really want to meet** Mr. Brown someday.)

350

28.7   sore ga taihen desu

In the expression, **sore ga taihen desu**, the particle **ga** is an emphasis marker and places extra importance on the subject of the sentence, **sore** (that). **taihen**, which was previously introduced as an adverb meaning 'very much' or 'a great deal' can be used as a noun predicate followed by **desu** to mean 'a thing of great concern' or 'an event of great importance.'

sore ga taihen desu.	(**That's** a big problem.)
nani ga taihen na n desu ka?	(**What** is the problem here?)
taihen desu! dareka kite kudasai!	(**Help!** Someone come here, please!)

28.8   isshookemmei ni

Japanese people value sincere efforts and hard work, and like to express this particular cultural trait by the word **isshookemmei** which means 'to put one's best efforts into life.' This word is usually used as an adverb--but may occur either with the adverb marker **ni** (as in **isshookemmei ni**) or without it. When it is used as a modifier of a noun, it takes **na**--as it is a copula noun.

isshookemmei ni benkyoo shinakereba narimasen.
> (We'll have to study **as hard as we can**.)

Buraun-san wa **isshookemmei** kanji o oboete imasu.
> (Mr. Brown is memorizing kanji **with all his might**.)

Buraun-san wa honto ni **isshookemmei na** hito desu ne!
> (Mr. Brown is certainly a **sincere, hardworking** person!)

28.9   shikkari gambarimashoo

When Japanese people depart from their friends they often say '**shikkari gambarimashoo**' as their departing remark. **shikkari** literally means 'to put your sound mind firmly into [your] conduct' and **gambarimashoo**, the **-mashoo form** of the verb **gambaru**, means '[let's] work very hard to attain [our] goals.' Of course, all Japanese people may not literally mean these words each time they speak, but most people like to encourage each other with these phrases as they part, rather than by saying 'don't work too hard,' or 'take it easy.'

shikkari   gambarimashoo!
> (**Well, let's keep up the good work** [till we see each other again]!) or
> (**Let's give it our best!**)

EXERCISES

28E.1 Oral Translation: Say the following sentences in Japanese.

Example 1: In order to understand Japanese culture, you must study the Japanese language.

--> 日本の文化を、よくりかいするために、日本語を
勉強しなければなりません。

1. In order to read Japanese newspaper, you must learn kanji.

2. In order to study kanji, you must buy a Japanese dictionary.

3. In order to make good grades, you must study very hard.

4. In order to understand Japanese culture, you must go to Japan.

5. In order to understand American culture, you must study American history.

6. In order to play the piano well, you must practice a lot.

7. In order to do research in medicine, you must study chemistry and biology.

Example 2: I really want to read a Japanese novel in the original text.

--> 日本の小説を、原書で読んでみたいなあと思います。

1. I really want to go to Japan some day.

2. I really want to read Japanese magazines.

3. I really want to climb Mt. Fuji some day.

4. I really want to meet Mr. Brown sometime.

5. I really want to play the piano well.

6. I really want to speak Japanese well.

7. I really want to read Soseki's novels in the original texts.

Example 3:   I am interested in music.

--> わたくしは、音楽にきょうみがあります。

1. I am interested in Japanese history.

2. I am interested in Japanese culture and literature.

3. I am interested in research in medicine.

4. I am interested in research in chemistry.

5. I am interested in classical music.

6. What are you interested in?

28E.2   つぎのしつもんにこたえなさい。

1. あなたは、日本語が上手になったら、何をするつもり
   ですか。

2. 日本に行ったら、どんな所にりょこうするつもりですか。

3. 東京に行ったら、どこにすむつもりですか。

4. 日光に行ったら、どんな所をしゃしんにとるつもり
   ですか。

5. かまくらに行ったら、何を見るつもりですか。

6. 大学をそつぎょうしたら、しょうらい、何をするつも
   りですか。

7. けっこんしたら、どんな家にすみたいと思いますか。

8. 漢字をたくさんおぼえたら、どんな本を読みたいと、
   思いますか。

9. しょうらい、医学の研究を、したいと思いますか。

10. お金がたくさんあったら、何を買うつもりですか。

28E.3 つぎのかんじを正しく書いて、おぼえなさい。

149. 医 (medicine) 医学 一 ア ア 三 至 医 医

150. 研 (to polish) 研究 一 ア ア 石 石 石 石 研
研

151. 究 (research) 研究 ` ` 宀 宀 宛 究 究

152. 物 (thing) 生物 ノ ト 牛 牛 牜 物 物 物

153. 化 (to transform) 化学 ノ イ 仁 化

154. 数 (number; math) 数学 ` ` ⺍ 半 米 米 类 娄
娄 数 数 数 数

155. 科 (task) 学科 一 二 千 禾 禾 禾 禾 禾
科

156. 文 (sentence) 文化 ` 一 ナ 文

157. 歴 (chronology) 歴史 一 厂 厂 厈 厤 厤 厤 厤

厤 厤 厤 歷 歷 歷

158. 史 (history) 歴史 丶 ロ ロ 史 史

159. 説 (to narrate) 小説 丶 ニ ㇡ ㇢ 言 言 言 言

言 訁 訮 説 説 説

160. 原 (origin) 原書 一 厂 厂 厂 厉 原 原 原

原 原

161. 漢 (Chinese) 漢字 丶 ㇡ ㇢ 汀 汫 汫 浐

浐 浐 漢 漢 漢

162. 字 (character) 漢字 丶 ㇒ 宀 宇 宇 字

28E.4 こえをだして、読んでごらんなさい。つぎに、英語で、い
みをいってごらんなさい。

1. 山田さんは、しょうらい、医学の研究をしたいと思っ
    ているので、生物や化学や数学を、勉強しなければな
    りません。

2. ブラウンさんは、今学期、歴史と日本文学と文化史を
   とっているので、たくさん本を読まなければなりません。

355

4. 化学や生物は、大変むずかしい学科なので、いっしょうけんめい勉強しなければなりません。

5. 日本文化をりかいするためには、日本歴史の本や、文学書などをたくさん読まなければなりません。

6. 日本語の新聞を読むためには、漢字をおぼえなければなりません。カタカナも大切_{たいせつ}です。

7. できたら、日本の和歌_{わか}や、俳句_{はいく}や、小説などを、原書で読んでみたいなあと思います。

8. 去年、夏目漱石_{そうせき}の小説を、ほんやくで読んでみました。

9. 医者になるためには、生物や化学などのむずかしい学科を勉強して、医大に入って、医学の研究をしたりインターンをしたり、しなければなりません。

10. 日本文学をおしえるためには、文学書を原書で読んだり、英語にほんやくしたり、しなければなりません。

11. 日本文学史の研究には、大変きょうみがあります。

12. あなたは、日本で一番大きい都市の名前を、知っていらっしゃいますか。

28E.5　「...と思います」をくわえて、こたえてごらんなさい。

1. ブラウンさんは、もう日本の生活になれましたか。

2. 本州、四国、九州、北海道の中で、どの島が一番大きいですか。

3. 京都は、富士山_{ふじさん}の西の方にある都市ですか。

4. ブラウンさんの家族は、みんな、元気ですか。

5. 日本語の文学を読むためには、漢字をおぼえなければ
なりませんか。

6. 日本の一番北にある大きい島の名前を、漢字で書くこ
とができますか。

7. つゆの間は、毎日かさを持って出た方がいいですか。

8. 日本のつゆは、三週間も続きますか。

9. 日本では、さくらの花が咲くころに、学校の新学年が
始まりますか。

10. 冬、北風がふく日にゆきがふると、大変さむいですね。

11. ブラウンさんが、はこねに行った時、天気がよかった
ですか。

12. 今学期（こんがっき）の日本語のクラスは、むずかしかったですか。

13. あなたは、日本語が上手（じょうず）になりましたか。

14. もっと日本語を勉強して、日本の小説をどんどん読ん
でみたいですか。

15. 日本語のクラスは、楽しかったですか。

VOCABULARY

VERBS

sotsugyoo shitara	(when I graduate; after I graduate: -tara form of sotsugyoo suru)
dekitara	(if possible; if I can: -tara form of dekiru)
shinakereba narimasen	(I must do...: -nakereba narimasen construction of suru, 28.1)
motte imasu	(I have; I own: -te form of motsu + imasu)
motsu	(to have; to own)
yonde mitai	(I'd like to try reading [such and such]: -te form of yomu + -tai form of miru)
rikai suru	(to understand; to comprehend)

yomanakereba narimasen   (I must read: -nakereba narimasen construction of yomu, 28.1)

oboenakereba narimasen   (I must memorize; I must remember, 28.1)

oboeru   (to learn; to memorize)

benkyoo shinakereba narimasen   (I must study: -nakereba narimasen construction of benkyoo suru, 28.1)

gambarimashoo   (let's work hard: -mashoo form of gambaru, 28.9)

gambaru   (to work diligently toward specific goals, 28.9)

ADJECTIVES   (---)

NOUNS

sotsugyoo	(graduation)
shoorai	(the future)
igaku	(the study of medicine)
kenkyuu	(study; research)
seibutsu	(biology)
gakka	(subject [of study]; scholastic fields)
kiboo	(hope; desire; ambition)
kyoomi	(interest; curiosity)
bunka	(culture)
rikai	(understanding; comprehension)
bungakusho	(literary works)
hon'yaku	(translation; a work in translation, 28.5)
bungaku	(literature)
isha	(medical doctor, physician)
idai	(medical school)
Natsume Sooseki	(twentieth-century Japanese author, 28.4)
shoosetsu	(novel)
gensho	(original [untranslated] text, 28.5)

OTHERS

-nakereba naranai	(I must do [such and such]: an idiomatic expression, 28.1)
yama no yoo ni arimasu	(to be swamped with; to have a million things [one would like to do])
mazu	(first; first of all; initially)
dondon	(sequentially; one after another; an adverb)
-te miru	(to try doing [suh and such]: -te form of the verb + miru)
tatoeba	(for example)
kyoomi ga aru	(to be interested in ..., 28.2)
tame ni	(in order to do [such and such], 28.3)
soshite	(and; also; too)
itsuka	(sometime)
-tai naa!	([I] would really like to do: -tai + the interjection naa, 28.6)
sore nara	(in that case; if that's so)
sore ga taihen desu	(that's a big problem; that's terrible, 28.7)
otagai ni	(each other; [to do something] each other: honorific prefix o- + tagai + ni)
isshookemmei ni	(putting all one's efforts into one's life, 28.8)
shikkari gambarimashoo	(let's do our very best; let's keep up the good work, 28.9)

hiragana

a	i	u	e	o
あ	い	う	え	お

ka	ki	ku	ke	ko
か	き	く	け	こ

sa	shi	su	se	so
さ	し	す	せ	そ

ta	chi	tsu	te	to
た	ち	つ	て	と

na	ni	nu	ne	no
な	に	ぬ	ね	の

ha	hi	fu	he	ho
は	ひ	ふ	へ	ほ

ma	mi	mu	me	mo
ま	み	む	め	も

ya		yu		yo
や		ゆ		よ

ra	ri	ru	re	ro
ら	り	る	れ	ろ

wa				(w)o
わ				を

N
ん

katakana

a	i	u	e	o
ア	イ	ウ	エ	オ

ka	ki	ku	ke	ko
カ	キ	ク	ケ	コ

sa	shi	su	se	so
サ	シ	ス	セ	ソ

ta	chi	tsu	te	to
タ	チ	ツ	テ	ト

na	ni	nu	ne	no
ナ	ニ	ヌ	ネ	ノ

ha	hi	fu	he	ho
ハ	ヒ	フ	ヘ	ホ

ma	mi	mu	me	mo
マ	ミ	ム	メ	モ

ya		yu		yo
ヤ		ユ		ヨ

ra	ri	ru	re	ro
ラ	リ	ル	レ	ロ

wa				(w)o
ワ				ヲ

N
ン

359

hiragana

ga が	gi ぎ	gu ぐ	ge げ	go ご
za ざ	ji じ	zu ず	ze ぜ	zo ぞ
da だ	ji ぢ	zu づ	de で	do ど
ba ば	bi び	bu ぶ	be べ	bo ぼ
pa ぱ	pi ぴ	pu ぷ	pe ぺ	po ぽ

katakana

ga ガ	gi ギ	gu グ	ge ゲ	go ゴ
za ザ	ji ジ	zu ズ	ze ゼ	zo ゾ
da ダ	ji ヂ	zu ヅ	de デ	do ド
ba バ	bi ビ	bu ブ	be ベ	bo ボ
pa パ	pi ピ	pu プ	pe ペ	po ポ

hiragana

kya きゃ	kyu きゅ	kyo きょ
sha しゃ	shu しゅ	sho しょ
cha ちゃ	chu ちゅ	cho ちょ
nya にゃ	nyu にゅ	nyo にょ
hya ひゃ	hyu ひゅ	hyo ひょ
mya みゃ	myu みゅ	myo みょ
rya りゃ	ryu りゅ	ryo りょ
gya ぎゃ	gyu ぎゅ	gyo ぎょ
ja じゃ	ju じゅ	jo じょ
ja ぢゃ	ju ぢゅ	jo ぢょ
bya びゃ	byu びゅ	byo びょ
pya ぴゃ	pyu ぴゅ	pyo ぴょ

katakana

kya キャ	kyu キュ	kyo キョ
sha シャ	shu シュ	sho ショ
cha チャ	chu チュ	cho チョ
nya ニャ	nyu ニュ	nyo ニョ
hya ヒャ	hyu ヒュ	hyo ヒョ
mya ミャ	myu ミュ	myo ミョ
rya リャ	ryu リュ	ryo リョ
gya ギャ	gyu ギュ	gyo ギョ
ja ジャ	ju ジュ	jo ジョ
ja ヂャ	ju ヂュ	jo ヂョ
bya ビャ	byu ビュ	byo ビョ
pya ピャ	pyu ピュ	pyo ピョ

List of Kanji

Lesson 10

1. 一　(one)　　　いち　ひと　　ひとり　　ついたち　いっぽん
一、一つ、一人、一日、一本

2. 二　(two)　　　に　ふた　ふたり　ふつか
二、二つ、二人、二日

3. 三　(three)　　さん　みっ　さんにん　みっか
三、三つ、三人、三日

4. 四　(four)　　　よん　よっ　よにん　よっか　しがつ
四、四つ、四人、四日、四月

5. 五　(five)　　　ご　いっ　ごにん　いつか
五、五つ、五人、五日

6. 六　(six)　　　ろく　むっ　ろくにん　むいか
六、六つ、六人、六日

7. 七　(seven)　　しち　なな　しちにん　なのか
七、七つ、七人、七日

8. 八　(eight)　　はち　やっ　はちにん　ようか
八、八つ、八人、八日

9. 九　(nine)　　きゅう　ここの　きゅうにん　ここのか
九、九つ、九人、九日

10. 十　(ten)　　　じゅう　とお　じゅうにん　とおか
十、十、十人、十日

11. 日　(sun; day)　にち　じゅうよっか　はつか　なんにち
日、十四日、二十日、何日
　　　　　　　　にちようび　ひ　きょう　きのう
日曜日、日、今日、昨日

12. 月　(moon; month)　げつ　つき　なんがつ　げつようび　ひとつき
月、月、何月、月曜日、一月
　　　　　　　　しちがつ　ろっ　げつ
七月、六か月

Lesson 11

13. 本　(book)　　　ほん　いっぽん　さんぼん
本、一本、三本

14. 人　(person)　　ひと　なにじん　ひとり　ふたり　さんにん
人、何人、一人、二人、三人

15. 語　(language)　にほんご
日本語

List of Kanji

16. 何　(what)　何、何人、何人
　　　　　　　　なに　なんにん　なにじん

17. 英　(English)　英語
　　　　　　　　えい ご

18. 話　(to speak)　話します、電話
　　　　　　　　はな　　　　でん わ

Lesson 12

19. 火　(fire; Tuesday)　火曜日、火
　　　　　　　　か よう び　ひ

20. 水　(water; Wednesday)　水曜日、水
　　　　　　　　すい よう び　みず

21. 木　(tree; Thursday)　木曜日、木
　　　　　　　　もく よう び　き

22. 金　(gold; Friday)　金曜日、お金、金
　　　　　　　　きん よう び　かね　きん

23. 土　(earth; Saturday)　土曜日、土
　　　　　　　　ど よう び　つち

24. 曜　(day of week)　日曜日
　　　　　　　　にち よう び

Lesson 13

25. 男　(male; man)　男、男子
　　　　　　　　おとこ　だん し

26. 女　(female; woman)　女、女子
　　　　　　　　おんな　じょ し

27. 先　(ahead)　先生、先
　　　　　　　　せん せい　さき

28. 生　(to be born; life)　先生、学生、生きる、生活
　　　　　　　　せん せい　がく せい　い　　　せい かつ

29. 時　(time; o'clock)　六時、時、時計
　　　　　　　　ろく じ　とき　と けい

30. 分　(minute)　五分、十分、分かる
　　　　　　　　ご ふん　じゅっぷん　わ

Lessson 14

31. 上　(on; top)　上、上手
　　　　　　　　うえ　じょう ず

362

32. 下 (under) 　　下、上下、下手

33. 中 (in; center) 　中、中国語、中学生

34. 大 (large) 　　大きい、大すき、大変

35. 小 (small) 　　小さい、小学校

36. 今 (now) 　　　今、今度、今日

Lesson 15

37. 田 (rice field) 　田中、中田、山田

38. 父 (father) 　　父、お父さん

39. 母 (mother) 　　母、お母さん

40. 毎 (every) 　　　毎日

41. 学 (learning) 　学校、学生

42. 校 (institution) 学校

Lesson 16

43. 口 (mouth) 　　口、入り口

44. 食 (to eat) 　　食べる、食事、夕食

45. 目 (eye) 　　　目、二つ目

46. 見 (to see) 　　見る、見物

47. 手 (hand) 　　　手、上手

48. 読 (to read) 　　読む、読書

Lesson 17

49. 山 (mountain) 山田、富士山

50. 勉 (effort) 勉強

51. 強 (strong) 勉強、強い

52. 午 (noon) 午後、午前

53. 後 (after) 午後、後、後ろ

54. 間 (interval) 時間、間

55. 行 (to go) 行く、旅行

Lesson 18

56. 来 (to come) 来る、来年

57. 年 (year) きょ年、年

58. 家 (house) 家、家、家族

59. 歩 (to walk) 歩く、歩行者

60. 近 (near) 近い、近所

61. 遠 (far) 遠い、遠方

62. 朝 (morning) 毎朝、朝食

Lesson 19

63. 度 (occasion) 今度、度々

64. 所 (place) 所、近所

65. 出　(to get out)　出かける、出来る、出口

66. 東　(east)　東京、東

67. 京　(capital)　東京、京都

68. 作　(to make)　作る、作文

69. 買　(to buy)　買う、買い物

Lesson 20

70. 屋　(store)　くすり屋

71. 方　(direction)　…の方、方

72. 右　(right)　右、左右

73. 左　(left)　左

74. 前　(in front)　前、午前

75. 銀　(silver)　銀行、銀

76. 百　(hundred)　百、三百

77. 千　(thousand)　千、三千

78. 万　(ten thousand)　万

79. 円　(yen)　円

Lesson 21

80. 音　(sound)　音楽、音、

81. 楽　(to enjoy)　音楽、楽しい、楽

82.	聞	(to hear)	聞く、新聞
83.	歌	(song)	歌、和歌
84.	番	(order)	一番
85.	思	(to think)	思う
86.	耳	(ear)	耳
87.	書	(to write)	書く、読書
88.	美	(beautiful)	美しい、美人、美恵子

Lesson 22

89.	光	(to shine)	日光、光、光る
90.	変	(to change)	大変、変な、変わる
91.	有	(to have)	有名、
92.	名	(name)	有名、名前
93.	入	(to enter)	入る、入れる、入り口
94.	高	(high)	高い、高校生
95.	少	(a little)	少し、少々
96.	天	(heaven)	天気
97.	気	(feeling)	天気、気持ち、気分

Lesson 23

| 98. | 春 | (spring) | 春、春夏秋冬 |

99. 夏 (summer) 夏 [なつ]

100. 秋 (autumn) 秋 [あき]

101. 冬 (winter) 冬 [ふゆ]

102. 休 (vacation) 休み [やす]

103. 海 (sea) 海、海岸 [うみ][かいがん]

104. 正 (correct) 正月、正しい [しょうがつ][ただ]

105. 友 (friend) 友だち、友人 [とも][ゆうじん]

106. 花 (flower) 花 [はな]

Lesson 24

107. 咲 (to bloom) 咲く [さ]

108. 新 (new) 新しい、新聞、新学年 [あたら][しんぶん][しんがくねん]

109. 始 (to begin) 始まる [はじ]

110. 子 (child) 子供、男の子 [こども][おとこ][こ]

111. 供 (follower) 子供 [こども]

112. 着 (to wear) 着る [き]

113. 開 (to open) 開く、開始 [ひら][かいし]

114. 々 (repetition sign) 人々、度々、山々 [ひとびと][たびたび][やまやま]

115. 若 (young) 若い [わか]

116. 風 (wind) 風、風邪 [かぜ][かぜ]

Lesson 25

117.	昨	(yesterday)	昨日、昨日、昨年
118.	頭	(head)	頭
119.	雨	(rain)	雨、梅雨、梅雨
120.	電	(electric)	電車、電話
121.	車	(car)	電車、車
122.	持	(to hold)	持つ、気持ち
123.	空	(sky)	空、空港
124.	多	(numerous)	多い、多数
125.	続	(to continue)	続く
126.	週	(week)	週間、今週

Lesson 26

127.	島	(island)	島、日本列島
128.	知	(to know)	知る
129.	北	(north)	北、北海道
130.	道	(road)	北海道
131.	州	(state)	州、本州
132.	南	(south)	南、南北
133.	国	(country)	四国、中国、中国人

134.	西	(west)	西、関西
135.	都	(capital)	京都、都、首都
136.	市	(city)	都市
137.	阪	([O]saka)	大阪

Lesson 27

138.	夫	(spouse)	夫人、夫
139.	去	(past)	去年、去る
140.	活	(active)	生活
141.	族	(clan)	家族
142.	皆	(all)	皆さま、皆、
143.	元	(origin)	元気
144.	兄	(older brother)	兄弟、兄、お兄さん
145.	弟	(younger brother)	弟
146.	姉	(older sister)	姉、お姉さん
147.	妹	(younger sister)	妹、姉妹
148.	夕	(evening)	夕食、夕方

Lesson 28

149.	医	(medicine)	医学、医者
150.	研	(to polish)	研究

151. 究 (research) 研究 (けんきゅう)

152. 物 (thing) 生物、着物 (せいぶつ、きもの)

153. 化 (to transform) 化学、お化け、化ける (かがく、ば、ば)

154. 数 (number; math) 数学、数、数える (すうがく、かず、かぞ)

155. 科 (task) 学科、日本語科 (がっか、にほんごか)

156. 文 (sentence) 文化、文、文学、文字 (ぶんか、ぶん、ぶんがく、もじ)

157. 歴 (chronology) 歴史 (れきし)

158. 史 (history) 歴史、日本史 (れきし、にほんし)

159. 説 (to narrate) 小説、説明 (しょうせつ、せつめい)

160. 原 (origin) 原書、原、野原 (げんしょ、はら、のはら)

161. 漢 (Chinese) 漢字、 (かんじ)

162. 字 (character) 漢字、ローマ字、文字 (かんじ、じ、もじ)

Vocabulary

【a】

aa   (oh; ah; well) ···· 24, 182

achira   (that way over there, over yonder; 3.6) ···· 36, 182

achira kochira ni   (here and there) ···· 310

aimashoo   (let's meet: -mashoo form of a[w]u) ···· 125

aimashoo ka   (shall we meet? ,10.7) ···· 125

aisukuriimu   (icecream, 8.11) ···· 98,114

aka   (red color, 14.6) ···· 182

akai   (red, 14.6) ···· 62, 181

akeru   (to open; something lifts off; [rainy season] ends) ···· 334

akete kudasai   (Please open) ···· 36

aki   (fall; autumn) ···· 298

amai   (sweet tasting) ···· 98,169

amakute   (tasting aweet and ...: -kute form of amai) ···· 169

ame   (rain) ···· 322

amerika   (America; USA) ···· 14

amerikajin   (US citizen; American) ···· 86

ammari + -masen   (not very ...; not so ...) ···· 140

anata   (you, 1.8) ···· 13

ane   (my older sister, 13.1, 27.1) ···· 168,   346

ani   (my older brother, 13.1) ···· 168

anna   (that ... sort of, 7.8) ···· 85

ano   (that ... over there, 4.1) ···· 46

ano ...   (well; umm ..., 14.2) ···· 182

ano hito   (that person over there; that person mentioned; he; she) ···· 47

ao   (blue color, 14.6) ···· 182

aoi   (blue, 14.6) ···· 62, 181

Aoki   (a Japanese surname) ···· 14

apaato   (apartment) ···· 238

are   (that over there, 3.5) ···· 36

are o   mite kudasai.   (Please look at that thing over there.) ···· 36

arigatoo gozaimasu   (thank you very much) ···· 24

arimasu   (something is located; there is; there are; I have: -masu form of aru 'to exist',12.2)····73, 153)

aru   (to exist; to be; to be located at such and such place) ···· 73, 153

aru   (a certain; some) ···· 310

aruite   (on foot; to go by walking: -te form of aruku,16.4, 18.8)···· 208, 237

arukimashita   (I have walked; I walked: -mashita form of aruku, 11.1) ···· 139

aruku   (to walk, 18.8) ···· 237

asagohan   (breakfast; morning meal) ···· 113

Asakusa   (the merchants' center in   downtown Tokyo, 15.10) ···· 193

ashita   (tomorrow) ···· 24,125

asobi ni   kite kudasai   (Please come and visit, 18.9) ···· 237

asobu   (to play; to enjoy oneself; to have fun) ···· 297

asoko   (over there) ···· 61

asondari   (I [can] play or ...: -tari form of asobu) ···· 297

asupirin   (aspirin) ···· 262

atama   (head) ···· 322

atarashii   (new) ····250

atarimashita   (you have hit the target; you have given the right answer: -mashita form of atarimasu, ataru)   ···· 208

ataru   (to strike the target; to guess [something] right) ···· 208

atatakai   ([comfortably] warm; nice and warm) ···· 309

atatakaku   (warm: -ku form of atatakai) ···· 309

ateru   (to guess or to come up with a correct answer) ···· 208

Vocabulary

atete kudasai (please guess; please come up with a right answer: -te form of ateru + kudasai) ···· 208

atsui (warm; hot to touch) ···· 24, 98

atte (there is ... and ...; I'll see ... and ...: -te form of aru) ···· 261, 297

a[w]u (to meet [someone]) ···· 125

【b】

bakari (nothing but; only) ···· 346

banana (banana, 8.11) ···· 98

bangoo (number) ···· 85

basu (bus) ···· 140

Beetooven (Beethoven, a famous composer) ···· 274

benkyoo shimasu (I study: -masu form of benkyoo suru, 9.9) ···· 61,113

benkyoo shinakereba narimasen (I must study: -nakereba narimasen construction of benkyoo suru, 28.1) ···· 358

benri (na) (convenient: a copula noun, 13.5) ···· 169

(o)bentoo (boxed or sack lunch; picnic lunch) ···· 250

betsu ni ... -masen (not particularly; nothing in particular) ···· 126

bin (bottle) ···· 153

bisshori (soaking wet) ···· 322

booshi (hat; cap) ···· 309

Bosuton (the city name 'Boston' as pronounced in Japanese) ···· 238

bumpoo (grammar) ···· 226

bungaku (literature) ···· 358

bungakusho (literary works) ···· 358

bunka (culture) ···· 358

Buraun (the English surname 'Brown' as pronounced in Japanese) ···· 13

【c】

chairo (brown, 14.6) ···· 183

Chen-san (Mr. [Mrs. or Miss] Chen) ···· 46

chichi (my father, 13.1, 27.1) ···· 168, 346

chigaimasu (that is incorrect; that's wrong; you are mistaken) ···· 14

chiisakute (small and ...: -kute form of chiisai, 13.10) ···· 169

chiisai (small; little)

chikai (near) ···· 238

chikaku (nearby) ···· 262

chikatetsu (subway, 11.13) ···· 139

chirachira to (flickering down: a reduplicated onomatopoetic word, 24.3, 24.8) ···· 310

chiru (to fall: an intransitive verb used for flowers or leaves to fall from trees) ···· 309

chitte (fall from trees and ...: -te form of chiru) ···· 309

chittomo ...-masen (not ... at all, 15.5) ···· 193

chizu (map) ···· 334

choodo (just, exactly, it so happens that ...) ···· 61, 298

chotto (a littel bit) ···· 24, 47

chuugoku (China) ···· 14

chuugokugo (the Chinese language) ···· 14

chuugokujin (Chinese person) ···· 86

chuuka-ryoori (Chinses cuisine or cooking) ···· 98

【d】

-dai (counter for machinery) ···· 250

daibutsu (the Great Buddha, 19.2) ···· 250

daigaku (university; college) ···· 238

daigakusei (college student: daigaku + [gaku]sei) ···· 86

daijoobu (I'm fine; I'm all right) ···· 322

daisuki (very pleasing; I like ... very much, 8.1) ···· 97

daitai (in general) ···· 322

dakara (therefore; and so; that's why) ···· 193

dake (only, 5.10) ···· 62

dame (no good: a copula noun, 17.3) ···· 226

dare (who [neutral], 4.2) ···· 47

dare no (whose, 4.5) ···· 47

dareka (someone, 11.5) ···· 140

dashite kudasai (please take [something] out: -te form of dasu + kudasai) ···· 153

dasu (to take [something] out) ···· 153

datta (the past form of da, the plain form of deshita, 25.6) ···· 322

de (particle denoting the location of activity or event, 12.4) ···· 153

de (using such and such; by: a particle denoting the means of transportation, 11.10) ···· 139

de (by means of; in (the ... language): a particle marking the agent, 1.14) ···· 13

de (at; in; on: a particle marking the place of activity, 5.8) ···· 62

de [yuumei] ([famous] for [such and such], 22.3) ···· 286

de gozaimasu (it is: salesperson's honorific style of saying desu) ···· 262

[shashin] de miru (to see [something] in [photographs], 22.5) ···· 286

de wa arimasen (is not: negation of NOUN + desu, 3.10) ···· 36

de wa arimasen.deshita (the negative past form of desu, 11.4) ···· 140

deeto (date) ···· 154

deguchi (exit, 10.10) ···· 126

dekakemashoo (let's go out; let's leave: -mashoo form of dekakeru) ···· 125

dekakeru (to leave home [to go somewhere]; to go out) ···· 125

dekimasu ([someone] is able to do such and such: -masu form of dekiru) ···· 85

dekiru (to be able to do such and such; to be able to speak the language) ···· 85

dekitara (if possible; if I can: -tara form of dekiru) ···· 357

[ni] demasu (you turn up [at]...; I come to [the place of]: -masu form of deru) ···· 261

... demo (... or something, 8.10) ···· 97

demo (but) ···· 24

denki (electricity; electric light) ···· 322

denki o tsukeru (to turn on the light) ···· 321

densha (train) ···· 139

denwa (telephone) ···· 85, 322

denwa o kakeru (to call [someone] on [the telephone]) ···· 321

depaato (department store) ···· 139

deshita (was: the past form of desu, 11.3) ···· 140

deshoo (probably is; maybe: tentative form of desu 10.6) ···· 126

desu (is; equivalent to: a copula, 1.6) ···· 13

dewa (well; then; hmmm) ···· 13

dezaato (dessert) ···· 114

dezain (design) ···· 182

dochira (which way; where [politely spoken]; which one of the two, 3.6) ···· 14, 36

dochira kara desu ka? (Where are you from?) ···· 14

dochira no hoo (which way to ...; which one of the two, 8.6, 20.3) ···· 97, 262

doko (where, 5.7) ···· 62, 126

dokoka (somewhere, 11.5) ···· 140

donata (who [exalted], 4.2) ···· 47

dondon (sequentially; one after another: an adverb) ···· 358

donna (what sort of, 7.8) ···· 85

dono (of which, 4.1) ···· 46

dono gurai (about how long; how much; how long, 18.2) ···· 226, 238

(dono) hen (whereabout; in what neighborhood) ···· 238

doo (how, 2.8) ···· 24

doo itashimashite (you are welcome, 6.9) ···· 73

dooka shita (something has happened, 25.1) ···· 322

doomo arigatoo gozaimashita (thank you very much for what you have done, 6.9) ···· 73

dooshite (why) ···· 298

doozo (please) ···· 13

doozo okamai naku (Please don't do anything special, 27.8) ···· 346

dore (which one, 3.5) ···· 36

dore desu ka? (Which one?) ···· 36

doyoobi (Saturday, 10.3) ···· 125

【e】

e (to: a particle denoting destination or direction, 11.6) ···· 140

ee (yeah; informal way to say 'yes') ···· 24

ee to (let me see...; ummm ...) ···· 154, 262, 334

eiga (movie) ···· 139

eigo (the English language) ···· 13

empitsu (pencil, 3.7) ···· 35

en (yen: the Japanese currency, 14.12) ···· 182

enryo (the virtue of modesty and humility, 27.9) ···· 346

erebeetaa (elevator) ···· 262

esukareetaa (escalator) ···· 262

【f】

Foodo (the personal name 'Ford' as pronounced in Japanese) 238

fude (writing brush, 16.8) ···· 209

Fujisan (Mt. Fuji, 15.7) ···· 193

fuku ([the wind] blows) ···· 309

fukushuu (review of previous lesson) ···· 250

-fun, -pun (minute: bound words indicating minutes, 9.4) ···· 113

furansu-ryoori (French cuisine or cooking) ···· 98

furansugo (the French language) ···· 24

furu (to fall: rain, snow, or hail to fall from the clouds) ···· 321

furui (old; ancient; historical) ···· 168, 250

furukute (old and ...: -kute form of furui, 13.10) ···· 168

furuutsu (fruit) ···· 114

futatsume (the second object, 20.7) ···· 262

futte imashita (it was raining: -te form of furu + imashita) ···· 321

fuyu (winter) ···· 298

【g】

ga (a particle marking the subject in emphasis) ···· 168

ga (particle denoting the subject of the verb aru, 12.2) ···· 153

ga (a particle marking the subject, 1.11) ···· 13

ga (but: a conjunctive particle, 5.12) ···· 62

ga (a particle marking the subject of a subordinate clause) ···· 238

ga (a particle marking the subject of the question which begins with an interrogative word) ···· 182

gakka (subject [of study]; scholastic fields) ···· 358

gakki (school term; session; semester) ···· 226

gakki (musical instrument) ···· 274

gakki-shiken (final examination, 17.1) ···· 226

gakkoo (school) ···· 24

gakusei (student) ···· 47, 61

gambarimashoo (let's work hard: -mashoo form of gambaru, 28.9) ···· 358 gambaru (to work diligently toward specific goals, 28.9) ···· 358

.(o)genki (in [your] good health; fine, 2.6) ···· 24

gensho (original [untranslated] text, 28.5) ···· 358

getsuyoobi (Monday, 10.3) ···· 126

ginkoo (bank, 20.1) ···· 262

Ginza (The Ginza, Tokyo's most beautiful and fashionable shopping district, 10.9) ···· 125, 139)

go (five; 5, 7.9) ···· 85

(go)enryo naku (Please don't worry about a thing, 27.9) ···· 346

gogo (p.m.; afternoon, 9.2) ···· 113

goji (five o'clock, 9.1) ···· 114

(go)kazoku (your family; honorable family: exalted prefix go- + kazoku) ···· 168, 346

gokigenyoo (Farewell; good-bye, 2.1) ···· 24

(go)kyoodai (your brothers and sisters, 27.1) ···· 346

gonin-kyoodai (five brothers and sisters [including myself]) ····168

-goro (approximate time, 9.7) ···· 113

(go)shujin (your husband, 13.1) ···· 169

(go)yukkuri (please take time; [do] slowly and leisurely; in a relaxed way or leisurely manner, 27.9: the honorific prefix -go + yukkuri meaning slowly) ···· 183, 346

gozaimasu (there is; there are; we have: -masu form of the archaic verb gozaru used by salespersons to add politeness to arimasu, 14.5) ···· 181

gozen (before noon; a.m., 9.2) ···· 113

-gurai (approximately; about, 17.9) ···· 226

guramu (gram, 20.5) ···· 262

【h】

haburashi (tooth brush) ···· 262

hachi (eight; 8, 7.9) ···· 85

hachiji (eight o'clock, 9.1) ···· 113

haha ([my] mother, 13.1, 27.1) ···· 168, 346

hai (yes) ···· 13

hai doozo (yes please; here you are, 4.7) ···· 47

hai, sore desu. (Yes, that is the one; that's right, 3.12) ···· 36

haiku (17-syllable Japanese poem) ···· 310

hairimashita (I went into; I took a dip in: -mashita form of hairu, 22.1) ···· 285

hairu (to enter; to go in) ···· 285

haite (I wear on my feet: -te form of haku, 24.5) ···· 309

haitta (I have entered: -ta form of hairu, 22.1) ···· 285

hajimarimasu (it starts; it begins: -masu form of hajimaru) ···· 113

hajimaru (something begins) ···· 113

hajime ni (at first) ···· 183

hajimemashite (How do you do? 1.1) ···· 13

hakkiri (clearly; distinctly) ···· 73

hako (box) ···· 153

Hakone (a scenic national park southwest of Tokyo, 22.4) ···· 286

haku (to wear on one's legs or feet, 24.5) ···· 309

hambaagaa (hamburger, 8.11) ···· 97

han (half; half past the hour, 9.5) ···· 113

hana (flower; blossom) ..169,298

(o)hanami (flower-viewing, 24.6) 310

hanashimasen (I don't speak someone doesn't speak: negative f.of hanashimasu) ...61

hanashimashoo (let's speak, 1.15)....13

hanashimasu (I speak/ someone speaks; the -masu form of hanasu) ···· 61

hanashite (-te form of hanasu, 16.2, 16.4) ···· 208

hanashite kudasai (please speak, 3.4: -te form of hanasu + kudasai, 6.5) ···· 35, 73

hanaya (florist, 20.1) ···· 262

haru (spring) ···· 298

(o)hashi (chopsticks, 8.4) ···· 97

Hawai (Hawaii: the state name 'Hawaii' as pronounced in Japanese) ···· 14, 238

hayaku (fast; rapidly) ···· 73

hayaoki (earlybird; a person who wakes up early) ···· 113

hen (approximate point in space) ···· 238

heta (na) (to be unskillful at; to be no good at) ···· 274

heya (room) ···· 193

hi (day) ···· 126

hidari (left hand side; left) ···· 36, 262

hidarite (on [your] left) ···· 262

higashi (east, 10.10) ···· 126

hiite shimatta (I ended up catching [a cold]: -te form of hiku + -ta form of shima[w]u, 25.2) ···· 321

-hiki, -piki, -biki (counter for animals, 13.8) ···· 168

hiku (to play a musical instrument) ···· 273

hiku (to catch [a cold]; to pull; to draw in) ···· 321

hinamatsuri (the Doll Festival, 23.4) ···· 298

hiragana (hiragana syllabary) ···· 73

hirakimasu ([it] opens; to blossom: -masu form of hiraku) 309

(o)hiru (noon) ···· 125

(o)hirugohan (lunch) ···· 97, 114

hito (person [neutral]) ···· 46

hitobito (people; many people) ···· 310

hitori de (alone; by oneself) ···· 140

hitori, futari, sannin ... (one, two, three ... : number + -tari or -nin [counters for people], 13.6) ···· 168

hitorikko (the only child) ···· 169

hodo (about; roughly as many as...; approximately, 20.6) 154, 262

Hokkaidoo (one of the major islands of Japan, located north of Honshu, 26.4) ···· 334

hon (book) ···· 35

hon'ya (bookstore) ···· 262

hon'yaku (translation; a translated work, 28.5) ···· 358

-hon, -bon, -pon (counter for slender and long objects, 12.7) ···· 153

Honshuu (the largest island of Japan, located in the center of the island chain, 26.4) ···· 334

honto ni (really; truly, 2.10) ···· 24

hontoo ni (truly; indeed: more formal or written style variant of honto ni) ···· 310

hoo (direction, 20.3) ···· 261

hoomusutei (home-stay; a Japanese style room and board arrangement, 18.7) ···· 238

hooseki (jewelry) ···· 262

hoshii (wish to obtain, 14.4) 181

hosoi (slender; thin) ···· 169,183

hotondo (almost; for the most part) ····226

hyaku (one hundred,14.10) 182

【i】

i[w]u (to say) ···· 35, 208

ichi (one; 1, 7.9) ···· 85

ichiban [suki] (the best; the most; I [like] ... the best, 21.5) ···· 274

ichido (once; one time) ····298

ichido ni (all at once) ····310

ichiji (one o'clock, 9.1) ····113

ichiman-gosen (fifteen thousand, 14.10) ····182

idai (medical school) ····3

itta koto ga arimasu (I have been [there]; I have gone [there] before, 22.2) ···· 285

itte (I go and ...: -te form of iku) ···· 225

itte (-te form of i[w]u (to say), 16.2, 16.4) ···· 208

itte kudasai (please go: -te form of iku + kudasai) ···· 261

itte kudasai (please say : -te form of i[w]u + kudasai, 6.5) ···· 35, 73

itte miru (to go and see [how it is], 22.8) ···· 285

〖j〗

ja (contracted form of de wa, 3.11) ···· 36

ja, mata (I'll see you, 2.11) ···· 24

jazu (jazz) ···· 274

jetto (jet: a loan word from English) ···· 238

ji (written symbol, character or letter) ···· 73

jikken (experiment) ···· 226

jisho (dictionary) ···· 47

Jooji (the English name 'George' as pronounced in Japanese) ···· 13

joozu (being skillful at; be proficient in) ···· 85

joozu (to be good at ...; skillful, 27.3) ···· 346

joozu (na) (to be skillful at; to be good at) ···· 274

juu (ten; 10, 7.9) ···· 85

juubun (enough; sufficient) ····154

juuichiji (eleven o'clock, 9.1) 114

juuji (ten o'clock, 9.1) ···· 114

juunigatsu (December, 10.1) ···· 125

juuniji (twelve o'clock, 9.1) ···· 114

juusho (address) ···· 85

〖k〗

[A] ka [B] ([A] or [B], 14.7) ···· 182

ka (a particle marking the question, 1.12) ···· 13

... ka, ... ka? (a question giving a choice among alternatives, 3.8) ···· 36

ka[w]u (to buy) ···· 250

kaban (briefcase; bag) ···· 46

kaburu (to wear on one's head, 24.5) ···· 309

kabutte (I wear [a hat] on my head and ...: -te form of kaburu, 24.5) ···· 309

kado (corner; street corner, 20.4) ···· 261

kaeri (returning home; return trip) ···· 139

kaerimashita (I have returned; I went [or came] home: -mashita form of kaeru, 11.1) ···· 139

kaerimasu (I go home: -masu form of kaeru) ···· 113

kaeru (to return; to go home) ···· 113

kagaku (chemistry) ···· 226

-kagetsu (month[s]: a counter for months, 18.4) ···· 238

kagi (key) ···· 36

kaigan (beach; seashore) ···· 250

kaimasen deshita (I didn't buy: negative past form of ka[w]u, 11.2) ···· 139

kaimashita (I have bought; I bought: -mashita form of ka[w]u, 11.1) ···· 139

kaimashoo (I will buy; let's buy: -mashoo form of ka[w]u) ···· 250

kaimono (shopping) ···· 125

kaite imasu (he is writing: -te form of kaku + imasu) ···· 208

kaite kudasai (please write: -te form of kaku + kudasai, 6.5) ···· 73

kakarimasu (it takes such and such length of time: -masu form of kakaru, 18.8) ···· 237

kakaru (to take a certain length of time or amount of money, 18.8) ···· 237

kakeru (to wear [glasses]) ···· 310

kaki (persimmon; native Japanese fruit ripe and sweet in autumn) ···· 298

kakimasu (I write/ someone writes: -masu form of kaku 'to write') ···· 73

kaku (to write) ···· 73

Kamakura (a famous historical site located southwest of Tokyo, 19.2) ···· 250

kamera (camera) ···· 183, 250

kami (paper) ···· 36

kanai (my wife, 13.1) ···· 169

kanari (quite; considerablly; pretty much) ···· 47, 193

kangaemasu (I'll think [about it]: -masu form of kangaeru) ···· 182

kangaeru (to think; to contemplate) ···· 182

kanji (Chinese characters adopted in Japanese) ···· 73

kankoku (South Korea) ···· 14

kankoku-ryoori (Korean cuisine or cooking) ···· 98

kankokugo (the Korean language) ···· 14

kankokujin (Korean person) ···· 86

kankoo (tour; sight-seeing) ····193

kankoo-kyaku (tourist) ···· 193

kankoo-basu (sightseeing bus) ···· 193

kara (because; a particle denoting a reason or cause, 17.5) ···· 226

kara (from: a particle denoting the point of departure, 11.12) ···· 140

Kariforunia (the state name 'California' as pronounced in Japanese) ···· 14, 238

kasa (umbrella) ···· 182

(o)kashi (cookies, crackers; snacks) ···· 98

kata (person [exalted]; honorable person) ···· 46

katakana (katakana syllabary) ···· 73

-katta desu (the affirmative past form in an adjective construction, 15.1, 15.3) ···· 193

katte (I bought [something] and..: -te form of ka[w]u) ···· 334

kawa (leather) ···· 183

kawa (river) ···· 194

kawaii (loveable; cute) ···· 169

kawaite imasu (I am thirsty; something is dry: -te form of kawaku + imasu, 16.2, 16.3) ···· 208

kawaku (to get dry; to be thirsty [nodo ga] kawaku) ···· 208

kawariyasui ([something] is changeable: the bound form of kawaru + yasui, 25.7) ···· 321

kawaru (to change) ···· 321

kayo[w]u (to commute; to go to [school]) ···· 309

kayoimasu (I commute; I go to: -te form of kayo[w]u) ···· 309

kayoobi (Tuesday, 10.3) ···· 126

kazarimasu (I decorate; I put out a display of ...: -masu form of kazaru) ···· 297

kazaru (to decorate; to display) ···· 297

kaze (a common cold [that people catch in cold weather]) ···· 322

kaze (wind; breeze) ···· 310

kaze o hikimashita (I've caught a cold; I have a cold) ···· 24

kazoeru (to count) ···· 153

kazoete kudasai (please count: -te form of kazoeru + kudasai) ···· 153

kazoku (family) ···· 168

keeki (cake, 8.11) ···· 98

kekka (results) ···· 250

kekkon (marriage, 27.5) ···· 346

kekkon shite iru ([someone] is married, 27.5) ···· 346

-ken (counter for stores and buildings, 20.1) ···· 262

kenkyuu (study; research) ···· 358

kenkyuushitsu (professor's office; research room)) ···· 62

kesa (this morning) ···· 226

keshigomu (eraser) ···· 73

keshiki (scenery) ···· 286

ki (tree) ···· 169

ki o tsukeru (to take particular note of; to be careful about ...) ···· 321

kiboo (hope; desire; ambition) 358

kiiroi (yellow, 14.6) ···· 181

kiita (I have heard: -ta form of kiku, 22.2) ···· 285

kiite imasu (he is listening; he is hearing: -te form of kiku + imasu) ···· 208

kiite kudasai (please listen, 3.4) ···· 35

kikoemasu (I can hear; [something] is audible: -masu form of kikoeru, 21.8) ···· 273

kikoeru (to be audible: an intransitive verb, 21.8) ···· 273

kiku (to listen; to hear) ···· 35

kimashita (to have come; I came: -mashita form of kuru) ···· 237

kimasu (someone comes; someone is coming: -masu form of kuru) ···· 153

Kimu (the Korean name 'Kim' as pronounced in Japanese) ···· 24

Kimura (a Japanese surname) 14

kin'yoobi (Friday, 10.3) ···· 125

kinodoku ([I] feel sorry for [you]) ···· 322

kinoo (yesterday) ···· 139

kinu (silk) ···· 182

kippu (ticket) ···· 154

kirai (displeasing; I don't like; I dislike, 8.1)) ···· 97

kirei (na) (pretty; beautiful: a copula noun, 13.5) ···· 168

kiro-meetoru (kilometer, 20.5) ···· 262

kiroguramu (kilogram, 20.5). 262

kiru (to wear on the upper part of the body, 24.5) ···· 309

kisetsu (season) ···· 298

kissaten (the Japanese version of a coffeeshop, 11.14) ···· 139

kita (north, 10.10) ···· 126

kite (-te form of kuru (to come), 16.3, 16.4) ···· 209

kite (I wear and ...: -te form of kiru, 24.5) ···· 309

kite [kara] ([after] coming: -te form of kuru + kara, 18.1) ···· 237

kochira (this way, 3.2 & 3,6) 36

kochira (this way; my way; for me to say) ···· 13

kochira (over here; this way) ···· 182

kochira koso (it's for me to say that; it's my pleasure to say that) ···· 14

kodomo (child/children) ···· 85

kodomotachi (children: kodomo+tachi 'explicit plural marker') ···· 309

koko (here; at this place: part of a paradigm, 13.1) ···· 61, 169

kokuban (chalkboard; blackboard) ···· 36

kombanwa (good evening, 2.1) 24

kon iro (navy blue, 14.6) ···· 183

kon'ya (tonight) ···· 126

kon-gakki (this semester) ···· 226

kondo (this time; the next time; the coming occasion; some time, 17.1) ···· 86, 226

kongetsu (this month, 22.6) 286

konna (this sort of, 7.8) ···· 85

konnichiwa (good afternoon; good day; hello, 2.1) ···· 24

kono (this ..., 4.1) ···· 46

konsaato (concert) ···· 154

konshuu (this week) ···· 154,286

koo (this way, 6.9) ···· 73

Koobe (one of the major seaports in western Japan) ···· 334

koocha (red tea; black tea, 8.8) ···· 98

kooen (park) ···· 310

koohii (coffee, 8.11) ···· 98

Koojoo no Tsuki (the title of a famous Japanese song about the moon over a ruined castle) ···· 274

kookoosei (high school student: kootoo-gakkoo 'high school' + [gakus]sei, 27.6) ···· 86,346

kookyo (the Imperial Palace, 15.8) ···· 193

【l】

【m】

nanji (what time, 9.1) ···· 113

nanjikan (how many hours, 17.8) ···· 226

nannichi (what day of the month, 10.2) ···· 125

nannin (how many persons; nan(i) + -nin [a counter for human beings], 13.3) ···· 168

nansatsu (how many volumes, 12.9) ···· 154

napukin (napkin) ···· 154

Nara (the quaint ancient capital of Japan located south of Kyoto) ···· 334

nara[w]u (to learn; to take lessons) ···· 273

naratte imasu (I am learning; I am taking lessons: -te form of nara[w]u + imasu) ···· 273

naremashita (I have become familiar with ...: -mashita form of nareru) ···· 237

nareru (to get used to [a situation]; to become familiar with such and such) ···· 237

(ni) narimasu (it comes to; it amounts to, 18.1) ···· 237

(ni) naru (to become; to turn into, 24.1) ···· 309

naru (to change to; to become) ···· 333

narubeku (as ... as possible, 19.4) ···· 250

narubeku hayaku (as early as possible; as soon as or as quickly as possible, 19.4) ···· 250

naruhodo (indeed; I see) ···· 182

natsu (summer) ···· 298

natsu-yasumi (summer vacation) ···· 298

Natsume Sooseki (twentieth century Japanese author, 28.4) ···· 358

nattara (when [it] becomes that way; when such and such happens: -tara form of naru) ···· 333

nedan (price) ···· 182

neko (cat) ···· 169

nemasu (I go to bed: -masu form of neru) ···· 113

nempai (mature age; older) ···· 85

[go]nen ([five] years: a counter for years) ···· 274

nen (year) ···· 274

neru (to go to bed; to sleep) ···· 113, 208

nete imasu (I am sleeping: -te form of neru + imasu, 16.2) ···· 208

ni (a prticle denoting purpose; for, 8.9) ···· 97, 113

ni (at: a particle indicating the time for an activity, 9.6) ···· 113

ni (the particle marking indirect object, 7.6) ···· 86

ni (two; 2, 7.9) ···· 85

ni (particle marking location of existance, 12.3) ···· 153

ni (to: a particle indicating direction when used with verbs of movement, 9.8) ···· 113

ni (onto; towards: a particle of direction, 6.10) ···· 73

[A] ni ittari [B] ni ittari dekiru (I can go to either [A] or [B]: -tari form of iku in an idiomatic expression -tari -tari suru, 23.2) ···· 297

ni tsuite (concerning; about; on the subject of) ···· 286

nichiyoobi (Sunday, 10.3) ···· 126

nihon no (of Japan; Japanese ...) ···· 47

nihon-ryoori (Japanese cuisine or cooking) ···· 98

nihon-shoku (Japanese food, 8.8) ···· 97

nihongo (the Japanese language) ···· 13

nihongo no (of the Japanese language; Japanese...) ···· 47

nihongo no sensei (teacher of Japanese; Japanese language instructor, 4.4) ···· 46

nihonjin (Japanese national) ···· 86

niji (two o'clock, 9.1) ···· 114

nikai (second floor) ···· 61

Nikkoo (a famous cultural site north of Tokyo, 22.4) ···· 286

niku (meat) ···· 98

nishi (west, 10.10) ···· 126

niwaka ame (sudden shower; cloudburst) ···· 322

[akai] no (the [red] one, 14.8) ···· 182

no koto (with reference to; concerning) ···· 322

no naka de (out of; within the choices of ..., 23.1) ···· 298

no aida (during the time ...) 322

noborimashita (I have climbed; I climbed: -mashita form of noboru) ···· 193

noboru (to climb; to go up to the top of [some place]) ···· 193

node (because, 22.9) ···· 286

nomimashita (I have drunk; I drank: -mashita form of nomu, 11.1) ···· 139

nomimasu (I drink/someone drinks: -masu form of nomu) 97

nominagara (while drinking: the bound form of nomu + nagara, 24.7) ···· 309

nomu (to drink) ···· 97

nonde imasu (he is drinking, 16.2, 16.4) ···· 208

noosakubutsu (agricultural products) ···· 334

nooto (notebook) ···· 36

norimono (means of transportation) ···· 139

nureru (to get wet) ···· 321

nureta (I got wet: -ta form of nureru) ···· 321

Nyuuyooku (the city name 'New York' as pronounced in Japanese) ···· 238

【o】

o (a particle marking the direct object of the verb, 3.9, 5.9) ···· 36, 62

o(verb) ni naru (an exalted verb construction, 27.2) ···· 346

oazukari itashimasu (I humbly take [your money] in my custody) ···· 181

oboenakereba narimasen (I must memorize; I must remember, 28.1) ···· 358

oboeru (to learn; to memorize) ···· 358

ocha (Japanese green tea, 8.8, 8.4) ···· 97

(o)daiji ni (please take care of yourself) ···· 24, 322

odoru (to dance) ···· 309

odottari (I dance or ...: -tari form of odoru) ···· 309

ohayoo gozaimasu (good morning, 2.1) ···· 24

ohinasama (Hina dolls, 23.4) 298

oishii (good tasting; delicious; good) ···· 97, 169

okaasan (mother; your mother, 13.1) ···· 86, 168

okagesamade (fortunately; thank you for asking, 2.6) ···· 24

okane (money) ···· 209

okimasu (I get up: -masu form of okiru) ···· 112

okiru (to get up) ···· 112

okusan; okusama (your wife, 13.1) ...169

omatase itashimashita (Thank you very much for waiting) 181

omo[w]u (to think; to hold in mind) ···· 113, 333

omoimasu (I think: -masu form of omo[w]u) ···· 113

omoshiroi (interesting; fun, 2.9) ···· 23

omoshirosoo (looks like or sounds like fun: the stem of the adjective omoshiroi + soo, 19.3) ···· 250

omotte (I am thinking ... and ...: -te form of omo[w]u) ···· 333

onaji (same) ···· 226

onaka (stomach, 8.7) ···· 97

onamae (your name: the exalted form of namae meaning 'name') ···· 14 onare ni narimashita (you have become accustomed to; you have gotten used to: -mashita form of the exalted construction of nareru) ···· 346

oneesan (older sister, 13.1) 169

ongaku (music) ···· 209, 274

oniisan (older brother, 13.1) 169

onna (female, 4.3) ···· 46

onna mono (clothing made for women; ladies', 14.3) ···· 182

onna no kata (lady, 4.3) ···· 46

onna no ko (girl, 4.3) ···· 46

onsen (hotspring) ···· 286

ooi (numerous; many; lots; frequent) ···· 322

ookii (large; big) ···· 61

ookiku arimasen (not large, 5.2) ···· 61

ookikute (large and ...: -kute form of ookii, 13.10) ···· 168

Oosaka (Osaka, the second largest city in Japan) ···· 334

oosooji o suru (to do a big cleaning; to clean up the room) ···· 310

oozei (many people) ···· 153

orenji-juusu (orange juice, 8.11) ···· 98, 114

orimasu (there is; there are; I have: -masu form of oru) ····346

[... o] oriru (to get off [the vehicle]; to descend [the slope]) ···· 321

orita (I got off [the vehicle]: -ta form of oriru) ···· 321

oru (to be: a humble verb, 27.2) ···· 346

oshaberi (chatting; talking; friendly conversation) ···· 310

oshiemasu (I [or someone] teach[es]: -masu form of oshieru 'to teach') ···· 85

oshieru (to teach; to inform; to instruct) ···· 85

oshiete kudasai (please teach; please inform: -te form of oshieru + kudasai) ···· 85

otagai ni (each other; [to do something] each other: honorific prefix o- + tagai + ni) ···· 358

otaku (your house hold: exalted word, 13.7) ···· 168

otearai (restroom; place to wash hands; toilet) ···· 62

oto (sound) ···· 274

otoko (male, 4.3) ···· 46

otoko mono (for men; men's, 14.3) ···· 182

otoko no hito (man; gentleman, 4.3) ···· 46

otoko no ko (boy, 4.3) ···· 46

otona (adult; grown-up people) ···· 85

otoosan (father) ···· 86

otoosan (your father, 13.1) 168

otooto ([my] younger brother, 13.1, 27.1) ···· 168, 346

otsuri (change, 14.13) ···· 182

owarimasu (it ends: -masu form of owaru) ···· 113

owaru (to be over; something ends: intransitive verb) ···· 113, 225

owatte [kara] ([after] something is over: -te form of owaru) 225

oya (hey; well, 25.1) ···· 322

oyasuminasai (good night, 2.1) 24

【p】

paasento (percent; %) ···· 182

paatii (party; gathering)···· 153, 298

painappuru (pineapple, 8.11) ···· 98, 114

pan (bread) ···· 262

pan'ya (bakery, 20.1) ···· 262

patto (suddenly [open]) ···· 310

pen (pen) ···· 35

petto (pet) ···· 168

piano (piano) ···· 154, 274

pokapoka to (comfortably or cozily [warm]: a reduplicated onomatopoetic adverb, 24.2) 310

poriesuteru (polyester) ···· 182

potetochippusu (potato chips) ···· 310

purezento (gift; present) ···· 126

【r】

rabo (laboratory) ···· 226
raigetsu (next month, 22.6) 286
rainen (next year, 22.6) ···· 286
raishuu (next week, 22.6) ···· 286
rei, zero (zero; 0, 7.9) ···· 85
reinkooto (raincoat) ···· 262
rekishi (history) ···· 47
remon (lemon) ···· 262
renshuu (practice; exercise) 209
renshuu suru (to practice:
    compound verb made up of
renshuu + suru) ···· 208
resutoran (restaurant) ···· 98
rikai (understanding;
    comprehension) ···· 358
rikai suru (to understand; to
    comprehend) ···· 357
rippa (na) (distinguished looking;
    impressive: a copula noun, 13.5)
    ···· 168
risaitaru (recital) ···· 154
roku (six; 6, 7.9) ···· 85
rokuji (six o'clock, 9.1) ···· 113
Rosanzerusu (the city name 'Los
    Angeles' as pronounced in
    Japanese) ···· 238
ruumu-meeto (roommate) ···· 47
ryokoo (traveling; touring) ···· 334
ryoo (dormitory; student housing
    offered by the school) ···· 238
ryoohoo (both [of them], 8.6) 97
ryoori (cuisine) ···· 98

【s】

saa (well; let me think) ···· 47,334
saifu (wallet) ···· 36
sakana (fish) ···· 98
(o)sake (Japanese style liquor;
    sake) ···· 310
sakimasu ([flowers] bloom: -masu
    form of saku) ···· 297
saku (to bloom: intransitive verb)
    ···· 297
sakura (cherry tree; cherry
    blossoms) ···· 274

Sakura, Sakura (the title of a
    Japanese song praising the
    beauty of cherry blossoms) 274
samma (a kind of fish plentiful
    and delicious in autumn) ···· 298
samui (cold weather; [to feel]
    cold) ···· 24
samukatta (it was cold: -katta
    form of samui, 15.1) ···· 193
-san (Mr., Mrs., Miss, 1.8) ···· 13
san (three; 3, 7.9) ···· 85
sandoitchi (sandwich) ···· 114
Sanfuranshisuko (the city name
    'San Francisco' as pronounced in
    Japanese)   ···· 238
sangai (third floor) ···· 262
sanji juugofun (3:15, 9.1, 9.3,
    9.4) ···· 113
Santosu (the Spanish name
    'Santos' as pronounced in
    Japanese) ···· 14
sara (plate[s]; dish[es])   ···· 153
sararii-man (salaried worker) 168
-satsu (counter for books and
    other bound volumes, 12.9) 154
sayoonara (good-bye, 2.1) ···· 24
seetaa (sweater) ···· 36
seibutsu (biology) ···· 358
seikatsu (life; living) ···· 238
seki (seat) ···· 194
sekken (soap) ···· 262
senchi-meetoru (centimeter,
    20.5) 262
sengetsu (last month, 22.6) 286
senkoo (major field of study) 226
sensei (teacher; instructor) ···· 46
senshuu (last week, 22.6) ···· 286
setsumei shimasu (I explain;
    someone explains; the -masu
    form of setsumei suru) ···· 61
shakuhachi (a Japanese-style
    flute) ···· 274
shashin (photograph; picture)168
shashin (photograph; picture)286
shatsu (shirt) ···· 183
shi (and; moreover; and in
    addition: a conjunctive particle,
    17.7) ···· 226
(s)hichiji (seven o'clock, 9.1) 114

shika ... nai (only; nothing but ...,
23.7) ···· 298

shikata ga arimasen (it couldn't
be helped; it can't be helped,
17.4) ···· 226

shiken (exam; test; quiz) ···· 154,
226

shikkari gambarimashoo (let's do
our very best; let's keep up the
good work, 28.9) ···· 358

shikke (humidity) ···· 334

Shikoku (one of the major islands
of Japan, located south of
Honshu, 26.4) ···· 334

shima (island) ···· 334

shima[w]u (to completely do ...;
to put something away) ···· 321

shimasen deshita (I didn't do:
negative past form of suru,
11.2) ···· 139

shimashita (I have done; I did:
past form of suru, 11.1)....139

shimashoo (let's do..., 1.15)...13

shimbun (newspaper) ···· 35

shin- (new--: a prefix indicating
newness, 24.4) ···· 310

shin-gakunen (new academic
year, 24.4) ···· 309

shinakereba narimasen (I must
do...: -nakereba narimasen
construction of suru, 28.1) 357

shingoo (traffic signal) ···· 262

Shinjuku (a major shopping center
in Tokyo, 11.15) ···· 139

shiraberu (to check; to
investigate) ···· 334

shirabete ita (I was checking [it]:
-te form of shiraberu + ita, the
plain form of imashita) ···· 334

shiriai (acquaintance, 7.4) ···· 85

shirimasen (I don't know, 7.1) 85

shiroi (white, 14.6) ···· 62, 181

shiru (to know) ···· 85

shita (down; below; under
beneath: a noun of location,
12.1) ···· 36, 153

shite imasu (he is doing: -te form
of suru+imasu, 16.2, 16.4) 208

shitsumon (question) ···· 73

shitsurei shimashita (I'm sorry;
excuse me; I was rude) ···· 14

shitte imasu (I [or someone]
know[s]: -te form of shiru +
imasu, 7.1) ···· 85

shiyoo (I'm thinking of doing such
and such: -yoo form of suru,
26.6) ···· 333

shizuka (na) (quiet; peaceful: a
copula noun, 13.5) ···· 169, 238

shokuji (meal) ···· 139

(o)shoogatsu (New Year's, 23.4)
···· 298

shookai shite kudasai (please
introduce: a compound verb
made up of shookai
(introduction) + suru (to do))
···85

shoorai (the future) ···· 358

shoosetsu (novel) ···· 358

shujin (my husband, 13.1) ····169

shukudai (homework assignment)
···· 226

shuu (state) ···· 334

(o)shuuji (traditional Japanese
brush writing; calligraphy, 7.3)
···85

shuukan (week) ···· 322

shuumatsu (weekend) ···· 193

(o)soba (buckwheat noodles;
Japanese peaple's favorite lunch
item) ···· 97

soba (near; near-by, 12.1) ····154

sochira (that way; that one; your
way, 3.6) ···· 36, 182

soko (there) ···· 61

sonna (that sort of, 7.8) ···· 85

sonna ni (in that manner; that
way; not so ..., 5.4) ···· 61

sono (that ..., 4.1) ···· 46

sono hoka (apart from that; other
than that) ···· 193

sono toori (exactly [as you said]; I
agree) ···· 334

-soo (to look like; to sound like: a
bound copula noun, 19.3) 250

soo (in that way; so) ···· 13

soo datta n desu ka? (Is that
what it was?, 26.8) ···· 334

soo desu (that's right; you are correct) ···· 13

soo na n desu (that's right, 25.4) ····322

soo suru to (if you do that, 20.8) ····262

sora (sky) ···· 194

sore (that, 3.5) ···· 24, 36

sore ga taihen desu (that's a big problem; that's terrible, 28.7) ····358

sore hodo demo arimasen (not really so; not exactlly as you say: a humble response to a compliment given) ···· 168

sore kara (and after that; afterwards; and then) ···· 113, 182, 154

sore mo soo desu ne (that's true; you have a point) ···· 298

sore nara (in that case; if that's so) ···· 358

sore ni shite wa (taking that into consideration) ···· 346

sore wa nan desu ka? (What is that [thing near you]?) ···· 36

sore wa soo to (by the way, 18.6) ···· 238

sore wa yokatta desu ne! (I'm glad to hear that; that was good!) ···· 24

soro soro (nearly; gradually or slowly approaching) ···· 238

soshite (and then; also; too) ···· 114, 358

soto (outdoors; outside) ···· 193

sotsugyoo (graduation) ···· 358

sotsugyoo shitara (when I graduate; after I graduate: -tara form of sotsugyoo suru) ···· 357

subarashii (excellent; wonderful, 22.1) ···· 193, 274

subarashikatta ([it] was wonderful: -katta from of subarashii) ···· 286

sugi (past the hour, 9.5) ···· 113

sugiru ([for time] to elapse; to be over) ···· 309

sugite ([it] is past and ...: -te form of sugiru) ···· 309

sugu (immediately; right away) ···· 262

sugu wakarimasu ka? (Will I recognize it right away?) ···· 262

suisu (Switzerland) ···· 183

suite imasu (I am hungry: -te form of suku+imasu, 16.2, 16.4) 208

suiyoobi (Wednesday, 10.3) 126

sukaafu (scarf) ···· 183

sukeeto o suru (to skate) ···· 298

suki (pleasing; likeable; I like, 8.1) ···· 97

sukii o suru (to ski) ···· 298

sukimashita (... has become empty/is empty: -mashita form of suku, 8.7) ···· 97

sukiyaki (Japanese dish, 8.8) 97

sukkari (completely; really; terribly) ···· 238, 322

sukoshi (a little) ···· 13

suku (to become less filled; to be hungry) ···· 97

sumi (charcoal ink for calligraphy art, 16.8) ···· 209

sumi (inside corner) ···· 262

sumimasen (excuse me) ···· 73

Sumisu (the English name 'Smith' as pronounced in Japanese) 14

sumu (to live in or at; to reside at ...) ···· 237

sunde imasu (I am living: -te form of sumu + imasu) ···· 237

supeingo (the Spanish language) ···· 14

supootsu (sports) ···· 274

suppai (sour) ···· 169

(o)sushi (Japanese dish, 8.8) 97

suwatte kudasai (please sit down) ···· 36

suzuri (ink plate for calligraphy art, 16.8) ···· 209

【t】

-ta hoo ga ii (I had better do [such and such], 25.8) ···· 322

-ta toki (when [I] did such and such) ···· 322

389

-ta tokoro (such and such has just happened; [I have] just been doing [such and such]; [I was] just now doing [such and such], 26.7) ···· 334

-ta koto ga aru (I have done [such and such], 22.2) ···· 286

tabemashoo (let's eat: -mashoo form of taberu) ···· 97

tabemasu (I eat/someone eats: -masu form of taberu) ···· 97

tabenagara (while eating: the bound form of taberu + nagara) ···· 309

taberu (to eat) ···· 97

tabete imasu (he is eating, 16.2, 16.4) ···· 208

tabun ... deshoo (probably is ...) ···· 334

-tachi (a suffix expressing plurality of people) ···· 310

-tai (want to; would like to: a bound adjective, 19.5) ···· 250

-tai naa! ([I] would really like to do: -tai + the interjection naa, 28.6) ···· 358

-tai to omo[w]u (I'd like to [do such and such]) ···· 298

taihen (extremly; exceedingly; very much) ···· 193, 286

taisetsu (na) (important) ···· 334

taitei (usually) ···· 62

Taiwan (Taiwan) ···· 14

takai (high; expensive; tall) ···· 169, 183

taki (waterfall) ···· 286

takushii (taxi; cab) ···· 139

tame ni (in order to do [such and such], 28.3) ···· 358

Tanaka (a Japanese surname) 13

tango (vocabulary word) ···· 226

tani (valley; gorge) ···· 286

(o)tanjoobi (birthday) ···· 126

tanoshii (enjoyable; fun) ···· 23, 153

tanoshikatta (it was enjoyable: -katta form of tanoshii, 15.1) ···· 193

tanoshimi (something to look forward to) ···· 286

-tara (when; if: an inflectional ending denoting a 'condition,' 23.5) ···· 298

-tari -tari suru (to do [such and such] alternating with [such and such], 23.2) ···· 298

tatemono (building) ···· 61

tatoeba (for example) ···· 358

tatte kudasai (please stand up) 36

-te shima[w]u ([something] is completely done; [someone] ended up doing [something], 25.2) ···· 322

-te kara (after doing such and such, 17.10) ···· 226

-te kara moo ... ni naru (it has been .... since I did such and such, 18.1) ···· 238

-te miru (to do [such and such] and see [how it is], 22.8: -te form of the verb + miru) ···· 286, 358

-te... (doing such and such and..., 17.11) ···· 226

teeburu (table) ···· 153

teepu (tape) ···· 226

tegami (letter; correspondence) ···· 86

tempura (Japanese dish, 8.8) 97

(o)tenki (weather, 2.3) ···· 24

(o)tera (Buddhist temple) ···· 250

terebi (T.V.; a Japanese abbreviation for the English word 'television') ···· 113

tetsuda[w]u (to assist someone's work; to help) ···· 153

tetsudaimashoo ka? (Shall I assist [you]? Shall I help [you]? ····153

(naru) to (when; whenever; if: a particle marking a subordinate clause, 24.1, 24.2) ···· 310

to ('and' in complete enumeration, 13.4) ···· 168

to issho ni (together with..., 11.7) ···· 139

to omoimasu (I think that ..., 26.2) ···· 333

... to ... to (... and ... compared, 8.6) ---- 97

to mo (inclusive of ... ; both of them, 8.6) ---- 97

tojite kudasai (Please close [the book]) ---- 36

(A) toka (B) toka ([A] and [B] and such things, 21.6) ---- 274

tokei (clock) ---- 36

toki (time; when [something happened], 22.7) ---- 286

tokidoki (sometimes) ---- 62

tokoro (place) ---- 193

tokoro de (by the way) ---- 322, 346

(o)tomodachi (friend) ---- 47

tonari (next-door neighbor) 262

tooi (far away; distant) ---- 238

tooku arimasen (not far: negative of tooi desu) ---- 238

Tookyoo-eki (Tokyo Station) 125

Tookyoo-tawaa (Tokyo Tower, 15.7) ---- 193

Toomasu (the English name 'Thomas' as pronounced in Japanese) ---- 14

Tooshooguu (a famous shrine in Nikko, 22.4) ---- 286

toosuto (toast) ---- 114

tori (bird) ---- 169

torimashita (I took; I have taken: -mashita form of toru) ---- 285

toru (to take) ---- 226, 285

toshi (city) ---- 298, 334

toshokan (library) ---- 61,226

totemo (very much, 2.10) ---- 24

-tsu (the general counter for small objects, 12.8) ---- 154

tsuitachi (the first day of the month, 10.2) ---- 125

tsuka[w]u (to use, 16.4) ---- 208

tsukatte imasu (he is using: -te form of tsuka[w]u + imasu, 16.4) 208

tsukeru (to wear accessories; to attach on clothing) ---- 310

tsukue (desk) ---- 35

tsukuru (to make, 16.4) ---- 208

tsuma (my wife [formal use], 13.1) ---- 169

tsumaranai (uninteresting; dull; boring) ---- 62

tsumetai (cold to touch; cold referring to food or other things but not to weather) ---- 98

tsumori (intention; plan: a noun usually preceded by a verb in its dictionary form, 19.1) ---- 250

tsuukoonin (passerby) ---- 261

tsuyoi (to be strong; intense) 334

tsuyu (the rainy season in Japan during June and July, 25.9) 322

tsuyu ga akeru ([the rainy season] ends; clouds lift or break up) ---- 322

tsuzuku (to continue; something continues) ---- 321

【u】

uchi (home; house) ---- 61

udon (regular white noodles; a favorite lunch item) ---- 97

ue (up; above; on top of: a noun of location, 12.1) ---- 36, 153

Ueno (the cultural center in downtown Tokyo, 15.9) ---- 193

ukaga[w]u (to visit; to go: humble verb) ---- 237

ukagaimasu (I will visit; I'll drop in: -masu form of ukaga[w]u) 237

ume (plum) ---- 309

umi (sea; ocean; beach) ---- 298

ureshii (happy; delighted) ---- 153

uriba (department or section of a store; sales counter) ---- 262

uta (song) ---- 274

uta[w]u (to sing a song) ---- 273, 309

utattari (I sing or ...: -tari form of uta[w]u) ---- 309

utsukushii (beautiful) ---- 193

utsukushikatta (it was beautiful: -katta form of utsukushii, 15.1) ---- 193

utsukushiku ([something looks or sounds] beautiful: -ku form of utsukushii) ---- 274

【v】

Vikutaa   (the personal name 'Victor' as pronounced in Japanese) ···· 238

【w】

wa   (a particle marking the topic, 1.4) ···· 13

waka   (31-syllable Japanese poem) ···· 310

wakai   (young) ···· 86, 309

wakaranai koto bakari   (nothing but things I don't understand, 27.4) ···· 346

wakarimasen   (I'm not sure; I don't understand: -masen form of wakarimasu, 1.13) ···· 46

wakarimashita   (I have understood: -mashita form of wakaru 'to understand, 6.6) 73

warito   (relatively) ···· 238

warui   (bad) ···· 62, 286

warukatta   ([it] was bad: -katta from of warui, 22.1) ···· 286

Washinton D.C.   ('Washington D.C.' as pronounced in Japanese) ···· 238

wasureru   (to forget) ···· 321

wasurete shimatta   (I have completely forgotten about ...: -te form of wasureru + shimatta, 25.2) ···· 321

watakushi   (a formal and polite form for 'I', 1.2) ···· 13

watakushi no   (my...; mine, 4.5) 47

watakushitachi   (we) ···· 46,62

watakushitachi no   (our, 4.5) ···46

【y】

-ya   (store: a bound noun usually suffixed to a noun indicationg a specific merchandise, 20.1) ···· 262

ya   (and: a particle meaning 'and' in incomplete enumeration, 8.3) ···· 97

yama   (mountain) ···· 194, 286

yama no yoo ni arimasu   (to be swamped with; to have a million things [one would like to do]) ···· 358

Yamada   (a Japanese surname) ···· 13

yaoya   (green grocer) ···· 262

yasai   (vegetable) ···· 98

yasashii   (easy, 5.1) ···· 61

yasashiku arimasen   (not easy, 5.2) ···· 61

-yasui   (easy to ..., 25.7) ···· 322

yasui   (inexpensive; cheap) ···· 181

yasumi   (holiday; vacation) ···· 298

yasumimashita   (I was absent from work or school: -mashita form of yasumu) ···· 321

yasumu   (to take a rest from ...; to be absent from regular work) ···· 321

yo   (particle of emphasis, 7.5, 12.5, 22.10) ···· 86, 153, 286

yoji-han   (4:30, 9.1, 9.4, 9.5)113

yokatta   ([sometnig] was good): the past form of ii or yoi, 15.3) ···· 23, 193

yokatta desu ne!   (I'm glad to hear that! 15.6) ···· 193

yokattara   (if it's good [for you]; if you'd like: -tara form of ii, 23.5) ···· 298

yoku   (well) ···· 61

yokute   (it [was] good and ...: -kute form of ii) ···· 322

yokute mo   (even if it is good) ···· 334

yomanakereba narimasen   (I must read: -nakereba narimasen construction of yomu, 28.1) ···· 358

yomimashoo   (let's read: -mashoo form of yomu, 1.13) ···· 73

yomu   (to read) ···· 73

yon, shi   (four; 4, 7.9) ··· 85

yonde imasu   (he is reading: -te form of yomu + imasu, 16.2, 16.4) ···· 208

yonde kudasai   (please read: -te form of yomu + kudasai, 6.5) ···· 73 yonde mitai   (I'd like to try reading [such and such]: -te form of yomu + -tai form of miru) ···· 357

yoo   (appearance; looks: a bound copula noun, 17.6) ···· 226

-yoo to omo[w]u   (I'm thinking of doing such and such, 26.6) ···· 334

yoofuku   (Western-style clothing; dress) ···· 309

(A) yori (B) no hoo ga   ([choosing] (B) over (A); I [like] (B) better than (A), 23.3) ····298

yoroshii   (good: an exalted adjective, honorific equivalent of ii) ···· 181, 346

yoroshikattara   (if it's good; if it's convenient for you: -tara form of yoroshii, 27.7) ···· 346

yoroshiku   (be favorable [to me], 1.7) ···· 13

yoshuu   (preparation for the next lesson) ···· 250

yotei   (plan) ···· 154

Yotsuya   (a place in central Tokyo) ···· 238

yuki   (snow) ···· 310

yukkuri   (slowly; slow) ···· 73

yuubinkyoku   (post office) ···· 262

yuugohan   (supper; dinner) ····114

yuumei (na)   (famous: a copula noun, 22.3) ···· 286

【z】

zaazaa   (pouring; [raining] cats and dogs) ···· 322

zannen   (too bad; regrettable) ···· 140

zasshi   (magazine) ···· 35

zehi   (for sure; definitely: emphatic expression approving the proposed action) ···· 126, 298

zenzen   (absolutely; completely: adverb expressing intense degree, 17.2) ···· 226

zuibun   (quite; extremely) ···· 47